Cessna War

A Detailed & Personal History of Cessna's Involvement in the Armed Forces

By Walt Shiel
Foreword by Bill Sweetman

Publisher/Acquisitions Editor
Gregory W. Bayer

Editors
Frank Hamilton
Gregory W. Bayer
Kim Shields

Art Director
Joni Clarke
Beth Jolin

Production Team
Jean Adams
Cindy Boutwell
Cindy McCarville

Information Systems Management
Bruce Loppnow

Published By:
Jones Publishing, Inc.
P.O. Box 5000
N7450 Aanstad Road
Iola, WI 54945-5000

Phone: 715-445-5000
Fax: 715-445-4053

Cessna Warbirds
A Detailed & Personal History of Cessna's Involvement in the Armed Forces

By Walt Shiel

Published by: **Jones Publishing, Inc.**
P.O. Box 5000
N7450 Aanstad Road
Iola, WI 54945-5000

Phone: 715-445-5000
Fax: 715-445-4053

This book is available at special quantity discounts for bulk purchases. For details, contact Greg Bayer at the above address or phone number.

Jones Publishing, Inc. also publishes:
CESSNA OWNER magazine
PIPERS magazine
Standard Catalog of Cessna Single Engine Aircraft
Standard Catalog of Piper Single Engine Aircraft
Standard Catalog of Piper Twin Engine Aircraft
A Guide to Purchasing Aircraft
Aircraft Modifications & Avionics for Piper & Cessna Airplanes
Generalities, Truths, & Assorted Fables
Cockpit Companion: Flight Assistance From the Right Seat

10 9 8 7 6 5 4 3 2 1
First Edition

Manufactured in the United States

ISBN 1-879825-25-2 $29.95

Library of Congress Catalog Card Number: 95-79371

About the Author

Walt Shiel has spent most of his life around military aircraft. He was raised as an "Air Force Brat" on a variety of bases across the country and around the world.

While attending Michigan State University, he married the love of his life, Kerrie. Upon earning his BS degree in electrical engineering in 1969, he went directly into the U.S. Air Force and the Undergraduate Pilot Training (UPT) program at Webb AFB in Big Spring, Texas, a base long since closed. He graduated a year later and was selected to remain at Webb AFB as an instructor pilot in the Cessna T-37B primary jet trainer. He later served as an instructor pilot in the Air Force's Cessna T-41 propeller-driven basic trainer. After seven years and 1,500 flying hours (surviving innumerable stalls, spins, loops, rolls, and brutal student landing attempts), he left the Air Force and went to work as a civilian engineer. By that time, he had two lovely daughters — Laura and Lisa. But he couldn't get away from those military Cessnas.

Walt joined the Michigan Air National Guard's 172nd Tactical Air Control Squadron at Battle Creek, Michigan. He was flying the Cessna O-2A, a militarized twin-engine, push-pull Model 337. Three years later, he found himself back on Air Force active duty flying and instructing in a variety of missions including intercept training, simulated ground attack, photographic reconnaissance, and dissimilar air combat tactics training with local F-4s — all in the 30-year-old Lockheed T-33. After three years flying over the rugged mountains and desolate glaciers of Alaska in a 3-decade-old single-engine jet, he returned to UPT instructor pilot duties, this time in the supersonic Northrop T-38 at Columbus AFB in Mississippi.

Seemingly undecided about what he wanted to be when he grew up, Walt got out of the Air Force once more in 1985, and went to work for Northrop in California as a project engineer on the B-2 stealth bomber program. He served in the Air Force Reserves as a mobilization augmentee in the 6521st Range Squadron at Edwards AFB in California. Shortly after the first flight of the B-2, Walt switched jobs and moved to North Texas to work for General Dynamics (GD). One of his first assignments was to work on the joint GD-Cessna proposal for the Tanker Transport Training System contract. Alas, they did not win, but Walt refuses to accept the blame.

Walt later worked on GD's Air Defense F-16A training system. In 1990, he began working on the GD-Boeing-Lockheed team proposal for the F-22 stealth fighter's training system. When the team actually won the contract (for which Walt is quite willing to accept credit), he went to work to turn the proposal into reality — and that's where he is today. However, due to mergers and buy-outs, he has managed to work for three companies from the same desk — GD, Lockheed Fort Worth Company, and now Lockheed Martin Tactical Aircraft Systems.

With 4,000 flying hours in aircraft ranging from the Aeronca Champ to the T-38, Walt has accumulated almost 1,800 hours in military Cessnas. He is a graduate of the Air Force's Air War College, an AF command pilot, and a Lieutenant Colonel in the AF Reserves. He is a member of the Air Force Association, the AOPA, the EAA, and the Warbirds of America. He writes regularly for general aviation publications such as *Cessna Owner* magazine, and is the author of the monthly "Military Aviation and Warbird News" column in *US Aviator* magazine. These days, Walt flies mostly for his own pleasure in lightplanes with his favorite copilot, Kerrie. His three-year-old grandson, however, seems to have acquired Walt's passion for airplanes. Walt and Kerrie live on a mini-ranch west of Fort Worth, Texas, with three horses, five dogs, and a dozen or so cats. His near-future goal is to own his very own Cessna warbird — maybe an O-2A. ✝

Please Read This!

Dedication

This book was produced for the entertainment and enlightenment of Cessna warbird enthusiasts, researchers, and anyone interested in Cessna military aircraft. It is intended as a reference manual, not as an operator's manual for any of the aircraft described within. While every effort has been made to ensure the information contained herein is correct and up-to-date, the editor, author, and publisher extend no warranty as to the accuracy or completeness of the information — there may be mistakes, both typographical and in content. It is inevitable that a publication this comprehensive contains errors, even though we eliminated them to the best of our ability. Therefore, this text should be used only as a general guide and not as the ultimate source of information. Any errors, inconsistencies, or omissions discovered in reading *Cessna Warbirds* may be brought to our attention by returning the form located in the back of this book.

This book is sold with the understanding that the publisher and author are not engaged in rendering product endorsements or providing instruction as a substitute for appropriate training by qualified sources. Therefore, Jones Publishing, Inc. and the author, Walt Shiel, shall have neither liability nor responsibility to any person or entity with respect to any loss or damage caused, or alleged to be caused, directly or indirectly, by the information contained in this book.

The author and staff of Jones Publishing hope you enjoy reading *Cessna Warbirds: A Detailed & Personal History of Cessna's Involvement in the Armed Forces.* ✝

To my delightful wife Kerrie, without whose constant support, unflagging enthusiasm, periodic pep talks, and tolerant love this book would never have been completed. Without complaint, she endured my apparent love affair with a computer, while meticulously assisting me with research on topics about which only I felt passionate. She read every word of the finished product, searching out the jargon, mistakes, and general readability flaws I likely would have missed. Whatever success this book may enjoy is due in large part to her — whatever failings it may have are solely my own. ✝

Table of Contents

Acknowledgements 1

Foreword 6

Introduction 7

Abreviations & Definitions 10

Chapter 1
    The Cessna Dynasty 13

Chapter 2
    Aircraft Model and Serial Numbers 25

Chapter 3
    The First Military Cessnas 29

Chapter 4
    The T-50 Bobcat 35

Chapter 5
    A C-195 in Uniform: the LC-126 53

Chapter 6
    Tactical Weapons and FAC Tactics 63

Chapter 7
    The L-19/O-1 Bird Dog 77

Chapter 8
    The U-3 Blue Canoe 127

Chapter 9
    The T-37 Tweety Bird 137

Chapter 10
    The A-37 Dragonfly 187

Chapter 11
    The O-2 "Fighting Skymaster" 209

Table
of Contents

Chapter 12
    The T-41 Mescalero 259

Chapter 13
    The YH-41 Seneca 283

Chapter 14
    U-17: Cessna 180s and 185s Go to War 295

Chapter 15
    The T-47: Navy Citations 305

Chapter 16
    Other Cessnas That Served 311

Chapter 17
    The JPATS/CitationJet 315

Associations and Museums 321

Bibliography 325

Acknowledgements

"Writing, when properly managed (as you may be sure I think mine is), is but a different name for conversation."
— *Laurence Sterne*

I tried to observe Sterne's admonition in two ways during the writing of this book: first, I tried to converse with the reader, to keep the stories from becoming dry historical compilations; second, I invested many hours conversing with people across this country and around the world. It is to this second phase, which actually came first, that I now turn my attention.

I approached with some trepidation the subject of acknowledging all of the people who have contributed to this book. So many have contributed their time, advice, assistance, and stories that I was sure I would forget someone. If I have, it was wholly unintentional and merely the fault of the incredible volume of material I accumulated and my less-than-perfect filing system. I tried to keep track of those who touched this project in any way — but I may still have failed to be as complete as I intended. Having salved my conscience beforehand, I shall recognize the people who made the research task so much easier than it might have been.

When I began the project, the first place I turned for help was the one place with which I was most familiar — the U.S. Air Force Museum at Wright-Patterson Air force Base (AFB) at Dayton, Ohio. Mr. David Menard was quick to respond with background information, photos of various United States Air force (USAF) Cessnas, and suggestions for other material that could be included.

My next concern regarded all of those Bird Dogs the U.S. Army had operated, which led me eventually to the U.S. Army Aviation Museum at Fort Rucker, Alabama, and Ms. Regina Burns. This proved to be most fortuitous as Regina was a godsend. She immediately offered to provide me with lists of the museum's photographs, Army technical manuals, and articles from past issues of *Army Aviation Digest*. It seemed, no matter how extensive my requests, or how many times I bugged her for "just one more group of photos," she cheerfully complied. She loaned me dozens of photographs, researching the museum's archives every time I found one more Cessna the Army had flown. And even when she was unable to find what I was looking for in the museum's records, she offered suggestions as to where to look next. For her patience, persistence, and invaluable assistance, I thank her. I only hope the Army Aviation Museum appreciates her efforts as much as I do.

While casting about for leads on military Cessnas, I naturally turned to Cessna Aircraft Company. Although Renee Sarver of the Cessna Press Relations office was eager to help, the once-extensive Cessna archives had, some time ago, been released to private care. Cessna was in the process of rebuilding their historical files, but had little to offer. Renee did, however, track down a nice series of photos of many of the military Cessna models.

In an attempt to contact service members who had flown Cessnas while on active duty, I posted a notice requesting assistance in the "Bulletin Board" department of *Air Force Magazine*. The first to respond was Don Sampsel of Billings, Montana. Don had trained in the AT-17 and UC-78 during World War II and took the time to write several pages of reminiscences. He also allowed me to bother him on the telephone a couple of times. His personal anecdotes of flying the Bobcat when it was new proved indispensable.

When I started researching the book, I was actively involved in the *Aviation Forum* and *Veterans Forum* on

CompuServe. I put out a few feelers to see if anyone on-line could offer "war stories" or point me towards sources of data and photographs. I never envisioned the amount of material that would result from those few on-line queries. Anyone who doubts there is a true on-line community, or who thinks the on-line services are anonymous and confrontational, has been spending too much time in the wrong electronic places. Denizens of both the *Aviation Forum* and the *Veterans Forum* responded with stories, other possible sources, names of people who had flown the aircraft and might be willing to help, and offers to provide narratives and personal photos.

George Kyer, retired U.S. Army officer from Arkansas, was one of the first to respond. Everyone who knew George on-line recognized him as a first-class gentleman and one of those people who was always willing to go "above and beyond" to help anyone who asked. Despite his advanced years and recurring health problems that periodically kept him off-line, his mind was sharp and his memories vivid. George recalled an old Army buddy who had spent many hours above Vietnam in a Bird Dog. George soon came up with the man's name, address, and phone number, as well as a string of personal tales about him. George also put me in touch with an ex-Bird Dog instructor he knew personally. More than just providing me with information and names, George maintained an active interest in my project and regularly prodded me with E-Mail messages to check on my progress. George passed away before I was halfway finished, so he will never know how the book finally came out. I hope he would have been pleased.

Alan O'Hollaran is the retired Army Bird Dog pilot with whom George put me in touch. Alan took time from his busy schedule to compose a lengthy history of his year in the Southeast Asia war games. He also loaned me his personal copy of the 212th Combat Aviation Battalion's 1971 Vietnam yearbook. I am grateful to him for sharing his stories, as they filled in some of the gaps regarding the Army's use of Cessnas in Vietnam.

Jerry Robinson, Director of Aviation at Henderson State University in Arkansas, was the other friend George Kyer suggested I contact. Dr. Robinson wrote an excellent account of his many hours flying and instructing in the Bird Dog. I told him he should see about getting them published. I don't know if he has followed through on that idea yet, but he should. Besides writing interesting tales, his engaging style was thoroughly enjoyable and his personal observations on the character of the Bird Dog were indispensable. I would have graded his paper a solid A+.

Bill Sweetman and I corresponded on the *Aviation* and *Veterans Forums* about a variety of subjects. I knew Bill through his books and magazine articles and knew he must have had occasion to do more than a little research into aviation-related matters. When I asked if he had any ideas on sources of military Cessna information, he quickly passed along the name and address of a friend in Wichita, Kansas. Later, Bill graciously agreed to write the foreword for this book.

Bill's friend, John Davis, responded almost immediately to my query letter. He worked with what had been the Wichita Aviation Historical Foundation, now the Kansas Aviation Museum (KAM), and let me know, yes, they had lots of Cessna information. KAM had acquired the historical records and photographs that had once been maintained at Cessna by Robert Pickett. Between Christmas and New Year's Day, Kerrie and I trekked north from Weatherford, Texas to Wichita. John opened the KAM office suite, which was packed full of photos and records, and asked us to lock it up when we were finished. Those two days unearthed a wealth of material, some of it serendipitous and found in uncataloged boxes. For his willingness to trust a couple of strangers with an invaluable horde of history, I thank John Davis. He even let me borrow a couple of boxes of slides for more leisurely review at home.

Another Wichitan, Duane Moore, contacted me about the same time. His brother, a retired USAF officer, had seen my notice in *Air Force Magazine* and forwarded it to Duane. Duane had retired from Cessna after a 40-year career that included serving as production manager of Cessna's Military Division from the mid-1950s through the 1960s. This period featured the L-19, T-37, and A-37 programs. Duane was a true pack rat, and I am grateful for that. He had kept boxes and boxes of records and old Cessna publications. He and his wife opened their home to us and spent many hours discussing the history of Cessna and the people who worked there. Duane let us borrow stacks of material for reproduction. He filled in a lot of holes in my research and patiently answered my interminable questions.

Jerry DiGrezio was one of the first Bird Dog pilots to answer my plea for war tales. He spent what must have been several hours putting it all into his computer and E-Mailing me the results. His stories were interesting and welcome additions to the book. After reading his stories, I realized there was a very personal side of the entire "Cessna Warbirds" story needing to be told.

Other help came from around the world — literally. And all through the magic of CompuServe. Michael Jerram of the United Kingdom offered the results of his own research and the titles of several excellent books on Cessnas and their history. Jerome Grossman of France recalled having seen an article about the French Army's use of the L-19 in Chad, and he searched until he found it. Jerome willingly sent me his personal copy and put up with my pestering him for other details and assistance. He even suffered through my attempts at communicating in French (a skill once learned when I lived there for two years, but long since grown rusty from disuse). Yoshitaka Nishimura of Japan provided information on Fuji Industries' involvement with the L-19.

My Australian electronic buddy, Allan Elliott, went far beyond the call of friendship. Allan seemed to get as caught up in my research efforts as I was. He sent me Australian magazines, copies of historical articles, and a complete book on the Australian aerial participation in the Vietnam War. Allan also identified several potential Australian bookstore outlets for this book. So far, the only recompense he has asked for is a batch of USAF flight suit patches and a copy of this book. The patches have been sent, and the book is forthcoming.

Stephen Crocker is another Australian who has been more than willing to help. He flies a restored Cessna A-37B Dragonfly and has provided me with a wealth of information, from photos and historical records to his personal impressions of flying the aircraft. If Australian face-to-face hospitality is anything like their electronic hospitality, I've got to go visit "Down Under" someday.

Stephen Riethoff, John Macartney, and Clay Tice, Jr., all CompuServe acquaintances, provided tales and anecdotes from their Cessna recollections. I appreciate it.

When I ran into a research dead end on the subject of the U.S. Army's use of Cessna O-2s, someone mentioned Doug Powell, a retired Army officer and aviator. Doug had the information I was looking for and took the time to make copies of it, discuss everything he knew about the topic on the phone, and provide names and phone numbers of others who might know more. Through Doug's assistance, I tracked down Jim Grenier, who now owns one of the two original Army O-2s. Jim loaned me the only copies of some photographs of his aircraft, which he had restored to original Army configuration and colors.

There were two significant modifications made to the O-2 that never went beyond the prototype stage, and which were made by companies no longer in business — Wren Aircraft and Robertson Aircraft. Thanks again for suggestions received on the *Aviation Forum,* as they helped me track down the companies that now own all the Wren and Robertson records. Chip King, the engineering manager at Sierra Industries in Uvalde, Texas, willingly researched their old Robertson archives and found the photos and technical data on the Sandcrab prototype. You will find this information in the O-2 section of this book. Chip loaned me the photos on the strength of a phone call. Todd Peterson, who now supports the Wren modifications, put up with my interrupting his evening with a phone call. He discussed what he knew about the Wren O-2 conversion, which was a lot more than any other source I had found, and spent additional time finding and copying the drawing included herein.

Lest anyone think only old Army pilots contributed to this book, I want to thank my fellow USAF pilots. First, Darrell R. (Doc) Lambert with whom I have worked for five years. Doc devoted an entire evening to talking O-2s and the Vietnam War, explaining each and every photo he had accumulated during his year in Thailand, and letting me borrow the entire lot to make copies. He then spent additional time proofreading the transcript of the tape I had made that evening of our conversation. I would be remiss if I did not also thank Doc's charming "significant other," Debbi Blackmon, for letting us chase her from her own living room, and for feeding us.

Fred McNeill, now an Adjunct Professor of Law at the University of Phoenix, responded to my on-line queries early in my research. He offered to discuss his O-2 tour (taken late in the Vietnam War), and offered a little-known story about the symbiotic relationship between the high-flying Lockheed U-2 and the Cessna U-3 (Model 310). Besides taking time to spend a couple of evenings on the phone talking about his experiences, Fred went through his extensive personal photo collection, made copies of those photos he thought I would find useful, and mailed them to me. And then, he also provided some free legal advice on a personal matter having nothing to do with this book.

Airline pilot John Wiley, from Atlanta, was also ready and willing to provide assistance with both O-2 stories and photographs, after seeing my on-line query. We originally set up a meeting in Atlanta, but our schedules conflicted and we had to settle for a telephone interview. John also took time to sort through his personal photo files and sent me a bunch of them for copying, taking time to provide narratives for each slide. His candid description of the life of a USAF forward air controller in Vietnam enlivened the O-2 section of the book. He even assured me he will be one of the first to buy a copy — so I know I have at least one sale!

Although I had been a USAF T-41 instructor for many years, I wanted some tales other than just my own. I had worked for three years with then-Captain George Vierno and had considered him a friend, but we had not been in contact for almost 20 years. I tracked him down in Denver, and we spent some time recalling our T-41 years. The result of that reunion helped to flesh out the T-41 chapter.

I contacted Ed Reints of Colorado through my brief flirtation with America On-Line. Ed had a friend, Darrel Porter, who was restoring an O-2 that had been purchased from the aircraft bone yard at Davis-Monthan AFB. Ed and Darrel provided me with some photos of the in-progress restoration, and copies of the aircraft's official USAF historical records, in exchange for some of the photos I had accumulated that illustrated the configuration and paint schemes used on active duty O-2s.

When I tried to track down a now-defunct organization devoted to the preservation of the Cessna T-50 Bobcat, I eventually located Gary Montpelier (again thanks to on-line assistance and suggestions). Gary had acquired all the records and data from the original "T-50 Flying Bobcats." He was also in the process of restoring a T-50 to its AT-17 configuration. We bartered. I sent him some detailed photos of the AT-17 cockpit, and he sent me copies of some old Bobcat ads from the World War II era to use as fillers, along with some additional technical and historical data I needed.

USAF Public Affairs offices were also helpful. Captain Brent Boller, 12th FTW Public Affairs at Randolph AFB, had helped me with an earlier magazine project and came through one more time with some excellent and recent T-37 photos. Lieutenant Colonel James Thomas, commander of the USAF Academy's 557th Flying Training Squadron (FTS), provided an afternoon's hospitality while his unit still had T-41s. He ensured that I had access to the aircraft, the flightline, the maintenance operation, and several of his pilots. I came away with more information than I could possibly use, but also many T-41 photos made even more dramatic with the beautiful Colorado mountains as a backdrop.

Through the auspices of the Sheppard AFB Public Affairs office, I met Royal Netherlands Air Force Lieutenant Colonel Adriann Brouwer, operations officer of the 89th FTS. Lieutenant Colonel Brouwer's candid discussion of the Euro-NATO Joint Jet Pilot Training Program (specifically, the T-37 portion of that training) helped to fill-in the real story of what goes on there. He also arranged to have one of their T-37s set aside for photographic purposes, had the engine shop set-up an uninstalled engine for photographs, and provided me with a "seeing-eye lieutenant" for the duration of my visit.

Paul Zervos, Air Education and Training Command (AETC) historian at Randolph AFB, offered me access to their extensive historical files and was able to provide some T-41 and T-37 photos. Hill Goodspeed, National Museum of Naval Aviation's Emil Buehler Naval Aviation Library, was instrumental in providing data on the Navy T-47 program and historical data on the South Vietnamese L-19 that landed on the USS Ranger in 1975. Mike Starn, Marine Corps Museum, was likewise helpful with data on Marine use in various Cessna models.

In addition, I would like to thank my many co-workers who have provided both interest and support throughout this long ordeal, and who put up with my periodic complaints about overwork due to this project.

Finally, I'd like to thank Greg Bayer and Frank Hamilton of Jones Publishing, Inc. Without them, this book would never have been started. Without their support, encouragement, and patience, it might not have been finished. They tolerantly put up with my periodic phone calls, which were as much pleas for moral support as progress updates, I hope they are satisfied with the result. ✝

Foreword

Airpower is a seamless, tightly woven fabric in which no pilot, no unit and no aircraft does not depend on others. The hottest jet pilot was a trainee once. The most devastating strike mission must sit on the ground if a vital member of the planning team cannot get to the airfield, and it is of no use at all if it cannot find its target.

We can also forget too easily that reconnaissance satellites and drones, laser-guided weapons, high resolution radars, and high-speed secure datalinks are recent inventions. From World War II through Vietnam, pilots needed more direct, lower-tech help in hitting their targets; and "secure communications" often meant a courier with a locked dispatch case in constant view.

Many of these operations relied on the rugged if unglamorous products of the Cessna Aircraft Company. There is probably no more widely distributed type of airplane than a Cessna. Cessna is the only make of aircraft which every USAF pilot flies: a ling-time pilot with no Cessna time in his or her logbook is a rare bird indeed, as rare as a helicopter pilot who has never flown a Bell.

Does Cessna get respect for this performance? Probably not. Familiarity breeds contempt, and the Cessna usually passes unnoticed wherever it flies.

This is why Walt Shiel's detailed survey of the military Cessnas is so important. Some history must be captured before the record are dispersed or buried in musty vaults, especially when its importance was underrated at the time.

Here, then you will find the complete family of early military Cessnas, which trained and transported throughout the world in World War II; the amazing exploits and many versions of the O-1 Bird Dog observation aircraft and its Vietnam-era follow-on, the push-pull O-2; and the story of the T-37 Tweet and its armed cousin, the A-37 Dragonfly. There are also even less-known stories — one-offs such as barely recognizable as an O-2, and other almost forgotten stories such as Cessnas foray into the helicopter business.

Numbers sometimes climb out of the text and grab you. Towards the end of a fascinating discussion of the "Raven" forward air controllers who marked targets in the secret war over Laos, Shiel notes that "a total of 191 pilots served as Raven FACs, and 31 of them were killed in action." Dropping ordnance on a ground target is one thing: marking it with rockets and loitering over it for minutes on end is another. Nevertheless, the book is full of tales of O-1 pilots who ignored instruction to break off and stayed until the job was done or the enemy shot so many pieces off the airplane that it would no longer fly.

Congratulations Walt on a thorough history of an unjustly neglected family of aircraft, and welcome to the family of aviation writers ✝

Bill Sweetman
Author "Aurora: The Pentagon's Secret Spyplane"
Motorbroks, 1993

Introduction

"Silver Wings"

Some people think of those silver wings
      As glorious, glamorous li'l ole things
That shine like a beacon when a pilot makes love
      And reflect all the moonlight that comes from above.

But to a flyer they're not that at all!
      Those wings are an emblem of an uphill haul.
It's just a small way that a man's reimbursed
      For the numerous times he's been viciously cursed.

A hunk of cheap silver that's been shaped into wings
      The representation of lots of fine things,
Of sweatin' and swearin' and laughin' and tears,
      Of a few open posts with the boys, and some beers.

It just adds up to this in a pilot's eye
      The stuff that he went through to learn how to fly
Day after day in a classroom or cloud
      By gosh, it's enough to make any man proud!

— *Author Unknown*

Shortly before I received my commission through the Air Force Reserve Officers Training Corps at Michigan State University in June of 1969, the Air Force issued me a set of orders to report to Webb AFB in Big Spring, Texas, for Undergraduate Pilot Training (UPT). When I went home and told my wife, her first reaction was, "Where is Big Spring, Texas?" I certainly had no idea. We dragged out a map and located Big Spring — way out in West Texas, some 90 miles south of Lubbock. In other words, in the middle of absolutely nowhere. Somehow, it did not sound like a garden spot to either of us.

Big Spring failed to exceed our expectations. However, I was soon immersed in the 12-hour days of UPT and really did not pay much attention to the surrounding dust and mesquite trees. What did get my attention was the first aircraft the Air Force assigned me and my Class 71-01 cohorts to fly (71-01: first graduating Webb class of fiscal year 1971). We were bussed out to the nearby Howard County Airport, introduced to a bunch of civilian instructors, and shown the aircraft in which we would be taking our first military training — a Cessna Model 172!

I had already earned my private pilot's license and was somewhat underwhelmed by the prospect of continuing to fly a lightplane, while watching and listening to the jets from Webb zip by overhead. However, soon we all learned that even the 172, or T-41 as the military called it, could be a challenge when combined with learning the "military way" of flying airplanes in the midst of the USAF's high-pressure pilot training.

Leaving Howard County Airport behind, we were beginning to understand the military approach to aviation, but were more than ready to wrap our fists around the sticks of a bona-fide Air Force jet aircraft. We were next introduced to yet another Cessna — the T-37. We learned to appreciate the intricacies of its systems, the procedures for flying it, and the excruciatingly ear-piercing whine from the "6600-pound dog whistle's" screaming little turbojet engines. And we found out just how challenging that lovable beast could be as we learned a lot of new and wondrous things things like spins, aerobatics, and instrument flying. The worst part about flying the T-37 was our wives and girlfriends all insisted the airplane was *cute*!

And, besides, we wanted speed.

We soon left those Cessnas behind and moved on to the beautiful and supersonic Northrop T-38 Talons. Six months later, they pinned silver wings on us.

But the Air Force was determined to keep me humble. They decided I should stay at Webb as an instructor — in the Cessna T-37, of course. Later, I found myself flying the T-41 at Howard County Airport (as one of the Air Force instructors supervising the civilian contract operation) and then at Hondo, Texas, when we consolidated all T-41 operations at that ex-World War II navigator training base west of San Antonio. When I got out of the Air Force in 1976, I went to work as a civilian engineer, but soon found myself longing for military flight again. So I joined the Michigan Air National Guard to fly the Cessna O-2A (a military version of the Model 337 Skymaster). When I stopped flying O-2s in 1979, I found I had accumulated 2,000 hours of military flying time, and all but 120 hours of it had been in Cessnas. I later flew other Air Force airplanes, but I guess there remained a certain soft spot in my heart for Cessnas (although some have alleged the soft spot might be elsewhere).

I relate all of the above events and experiences by way of explaining how I came to write this book. In June of 1994, I proposed to Frank Hamilton of Jones Publishing, Inc. (editor of *Cessna Owner* and *Pipers* magazines) a series of articles on military Cessna aircraft. I knew there had been quite a few of them, and I figured I could start out with the ones I knew best — the T-41, the T-37, and the O-2. Frank thought it sounded like a good idea, but soon turned the whole thing over to Jones Publishing's book publisher, Greg Bayer. Greg suggested, hey, what the hell, why not just make it into a book? Now, I had been doing some free-lance writing, mostly magazine articles for a variety of aviation and equine magazines, plus a few short stories and even a few novels (well, every writer has novels in his desk drawer), but I had never even considered a nonfiction project like this. However, I let Greg twist my arm (okay, he didn't have to twist all that hard) and I said yes.

Greg's first question concerned how long I would require to complete the book. I had no idea, but that had never stopped me before. I worked as an engineer for a defense company (most writers have to have a "day job") and routinely estimated projects I had never done before, so I just put on my engineer's cap and laid out a plan. It looked good (I was impressed with my foresight and careful attention to detail), and I quickly determined one year ought to be more than enough time. (If I only knew then what I know now!)

Well, let me just note that the last year has been an educational experience. I started out by calling various military museums. They were helpful, but mostly with pictures. Then I started scouring the book stores and libraries (thank God for the interlibrary loan system). And, finally, I wised up and used the one tool that had been sitting in front of me all along — my computer. I had been a member of CompuServe for almost a year at that point, but had never really used it for serious research. So, I put out my electronic feelers and asked the denizens of cyberspace (in places like the *Aviation Forum* and the *Military Forum*) for help and ideas and suggestions and — well, most anything.

Believe me, there is a real honest-to-God community out there on the "Information Superhighway." (Damn! I promised myself I wasn't going to use the phrase "Information Superhighway.") I was amazed at the numbers of people, from all over the world, who volunteered to help. You'd think I was offering to pay them (which I most definitely was not). Pilots and airplane fanatics just love to talk about airplanes, particularly airplanes they own or have flown.

Before long, I found myself piling up stacks of photos, receiving pages and pages of "war stories," and buying a lot of books. One source led to another source. I interviewed people face-to-face, on the telephone, and via E-Mail. It was fun, it was fascinating, and it was educational. But, you know, I wasn't really doing any writing. Doing lots of research, having lots of fun, but not *writing*. Finally, I looked at the stacks of material I had accumulated (by February of 1995 it had taken over our once-neat dining room) and realized if I was going to turn all of this material into 100,000 or so words of illuminating text, I had damn well better get started. The time had come to pull the plug on research and crank up the writing engine.

What does that mean? It means I would never be so foolish as to claim this book represents the definitive study of military Cessna aircraft. I could continue my research for another two years and maybe still not achieve such a lofty goal. But I think it does provide a concise history of Cessna's involvement in military aviation, with lots of personal stories (my own and those of others) added in an attempt to breathe life into the usual historical accumulation of dates and numbers and who-did-what-when. I hope I have succeeded. And I hope the reader gets even a fraction of the enjoyment out of reading it that I got out of writing it.

As the project wound down to the last few weeks, I told my wife it was beginning to resemble pregnancy. After almost a year's gestation, I was more than ready to just deliver the damn thing. Finally, I did. It was fun, but I have to admit to being relieved it's over.

If you enjoy it, let me know. If you find errors, let me know about those, too.

As we say in the flying game — keep the pointy end forward and the dirty side down! ✛

Walt Shiel
E-Mail: 72624.3632@compuserve.com
Weatherford, Texas
1 November 1995

Abreviations & Definitions

AAA	Anti-Aircraft Artillery
AAF	Army Air Force
ABCCC	Airborne Command and Control Center
ADF	Automatic Direction Finder
AETC	Air Education and Training Command
AFB	Air Force Base
AFFTC	Air Force Flight Test Center
AGL	Above Ground Level
ALAT	Aviation Légère de l'Armée de Terre (French Army Light Aviation)
AM	Amplitude Modulation
ANG	Air National Guard
AO	Area of Operation
AOA	Angle of Attack
API	Armor Piercing Incendiary
ARVN	Army of the Republic of (South) Vietnam
ATC	Air Training Command
BDA	Battle Damage Assessment
BLC	Boundary Layer Control
BuNo	Bureau Number
c/n	Constructor Number
CAA	Civil Aviation Administration
CAS	(1) Calibrated Air Speed
	(2) Close Air Support
CDI	Course Deviation Indicator
CIA	Central Intelligence Agency
DASC	Direct Air Support Center
Dash One	USAF Pilot's Flight Manual
DFC	Distinguished Flying Cross
DMZ	Demilitarized Zone
DoD	Department of Defense
FAA	Federal Aviation Administration
FAC	Forward Air Control(ler)
FFAR	Folding Fin Aircraft Rocket
FM	Frequency Modulation
FTS	Flying Training Squadron
G	Force of Gravity
GCA	Ground Controlled Approach

GCI	Ground Controlled Intercept
GFE	Government Furnished Equipment
GI	Government Issue
GPH	Gallons Per Hour
Guard	UHF Emergency Radio Frequency (243.0 MHz)
HE	High Explosive
HEI	High Explosive Incendiary
IAS	Indicated Air Speed
IFF/SIF	Identification Friend or Foe / Selective Identification Feature
IFR	Instrument Flight Rules
IP	(1) Initial Point (2) Instructor Pilot
JPATS	Joint Primary Aircraft Training System
KAF	Khmer Air Force
KBA	Killed By Air
KCAS	Knots Calibrated Air Speed
KIA	Killed In Action
KIAS	Knots Indicated Air Speed
Klick	Kilometer
Knot	One Nautical Mile Per Hour
KTAS	Knots True Air Speed
LF	Low Frequency
MAAG	Military Assistance Advisory Group
MAP	Military Assistance Program
mm	Millimeter
N Number	FAA Aircraft Registration Number (All Begin With The Letter "N")
Nautical Mile	6,080 Feet
NG	National Guard (Army)
NVA	North Vietnamese Army
PPH	Pounds Per Hour
PSP	Pierced Steel Planking
RAAF	Royal Australian Air Force
RCAF	Royal Canadian Air Force
Recce	Reconnaissance
RKA	Royal Khmer Army

RLAF	Royal Laotian Air Force
ROE	Rules of Engagement
rpm	Revolutions Per Minute
RTAF	Royal Thai Air Force
SAWC	Special Air Warfare Center
s/n	Serial Number
SCAMP	Standard Configuration and Modification Program
SRW	Strategic Reconnaissance Wing
Statute Mile	5,280 Feet
STOL	Short Takeoff and Landing
T.O.	Technical Order
Tac Air	Tactical Aircraft/Airstrike
TACAN	Tactical Aid to Navigation
TACS	Tactical Air Control System
TAS	True Air Speed
TASS	Tactical Air Support Squadron
TFG	Tactical Fighter Group
TFS	Tactical Fighter Squadron
TFW	Tactical Fighter Wing
Triple-A	Anti-Aircraft Artillery
UHF	Ultra-High Frequency
ULG	Universal Landing Gear
U.S.	United States
USAF	United States Air Force
USN	United States Navy
V-J Day	Victory Over Japan Day
VC	Viet Cong
VFR	Visual Flight Rules
VHF	Very High Frequency
VIP	Very Important Person
VNAF	(South) Vietnamese Air Force
VOR	VHF Omnidirectional Range
VR	Visual Reconnaissance
VTOL	Vertical Takeoff and Landing
Willie Pete	White Phosphorous (Rocket)
WW II	World War Two
✠	

The Cessna Dynasty
A History of the Cessna Aircraft Company

-chapter 1-

In 1911, Clyde Vernon Cessna, a 31-year-old farmer/mechanic from Rago, Kansas, became fascinated with the embryonic technology of aviation. Cessna was an Overland automobile dealer in Enid, Oklahoma, but after watching the exhibitions of the Moisant International Aviation Air Circus in Oklahoma City in February, he switched his focus from automobiles to airplanes. This changed his life, and ultimately made the Cessna name synonymous with lightplanes and general aviation.

Shortly after seeing the Air Circus, Cessna built a copy of the French Bleriot monoplane. When he lifted off on the craft's maiden voyage, he established himself as the first person between the Mississippi River and the Rocky Mountains to build and fly his own airplane. As was common in those early years of aviation, Clyde Cessna taught himself to fly. Before the year was out, he had mastered the airplane — despite a dozen "unsuccessful" attempts — and had made four demonstration flights over the Great Salt Plains near Jet, Oklahoma. For the next several years, he modified and improved his aircraft during the winter months and conducted flying exhibitions throughout Oklahoma and Kansas during the warmer months. His modifications included improved landing gear and an air-cooled engine. He dubbed the revised aircraft "Silver Wings."

In 1916, Cessna moved his aircraft operation to Wichita, Kansas, under the auspices of J. J. Jones of the Jones Motor Car Company. This move prophesied the eventual coronation of Wichita as the "Air Capital of the World" — where more aircraft manufacturers established their headquarters than in any other single location in the world. In exchange for space in the Jones Motor Car Company plant to construct a new aircraft of his own design, Cessna agreed to paint the name "Jones Six" on the underside of his new airplane's wing to advertise the Jones Light Six automobile. Cessna later flew his new "Cessna Comet," with its partially enclosed cockpit, from Wichita to Blackwell, Oklahoma, at the heady average speed of 124.62 miles-per-hour. Cessna anticipated an active flying demonstration season in the summer of 1917, but America's involvement in World War I interrupted his flying enterprises. As a result, he returned to farming in Rago, Kansas.

But destiny was not thwarted so easily. At the end of the "War to End All Wars," Cessna returned to aviation. In 1925, he joined forces with Walter Beech and Lloyd Stearman to form the Travel Air Manufacturing Company. Cessna was the company's first president and designed the four-place cabin monoplane on which a successful series of Travel Air models was based, including the first civilian aircraft to fly from the United States to Hawaii.

However, unsatisfied with the emphasis on biplane designs at Travel Air, Cessna resigned in 1927 and moved into a small shop on West Douglas Street in Wichita. In August, he completed a new four-place Comet with a fully-cantilevered wing and 120-horsepower Anzani radial engine. The following month,

• *Clyde Cessna, circa 1911* •
(Kansas Aviation Museum/Robert J. Pickett Collection)

• *Clyde Cessna and the "Jones Six"* •
(Kansas Aviation Museum/Robert J. Pickett Collection)

• *Clyde Cessna in his 1927 prototype "A" series airplane, 20 August 1927* •
(Kansas Aviation Museum/Robert J. Pickett Collection)

• *Part of the original Cessna crew, 1927 (Left to Right): Romer Wiant, test pilot; George Bassett, financier (squatting); Clyde Cessna (dark suit); George Siedhoff, building contractor for Cessna plant (squatting); Frances Bowhan, test pilot; Mead Hargiss, early Cessna official* •
(Kansas Aviation Museum/Robert J. Pickett Collection)

Victor Roos of Omaha, Nebraska, joined with Cessna to form the Cessna-Roos Aircraft Company. By October, Roos had left the company to join a competitor. In December, Clyde Cessna's company was incorporated as the Cessna Aircraft Company, a name it still carries.

In 1928, Cessna designed and built the prototype of the "A" series of fully-cantilevered monoplanes — the three-seat Phantom. To demonstrate the design's integrity and to meet the new Department of Commerce stress test requirements, Cessna loaded an inverted "A" series wing with 14,800 pounds of sand bags, and then had five men stand on top of the load. The wing survived the 15,752-pound load and exceeded the government certification requirements by a factor of two.

Cessna Aircraft was issued Type Certificate Number 65 for the Anzani-powered, 2,260-pound Model "AA." The "A" series was the first light airplane with a fully-cantilevered wing produced in the United States. By the end of 1928, Cessna production included five models in the "A" series (with engines ranging from the 120-horsepower Anzani to the 150-horsepower Floco), the three-place BW (a beefed-up "A" with a 220-horsepower Wright J-5 engine), and the six-place CW-6 (with a 225-horsepower Wright J-5 engine). In September of 1928, test pilot Francis Bowhan won the New York-to-Los Angeles Transcontinental Air Derby in an "AW." Another "AW" placed first on the 50-mile closed-course portion of the National Air Races.

In 1929 Cessna built a fourth design, the four-place DC-6 with a 170-horsepower Curtiss Challenger engine, at what was to become the legendary Pawnee Division plant on East Pawnee Road. Located on the southeast side of Wichita, this is where most of the single-engine Cessnas would be built for the next 50 years. By the end of 1929, two new versions of the DC-6 were in production — the 3,180-pound, 330-horsepower DC-6A Scout Chief and the 3,100-pound, 250-horsepower DC-6B Scout — and 96 aircraft were back-ordered. Production rates peaked at 2.5 airplanes per week. Later, Cessna's foray into military aviation began when the Army Air Force put eight DC-6s into service.

The Great Depression struck just as production began at the Pawnee Road plant. Sales dwindled despite the excellent performance of the firm's designs. Cessna resorted to producing the CG-2 glider, which sold for $398, and some small aircraft prototypes in an attempt to develop something marketable in the midst of the Depression's poor economy. Designs included the FC-1 two-place monoplane, the GC-1 and GC-2 Racers, the single-seat EC-1 "Baby Cessna" (a variation of the CG-2 glider with a 25-horsepower Cleone engine), and the two-place EC-2. Despite these efforts, in 1931, after producing about 250 airplanes, Cessna Aircraft boarded up the Pawnee Road plant and put the buildings up for rent.

• Line-up of new Cessna models at the factory, 1928 (front to rear): BW, BW, AS, AA, AW, BW, AF •
(Kansas Aviation Museum/Robert J. Pickett Collection)

Still in the thick of the Depression, Clyde and his son Eldon formed the C.V. Cessna Aircraft Company with the backing of a small group of investors. Their first design was the CR-1 racing airplane. The CR-1 was soon modified to become the CR-2 and CR-2A. In 1933 Roy Liggett won the Colonel Green Cup Race with the 145-horsepower CR-2, and earned a second-place finish in an unlimited race with an average speed of 194.46 miles-per-hour. Liggett died later that year when his CR-2A crashed.

Johnny Livingston, a well-known race pilot, ordered a custom-built CR-3 for the race circuit. In 1933 the aircraft set a speed record of 237.4 miles-per-hour in the under 500-cubic-inch engine class. A fourth prototype design, the C-3 cabin monoplane, was built and sold to Walter Anderson, founder of the White Castle hamburger chain.

In January of 1934, Clyde Cessna joined his two nephews, Dwight and Dwane Wallace, in re-opening the Pawnee Road plant. Dwane Wallace, a recent Wichita University aeronautical engineering graduate, had worked briefly for Beech Aircraft Company. With Clyde as company president, Dwight as secretary-treasurer, and Dwane as plant manager, the revitalized company built a few more DC-6A and DC-6B aircraft while designing and

developing the modern, cabin class C-34 monoplane, a success even in the midst of the Depression. George Hart won the Cleveland Air Races in 1935 with the prototype C-34, while another C-34 with Dwane Wallace at the controls won the 1936 Detroit News Trophy and the appellation "World's Most Efficient Airplane." As this was the third time a Cessna had won that particular trophy, the company was given permanent possession of it.

In 1935, with the new company's success seemingly assured, Clyde Cessna sold out to the Wallaces and returned to his 640-acre homestead near Rago. He continued as company president until October 8, 1936, when he completely retired from aviation. Until his death in 1954 at the age of 74, he operated his farm and invented farming implements.

Late in 1936, an improved C-34, christened the C-37, was designed and built. In early 1938, the C-38 Airmaster rolled out of the factory with its curved landing gear legs, one foot wider main gear tread, lockable tail wheel, and plexiglass windshield. When hydraulic brakes and electric wing flaps were added to the airplane later that year, the new design was dubbed the C-145 Airmaster.

As the C-145 went into production, a young man, who had been fired from his 25¢-per-hour job as shop foreman with a Wichita venetian blind manufacturer, came to work at Cessna for a 40-percent raise, increasing his wages to a whopping 35¢-per-hour. This man, Duane Moore, stayed on for the next 40 years (except for two years in the Navy during WW II), eventually retiring as Cessna's configuration control manager after serving almost two decades as production manager for the Military Aircraft Division.

Cessna's first twin-engine design, the Cessna T-50 Bobcat sporting Cessna's first retractable landing gear, was added to the company's Airmaster series and completed its initial flight in 1939. Bobcats and Airmasters were selling, but the company was financially depleted. Dwane Wallace, with a mere $5.03 in the corporate bank account, convinced the Royal Canadian Air Force (RCAF) the T-50 would be an ideal training aircraft for bomber pilots. Soon, the U. S. Army Air Corps (later the Army Air Force — AAF) ordered its own version of the plane in what was to be Cessna's largest production order to date. The Army Air Corps designated their new multi-engine trainer the AT-8, while the RCAF called theirs the Crane I. With orders for hundreds of T-50s, Wallace was able to acquire financing from a Wichita bank. Production quickly soared.

Duane Moore remembers that Cessna's production manager had to double-up on the production lines to meet the delivery timetable for the Canadian T-50 contract, putting the plant on an around-the-clock schedule. The production manager induced Moore to work a second shift by providing him with a motor scooter on which to

• *Clyde Cessna and his CG-2 glider on floats* •
(Kansas Aviation Museum/Robert J. Pickett Collection)

fetch and deliver parts all over the plant. After hand-building the prototype T-50, Moore says they built a jig around the welded fuselage to build the next ones. However, the tubing in the new jig shrunk just a bit and the subsequent T-50s turned out to be slightly smaller than the original.

New manufacturing facilities and a two-story administration building were built. Total company-owned real estate increased to 640 acres. In 1941, Cessna's employment swelled from 200 employees to 1,500 in just seven months. Production soon increased even more as the Army Air Corps ordered new AT-17 trainer and UC-78 utility and cargo models of the T-50. By the completion of the T-50 production run, a total of 5,399 aircraft had been delivered. During the war years, Cessna designed and built several experimental aircraft for the military market — the P-7/T-50A, P-10, C-106, and C-106A — but none of these were fielded.

Cessna's Depression-era experience with gliders was called upon again during World War II. On September 4, 1942, Cessna was one of 16 companies receiving orders to build 1,500 Waco-designed CG-4A gliders in preparation for the invasion of Europe. Cessna was designated the prime contractor for their portion of the production, but sub-contracted assembly to other Wichita manufacturers, mostly Boeing. Half of the orders were eventually cancelled, and the last

• *The C.V. Cessna Aircraft Company model CR-3 just after its initial test flight in 1933* •
(Kansas Aviation Museum/Robert J. Pickett Collection)

CG-4A was delivered in January of 1943. Parts and subassemblies were manufactured by a multitude of small manufacturers from communities across the country — among them, wings from Grand Rapids, Michigan, and Beatrice, Nebraska — and all three major aircraft companies in Wichita (Cessna, Beech, and Boeing) had a hand in the final assembly. Colonel Ray G. Harris, Army Air Force supervisor of the Midwestern Procurement District, said, "It is a story of industrial and Army cooperation and evidence of the ability of American industries to undertake a job that even a year ago would have been unbelievable."

The fuselage of the CG-4A featured welded steel tubing, the cockpit framework consisted of chrome molybdenum steel, the wings and tail were wood, and the entire aircraft was covered with fabric. The fuselage was box-shaped to accommodate either 15 fully-equipped infantry troops, a standard Army Jeep, a one-quarter-ton truck with a four-man crew, or a 75mm howitzer with a three-man crew. Normal personnel entry was through the aft doors, but the entire nose section (including the cockpit) hinged upward to allow loading vehicles or howitzers. The CG-4A's maximum gross weight was 7,500 pounds and could be towed at speeds up to 150 miles-per-hour behind aircraft such as the C-46 and C-47. The first combat use of the new gliders was during the invasion of

Sicily in July of 1943. Serial numbers for the Cessna contract aircraft, designated the CG-4A-CE even though they were actually assembled by Boeing-Wichita, were 42-61101 through 42-61460 and 42-61821 through 42-62210. After the war, none of the troop gliders were authorized for civilian use. Many were sold as war surplus — but the customers discarded the aircraft and kept the excellent packing crates (each glider came in a three-crate kit) for use as storage buildings or to reuse the high-grade lumber from which they had been built.

In September of 1942, Cessna was awarded the Army-Navy "E" Award for production quality, work stoppage avoidance, solving production problems, maintaining fair labor practices, management, labor force, accident record, and subcontracting — the first Wichita-based company to win this prestigious award. Cessna received the award four more times during the war years.

During World War II, Cessna also built components of the Boeing B-29 Super Fortress and the Douglas A-26 Invader. Employment peaked at 6,074 employees working in 468,000 square feet of facilities. When the war ended, with $191,753,000 of wartime sales, Cessna returned to civilian aircraft production.

By V-J Day, Cessna employment had dropped to 1,800 and soon plunged even further to 450. Cessna concentrated on single-engine airplanes with the highly-

successful Model 120 and 140 series, designed with post-war GI Bill flight training in mind, and the more powerful and comfortable four-place Models 190 and 195. The Model 120 and 140 became popular in 1946, and employment again surged to 1,873 as production jumped to 30 airplanes per day. Sales in 1946 climbed to $6,327,663.

In 1946, Duane Moore was responsible for determining where and how to mount the radios and antennas in the new aircraft. He established the company's first radio laboratory near an abandoned radio tower, and put the aircraft radio antennas on top of the tower to test them. Moore also recalls that the door between the production line and the flight test hangar was not as wide as the aircraft's wingspan. As a result, they left the landing gear off until the aircraft was in the hangar, and used dollies with castering wheels to carefully manipulate each aircraft through the narrow door.

Soon, a lot of competition developed in the two-place airplane market, and production rates slipped to five aircraft per day by the end of 1947,

• *Cessna Model C-145 over Golden Gate Bridge, San Francisco, 6 April 1939* •
(Kansas Aviation Museum/Robert J. Pickett Collection)

despite deliveries of the new Model 190/195 and Model 170 series for the business travel market. In 1948, prices for Cessna aircraft started at $2,845 for a Model 120 and peaked at $13,750 for a Model 195. Cessna had branched out into non-aircraft manufacturing with Quartermaster Corps Furniture for the military market, farm hydraulic equipment, and aluminum lockers. The year 1948 also witnessed Cessna's gradual return to military aircraft production with sales of Model 195s to the Army and Air Force as LC-126s. Cessna's 1948 annual report stated unequivocally that "management is in close touch with the needs of the military, and will aggressively attempt to secure such military business as may fit into Cessna's picture, either on a prime contract or subcontract basis."

Although 18 companies had been producing general aviation aircraft in 1946, only five were still doing so by the end of 1949. Cessna Aircraft Company was one of them, despite an employment of only 504 workers — with only 18 of them engineers.

In 1949, the Army issued a "Request for Proposals" for a liaison aircraft able to operate from small, unprepared airstrips — the U.S. Army Observation Aircraft. Cessna won the competition, and the renowned L-19 (later the O-1) Bird Dog was born, marking Cessna's first use of high-lift wing flaps. The Bird Dog saw combat service in the Korean War beginning in early 1951.

During the 1950s, Cessna military production included rudders for Boeing's B-47 and B-52 jet bombers, aft sections and empennages for Lockheed's T-33 Shooting Star jet trainer and F-94 Starfire all-weather fighter, and empennage assemblies for Republic's F-84F Thunderstreak and F-105 Thunderchief fighters.

In 1950, Cessna opened the Prospect Plant on the west side of Wichita, where all of the hardware for the military contracts was produced. Initially, there was no running water at this refurbished Aero Parts Company facility, and no cafeteria. Everyone packed their lunches and water was provided in insulated jugs. The staff numbered 17 when the first B-47 rudder contract was awarded, but increased to 2,400 by 1965.

In 1953, the company returned to the twin-engine market with the beautiful Model 310, the first in a long string of 300-series light twins. The prototype of Cessna's first jet aircraft, the Model 318, flew in 1954, later becoming the Air Force's ubiquitous T-37 twin-jet basic trainer. In April of 1957, the new Military Aircraft Division name was assigned to the Prospect Plant, home of T-37 production.

Cessna pursued corporate jet business with their Fanjet 500 in 1960, redesignated the Cessna 500 Citation in 1961 — the first in a long and auspicious line of business jet aircraft.

With Army aviation refocusing on helicopters and the commercial helicopter market growing, Cessna purchased Seibel Helicopter Company in March of 1952 through an exchange of 21,109 shares of Cessna common stock. Seibel's minuscule four-employee staff, almost miraculously, had designed, built, and certified a helicopter on a meager investment of only $125,000. Although the Army

• Prototype Cessna Model T-50, NX20784 •
(Kansas Aviation Museum/Robert J. Pickett Collection)

had bought two of the Seibel YH-24s for flight evaluations, they had no plans to purchase more. Cessna president Dwane Wallace was interested in Seibel more for its expertise than its rudimentary initial design. Cessna added its own management and production team to form the Cessna Helicopter Division. The Army eventually ordered ten YH-41 Senecas in 1957, and the Air Force acquired 15 more in 1962-1963 for use by South American countries under the Military Assistance Program (MAP). The company developed a civilian version, the Model CH-1D Skyhook, and sold it to several commercial operators. In 1962, after some problems and bad publicity, Cessna discontinued all helicopter development and production.

The 3,000th military L-19 was delivered in November of 1957, and the 30,000th Cessna aircraft was delivered by the end of the year. The four-engine, 282 mile-per-hour prototype Model 620 airliner was developed the same year, with 350-horsepower supercharged engines. With the advent of jet airliners, the Model 620 never went into production.

Cessna continued to grow and broaden its business base. The Aircraft Radio Corporation was purchased in

1959 to gain a foothold in the avionics market. Also in 1959, Cessna won the design competition for the Boeing Minute Man ICBM transporter-erector, with first deliveries made the following year. Cessna acquired propeller manufacturer McCauley Industrial Corporation as a subsidiary in 1960 and established an industrial hydraulics plant in Glenrothes, Scotland. Cessna acquired a 49 percent interest in Avions Max Holst of Reims, France, in 1960 and purchased the company in 1962, renaming it Reims Aviation. Reims provided Cessna a European manufacturing facility for modified versions of its American-designed products.

By 1962, military contracts were again thriving, with subcontracts to McDonnell Aircraft Corporation for F-4 bomb and missile rack assemblies, spares for the Boeing B-52, modifications for the L-19, and a classified contract for ordnance for the Army. The 50,000th Cessna was delivered in February of 1963.

President Lyndon Johnson presented Cessna president Dwane Wallace with the President's "E" Award, for exporting excellence, at a White House ceremony in 1964. That year also saw the start of Model 172 production at the Reims Aviation facility in France.

Nineteen sixty-five was a watershed year for Cessna. Total sales achieved a corporate record of $148,400,000 with 5,629 aircraft delivered — 48 percent of the total general aviation market. This marked the tenth consecutive year Cessna had sold more aircraft than any other company in the world, and the eighth consecutive year as worldwide civilian aircraft dollar-volume leader. By 1965, Cessna was also the industry leader in twin-engine general aviation aircraft sales. It was the year Cessna initiated its campaign to increase student pilot starts by offering special introductory rates for flight lessons through its "Learn to Fly" program. As a result, some 3,000 Cessna Model 150s were sold over the next year through 860 wholesale and dealer outlets. Almost one million square feet of new manufacturing plant facilities were built, and employment topped 11,000.

Overseas manufacturing expanded in 1967. The French Reims plant began to make the F-150, and DIN-FIA (an Argentinian industrial complex) started production of the Model A182. Cessna sold the 14,000th Model 172 Skyhawk in 1967. Additional military production of T-37s, T-41s, U-17s, and A-37s began, and the U.S. Army issued a contract to modify and update 179 O-1 Bird Dogs. By 1968 the Cessna general aviation line included 30 different aircraft models, sold through more than 900 retail outlets.

On 15 September 1969, the prototype Cessna Citation flew for the first time, marking the company's next step in the burgeoning civilian business jet market. Despite a flagging economy, Cessna inaugurated a nation-wide network of Cessna Pilot Centers in 1970 with a 39-model civilian product line. In 1971, Cessna claimed 53 percent of all civilian aircraft sales in the United States, although the corporate emphasis moved from personal to business transportation.

Sales of the new Citation business jet zoomed in 1972 when 35 aircraft were delivered. The following year, Cessna delivered 71 Citations, then 79 in 1974, plus another 877 multi-engine propeller-driven aircraft. Cessna had established itself as a major supplier of corporate aircraft. Cessna's financial enterprise expanded during this period as well, with Cessna Finance Corporation building its fourth North American branch and its first European branch.

Dwane Wallace retired in 1975 as chairman of the board, 40 years after taking office as the company president. During his tenure, Cessna Aircraft Company produced over 126,000 aircraft and became the world's largest manufacturer of aircraft for the general aviation market. In the year Wallace retired, Cessna delivered 90 Citation business jets, and the Pawnee Division rolled out its 100,000th single-engine airplane. The following year, the 27,000th Model 172 was delivered, and employment exceeded 15,000.

By 1977, Cessna was producing 47 different models for the general aviation market. The 400th Citation was produced in September of 1977, and the first Conquest turboprop was sold. Employment topped 16,000. In 1978, Cessna became the first manufacturer to offer weather radar as an option for its single-engine aircraft. The Ag Husky was introduced that year — the world's first turbocharged agricultural aircraft — and Clyde Cessna was inducted posthumously into the Aviation Hall of Fame on 22 July at the 17th Annual Enshrinement Ceremonies at the Convention Center in Dayton, Ohio.

Another major aviation milestone was reached in 1979 when Cessna's Turbo Centurion and Pressurized Centurion achieved FAA approval as the only production single-engine airplanes certified for flight into known icing conditions.

In 1980, Cessna sales topped $1 billion with a 54 percent share of the U.S. lightplane market. By 1982, over 1,000 Citations had been delivered. Despite a downturn in the lightplane industry, Cessna continued to prosper in 1983 with a major order from Federal Express® for a fleet of Caravan I single-engine turboprops, and a Navy contract for the lease of 15 Citations, designated T-47A, for Naval Flight Officer training. In 1985, Cessna merged with defense contractor General Dynamics Corporation as

• *U.S. Air Force Museum's Army Air Force Waco CG-4A* •
(U.S. Air Force)

• Line-up of a variety of military Cessna aircraft (Left to Right, starting on back row): U-17, L-19, U-3, O-2A, O-2B, A-37B •
(Kansas Aviation Museum/Robert J. Pickett Collection)

a wholly-owned subsidiary. The following year, Cessna received the Robert J. Collier trophy for the Citation fleet's outstanding safety record.

Federal Express® orders for Caravans reached 199 units in 1988, and the 1,500th Citation was delivered. The Fluid Power Division was sold to Eaton Corporation that same year. The next year, Reims Aviation was sold, and the Citation fleet reached 5,000,000 total flying hours. In 1990 Cessna opened a training and manufacturing center in an economically depressed portion of Wichita to train and employ people previously considered unemployable.

On 29 April 1991, the CitationJet engineering prototype made its maiden flight, making its first trade show appearance at the National Business Aircraft Association convention in Houston later that year. Also in April, Cessna delivered the 100th Citation V to a French company. On 20 November, the CitationJet pre-production prototype made its first flight.

General Dynamics Corporation sold Cessna to Textron, Incorporated in January of 1992, the same month FAA certification was received for the Citation VII. In October of that year, the CitationJet was certificated, and the first delivery of the new jet was made on 30 March 1993. "Citation Celebration 2,000" was launched in 1993,

culminating with the delivery of the 2,000th Citation — a Citation VII — 21 years after delivery of the first Citation.

Beyond the thousands of L-19 observation aircraft and T-37 jet trainers, Cessna produced many other aircraft for military use. Hundreds of T-41 trainers (militarized Model 172s) have been sold to both United States and foreign military services. The centerline-thrust Model 337 was adapted for forward air control duties and served admirably as the O-2 throughout the Vietnam War. The T-37 design was beefed-up and re-engined to become the A-37 — the world's smallest attack jet.

Besides those specific models built for military use, many other off-the-shelf civilian Cessnas have seen military service. In fact, it is difficult to identify a Cessna model since 1950 that has not seen some kind of military service somewhere in the world.

Since 1929, Cessna has operated three domestic aircraft manufacturing facilities. The original 1929 plant is now the Commercial Aircraft Division, where all commercial and military aircraft through the initial Model 310s were built. The Military Aircraft Division, located next to Mid-Continent Airport on the west side of Wichita and also called the Wallace Division, was established in 1956. In 1961, this facility assumed responsibility for

• *Cessna Model DC-6B* •
(Kansas Aviation Museum/Robert J. Pickett Collection)

building all commercial twin-engine aircraft. Cessna opened a third factory at Winfield, Kansas in 1967, to build the Models 150, 152, and 172 aircraft. The 1986 model year marked the end of single-engine production for Cessna, due in large part to a proliferation of large settlements in aviation liability suits. In 1994, the General Aviation Revitalization Act was passed by Congress and signed into law by President Bill Clinton. The new law restricts the period of liability for manufacturers of general aviation aircraft to 17 years from the date of manufacture. Following its passage, Cessna announced plans for resumption of Model 172 and 182 production.

Is Cessna now out of the military aircraft business? Not with hundreds of T-37s still training United States and foreign student pilots. Cessna did have a shot at potentially the largest military aircraft purchase in the foreseeable future — the Joint Primary Aircraft Training System (JPATS) — intended to replace both the Air Force's T-37B jet trainers and the Navy's T-34C turboprop trainers. Cessna's entry in the competition, the CitationJet/JPATS, was the only one of the seven contenders completely designed and built in the United States, and Cessna was the only competitor with a 40-year history of providing trainers for U.S. Air Force pilots. However, this was apparently not enough. Despite the aircraft's superb performance and twin-engine reliability, Cessna once again lost a major military trainer contract to Beech, which won with its Swiss-designed Pilatus PC-9.

When this book was completed, Cessna had filed a protest with the General Accounting Office, claiming the competition rules had changed without any notification to the contenders, thereby putting the Cessna entry at an unexpected disadvantage. It must be noted, however, that those who protest major defense contract awards rarely win those protests. ☩

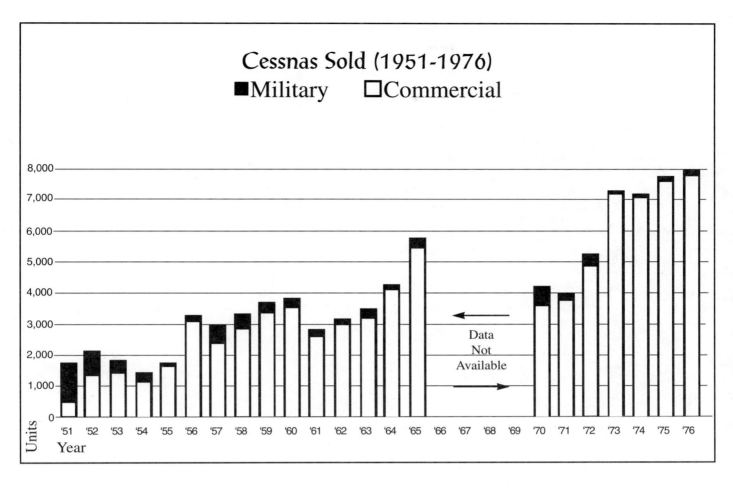

Cessnas Sold (1951-1976)
■ Military   □ Commercial

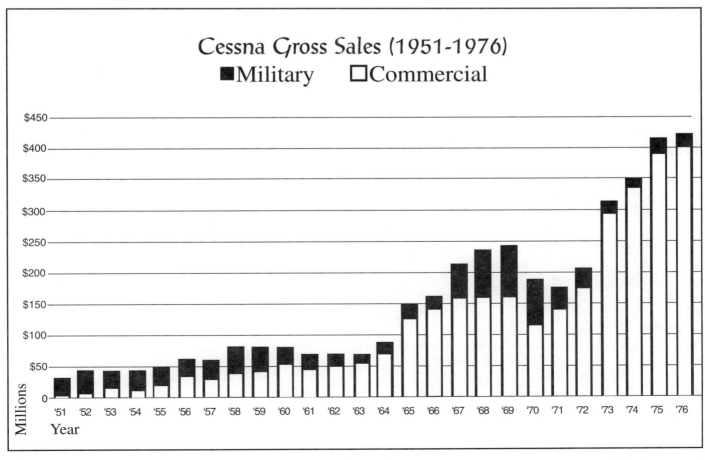

Cessna Gross Sales (1951-1976)
■ Military   □ Commercial

Aircraft Model And Serial Numbers

-chapter 2-

Military aircraft typically carry two identification numbers — the manufacturer's model number and the corresponding military designation. To further obscure things, since 1924 there have been three distinct military numerical designation systems used and, occasionally, the same letter has been used for different purposes in different systems. To relieve this confusion, I will attempt to explain what may seem, to the uninitiated, to resemble a random concoction of numbers and letters.

A basic understanding of the military and Cessna number and letter identification systems will help make sense out of apparent chaos. I will not try to provide an exhaustive reference, but will offer sufficient detail to familiarize the reader with the various schemes and enable the reader to interpret the designations appearing in subsequent chapters.

Cessna Model Indentification

Cessna model number identification began simply, with the first design referred to only as Cessna Design Number 1. In 1931, Cessna began using a two-letter code with its "A" series and "B" series, the second letter indicating the installed engine. Thus, the AW was an A-model with power by Wright. However, Cessna soon deviated from its own scheme with the DC-6 series — the DC-6 being powered by Curtiss, and the DC-6A and DC-6B powered by Wright engines. The nomenclature "CG" was used for Cessna gliders produced during the early 1930s.

In 1934, Cessna shifted to a single letter "C" followed by two digits to represent the year the design was started — the C-34 was designed in 1934, and the C-37 in 1937. This was changed again, in 1938, with new model numbers corresponding to engine horsepower — the C-145 was an Airmaster with 145 horsepower, and the C-165 was an Airmaster with 165 horsepower. However, the T-50 designation of 1938 seems to have been derived from the fact that the plane was a twin-engine aircraft with seating for five.

After World War II, Cessna adopted a new numbering system, which continued to evolve through 1961. The low-powered, single-engine aircraft became the "100" series (C-120, C-152, C-185, etc.), the higher-powered singles became the "200" series (C-210, for example), light twins composed the "300" series (like the C-310), heavier twins formed the "400" series (C-404), and jets were eventually assigned to the "500" series (the Citation series). The 400- and 500-series were not yet a part of the new scheme when the T-37 jet trainer was designed, so this twin-engine airplane was christened the Model 318.

Cessna used a single-letter suffix to indicate a significant change for a specific model year — thus the 1961 152A became the 1962 152B. The suffixes "O" and "I" were generally not used, to avoid confusion with zeroes and ones. A prefix letter usually indicated a more major change — consequently, the 150K Aerobat became the A150K, and the Cessna-Reims 172E became the R172E.

Military Nomenclature

If the constantly shifting designations used by Cessna over the years is perplexing, then the equally volatile military scheme can be even more confusing. Since 1924, the military model identification method has retained the basic organization of the original scheme:

(Status Prefix)(Type Symbol) - (Model No.)(Series Letter)

However, the meaning of the letters used for the Status Prefix and Type Symbol has changed several times over the intervening years. The system adopted in 1924 included the following Type Symbol definitions:

The 1924 Type Symbol System:

A	Attack
AT	Advanced Trainer
B	Bomber
BT	Basic Trainer
C	Cargo or Transport
HB	Heavy Bomber
LB	Light Bomber
O	Observation
P	Pursuit
PT	Primary Trainer

Several Type Symbols were Added during WWII:

AG	Assault Glider
CG	Cargo Glider

L	Liaison
R	Rotary Wing (helicopter)
TG	Training Glider

In 1948, the military system was expanded and modified to reflect changing roles and terminologies.

The 1948 Type Symbol System

A	Amphibian
F	Fighter (Replacing P)
G	Glider
H	Helicopter (Replacing R)
R	Reconnaissance
T	Trainer (Replacing AT, BT, and PT)
U	Utility (Added in 1952)
V	VTOL or STOL (Added in 1954)
X	Special Research

Following the implementation of this scheme, the three services (Air Force, Army, and Navy) each used slight variations of it. It was not until 1962 that the Department of Defense mandated a uniform system for use by all the U.S. services. The following basic system is still in use today:

The 1962 Tri-Service Type Symbol System

A	Attack
B	Bomber
C	Cargo or Transport
E	Special Electronic Installation
F	Fighter
G	Glider
H	Helicopter
O	Observation (Replacing L)
P	Patrol
R	Reconnaissance
S	Anti-Submarine
T	Trainer
U	Utility
V	VTOL or STOL
X	Special Research
Z	Airship

Frequently, additional Status Prefix letters are added to more clearly describe the aircraft and its mission. These are not additional or different Type Symbols, but only prefixes used in addition to the basic Type Symbols.

The 1962 Tri-Service Status Prefix System:

A	Attack
C	Transport
E	Special Electronic Installation
F	Fighter
H	Search and Rescue
J	Special Test Status (Temporary)
K	Tanker
L	Cold Weather
M	Multi-Mission
N	Special Test Status (Permanent)
O	Observation (or Forward Air Control)
P	Patrol
Q	Radio Controlled Drone
R	Reconnaissance
S	Anti-Submarine
T	Trainer
U	Utility
V	Staff (VIP Transport)
W	Weather
X	Experimental
Y	Service Test

Examples of the use of the Status Prefix include the RB-45 (Reconnaissance B-45), the XT-37 (Experimental T-37 — or Prototype), the EF-111 (a Special Electronic Installation on the F-111), and the OA-37 (Observation or Forward Air Control version of the A-37).

In addition, although not considered Status Prefixes, an R designation has been combined with either an S or a T prefix to indicate a Strategic or Tactical Reconnaissance mission (such as the SR-71 and the TR-1). The U Type Symbol of the UC-78, also, was not a Status Prefix designation, but instead a special prefix used in the 1940s to indicate a cargo or transport aircraft with a capacity of fewer than eight people, or less than 1,400 pounds of cargo.

As a result of the changing military designation schemes, many aircraft have carried a variety of designations over the course of their military careers. One of the most pronounced examples of this proliferation of nomenclatures for a single basic aircraft was the Cessna T-50 Bobcat, which has been known variously as the AT-8, the AT-17, the C-78, the UC-78, and the JRC-1, not to mention its Canadian incarnation as the Crane.

Beginning in 1924, the U.S. military assigned Model Numbers to indicate a sequential number within a specific Type Symbol. As an example, the B-19 was the nineteenth military bomber design. This sequential numbering scheme was not always obvious, since the Model Number was typically assigned early during the contract negotiations and was not reassigned even if the contract was cancelled. On occasion, the number was assigned later in the negotiations, such as when the contractor developed and tested a particular model using his own funds. In this case, the military Model Number would not be assigned until the military issued a contract, although the aircraft might enter service before another aircraft that had been assigned a lower Model Number early in the plane's design phase.

Prior to 1962's Tri-Service Type Symbol System, each service maintained its own sequential numbering scheme. Since 1962, however, the numbers have been maintained in common among the services, which led to the F-1 and F-9 being Navy fighters while the F-4 and F-5 were Air Force aircraft (although the F-4 was used by the Navy and Marines, as well). Some aberrations on this occurred when the Century Series fighters were introduced, beginning with the F-100. These ran in sequence, independently of the lower-numbered fighters, through the F-107. Then, with no regard to any sequential numbering system, the F-111 was introduced and, later, the F-117 stealth fighter appeared. As far as we know, there were never plans to build any aircraft in the F-108 to F-110 range, or F-112 to F-116 range. Perhaps the gaps in the would-be sequential numbers were created in an attempt to confuse those who track such things.

An additional suffix shows up on military aircraft numberings — the Series Letter. Under the 1924 System, the basic model of an aircraft received no Series Letter, and the first significant modification was assigned the "A" suffix, the second the "B" suffix, etc. However, beginning with the 1948 System, prototype aircraft were designated without a suffix and the first production version was assigned the Series Letter suffix "A." Sometimes, these suffixes seem out of sequence when compared to the dates of manufacture, usually due to conversions of earlier models receiving a later suffix while another version, with an earlier suffix, is still in production. As in the Cessna model number suffixes, the letters "O" and "I" are not used in order to avoid confusion with the similar numbers.

Besides the assigned official designation of letters and numbers, most military aircraft carry some form of official name or, at least, a nickname. Thus, the Cessna T-50 is officially known as the "Bobcat" — although it is more commonly referred to as the "Bamboo Bomber." Others, like the L-19/O-1 "Bird Dog," were named as the result of open contests and the official names became the most common name. Still others were either never officially named or rarely referred to by their sanctioned names. For instance, the Cessna T-37 was never officially named by Cessna or the Air Force, but became widely known as the "Tweety Bird." The Cessna O-2 forward air control aircraft was never given an official military moniker, although its pilots have dubbed it the "Oscar Deuce" or "Oscar Duck." Its civilian counterpart is the M-337 "Super Skymaster."

Serial and Constructor Numbers

Military aircraft also receive two sets of serial numbers — one assigned by the civilian manufacturer and another assigned by the military service. In the case of Cessna, all aircraft were assigned a sequential Constructor Number (c/n), even those aircraft specifically procured for exclusively military use. Meanwhile, the military assigned a corresponding Serial Number (s/n). This Serial Number usually reflected the year in which the contract was awarded plus a service-designated sequential number — thus, T-37A serial number 54-2729 was actually the first T-37A produced under a contract issued in 1954.

In the case of Navy and Marine aircraft, the Serial Number was called the Bureau Number (BuNo) and fell into one of five different series: A-51 through A-9206, 9207 through 9999, 0001 through 7303, 00001 through 100000 (although 9991 through 100000 were later canceled), and 100001 + (this is the current series and numbers are still being assigned).

The Navy's first numbering scheme developed in 1911 used a variety of initial letters — "A" for Curtiss hydroaeroplanes, "B" for Wright hydroaeroplanes, "C" for Curtiss flying boats, "D" for Burgess flying boats, and "E" for Curtiss amphibian flying boats. Within each letter designation, a sequential number beginning with 1 was assigned to each aircraft within a series. Soon, the variety of initial letters was dropped and all aircraft were assigned a serial number beginning with "AH." This system, however, was changed within 15 months of its initial use. The new system assigned sequential BuNos beginning with A-51. Starting with BuNo 9207, the "A" prefix was dropped.

In December 1940, the Navy began assigning four-digit BuNos in the 0001 - 7303 series, then switched to the five-digit 00001 - 10000 series in 1941 when aircraft production increased and the four-digit series proved inadequate. In the early 1960s, a sixth digit was added beginning with 100001, and this is the numbering system in use today. There were some exceptions to the Navy's sequential BuNo system: in the 1960s, a series of helicopter drones was produced and assigned six-digit BuNos beginning with 000000; the BuNos between 198003 and 999794, representing predominantly aircraft acquired from the Army or Air Force, are not sequentially assigned and there was no clear logic in the numbering scheme; and, finally, there were isolated cases of duplicate BuNos.

Military aircraft are also assigned tail numbers, much as civilian aircraft carry FAA-assigned N-numbers for identification. For the military, the tail numbers usually reflect at least some portion of the assigned serial number. In the case of the Cessna T-41 (a military C-172), the Air Force tail numbers were actually N-numbers, since the aircraft were maintained under a civilian contract to FAA standards.

Armed with an understanding, or at least a recognition, of the above variations in Cessna and military model designations, and military serial numbers and Cessna constructor numbers, you should be able to follow the numerical history of military Cessna aircraft. ✛

The First Military Cessnas
-chapter 3-

Cessna Aircraft Company is usually considered a manufacturer of civilian aircraft — single-engine, high-wing planes, light to medium twins, or even the Citation series of corporate jets. Military aircraft are usually considered the province of companies like McDonnell Douglas, North American, Grumman, Lockheed, or General Dynamics. And yet Cessna, that premier manufacturer and marketer of general aviation aircraft, has played a significant role in the annals of military aviation since the start of World War II. True, Cessna has never produced a state-of-the-art air superior fighter, or a long-range strategic bomber (although Cessna did churn out parts for front-line aircraft throughout the 1940s and 1950s). But if we count all those small, versatile, and necessary adjunct aircraft used for observation, pilot training, forward control of air and artillery strikes, and miscellaneous utility applications, Cessna probably has provided as many aircraft for the military forces of the United States and its allies as any but the largest manufacturers of front-line war machines.

Cessna's entry on the military landscape coincided with the entry of the United States into World War II. By that time, Cessna had established itself as a leading designer and manufacturer of cabin-class aircraft for the business traveler, and the military was quick to recognize military applications for those already-produced Cessnas.

• *This 1941 photo depicts a Cessna prototype experimental model P-7 derived from the T-50* •
(Kansas Aviation Museum/Robert J. Pickett Collection)

Chiefs and Scouts

Although there is some disagreement on the total number, in 1942 the U.S. Army Air Force (AAF) purchased at least four Cessna DC-6A Chiefs and four DC-6B Scouts for personnel and cargo transport. (There may have been three others acquired later, but if so, records do not indicate clearly whether these were DC-6A or DC-6B aircraft, and the associated serial numbers were not recorded.) The Army assigned the DC-6A the military designation UC-77 along with military s/n 42-38290, 42-46637, 42-46638, and 42-46639, corresponding to Cessna c/n 238, 232, 231, and 226. These aircraft were originally issued civilian registration numbers NC302M, NC654K, NC6449, and NR6441, respectively. The DC-6B was redesignated UC-77A and assigned military s/n 42-38292 through 42-38295, with c/n 211, 219, 290, and 200. The civilian registration numbers were NC631K, NC633K, NC14452, and NC9865 respectively.

The DC-6 series aircraft featured four seats and a 3,100-pound gross weight, and was based on the earlier three-seat Model BW. The BW's heritage, in turn, can be traced to the four-seat A-series designs. The DC-6A (UC-77) was a DC-6 with a 300-horsepower Wright R-975 Whirlwind Nine engine, replacing the DC-6's 170-horsepower Curtiss engine. This change resulted in a 25 mph higher cruise speed and a 31 mph higher maximum speed. The DC-6B (UC-77A) was powered by the somewhat less muscular 225-horsepower Wright R760 Whirlwind Seven engine. The UC-77's cruise speed of 130 mph and top speed of 161 mph compared to the UC-77A's 120 mph cruise and 146 mph maximum speed. Cessna produced a total of 22 DC-6A aircraft and 22 DC-6B aircraft between 1929 and 1930 (an additional four of the original DC-6s were later converted to the DC-6B configuration). Wing span for all models was 40 feet, 2 inches with an overall length of 24 feet, 8 inches.

Airmasters

Cessna's popular C-38 was the first model officially called an Airmaster by the company, but all of the C-34 through C-165 models later became commonly known as Airmasters because they all shared that "Airmaster Look." Several of these pre-War aircraft were purchased and used by various military services during World War II.

Two C-34s were impressed into U.S. Army service under the designation UC-77B: c/n 321 and 309 (civilian registrations NC16402 and NC15470), corresponding to military s/n 42-78021 and 42-78025. In Australia, a C-34 Airmaster originally flown by Airflite Limited was impressed into the Royal Australian Air Force (RAAF) in July 1941 and assigned military s/n A40-1. This Airmaster served as a communications aircraft with the RAAF's Number Two Communications Flight, operating out of Mascot Airport until May 1945 when it was sold and reassigned a new civilian registration number.

The four-seat C-34 Airmaster was powered by a 145-horsepower Warner Super Scarab 40 radial engine providing a cruise speed of 145 mph and a top speed of 162 mph. The C-34 had a wing span of 33 feet, 10 inches, and stretched 24 feet, 7 inches from propeller to rudder. Maximum allowable gross weight was 2,220-pounds. Cessna built 42 C-34 Airmasters in 1935 and 1936.

The AAF also acquired three C-37 Airmasters, which they designated the UC-77D. These were c/n 381, 366, and 347 (civilian registrations NC18596, NC18047, and NC17087) with respective military s/n 42-78023, 42-78024, and 42-97412. Another C-37 Airmaster, one of eight exported, was impressed into service with the Finnish Air Force and assigned military s/n CE-1.

The C-37 was a four-place design almost identical to the C-34 in size and configuration, although it incorporated wheel fairings and other minor improvements. Maximum gross weight was 2,350-pounds. Of the 46 C-37s built, seven were camera-plane models, and two of these were purchased by the AAF in 1942 (Cessna c/n 347 and 381, and respective military s/n 42-97412 and 42-78023).

Between 1939 and 1942, Cessna built 38 four-seat C-165 Airmasters with 165-horsepower Warner Super Scarab radial engines providing a cruise speed of 157 mph. Three of the C-165s were bought by the Army Air Corps in 1942. Cessna c/n 591 (civilian registration NC32458) was designated a C-94 and assigned military s/n 42-107400. Constructor numbers 558 and 562 (civilian registration NC21942 and NC21946) were declared UC-94s and issued military s/n 42-78018 and 4278022.

Cargo and Trainer Prototypes

During World War II, Cessna expended its own funds to develop several trainer and cargo aircraft prototypes, hoping to convince the military to place production orders. The four designs that actually reached the flying prototype stage included the P-7/T-50A, the P-10, the

• The prototype experimental model P-10 photographed in early 1942 •
(Kansas Aviation Museum/ Robert J. Pickett Collection)

• Prototype model C-106 (P-260) •
(Kansas Aviation Museum/ Robert J. Pickett Collection)

C-106, and the C-106A. None, however, went into production.

The P-7 was essentially an upgraded T-50 model, with larger engines, beefed-up wings, and heftier landing gear. It first flew in June of 1941, bearing registration number NX34750.

• Prototype Model C-106A lifting off on its maiden flight on 9 April 1943 •
(Kansas Aviation Museum/ Robert J. Pickett Collection)

To compete with Curtiss' higher-performance AT-9 twin-engine trainer, Cessna designed and built the prototype P-10. This one-and-only P-10 (registration number NX34751) was an experimental two-place trainer completed on October 4, 1941, and first flown two days later. It incorporated many of the same design features, and even many of the same components, as the T-50 Bobcat series. When Cessna was unable to interest the AAF in these new designs, both the P-10 and P-7 prototypes were dismantled on October 14, 1942.

The P-10 was powered by a pair of 300-horsepower Jacobs L6MB engines driving two-bladed, constant speed, metal Hamilton Standard propellers. The wing and tail surfaces were plywood. To minimize the use of strategic war materials, only the welded-steel frame used the precious metal. The prototype was assigned constructor number NX34751. Compared to

• *C-106A prototype passing overhead* •
(Kansas Aviation Museum/ Robert J. Pickett Collection)

the T-50 or P-7, the P-10 was sleek with a streamlined fuselage, shorter wings, a cockpit encased in a bubble-style canopy, and the beefy landing gear from a North American AT-6. The result was a trainer with the stance and panache of a fighter, vaguely reminiscent of the Lockheed P-38.

Loadmasters

Another prototype developed by Cessna during the war was Engineering Project 260 (P-260) — later designated the C-106 or "Loadmaster." With constructor number NX24176, the C-106 was completed and flown in January of 1943. And like the P-10, the C-106 was an attempt to minimize the use of strategic war materials. The C-106 required a two-man crew and was designed to stuff maximum cargo into its 596 cubic feet of cargo space. The 9,000-pound empty weight of the aircraft allowed it to carry 2,440 pounds of useful load. The stocky fuselage was constructed of chrome-molybdenum steel tubingcovered with fabric. All control surfaces were fabric-covered, while the tail surfaces and wings were covered with ply-

wood. Only the engine nacelles and cockpit area used aluminum skin. The C-106 was powered by a pair of Pratt & Whitney R-1340-S3H1 radial engines producing 600 horsepower at takeoff power settings with two-bladed, constant-speed propellers. The dimensions of theC-106 were: wing span - 64 feet, 8 inches; length - 51 feet, 2 inches; height - 11 feet, 4-½ inches. The plane's maximum gross weight was 14,000 pounds with an empty weight of 9,000 pounds.

The Army signed a Letter of Intent to purchase 500 C-106s, so Cessna painted the prototype with the military insignia. After some flight tests, the AAF asked for some modifications, which led to development of a second model, the C-106A. The prospective order for the basic C-106 was cancelled, and the prototype was scrapped before the war ended.

In 1943, Cessna rolled-out the C-106A with redesigned fuselage and cargo door, and full-feathering, ten-foot-diameter Hamilton Standard three-bladed propellers driven by geared Pratt & Whitney R-1340-AN2 radial engines. The prototype C-106A was assigned a Cessna

• An artist's concept of Cessna's proposed model 300 •
(Kansas Aviation Museum/ Robert J. Pickett Collection)

constructor number of 10002 and carried registration number NX44600. The craft's first flight was on 9 April 1943. The Army Air Corps issued a contract for 500 of the 200 mph airplanes, but the contract was cancelled when the required materials could not be acquired in sufficient quantity to meet production schedules. This prototype, like that of the C-106, was scrapped. The dimensions of the C-106A were identical to those of the C-106.

On 31 October 1947, the Air Materiel Command issued a Request for Proposals for a new trainer aircraft, defined by military Type Specification MX955. Cessna responded with its Model 300 piston-engine tandem trainer design on 31 December. Beechcraft also responded with its Model 45. Neither were selected at that time, but a version of the Beechcraft design was selected six years later as the USAF T-34A Mentor. ✛

T-50 Bobcat

-chapter 4-

Of the many aircraft models Cessna sold to the military over the years, perhaps the most successful (if success is measured in numbers sold) was the series based on the T-50 Bobcat light twin transport. Work on the original prototype, bearing c/n 1000 and registration number NX20784, began in 1938. Dwane Wallace completed the 20-minute initial test flight himself on 26 March 1939. The T-50 was a five-place, retractable gear aircraft with a low wing and a pair of 225-horsepower Jacobs L-4MB radial engines driving Curtiss Reed fixed-pitch propellers.

A feature unique to the prototype was the pronounced V shape of the windshield. The T-50 wing spars were constructed of laminated spruce with the truss-style ribs fashioned from spruce and plywood. Plywood covered the wing's leading edge and the outboard portions of the wing tips.

The T-50 prototype was tested for more than 100 flying hours, and was eventually modified into the production configuration. The V-shaped windshield was replaced with a curved one, rear windows with a curved trailing edge replaced the prototype's angular ones, and the vertical tail was resized and reshaped. Hamilton-Standard 2B-20-213 hydraulically-actuated, constant-speed, non-featherable propellers replaced the original fixed-pitch propellers. The 225-horsepower L-4MB engines were retained, albeit rated at 245-horsepower for takeoff. The prototype was eventually sold to Pan American Airways and registered in Mexico as XA-BLU. In 1941, this aircraft was completely refurbished by the factory and reassigned c/n 1000A.

• The first photo of the original T-50 prototype, NX20784, in 1939 •
(Kansas Aviation Museum/Robert J. Pickett Collection)

• *The first T-50 after modification to production configuration,*
on 6 December 1939 •
(Kansas Aviation Museum/Robert J. Pickett Collection)

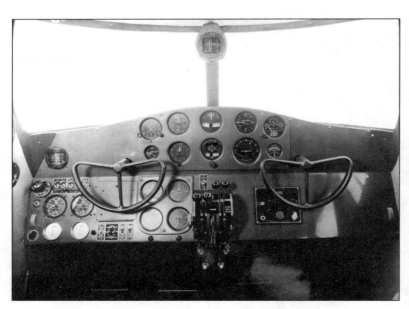

• *The instrument panel of the original T-50, NC20784,*
on 8 December 1939 •
(Kansas Aviation Museum/Robert J. Pickett Collection)

By December of 1939 the final configuration was determined, and the Bobcat was ready for production, selling on the civilian aviation market for $29,675. Eight aircraft from the original 19 aircraft production run were bought by the Civilian Aeronautics Administration (CAA). The CAA bought five additional T-50s from the 1941 production run of 22 aircraft, and Pan American Airways purchased 14 additional Bobcats. The gross weight of the civilian T-50 was 5,100 pounds, the service ceiling was 22,000 feet, and the maximum speed was 191 mph. Cruise speed was listed at 175 mph with a 750 mile range. Forty T-50s were produced between 1940 and 1942, and the Army Air Force (AAF) later put 17 of them into military service. With America's involvement in Europe's brewing war almost certain, Dwane Wallace and the Cessna management team realized the military would soon be needing advanced trainers to prepare new pilots for duties in the medium and heavy bombers that were rolling off assembly lines around the country. The T-50 seemed a logical candidate for the advanced trainer role, and Cessna set about positioning itself to capitalize on whatever large-scale production contracts came up. They began planning a $50,000 expansion project for June of 1941 — a new 28,000-square-foot assembly facility designed specifically for building the T-50 and Airmaster series.

$5 Into $5,000,000

Not content to wait for the Army to come knocking on his door and with only $5.03 in the corporate accounts, Dwane Wallace launched an aggressive lobbying campaign. He explained the T-50's capabilities as a multi-engine trainer to any military officers and civilian government officials who would listen. The AAF realized the deficiencies of the obsolete aircraft it was then using for trainers and was ready to procure new aircraft designed for the training role. They were agreeable to Cessna's new twin, but Congress was keeping a tight rein on budgets. Then, in May 1940, President Franklin D. Roosevelt proclaimed a goal of producing 50,000 aircraft to help the British, and Congress loosened its grip on the purse strings. On 19 July 1940, Assistant Secretary of War Louis Johnson awarded Cessna an $800,000 contract for 33 AT-8 multi-engine trainers based on the civilian T-50.

This, Cessna's biggest order to date, was the Army's first contract for purpose-built multi-engine trainers. The delivered aircraft bore c/n 1030 through 1062 and were assigned AAF s/n

• First production configuration T-50 with flaps down, 6 December 1939 •
(Kansas Aviation Museum/Robert J. Pickett Collection)

• Sperry hydraulic autopilots.

The Royal Canadian Air Force (RCAF), a major participant with England and Australia in the British Commonwealth Air Training Plan, needed multi-engine trainers — a lot of multi-engine trainers — fast. During the summer of 1940, the RCAF evaluated the T-50 in Wichita and found it possessed significant advantages over the competition. The predominantly wood and fabric construction (minimizing the use of strategic war materials such as steel and aluminum), economical operation, simplicity of

41-5 through 41-37. The contract called for the following modifications to the basic T-50:

• Windows in the cockpit roof.
• Hamilton-Standard constant-speed metal propellers.
• 290-horsepower engines (nine-cylinder R680-9 Lycomings).
• Military radio equipment.
• Aluminum silver paint job.

maintenance, and overall modern design (for 1940) impressed the Canadians. Cessna's foresight in preparing for large-scale production sealed the deal, and in September the RCAF signed a contract for 180 Bobcats. The Canadians designated the new aircraft the "Crane I." These aircraft carried c/n 1100 through 1279 and RCAF s/n 7657 through 7836. The RCAF order was not only Cessna's largest order, but the largest one ever awarded to a Wichita-based company at that time.

Now, with two major military orders in hand, Cessna faced a $5,000,000 backlog without the facilities or capital to make good on those orders. But the signed contracts provided sufficient leverage for Dwane Wallace to acquire funding from a local bank and press on with the needed expansions. Following a hectic two-month construction blitz that allowed another new 400-foot by 200-foot assembly building to open in November, the first AT-8 was delivered to the Army in December of 1940. Within six months

• A Lycoming-engined AT-8 from the first AAF order •
(Kansas Aviation Museum/Robert J. Pickett Collection)

• A Cessna exploded-view drawing of the AT-8 for an AAF technical manual •
(Kansas Aviation Museum/Robert J. Pickett Collection)

• This trio of RCAF Cranes is from the initial Canadian order •
(Kansas Aviation Museum/Robert J. Pickett Collection)

• Cessna's Bobcat assembly line in 1941 •
(Kansas Aviation Museum/Robert J. Pickett Collection)

• A line-up of 10 RCAF Cranes face an AAF AT-8 taxiing in •
(Kansas Aviation Museum/Robert J. Pickett Collection)

of contract award, the Army was conducting operational tests on the new aircraft at Wright Field in Dayton, Ohio.

Cranes Winging Northward

In November 1940, Cessna delivered the first RCAF Crane I and was promptly rewarded with a Canadian order for 460 more aircraft. Constructor numbers were issued in five lots: 1286 through 1299, 1350 through 1399, 1400 through 1689, 1280 through 1285, and 2201 through 2300. The respective RCAF serial numbers were 7843 through 7856, 7857 through 7906, 7907 through 8196, 8197 through 8202, and 8651 through 8750. The Canadian Crane I differed from its American twin, being outfitted with:

- Jacobs 225-horsepower engines.
- Hartzell fixed-pitch wooden propellers.
- Removable baffles to keep the cylinder heads and oil warm during the Canadian winters.
- Oil radiators designed to warm the oil in cold weather.

In 1941, Cessna's employees began working three shifts to fill the company's military contracts. Employment swelled to 1,900 workers by May of 1941

• *An early AAF Cessna AT-17. Note the main wheels that protrude from the engine nacelles even when retrated* •
(Kansas Aviation Museum/Robert J. Pickett Collection)

when Cessna delivered the 100th Crane I to the RCAF. Eleven assistant test pilots were hired primarily to ferry these aircraft north to Canada but also to serve as production test pilots when required. To reduce the time needed to accommodate meal breaks during this frenzied period, Dwight Wallace instituted the country's first corporate "rolling cafeterias" — 14 wheeled carts with electrical heating to keep the food warm as it was brought to the workers.

• *An RCAF Crane Ia (FJ-198) and an AAF AT-17 (c/n 2224) pair-up in flight* •
(Kansas Aviation Museum/Robert J. Pickett Collection)

Also in 1941, Cessna engineers developed an improved version of the T-50/AT-8/Crane I series and dubbed it the P-7 (the "P" being a standard Cessna designator for experimental designs), although it was often referred to as the T-50A. With two 300-horsepower Jacobs L-6MB engines, performance was expected to be much improved over the earlier versions. The higher speeds and increased gross weight necessitated beefing up the airframe with stiffer plywood skin over the whole wing surface. Cessna used modified North American AT-6 landing gear to handle the increased weight. First flight of the P-7 took place on 2 June

1941, with Morton W. Brown at the controls. Takeoff and climb performance were noticeably better than the T-50. Top speed on the initial flight was a bit over 200 mph. Despite the improved performance, both the AAF and the RCAF elected to continue with their original AT-8 and Crane I designs. After considerable flight testing, the single prototype was dismantled on 14 October 1941.

Orders and More Orders

However, all was not lost when Cessna scrapped the P-7, as the Army placed orders for 450 T-50s in the fall of 1941, redesignating them AT-17s (Cessna c/n 1701 through 2150, corresponding to Army s/n 42-2 through 42-451). The new models included some additional cockpit roof windows and the more readily available Jacobs R-755-9 seven-cylinder, air-cooled radial engines, which were rated at 245 horsepower for takeoff (225 maximum continuous horsepower). This configuration became the standard for all future AAF and RCAF T-50 series aircraft. The 14 Pan Am T-50s purchased in late 1941 were the same configuration as

• *String of AAF AT-17s. Aircraft closest to camera has engine nacelle covers installed* •
(Kansas Aviation Museum/Robert J. Pickett Collection)

these AT-17 aircraft. Constructor numbers up through 1762 were restricted to the original gross weight limit of 5,100 pounds, but subsequent aircraft incorporated wing spar modifications allowing the civilian-certified gross weight to be increased to 5,400 pounds. The AAF determined that the 5,100-pound aircraft could be safely flown at 5,300 pounds and cleared them for operational use at that weight, while the 5,400-pound aircraft were operated at a 5,700-pound gross weight. The original AT-17 aircraft were restricted to 5,300 pounds and were assigned the AT-17E model designation.

With the "day that will live in infamy" approaching, Cessna management worried about the worsening worldwide political climate. Once more, they gambled on disaster and bought a 320-acre plot of land to allow plant expansion and the construction of a new runway. By November of 1941, more than 360,000 square feet of factory was available. In addition, some 100 employees had banded together to form the Home

• *Original AAF AT-17 (top) and RCAF Crane I/AT-17A (bottom)* •
(Kansas Aviation Museum/Robert J. Pickett Collection)

Guard — personnel trained to combat enemy parachutists or in-country insurgents. All the planning and worry were vindicated on 7 December 1941, when Japan's carrier-born armada attacked Pearl Harbor at dawn. By that time, Cessna's production facilities had more than tripled and employment had increased almost sevenfold. Plant operations were running around the clock.

The RCAF ordered an additional 550 T-50s under the American Lend-Lease program, this time giving them the Crane Ia designation. However, only 182 were delivered when the AAF, following the Pearl Harbor debacle, took over the rest. The Crane Ia aircraft differed from the AAF's AT-17 only in the electrical systems and, as Lend-Lease aircraft, carried three different numbers: the Cessna c/n (2301 through 2440, and 2449 through 2490), the RCAF s/n (FJ-100 through FJ-239, and FJ-248 through FJ-289), and the AAF s/n (42-13617 through 42-13756, and 42-13765 through 42-13806).

Of the remaining 368 aircraft the AAF took over from the third RCAF order, four versions were produced, differing only in the radio and flight instruments installed: the basic AT-17, the AT-17A, the AT-17B, and the AT-17C. Most of these aircraft were delivered with constant-speed Hartzell wooden propellers due to the shortage of critical metals needed for aircraft destined for combat duty. Although early models had been equipped with metal constant-speed props, later models came with either the wooden constant-speed or wooden fixed-pitch props. None of the AT-8/AT-17/Crane series were outfitted with featherable props.

Of the total AT-17 series production, 450 were basic AT-17s, while 41 were AT-17A, 466 were AT-17B, 60 were AT-17C, and 131 were AT-17D aircraft. Also, 136 were designated UC-78C models, due primarily to a slackening demand for twin-engine trainers following the initial build-up. The AT-17Ds were later redesignated

• AAF AT-17B and AT-17C •
(Kansas Aviation Museum/Robert J. Pickett Collection)

UC-78Cs as well. The only real difference between the UC-78 and the AT-17 aircraft was the military's planned use of them — the ATs were destined solely for training use, and the UCs were destined for utility cargo and personnel transportation duties.

All AT-17B aircraft delivered after 15 May 1942 sported a silver paint scheme and the solid-star-in-roundel fuselage markings. Of the 655 aircraft originally ordered as AT-17Bs, the early aircraft (c/n 2901 through 3010, military s/n 42-38692 through 4238801) were restricted to a maximum gross weight of 5,300 pounds and were later redesignated as AT-17Gs. The remaining AT-17B aircraft (c/n 3011 through 3366, and s/n 42-38802 through 42-39157) were allowed gross weights up to 5,700 pounds. The last 189 aircraft in the order (c/n 3367 through 3555, s/n 42-39158 through 42-39346) were reassigned to transport duty and designated UC-78B, with 5,700-pound gross weights.

The production run of AT-17C aircraft was also the result of an interrupted Canadian order for Crane Ia airplanes. Constructor numbers ran from 2491 through 2550, and military serial numbers ran from 42-13807 through

• A UC-78 taking off from the grass prior to deleivery to the AAF •
(Kansas Aviation Museum/Robert J. Pickett Collection)

• A U.S. Navy JRC-1, BuNo 64456 •
(Kansas Aviation Museum/Robert J. Pickett Collection)

• An RCAF Crane I after suffering fire damage in a landing accident.
The steel tube construction of the fuselage is evident •
(Kansas Aviation Museum/Robert J. Pickett Collection)

42-13866. Some were later restricted to a gross weight of 5,300 pounds, and redesignated AT-17H. All sixty AT-17C/AT-17H aircraft featured the Hartzell fixed-pitch wooden propeller. The only major equipment difference between the AT-17B and the AT-17C was the installed radio gear.

Cargo and People Movers

In 1942, the AAF ordered production of the 5,700-pound gross weight C/UC-78 series for light cargo and personnel transport duties. The first 330 aircraft were delivered as C-78s (c/n 3601 through 3930, s/n 4258110 through 42-58439), with the remaining 101 aircraft designated UC-78 (c/n 3931 through 4031, s/n 42-58440 through 42-58540). The only difference between the two designations was the "U" for "Utility" in its military nomenclature. These aircraft featured an olive drab/gray paint scheme.

Orders for another 674 UC-78s soon followed, with contracts in 1942 and 1943. Six-hundred-and-seven aircraft went to the AAF. These AAF aircraft were c/n 3931 through 4031, 4801 through 4897, 4905 through 4942, and 4948 through 5373. Their respective military serial numbers were 42-58440 through 42-58540, 43-7281 through 43-7377, 43-7385 through 43-7422, and 43-7428 through 43-7853. Sixty-seven UC-78s were transferred to, or acquired for, the U.S. Navy and Marine Corps as JRC-1s. Twelve of these aircraft were c/n 4898 through 4904 (s/n 43-7378 through 43-7384) and 4943 through 4947 (43-7423 through 43-7427), and were assigned Navy Bureau Numbers 55772 through 55783. The remaining 55 Navy aircraft were procured from the 4948 through 5373 batch and assigned BuNos 64442 through 64496.

All C/UC-78 and JRC-1 aircraft were delivered with the Hamilton-Standard constant-speed props made of

metal. The AAF aircraft sported either an olive drab or an olive drab/gray paint scheme. The JRC-1s were painted a variety of colors including overall aluminum silver, two-tone dark blue and white, and two-tone light blue and white. Eventually, all C-78 aircraft were redesignated UC-78.

The most prevalent variety of T-50 series aircraft was the UC-78B, with 2,156 of this model built between 1943 and 1944. These were purchased in four lots and bore Cessna c/n 3367 through 3555, 4161 through 4800, 5374 through 5700, and 5701 through 6700. They corresponded to AAF s/n 42-39158 through 42-39346, 42-71465 through 42-72104, 43-7854 through 43-8180, and 43-31763 through 43-32762. Due to wing spar load problems, some of the UC-78B aircraft were later restricted to 5,300-pound gross weights and redesignated UC-78E. Propellers were provided by HamiltonStandard — of either the wood fixed-pitch or metal constant-speed variety, with most having the wooden props.

The Bobcat served in every theater of operation during World War II. Most spent their service time at training bases in the United States and Canada, but many hauled people and cargo throughout the European and Pacific the-

• A pair of UC-78B aircraft after a following-too-close taxi accident •
(Kansas Aviation Museum/Robert J. Pickett Collection)

aters from large, well-equipped air bases and small, impromptu forward airstrips.

Quite a few Bobcats found their way into the air forces of various foreign nations after World War II came to an end. The Nationalist Chinese and Brazilians were among those who put the aircraft to good use.

Civilian Bobcats in Olive Drab

To help fill the requirements for utility transports, the AAF impressed 17 of the 40 civilian T-50s into military service. Fifteen of these were acquired in 1942 and were designated UC-78A with military s/n 42-38276 through 42-38278 (c/n 1311, 1312, and 1315), 42-38374 through 42-38375 (c/n 1008 and 1005), 42-38377 (c/n 1018), 42-38379 (c/n 1001), 42-43844 (c/n 1012), 42-97033 through 42-97039 (c/n 1314, 1316, and 1318 through 1322). Another two were acquired in 1944, designated C-78As, and assigned military s/n 44-52998 and 44-53001 (c/n unknown).

In all, 5,376 AT-8, AT-17, C/UC-78, Crane I, Crane Ia, and JRC-1 aircraft were produced by Cessna between 1942 and 1944. The total T-50 production run consisted of 5,399 aircraft built either for military contracts or the civilian market. The average per-unit price of the military aircraft was $31,000 (in 1944 dollars). It was a busy and profitable two years for Cessna Aircraft Company. The chart shows a breakdown of the Model T-50 production run.

The last of the series, a UC-78C (later to become an F-model, c/n 4160, and military s/n 4272164), rolled off the assembly line on 7 June 1943. After the war, many were sold on the surplus market and later reconditioned to repair the ravages of military and training use, and to bring them up to the standards the Civilian Aviation Administration (CAA) demanded. Cessna produced a conversion kit which included such things as wiring and lighting changes, instrumentation modifications, the addition of a bungee spring in the elevator control system, new drain holes in the wing fuel tank compartment, and directions for inspection of the wing spar to determine the proper gross weight limitation. This last, requiring inspection through an underwing access door

T-50 Production Run		
Model	SubTotal	Total
T-50	40	23
(17 T-50s were modified into UC-78s)		
AT-8	33	33
Crane I	640	640
Crane Ia	182	182
AT-17	450	450
AT-17A through D	698	698
UC-78	3,029	2,974
(55 UC-78s were modified into JRC-1s)		
C-78A	332	332
JRC-1	12	67
(Includes 55 Modified from UC-78)		
TOTAL PRODUCTION		**5,399**

just ahead of the inboard flap, was the most important — a spruceplank spar meant a 5,100-pound limit while a plywood spar meant a 5,700-pound limit. In the 1950s, the popular television series "Sky King" initially costarred a civilianized UC-78 Bobcat as the Songbird. The specific c/n, military s/n, and exact model are not known.

Nicknames

As the AT-17 went into production, Cessna initiated a factory "name the plane" contest. Of the hundreds submitted, the winning entry was "Bobcat." However, the

• *5000th Bobcat (a UC-78) on display at the Cessna factory* •
(Kansas Aviation Museum/Robert J. Pickett Collection)

• *A Nationalist Chinese ex-AAF UC-78B at New Delhi, India, on 7 September 1945* •
(Kansas Aviation Museum/Robert J. Pickett Collection)

• *A Brazilian Air Force AT-17 at Salgado Filho Airport in Porto Alebra, Brazil, in the late 1940s* •
(Kansas Aviation Museum/Robert J. Pickett Collection)

aircraft's heavy reliance on wood, plywood, and fabric construction resulted in another endearing nickname — one that stuck throughout the plane's career. That nickname was "Bamboo Bomber." Today, all of the T-50 series aircraft are widely known as Bamboo Bombers.

Another common nickname, also reflecting the wood and fabric construction, was the "Double-Breasted Cub." The UC-78 series was frequently referred to as the "Useless 78," while the Navy and Marine Corps dubbed their JRC-1 Bobcat the "Box Kite."

The Lowdown

All military-contract T-50s were delivered with spartan seats designed to accommodate backpack parachutes.

The primary flight controls of the Bobcat were all conventional — elevator and ailerons controlled by dual control wheels, and rudders controlled by pedals with toe-operated brakes. Secondary flight controls included crank-operated adjustments for the elevator and rudder mounted in the cabin ceiling between the pilot and copilot, and an aileron trim tab, located on the inboard end of the right aileron, that was adjustable with a screwdriver during preflight.

The T-50's main landing gear was somewhat unique in that, when retracted, about half of each wheel protruded out of the engine nacelles. According to the AAF's pilot manual, this was designed to "bear the brunt of intentional wheel-up emergency landings." Extension or retraction of the main gear was controlled by an electrical switch mounted on the instrument panel in front of the pilot, and was actuated by a single electric motor through two chain-driven screws. Landing gear position was displayed by either a red/green light arrangement on the panel, or by a position-indicator and warning horn combination. There was a hand crank stowed beneath the pilot's seat for emergency extension of the gear, but there were no up or down locks. The aircraft's

• *Details of the Bamboo Bomber's wooden wing and flap construction* •
(Kansas Aviation Museum/Robert J. Pickett Collection)

nonretractable tailwheel could be locked in a centered position with a lever located between the rudder and elevator trim cranks in the cockpit ceiling. When unlocked, the tailwheel was fully swiveling.

Conventional wing flaps were activated by an electric switch in the cockpit and actuated by an electric motor through roller chains and drive screws. Travel was controlled by limit switches in both the up and down directions. Flap position was displayed on a panel-mounted indicator.

AT-8, AT-17A, AT-17C, UC-78C and Crane I and Crane Ia aircraft were all delivered with 12-volt electrical systems. Other models were delivered with 24-volt systems. The battery was located behind the copilot's seat and actually powered one set of spark plugs with a single magneto powering the other set. All aircraft later converted to civilian standards should have been modified to a dual-magneto configuration.

An interesting piece of equipment installed on AT-17A aircraft was a flare dispenser, which held one three-minute flare and three 1.5-minute flares. These were discharged electrically via a switch on the cabin wall to the pilot's left. The pilot's manual noted that "most effective ground illumination is afforded when the 1.5-minute flares are released at 1,200 feet (3-minute at 2,000 feet) above the ground." So, who needs runway lights?

For aircraft with the 225-horsepower Jacobs engines, takeoff thrust was limited to 245 horsepower at 2200 RPM, although maximum continuous operation was restricted to 225 horsepower at 2000 RPM. Maximum cruise power was achieved at 2000 RPM and 22 inches of manifold pressure — each engine producing 187 horsepower at 6,300 feet while consuming 17.6 gallons of fuel per hour. Maximum range power settings were achieved at 1950 RPM and 17 inches of manifold pressure at 13,300 feet. At those settings, total fuel consumption was 25 gallons per hour yielding a cruise speed of 138 mph. Standard fuel capacity was 120 gallons, although some aircraft were delivered with an optional tank to increase fuel capacity to 160 gallons. Normal oil consumption was listed as ranging from 2.1 to 4.2 quarts per hour for each engine, depending on the power setting.

Aircraft with wooden propellers had additional restrictions imposed on them. Climb power settings were limited to 23 inches of manifold pressure or 2,000 RPM. Normal cruise was limited to 1,900 RPM and 20 inches, while maximum sustained cruise was limited to 2,000 RPM and 21 inches of manifold pressure.

Flying Characteristics

The entire T-50 series was designed for a 200 mph maximum indicated airspeed and an engine overspeed limit of 2,400 RPM. The AAF pilot's manual calls out the following prohibited maneuvers:

- Loops, spins, rolls, Immelmanns
- Steep, tight turns
- Inverted flight
- Whip stalls

Although climb-out was a solid 1,000 feet per minute at 90 mph (110 mph was recommended for aircraft with wooden props), single-engine performance was marginal. Published data claims a 3,000-foot single-engine ceiling at 2,000 RPM (with a note that limited emergency operation could push that up to 5,700 feet at 2,200 RPM for the metal constant-speed props only), but practical experience indicated that 1,500 feet was a more realistic single-engine limit, which meant almost no climb rate was available on one engine. Since none of the installed props were

• *AAF UC-78, s/n 42-58125* •
(Kansas Aviation Museum/Robert J. Pickett Collection)

featherable, the best that could be done (if you were lucky enough to have the constant-speed props) was to push them into high pitch and hope for the best.

Cessna claimed a takeoff distance of 625 feet at a 5,700-pound gross weight. Service ceiling was 22,000 feet. Landing distance was a paltry 810 feet with an approach speed of 90 mph.

Stalls were docile at 63-66 mph with flaps and gear retracted or extended (the way those wheels dangle in the breeze, is it any wonder their position had little effect on stall speed?). The only variable affecting the stall speed was aircraft weight. Control response was excellent, reportedly very light for an aircraft in this weight class, and effective right down into the stalling regime.

In the event of an engine failure in flight, the pilot's manual seemed to be quite concerned about achieving and maintaining a magic speed — 90 mph. If above that speed, it recommended slowing down to it while applying "vigorous rudder action to compensate for yaw." If below 90 mph with sufficient altitude, "shove the control wheel

• *AAF Flight Manual warnings used humor to get the message across* •
(AAF Flight Manual)

• RCAF Crane I after a snow landing accident. This Bobcat could bite! •
(Kansas Aviation Museum/Robert J. Pickett Collection)

forward to pick up air speed of 90 mph." If the hapless pilot was below 90 mph and there just was not enough room to dive for speed, the book admonished him to:

(1) Close both throttles.
(2) Turn off ignition switches.
(3) Land straight ahead.

I would guess the prudent pilot would just plan to keep the old warhorse above 90 mph unless there were a lot of clear sky beneath him. Part of that old saw about "airspeed you don't have" being one of the three most useless things to a pilot (the other two being altitude above you and runway behind you).

Training in the Bamboo Bomber

Students generally spent three to four months in the AT-8/AT-17 training course, flying three to four hours per day. Each instructor was assigned up to five students. Some students, at least in the later years of the war, were training in B-25s, so those students flying Cessnas did not feel particularly privileged. But the aircraft's docile manners and stable handling were appreciated. To quote Don Sampsel, who was a student in Class 44-E at Waco, Texas, and is now retired in Billings, Montana:

"Stall characteristics were fabulous. In a full stall, holding the wheel all the way back, you could just sit there and let it fall straight down. If a wing started to drop, you hit the opposite rudder to bring it back up. I was so fascinated with how easy it was I would have a contest with myself to see just how long I could hold the stall. I could rudder-walk it down several thousand feet. And believe it or not, stall recovery was equally amazing. It was not necessary to come forward on the wheel to pick up speed. You continued to rudder-walk, if necessary, while applying power, and it flew out of that stall."

The partially-retracting landing gear was a blessing in a training environment, since those protruding wheels minimized damage if a student accidentally landed gear-up, or if a system failure necessitated it. According to Sampsel, when landing gear-up "with the two-bladed props, if you could stay cool, you cut the switches, then ticked the props over with starters until the props were horizontal ... Really made your instructor happy with you."

Apparently, some folks took advantage of the fact that the gear wouldn't retract while the plane's weight was on them. On takeoff from a smooth runway, you could hold the aircraft on the ground, tail-high, past normal liftoff speed and flip the retraction switch to the UP position. As the plane lifted off, the gear started up, fully retracting by about 20 feet. This practice embarrassed a few pilots when a slight runway dip bounced the aircraft just enough to start those main wheels retracting, and when the aircraft settled back down, propeller tips were ground away.

The Bobcat trainers were fully equipped for instrument flying with a vacuum-driven artificial horizon, a turn-and-slip indicator, and a magnetic compass. A few also included a radio-compass. (Remember, this was in the early '40s — this stuff was state-of-the-art!) A hood-and-goggle arrangement was typically used for student instrument flight training, consisting of a green windscreen panel (allowing the instructor to see out, albeit with a color-tinged view of the outside world) and red goggles for the student. The color combination completely blocked the student's view through the window. In the latter stages of training, "blind" instrument takeoffs were practiced.

Where Have All the Bobcats Gone?

In a recent issue of Trade-a-Plane, only two Bamboo Bombers were listed for sale:

"Cessna UC-78 (Bamboo Bomber) project, fuselage, engines, props, paperwork, $10,000." (Project = build-it-yourself. This one was in Oklahoma.)

• A UC-78B, s/n 42-71626, from the permanent collection of the U.S. Air Force Museum •
(U.S. Air Force Museum)

"Cessna UC-78C. This classic restored T-50 has 3150 TT, 652 SMOH ... polished props, dual taxi lights ... new interior, heavy duty battery, excellent records ... original Air Force markings." (Not too many hours for a training aircraft of this age, and somebody has obviously been working on it. Home based in Minnesota.)

• An ex-RCAF Crane Ia (FJ-176) converted to civil use as a floatplane in Vancouver, Canada, 1955 •
(Kansas Aviation Museum/Robert J. Pickett Collection)

At least 12 Bobcats exist in North American museums:

In the United States:
- *Alaska Aviation Heritage Museum*, Anchorage, AK (T-50)
- *Pima Air & Space Museum*, Tucson, AZ (UC-78/JRC-1)
- *Planes of Fame Air Museum*, Chino, CA (UC-78)
- *Liberal Air Museum*, Liberal, KS (T-50)
- *U.S. Air Force Museum*, Dayton, OH (UC-78B)
- *Lone Star Flight Museum*, Galveston, TX (T-50)
- *American Airpower Heritage Museum*, Midland, TX (UC-78)

In Canada (all Cranes):
- *Aerospace Museum of Calgary*, Calgary, AB
- *Canada's Aviation Hall of Fame*, Wetaskiwin, AB
- *Western Canada Aviation Museum*, Winnipeg, Manitoba
- *Canadian Warplane Heritage Museum*, Mount Hope, Ontario
- *Western Development Museum*, Moose Jaw, Saskatchewan ✛

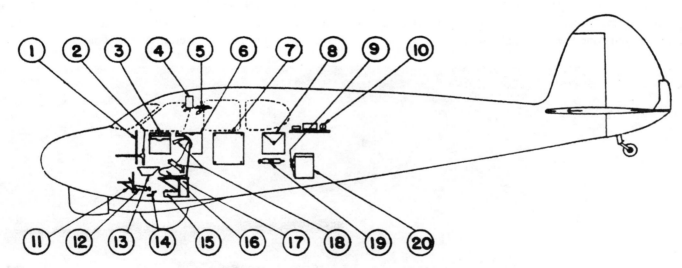

①	Instrument Panel	⑥	Flight Report Case	⑪	Rudder Pedals	⑯ Bucket Seat Pilot/Co-pilot
②	Control Wheel	⑦	Solenoid	⑫	Front Cabin Fire Extinguisher	⑰ Wing Spar (Ref.)
③	Map Case	⑧	Data Case	⑬	Radio Control Unit	⑱ Shoulder Harness & Safety Belt
④	Tab Control	⑨	Control Wheel Lock	⑭	Landing Gear Hand Crank	⑲ Rear Cabin Fire Extinguisher
⑤	Microphone Box	⑩	Radio Units	⑮	Fuel Selector Valve Box	⑳ Storage Box

• *AT-17/UC-78 internal arrangement diagram* •
(AAF Flight Manual)

Specifications

Wingspan . . . . 41 ft. 11 in.

      Length . . . . 32 ft. 9 in.

      Height . . . . 9 ft. 11 in.

Maximum Gross Weight

      Group I (Unmodified Wing Spar) . . . . 5,300 lbs.

      Group II (Modified Wing Spar) . . . . 5,700 lbs.

Engines . . . . Jacobs R-755-9, 7-cylinder, air-cooled, 245-horsepower radial

Propellers . . . . Hartzell wood fixed-pitch or Hamilton-Standard metal or wood constant-speed

Fuel Capacity . . . . 120 U.S. gallons

Maximum Allowable Speed . . . . 200 mph

Stall Speed

      5,200 Pounds . . . . 63 mph

      5,700 Pounds . . . . 66 mph

Takeoff Ground Roll, Paved Runway

      5,100 Pounds . . . . 525 ft.

      5,700 Pounds . . . . 575 ft.

Takeoff Distance Over 50-foot Obstacle, Grass Runway

      5,100 Pounds . . . . 1,450 ft.

      5,700 Pounds . . . . 1,950 ft.

Rate of Climb, 90 mph, Sea Level

      5,100 Pounds . . . . 1,150 fpm

      5,700 Pounds . . . . 950 fpm

Landing Ground Roll, Dry Paved Runway . . . . 600 ft.

Landing Ground Roll, Wet Grass Runway . . . . 800 ft.

Landing Distance Over 50-foot Obstacle, Dry Paved Runway . . . . 1,400 ft.

Landing Distance Over 50-foot obstacle, Wet grass Runway . . . . 1,600 ft.

Maximum Cruise, Sea Level

      TAS . . . . 175 mph

      Total Fuel Flow (Both Engines) . . . . 50 gph

      Range (No Reserves) . . . . 420 statute miles

Maximum Range Cruise @ 9,000 feet

      TAS . . . . 145 mph

      Total Fuel Flow (Both Engines) . . . . 22.6 gph

      Range (No Reserves) . . . . 637 statute miles

Single Engine Cruise, Sea Level

      TAS . . . . 106 mph

      Fuel Flow . . . . 22 gph

A C-195 In Uniform: the LC-126

-chapter 5-

As the Allied juggernaut steamed across Europe and the Pacific bringing World War II to a close, Cessna was developing a new line of single-engine airplanes to fill what management optimistically foresaw as a burgeoning post-war market for "family cars of the air." The 120/140 line was already in work in 1944, as was initial planning for the 170. And yet, the pre-war popularity of the Airmaster series (arguably one of the best-looking high-wing taildraggers) led management to authorize an updated version — the 190, retaining the basic Airmaster lines but with more interior room. The new aircraft was to capitalize on technological developments such as constant-speed propellers, Wittman spring-steel landing gear, control wheels to replace the sticks, and a semi-monocoupe metal fuselage (a design wherein the outer skin carries the majority of the stress).

As in the Airmasters, the 190's steel-tube front wing spar was full-depth and, in the fuselage carry-through section, protruded into the cabin's headroom such that the pilot and front seat passenger had to be wary of banging their heads, and the rear seat passengers could not see around it. To correct the problem on the prototype, a new spar was made from aluminum bar stock and secured with bolts and stress plates over-designed to 150% of the required strength to preclude problems due to the brittleness of the bar stock.

The first flight of the prototype 190, with fabric covering, was on 7 December 1944 with a 225-horsepower Jacobs engine borrowed from the AT-17 line. The second prototype, a five-place all-metal design, was upgraded to a 300-horsepower Jacobs engine and flew for the first time on 15 October 1945. Several problems cropped up during flight testing: directional over-control due to the large vertical tail and rudder (corrected with a dorsal fin); a tendency for the tailwheel to shimmy (corrected with a new tailwheel fork); a tendency to drop a wing at the stall (corrected by adding inboard stall strips); inadequate cabin heat (corrected with a gas-fired combustion heater under the rear seat); and some oil cooling problems. The only problem with the gas-fired heaters was that the intake and exhaust tubes coming through the aircraft's belly had to be individually trimmed and fitted by hand for every aircraft.

Development of both the 190 and 195 models continued in parallel, with the 190s eventually being delivered with only a 240-horsepower Continental W-670-23 radial engine and the 195s getting the 300-horsepower Jacobs radial engines. Options included the 245-horsepower R-755-9 (customer-furnished only), the 275-horsepower R-755-B2, and the more popular 300-horsepower R-755-A2.

• *A U.S. Army LC-126A, s/n 49-1967, at Fort Rucker, Alabama in 1958* •
(U.S. Army Aviation Museum)

Although the Continental engine on the 190 was smoother, it lacked the power of the bigger Jacobs, which tended to run rough and leak oil, leading to nicknames like "Shaky Jake" and "Bleeding Jake." In the 3,350-pound 195, the extra climb rate convinced most pilots to buy the bigger 300-horsepower engine. Production of the 195 started in July of 1947, while production of the 190

• A USAF LC-126A, s/n 49-1949, on skis in Alaska during the 1950s •
(Kansas Aviation Museum/Robert J. Pickett Collection)

the market in 1947, Cessna called it the "Cadillac of the Air" — the biggest and fastest civilian single-engine airplane available. The big radial engine provided a macho appeal and a distinctive roar on arrival and departure, but also complicated visibility when taxiing. Early in the production run, Cessna had to recall the Model 195s to replace a batch of bad pistons that were causing the engines to seize. Businessliners were produced continuously until 1954 with a total production run of 1,099 aircraft — 233 C-190s, and 866 C-195s. List price, in 1953, for the C-190 was $16,500 and ranged from $15,795 to $23,500 for the C-195 series, depending on the engine.

began in October of the same year. Both models were called Businessliners — the 190 seating four and the 195 seating five.

An uneven fuel-air mixture distribution to the seven cylinders in the Jacobs engine created the idiosyncratic "Jacobs cough." Cessna reworked the carburetor's butterfly valve, but the problem remained when the aircraft was operated at reduced throttle settings, with a fully leaned mixture, and at higher altitudes. The "cough" usually occurred just once, if all throttle and mixture settings were unchanged, but tended to rouse the attentions of both pilot and passengers when it did occur.

The 195 with the 300-horsepower Jacobs engine was designated the Model 195, while the 245-horsepower 195 was dubbed the Model 195A. When the 195 arrived on

"Off-The-Shelf" Purchases

In 1949, the U.S. Army requested that the Air Force purchase 15 Cessna 195s off-the-shelf to allow the Army to evaluate the aircraft's suitability for such duties as light cargo hauling, search-and-rescue missions, and liaison flights. The aircraft proved both rugged and dependable, and was able to haul loads from unimproved airstrips, leading the Army to eventually buy 67 more of them.

The easy-access engine compartment was certainly an important factor for the Army, as field maintenance was a necessity. The entire engine and cowl assembly on the C-195 aircraft was hinged on the left side with the engine on swing-out mounts. Once swung open, the entire assembly was held open by an over-center lock. With the engine in this position, a mechanic could easily get his hands on any of the engine components and accessories.

The original 15 aircraft were subsequently given the designation LC-126A and assigned military s/n 49-1947 through 49-1960, and 49-2773. All used the 300-horsepower Jacobs R-755-A2 engine. These original LC-126A aircraft were delivered with a seaplane door on the pilot's side, a spartan interior, the usual military avionics for that era, and provisions for interchangeable wheel, float, or ski landing gear. Following the Army's evaluation, the 195s were returned to the USAF and assigned duty in Arctic search-and-rescue work. In 1953, all were officially transferred back to the Army.

In 1950, the Army National Guard bought five C-195s

• An Army National Guard LC-126B, s/n 50-1253,
at Little Rock, Arkansas •
(Kansas Aviation Museum/Robert J. Pickett Collection)

• An Army LC-126C, s/n 51-16988, at Love Field in Dallas, Texas in November of 1952 •
(Kansas Aviation Museum/Robert J. Pickett Collection)

and designated them LC-126B, although they were virtually identical to the LC-126A. These were assigned s/n 50-1249 through 50-1253 and, in 1962, were redesignated U-20B. Three of the five aircraft continued to serve in the National Guard well into the 1960s.

With the success of the LC-126, the active duty Army elected to acquire 63 LC-126C aircraft. These planes were identical to the earlier aircraft except for a larger baggage door which allowed two stretchers to be placed in the passenger and baggage area for aeromedical evacuation. Many of these aircraft were also used as instrument flight training aircraft. They were assigned s/n 51-6958 through 51-6315 and, in 1962, were redesignated U-20C.

The A, B, and C Models

The differences between the three models of the LC-126 series include the following: oil and fuel system valves, circuit breaker panel, pilot and copilot seats, location of first aid kits, rudder trim, wing flap position indicator, lighting, radio equipment and antennas, baggage compartment and door, battery location, landing gear, and the control surface lock.

The LC-126A employed conventional landing gear and included a single lever to lock both the brakes and the flight control surfaces (aileron and rudder only — the elevators were secured with the pilot's seatbelt around the yoke). An elevator trim wheel was mounted in the center of the Y-shaped control column, but no in-flight adjustable rudder trim was provided. Only the A-model incorporated a wing flap position indicator, reading in degrees of extension, on the instrument panel in front of the pilot. Pilot and copilot seats were both constructed of foam rubber and springs. Two first aid kits were installed — one on the center of the utility shelf above the baggage compartment and the other on the front underside edge of the pilot's seat. The rear seat could be removed to permit loading a single stretcher through the cabin door. The LC-126A included standard navigation lights (red/green on the wingtips, and white on the tail) and a yellow tail position light, all operating in a steady mode only.

Radio equipment included a crystal-controlled (manually swapped-out to change frequencies) receiver and separate transmitter with a manually-controlled loop antenna (operated by a crank in the top center of the cabin roof between the pilot and copilot) for both voice and Morse code, and a fixed wire antenna on top of the fuselage. A trailing wire antenna was mounted on the underside of the fuselage (deployed by a crank on the left cockpit sidewall next to the pilot). The wire antenna was weighted to keep it near vertical when deployed, ensuring non-directional characteristics.

With the introduction of the B-model, the unique Goodyear crosswind landing gear was added, which swiveled when taxiing, taking off, or landing in a crosswind. This made crosswind landings easier, but complicated crosswind taxiing since the nose would not point in the direction of travel. The operating positions of two switches were reversed from the A-Model — the "Summer" and "Winter" positions of the Oil Dilution Tank-Hopper Valve were swapped (the winter position routed engine oil through only a subset of the full oil tank

• A typical U.S. Army LC-126 instrument panel •
(U.S. Army Aviation Museum)

• A U.S. Army LC-126A at Cairns Field of Fort Rucker, Alabama •
(U.S. Army Aviation Museum)

and, thus, decreased warmup time); and the Fuel Drain Valve's (on the left cabin sidewall just below the emergency exit door) "Closed" and "Open" positions were switched. Two self-locking drain valves were added for the wing tanks. These valves were located on the underside of the wings at the inboard aft corner of the tank bays. The circuit breaker panel was moved from the instrument panel to the left cockpit sidewall next to the pilot, and a rudder trim knob (actually, it only adjusted tension on the springs connected to the rudder bellcrank) was added to the center section

• A U.S. Army LC-126A overflying Cairns Field of Fort Rucker, Alabama •
(U.S. Army Aviation Museum)

of the control column. The construction of the pilot and copilot seats was altered to allow back and seat cushions to be removed to accommodate either seat or backpack parachutes. The two first aid kits were relocated to the cabin door (on the right side) and the lower front edge of the copilot seat. The combined parking brake/control lock was modified to lock the elevators as well as the other surfaces. A new stall warning system incorporated both a red light and a horn on the right side of the instrument panel. The map light (located between the pilot and the copilot in the cabin ceiling) was modified to allow adjustment of the beam's intensity and the installation of a red filter, plus it was removable for use as an extension light. An auxiliary rear seat back, located on the plane's right side, was provided to allow for an attendant when the stretcher was installed across the left seat bottom.

Radio equipment was modified to allow either voice or code reception on LF and ADF, and VOR, ILS, and marker beacon receivers were added. VHF transmission was available via a pair of crystal-controlled transmitters with six installed frequencies. VHF reception and transmission required a spike antenna mounted on top of the fuselage, ILS reception utilized a ramshorn antenna also mounted on top, ADF directional reception used a topside loop antenna (controlled by a radio control panel crank), both ADF and LF reception required the

• A U.S. Army LC-126B at Tiger Port, Fort Rucker, Alabama •
(U.S. Army Aviation Museum)

top-mounted wire antenna (switch selectable with the loop antenna), and marker beacon reception was via an antenna mounted on the underside of the fuselage.

Then along came the C-model and, inevitably, more changes. The stall warning indicator and the emergency oil shutoff valve were both deleted. Several items were relocated: the 12-volt battery was moved from behind the baggage compartment to inside the compartment and partially recessed; the external power receptacle was moved from the lower right side of the fuselage to the lower left side; and the first aid kits were moved to the underside front edge of both the pilot and copilot seats. Two position lights were added (one on top and one underneath the fuselage) and switch-selectable steady or flashing options were provided. The baggage compartment itself was stretched to 40 inches, and a longer access door (hinged at the top rather than on the forward edge) was incorporated to allow loading of two stretchers when the rear seat back was removed.

Radio equipment again changed, incorporating more modern equipment with a VHF transceiver (using a top-side spike antenna), VOR receiver (using the ramshorn antenna on top), a marker beacon receiver (using a belly-mounted antenna), and an ADF receiver (using either a top-mounted wire antenna or an underside motor-driven loop antenna).

According to the USAF pilot's flight manual (AN 01-125CAA-1), steep turns, stalls, lazy eights, and chandelles are permitted when the gross weight is less than 2,950 pounds. When the aircraft's weight is more than 2,950 pounds, none of these maneuvers are allowed. Whip stalls are prohibited at all weights.

Arctic Exploration Air Force Style

In 1949, while enrolled as a doctoral candidate in geology at California Institute of Technology in Pasadena under an Air Force Institute of Technology program, Air Force pilot Harry B. Allen (who, now deceased, retired as a colonel) was casting about for a doctoral thesis project. An arrangement was made between the departments of the Air Force and Interior for Allen to lead a team of Cal Tech graduate students in conducting geologic mapping of the arctic's St. Lawrence Island, which up to that time had never been completely mapped. The Soviet Union was claiming that St. Lawrence Island was not actually included in the original Alaskan Purchase, and President Truman wanted to find out what mineral resources might be on the island. Thus, Colonel Allen's adventure was ordered at the highest government level.

The Alaskan Air Command, with headquarters at Elmendorf AFB in Anchorage, provided him with a ski- and float-capable LC-126A, s/n 49-1949, from the inven-

• *A U.S. Army LC-126C, s/n 51-6962, c/n 7805. Note the marker beacon antenna in the housing on the underside of the fuselage* •
(U.S. Army Aviation Museum)

tory of its 10th Rescue Squadron. Colonel Bernt Balchen was the squadron commander and, as a well-known arctic explorer himself, fully supported Allen's mission, although the Alaskan Air Command staff was less enthusiastic. At that time, the 10th Rescue Squadron was often referred to as the 10th Hunting and Fishing Squadron since they frequently provided recreational aircraft services for visiting VIPs. Apparently, the loss of one of these assets was not appreciated.

The 10th Rescue Squadron also provided a crew chief for Allen — a former bartender from the Bronx who was less than thrilled at the prospect of

• *Eskimos in anti-exposure suits help refloat Colonel Allen's LC-126A, using strips of walrus hide strung under the floats and over six empty 50-gallon drums* •
(U.S. Air Force Museum)

an extended voyage into the Alaskan bush. To get to the Bering Straights and St. Lawrence Island, Allen and his crew flew 49-1949 from Anchorage to McGrath, landing on the Kuskokwim River where they overnighted. Then they continued on to Nome where Allen had to land in the open ocean since the Nome River was not wide enough for takeoffs or landings. The final 200-mile leg to the island was delayed by poor weather, and when they finally did taxi out from Nome they almost collided with a tug towing a barge. With only a magnetic compass for navi-

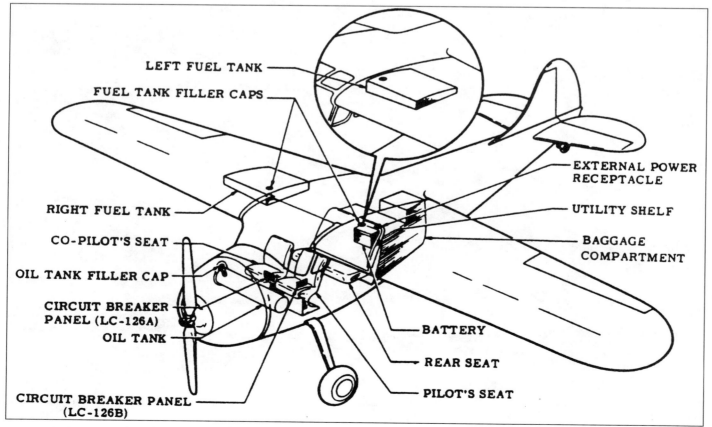

LEFT FUEL TANK

FUEL TANK FILLER CAPS

RIGHT FUEL TANK

CO-PILOT'S SEAT

OIL TANK FILLER CAP

CIRCUIT BREAKER
PANEL (LC-126A)

OIL TANK

CIRCUIT BREAKER PANEL
(LC-126B)

EXTERNAL POWER
RECEPTACLE

UTILITY SHELF

BAGGAGE
COMPARTMENT

BATTERY

REAR SEAT

PILOT'S SEAT

• *The internal arrangement of the LC-126A and LC-126B* •
(USAF Flight Manual)

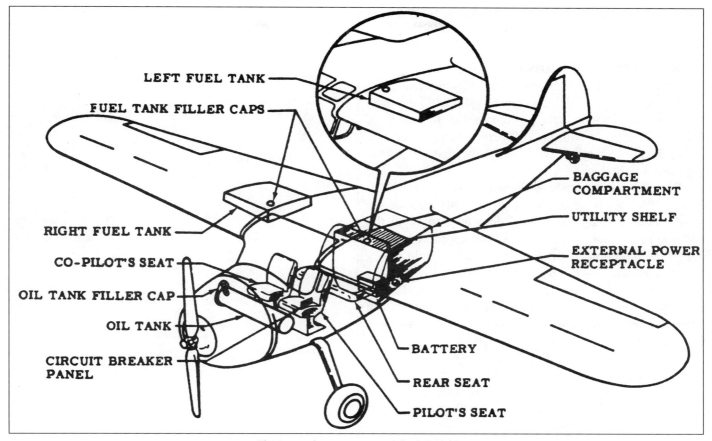

LEFT FUEL TANK

FUEL TANK FILLER CAPS

RIGHT FUEL TANK

CO-PILOT'S SEAT

OIL TANK FILLER CAP

OIL TANK

CIRCUIT BREAKER PANEL

BAGGAGE COMPARTMENT

UTILITY SHELF

EXTERNAL POWER RECEPTACLE

BATTERY

REAR SEAT

PILOT'S SEAT

• *The internal arrangement of the LC-126C* •
(USAF Flight Manual)

gation, Allen headed in the general direction of St. Lawrence Island. According to Colonel Allen in a letter to David Menard at the U.S. Air Force Museum, "After the longest hour, we could see the low-lying island as well as the Siberian mainland only 39 miles distant."

Allen found the rugged, radial-engined LC-126A ideal for its assigned duties of landing on whatever lakes or lagoons could be found during his expedition. He recalled, "Senior officials of the Alaskan Air Command would have put me up before a Flying Evaluation Board if they knew how I used and abused that pretty little bird. In true bush fashion, I lugged everything — lumber, rocks, supplies, fuel — anything that could be stuffed into the fuselage or pontoon ports, lashed to the struts, floats, or wherever. Sometimes it flew a little sideways, but that didn't seem to bother its flying characteristics unduly."

Allen recalls landing on a small lake on a calm, moonlit night (conditions which provide no depth perception) to pick up one of the geologists who had been missing for several days. "I thought I was just about to land and slowed the airplane for landing. I was 25-50 feet high and ended up doing a rudder exercise stall until I impacted the water. It was such a hard landing that I thought the struts would come up through the cabin. The little LC-126 gave nary a grunt and appeared to have suffered no pain."

Allen had to develop tactics to deal with the prevalent

summertime low ceilings and fog: "More than once I flew into a fog bank and would have to pull up into the overcast and fly clear of the land, out to sea, and begin a 50-foot per minute rate of descent until I was skipping through the tops of the swells and then slambanged into a trough." When the plane did not sink, he taxied towards the sound of breaking waves, sometimes having to drop anchor and wait out the weather for up to three days in a rolling airplane cockpit!

When Colonel Allen returned 49-1949 to the 10th Rescue Squadron at Anchorage in November of 1949, the aircraft sported a walrus-hide patch on one float. The float had to be repaired in the field following a sinking episode caused by an encounter with rocks. Also, one of the engine mounts was bent. But the LC-126A was still flying and floating. As Colonel Allen noted, "Not bad, after its long unsuffering service."

Colonel Allen went on to fly a variety of light aircraft on wheels, skis, and floats in the arctic and in China, Mongolia, and India. He offered an evaluation of the LC-126 compared to the L-3, L-5, Otter, Beaver, and C-64: "I have never flown a more reliable, sturdy, can-do, worthy steed as that LC-126. It was a part of my life. It breathed when I did and rested when I did. It was always ready to go. It required little or no maintenance other than filling it with gas and oil and pumping out the floats." A succinct testimony to a great airplane's capabilities, from a man who put it to the toughest of tests.

Where Are They Now?

There are still quite a few of the big-engined birds, along with many of the civilian C-190/C-195 models, cruising the skies at speeds comparable to many of today's singles, but with the distinctive throaty roar of a radial engine to remind everyone below that this is not your usual lightplane.

Recent issues of Trade-A-Plane list a half-dozen or so Model 195s, but none of the advertisements indicate the planes were military LC-126s. Prices tend to be in the $50,000 to $55,000 range. With a little appropriate paint and some attention to detail, any of them could easily become, at least, a semi-genuine warbird.

There are not very many examples of the LC-126, or even the civilian Model 195, on display in North American museums. The following three museums have LC-126s preserved in their collections:

- *Travis Air Force Base Museum*,
  Vacaville, California
- *Liberal Air Museum*, Liberal, Kansas
- *U.S. Air Force Museum*, Wright-Patterson Air Force Base, Dayton, Ohio ✝

• *A USAF LC-126A in Alaska during Harry Allen's 1949 mapping expedition of St. Lawrence Island* •
(U.S. Air Force Museum)

Specifications

Wingspan . . . . .36 ft. 2 in.
Length . . . . .27 ft. 10 in.
Height . . . . .8 ft. 3.5 in.
Maximum Gross Weight
        Landplane or Skiplane . . . . .3,350 lbs.
        Floatplane . . . . .3,600 lbs.
Fuel capacity . . . . .80 U.S. gallons
Engine . . . . .Jacobs R-755-A2, 300-horsepower, 7-cylinder, air-cooled radial engine
Propeller . . . . .2-blade, constant-speed Hamilton-Standard
Maximum Continuous Engine Speed . . . . .2,200 rpm
Normal Cruising Engine Speed . . . . .1,900 - 2,000 rpm
Maximum Allowable IAS (flaps up) . . . . .200 mph
Maximum Allowable IAS (flaps down) . . . . .130 mph
Stall Speed (Landplane)
        Power Off, No Flaps . . . . .53.5 mph
        Power Off, Full Flaps . . . . .51 mph
        Power On, No Flaps . . . . .44 mph
        Power On, Full Flaps . . . . .42 mph
Stall Speed (Floatplane)
        Power Off, No Flaps . . . . .53.5 mph
        Power Off, Full Flaps . . . . .48 mph
        Power On, No Flaps . . . . .46 mph
        Power On, Full Flaps . . . . .44 mph
Takeoff Ground Roll . . . . .760 ft.
Takeoff Distance Over 50-Foot Obstacle . . . . .1,690 ft.
Takeoff Distance (Floatplane) . . . . .3,050 ft.
Normal Takeoff IAS . . . . .55 mph
Rate of Climb
        Landplane . . . . .1,200 fpm
        Floatplane . . . . .760 fpm
        Climb IAS . . . . .104 mph
Landing Ground Roll . . . . .725 ft.
Landing Distance Over 50-Foot Obstacle . . . . .1,655 ft.
Landing Distance (Floatplane) . . . . .700 ft.
Normal Final Approach IAS . . . . .71 mph
Maximum Cruise (Sea Level)
        IAS . . . . .179 mph
        Fuel flow . . . . .23.6 GPH
Maximum Range Cruise (No Reserves)
        IAS . . . . .152 mph
        Fuel flow . . . . .12.6 GPH
        Altitude . . . . .10,000 ft.

Tactical Weapons and FAC Tactics

-chapter 6-

*"Short rounds cost us double;
our own that we lose,
and theirs that we don't get."*
- Anonymous Fighter Pilot

Various studies conducted by the U.S. military from World War II to the present indicate that airstrikes are responsible for a relatively small percentage of "friendly fire" accidents (such as short rounds) resulting in casualties. However, due to the great destructive potential of ordnance delivered by air, such accidents tend to cause more casualties per accident than either field artillery or naval guns. Short rounds and "friendly fire" accidents occurred due to normal ballistic dispersion of unguided weapons, possible aircrew errors in release parameters (especially if enemy ground fire was active), and aircraft or weapons equipment malfunctions.

• *USAF F-4E releasing a pair of MK-82 "Snakeye" 500-pound bombs* •
(U.S. Air Force)

Communications errors sometimes contributed to "friendly fire" accidents. Examples that have actually occurred include:

- An Army company commander inadvertently transmitted his own unit's coordinates rather than those of the enemy forces as the target for a blind air strike.
- For a radar controlled air strike, the initial portion of the target coordinates were encoded as "Yankee Foxtrot" but decoded as "Yankee Echo" — resulting in the bombs being dropped exactly 100 kilometers south of the intended target.
- An Army company commander radioed, "Do not bring the napalm closer." Unfortunately, the first two words of his transmission were blocked by a slow-keying transmitter — and napalm was spread over some of his own troops.

To be effective, a Forward Air Controller (FAC) had to know enough about a wide variety of air-to-ground weapons carried by fighter aircraft, artillery used by the Army, and naval guns based on ships to be sure he was directing the use of the best available type for a specific target. The FAC needed to know how the weapons were delivered, what fuzing options were available, what the likely effects would be, and what the minimum safe distance was to protect both himself and friendly ground forces. By ensuring that all fighter aircraft crews had the target in sight early, by properly choosing attack run-in headings, and by paying close attention to safe separation distances from the friendlies, "friendly fire" accidents could be at least minimized.

Before discussing the combat history and performance of the Cessna aircraft flight crews who completed thousands of combat missions in Korea and Vietnam, the reader ought to understand the weapons employed, the tactics required, and the depth of knowledge required by the pilots who flew those missions. If you have "been there, done that" — skip to the next chapter. If not, what follows will provide a basis for a better understanding of the stories presented in subsequent chapters.

Target Selection and Indentification

Most Army units possessed some organic capability to suppress enemy fire, such as field artillery or helicopter gunships. Therefore, calling for tactical fighter air support was usually reserved for those situations where the greater destructiveness of air-dropped weapons was needed or when organic firepower was not available. Other factors that had to be evaluated before requesting close air support sorties included:

- Ability of the pilots to identify the targets, with or without FAC marking rockets.
- Stability of the target (a target that would soon disperse or be overrun was not a good choice).
- Availability of proper aircraft ordnance to achieve the desired results for the specific targets.
- Determination that the potential gains from attacking the target justified risking the aircraft and crews.

• USAF F-111 releasing a load of low drag MK-82 bombs •
(U.S. Air Force)

Targets were generally grouped into three broad categories: armor (airstrikes were very effective against moving armor and armor staging areas); troops (airstrikes were more effective against grouped troops in the open than dispersed dug-in troops); and fortifications (airstrikes had to be concentrated on specific installations rather than broad fortified areas and typically needed to use heavy and accurately placed ordnance to be effective against any fortifications).

To pinpoint the specific target, the FAC needed to work hierarchically downward, starting with the least accurate references down to the most accurate. He had to be flexible enough to change identification methods depending on how much trouble the fighter pilots were having with the planned method. For instance, the FAC might use map coordinates or electronic navigation aids to get the fighters to the general target area and to an orbit point if one was necessary. Once the fighters were in the area, the FAC could use prominent landmarks and terrain features both as location markers and as size references (the width of a river bed or the distance from one bend to the next might be used to help estimate distances to the actual target). Smoke marking rockets or flares were, of course, standard references — sometimes, it was necessary and

• A pair of U.S. Army L-19s head out for target spotting duties during the Korean War •
(U.S. Army Aviation Museum)

desirable to bracket the intended target to provide both a distance reference and an attack run-in reference line.

Any friendly positions had to be carefully identified by all airstrike participants before the FAC could clear the fighters for the attack. Mirrors, colored panels on the ground, terrain features, smoke grenades, strobe lights, vehicle lights, fires, colored balloons, and flares were all used when available and time permitted.

The FAC also had to determine any restrictions for the fighters' attack patterns. Whenever possible, FACs allowed the fighters to set-up random attack headings — making it more difficult for the enemy to fire on them. FACs tried to avoid directing the fighters to attack over the heads of, or toward, friendly forces, since it was too easy for a short or long round to land on the friendlies. If necessary to attack perpendicular to a line of friendlies, the preferred attack would be over their heads heading away with the FAC or ground commander making the final "clear to release" call when certain that the attacker could not drop on the friendly troops. FACs, and the ground troops, preferred to direct airstrikes along an attack axis parallel to the line of friendly forces, since most errors in delivery would occur along that line of attack.

• A pair of O-2As on their way to their assigned patrol areas with a full load of rockets •
(U.S. Air Force)

Delivery Parameters and Planning

There are five basic weapons delivery patterns used by fighters: level, low angle, high angle, dive toss, and level toss. There were eight basic release modes in use during the Korean and Vietnam Wars: visual (manual), radar, Loran, inertial (onboard navigation computer), optical (laser and TV), beam seeker (homing on enemy radar beams), beacon, and TACAN (a military ground-based navigation aid). On a specific mission, the fighters might have been loaded with a variety of ordnance (e.g., conventional bombs, napalm, and/or 20mm guns), which might require different delivery patterns and release modes.

For preplanned missions, the FAC had time to coordinate his target requirements with the fighters' weapons load, and determine the best sequence and delivery patterns. However, for missions in which either the FAC or a ground commander requested immediate air support, the planning had to be accomplished "on the fly," based on the FAC's general knowledge of weapons and tactics. Once in the target area, both the FAC and the fighters were busy with aircraft control, identification of enemy defenses and friendly forces, target identification, and weapons settings, all while monitoring fuel and weather. This was not a good time to plan an airstrike. The accuracy of the attack and the success of the mission were often determined by the time available before the fighters dropped into the target area and by the FAC's overall knowledge of weapons and tactics.

Types of Weapons Deliveries

A level weapons delivery can be made at most any altitude from 50 feet to 50,000 feet and may use radar, Loran, beacon, or visual release modes. Level deliveries were generally only very accurate at very low altitudes. Errors tended to be directly along the line-of-flight (i.e., hitting short or long).

A low angle delivery was a release on a dive angle of 30 degrees or less. It was usually used with visual releases, sometimes combined with internal radar ranging, and was primarily useful in an area without extensive anti-air threats. Pattern altitudes, during the set-up prior to the dive itself, were typically 4,000 to 6,000 feet AGL. This was the preferred delivery for high drag bombs, finned napalm, unguided rockets, and for strafing. Low angle deliveries tended to be very accurate and kept the fighters in close to the target area. Typical accuracies were:

- Strafing - 90 percent within 50 feet of target.
- Low Drag Bombs - 90 percent within 300 feet.
- Rockets - 90 percent within 150 feet.

A high angle delivery entailed a dive angle of more than 30 degrees and used the same release modes as a low angle delivery. It was the best choice in areas with moderate to heavy anti-air threats, but was less accurate than a low angle delivery. Pattern altitudes were typically 9,000 to 12,000 feet AGL with an average pull-out altitude of 3,500 feet. Due to the reduced accuracy, it was imperative that the FAC have the fighters in sight during their roll-in and dive before clearing them to release, to be certain where they were aiming. The entire attack typically took only a few seconds and a minor error by either the FAC or the fighter pilot could potentially result in disaster for friendly troops — rather than a successful mission.

A dive toss delivery typically required a high angle dive and on-board radar ranging equipment. The pilot rolled in, held the pipper (gunsight reticle) on the target, held down the release button, and began a pull-out. The radar, through the aircraft's weapons release computer, determined the appropriate slant range and released the weapon at the proper moment.

Finally, a level toss delivery involved similar techniques as the dive toss, with the exception that the pull-out maneuver was begun from a level pass rather than a dive. It usually involved rippling a series of weapons rather than releasing a single weapon, to achieve a dispersed pattern for maximum target area coverage. The level toss delivery was primarily for areas with heavy anti-air threats and its accuracy depended on the precision of the computations.

Weapons Designation System

The letter and number system used to denote the various non-nuclear weapons carried on aircraft was similar to that used to designate military aircraft, and contained a considerable amount of information about the weapon itself. With a basic knowledge of this system, nomenclatures such as BLU-26/B and CBU-24 could be decoded.

The first two letters in a weapon's designation were the component or unit indicators and indicated what the item was and, sometimes, what it did. For high explosive "dumb" bombs, usually only the single "M" unit indicator was used. Typical component indicators seen during the Vietnam War and since included:

- AG - Air-to-ground guided weapon.
- AI - Air-to-air guided weapon.
- BD - Dummy practice and training bombs.
- BL - Live aerial bombs.
- CB - Various devices incorporating clusters of small bombs or missiles.
- CT - Containers for aerial delivery of supplies.
- GA - Integral aircraft guns.
- GB - Guided aerial bombs.
- GU - Other aircraft guns, such as gun pods.
- LA - Weapons launchers installed on aircraft.
- MA - Miscellaneous armament items.
- ML - Miscellaneous live munitions.
- RL - Non-guided live aircraft-launched rockets.
- MX - Miscellaneous.

• Prominent visual references were used by FACs and fighter crews in South Vietnam. This II Corps reference was known to all as "Pussy Mountain" •
(Fred McNeill)

• A pair of A-37Bs and an A-1E returning from combat missions, led by another A-1E •
(Kansas Aviation Museum/Robert J. Pickett Collection)

• SU - Suspension and release devices for stores (bombs, rockets, fuel tanks, launchers, etc.).

The third or last letter was almost always either a "K" or a "U." The "K" identifier referred to a component (fuze, mount, fins, relay, etc.) that was essential to the weapon's function. For example, the MK-82 500-pound bomb included high-drag fins while the M-117 750-pound bomb did not. The identifier "U" referred to an independent weapon unit with a specific function.

Subsequent models of the original or basic weapon were indicated by a number following a dash and might be followed by a letter indicating a follow-on modification of that model. After the version number a slash and a letter indicating the specific installation might be found. Common indicators included:

• B - Item dropped from an aircraft.
• C - Combination.
• M - Missile.
• S - Ground, self-propelled.
• U - Multiple installations.
• W - Water (surface or submerged).

For example, a BLU-4A/B would be a live aerial bomb unit, fourth model, first modification, aircraft transported.

However, just knowing all of the above designations was not enough to conduct an air strike. The system did not provide sufficient information to describe how the weapon was used, what its effects would be, or any of the specific safety information such as safe separation distances. In addition, some nomenclatures were, in fact, combinations of individual components. For example, a CBU designation described a "cluster bomb unit" but not what specific bombs were contained in the CBU or the type of dispenser used. One would have to know the kind of dispenser (SUU) and the type of bomblets (BLU) to know how to employ the resulting unit. For example, BLU-26/B bomblets loaded in an SUU-30 dispenser unit resulted in a specific combat unit — the CBU-24. Whereas the BLU-66/B bomblets loaded in an SUU-7 dispenser resulted in a CBU-46 "cluster bomb unit."

Types of Weapons

During the Vietnam War, a FAC had to have at least a modest familiarity with some 15 different weapons classifications and over 100 different specific weapon types, and a working knowledge of a large portion of them. He could never be certain what type of ordnance the fighters might be carrying when they arrived in the target area.

Aircraft guns ranged from the 7.62mm miniguns found on the Cessna A-37 Dragonfly, the Rockwell OV-10 Bronco, and some gunships to the standard M-61 Vulcan 20mm cannon found on most of the modern fighters. These were, of course, primarily useful against exposed personnel, although the 20mm gun loaded with Armor Piercing Incendiary (API) projectiles could be effective against lightly armored vehicles. Today, the Grumman A-10 Thunderbolt II carries an internal 30mm Gatling gun capable of piercing heavily armored vehicles.

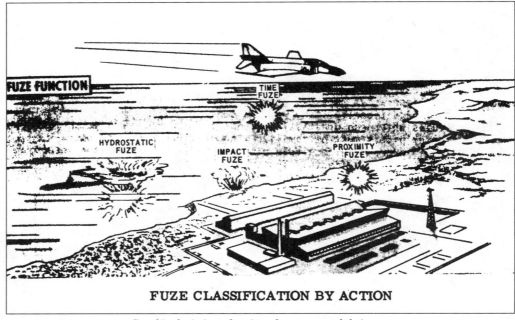

FUZE CLASSIFICATION BY ACTION

• Graphic depiction of various fuze types and their uses •
(U.S. Air Force Handbook)

There also was a wide variety of CBU munitions with varying effects and effectiveness, in addition to a broad range of fuzes. These fuzes ranged from airburst and impact fuzes to delayed fuzes up to 20 minutes. The following examples illustrate the wide variety of CBU munitions with which a FAC had to contend (there were at least 22 different CBU devices):

- CBU-12 (SUU-7 + BLU-17/B) - Airburst, white phosphorous incendiary with minimum safe distances of up to 500 meters.
- CBU-24 (SUU-30 + BLU-26/B) - Impact detonation, anti-personnel weapon with minimum safe distances of up to 600 meters.
- CBU-30 - Time delay detonation, anti-personnel weapon dispensing 385 pounds of CS gas (minimum safe distance depended on the surface winds).
- CBU-42 (SUU-38 + BLU-49/B) - Anti-personnel mines, detonated when disturbed by moving personnel.
- CBU-46 (SUU-7 + BLU-66/B) - Short time delay, anti-personnel, fragmentation, jungle penetrating bomblets with minimum safe distances of up to 250 meters.
- CBU-66 (SUU-51 + BLU-81/B) - Impact fuzed, jungle penetrating anti-personnel fragmentation bomblets with minimum safe distances of up to 700 meters.
- CBU-72 - 500 pounds of fuel-air explosive for defoliation and anti-personnel.
- CBU-78 (SUU-51 + BLU-91 + BLU-92) - "Gator" 1000-pound cluster of anti-tank and anti-personnel surface

• A photo of the immediate aftermath of dropping napalm on an enemy's exposed hilltop position, taken from a FAC's O-2A •
(Fred McNeill)

mines detonated by magnetic disturbance.

In addition, there were several CBU munitions that were guided units. A guided CBU-74 anti-material weapon was called a GBU-3/B, while the laser-guided "Rockeye" 3,000-pound cluster of anti-tank bomblets was the GBU-1B. The BLU components that were used to create the CBU combat units included the following:

- BLU-17 (Incendiary white phosphorous).
- BLU-24 (Cyclotol-filled jungle bomb).
- BLU-27 (750-pound napalm - BLU-32: 500-pound).
- BLU-54 (Anti-personnel mine).
- BLU-59 (Anti-personnel and anti-material delayed fuzing).
- BLU-61 (Anti-material incendiary and fragmentation bomblets).
- BLU-66 (Cyclotol-filled fragmentation jungle penetrating bomblets).
- BLU-73 (500-pound fuel-air explosive defoliation and anti-personnel bombs).
- BLU-81 (Anti-vehicle mines).
- BLU-82 (15,000-pound gelled slurry-filled parachute retarded bomb).
- BLU-91 (Surface anti-tank mines).
- BLU-92 (Surface anti-personnel mines).

There were also six standard high-explosive bombs (the basic "iron bombs") with minimum safe distances ranging from 900-meters for the MK-81 to 1,400-meters for the M-118. The basic nomenclatures for these weapons were:

- MK-25 - 2000-pound underwater mine.
- MK-36 - 500-pound mine (modified MK-82).
- MK-40 - 1000-pound mine (modified MK-83).
- MK-81 - 250 pounds.
- MK-82 - 500 pounds.
- MK-83 - 1,000 pounds.
- MK-84 - 2,000 pounds (a laser-guided version was called the KMU-351/B and weighed 2,052 pounds).
- M-117 - 750 pounds.
- M-117D - 750 pounds of mines.
- M-118 - 3,000 pounds (a laser-guided version was called the KMU-370/B and weighed 3,066 pounds).

Knowledge of fuze types and delay settings was also important. The type of target suggested the type of fuze and fuze delay setting that would produce the best results. Most weapons could be installed with a variety of fuzes — thus substantially altering the weapon effects. In addition, improper use of weapon and fuze combinations could lead to serious damage to the aircraft or injury to the crew. Bomb fuzes were classified by the position in which they were mounted on the bomb and by their function. Fuzes could be mounted in either the nose or the tail section of a bomb, sometimes both, with pilot action required to select the proper fuze prior to activating the master arming switch in flight. Tail fuzes were better for boring into the deep tunnels frequently used by the dug-in Viet Cong than nose-mounted fuzes. Five basic fuze types or functions could be mounted on a given bomb:

- Impact fuzes detonated when the fuze impacted the target and sometimes included cockpit-selectable time delays.
- Proximity fuzes sensed the nearness of a target (e.g., by radar) to initiate detonation prior to impact.
- Hydrostatic fuzes detonated on contact with water, sensing the build-up of water pressure.
- Target detection fuzes were the type used on air-dropped land or sea mines, which detonated when the target passed near the mine (through ground vibration detectors) or over the mine (by sensing pressure).
- Timed fuzes were used to detonate the bomb prior to impact, proper release altitude being critical to determining the correct timing.

• *NVA target illumination flares being used during a nighttime attack against the USAF airfield at Pleiku* •
(Fred McNeill)

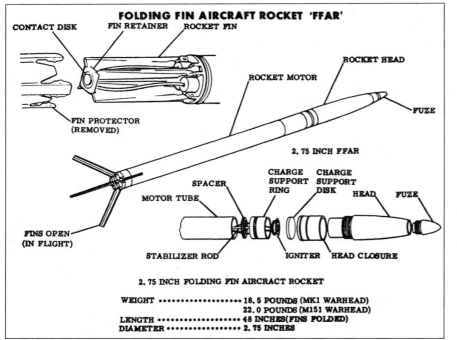

FOLDING FIN AIRCRAFT ROCKET 'FFAR'

CONTACT DISK
FIN RETAINER
ROCKET FIN
ROCKET HEAD
ROCKET MOTOR
FUZE
FIN PROTECTOR (REMOVED)
2.75 INCH FFAR
CHARGE SUPPORT RING
CHARGE SUPPORT DISK
SPACER
MOTOR TUBE
HEAD
FUZE
FINS OPEN (IN FLIGHT)
STABILIZER ROD
IGNITER
HEAD CLOSURE

2.75 INCH FOLDING FIN AIRCRACT ROCKET

WEIGHT ·················· 18.5 POUNDS (MK1 WARHEAD)
22.0 POUNDS (M151 WARHEAD)
LENGTH ·················· 48 INCHES(FINS FOLDED)
DIAMETER ················ 2.75 INCHES

*• Internal layout and specifications of a 2.75-inch FFAR rocket —
the FAC's main "weapon" •*
(U.S. Air Force Weapons Manual)

Impact fuzes could be set by the pilot for either instantaneous detonation or for a specific delay (up to a maximum of 20 seconds, although the most common delay settings were 0.25 second or less). By selecting delayed fuzing, particularly with the heavier bombs like the 750-pound M-117 or 1000-pound MK-83, the bomb's momentum drove it deep into the ground before detonation. This resulted in maximum destruction of fortified targets and deep tunnels. FACs rarely asked for instantaneous fuzing unless the targets were on the surface and lightly armored, like trucks and personnel. Sometimes, they might ask for a 0.025-second delay to get the bomb just barely into the ground or, more likely, a 0.25-second delay to allow it to drive eight feet or more into the ground.

FACs had little use for napalm since it was only effective against troops out in the open and was unable to penetrate into the tunnels or fortifications at all. However, by having the fighters arm their "iron bombs" with delayed fuzing to allow them to bore deep into the tunnel before detonating, a second pass with the napalm could be effective.

Flares and target markers were also commonly carried both by the fighters (in dispensers holding up to 16 flares or markers) and by the FACs for night missions. Possible flares and markers included:

* MK-6 Flare: Multi-candle flame and smoke ground illumination device with a 90-second delay fuze and a total burn

time of 40 minutes.

* MK-24 Flare: Parachute-retarded, falling at 15 feet per second before ignition and 7.5 feet-per-second after ignition, with a total burn time of 120 to 180 seconds depending on the specific model.

* MLU-32/B99 "Brighteye" Flare: Five million candlepower device that burned for up to five minutes under a 19-foot diameter hot air balloon descending at three feet per second).

* LUU-1/B & LUU-5/B Target Marker Flare: Modified MK-24 designed to burn for 30 minutes after reaching the ground with an easily-distinguished red flame for the LUU-1/B and a green flame for the LUU-5/B.

* LUU-2/B Flare: Similar to the MK-24 with a 4.5-minute burn time under a parachute.

Also, a range of miscellaneous weapons were available, such as:

* ANM-47A4: 100 pounds of smoke and incendiary.
* M-36E1: 182 slow-burning M-126 incendiary bomblets, 900 pounds total.
* M-36E2: 182 fast-burning M-126 incendiary bomblets, 900 pounds total.
* MLU-10/B: Blunt-nosed, 660-pound bomb containing up to 15 land mines.
* ANM-1A4: 800 pounds of fragmentation bomblets.

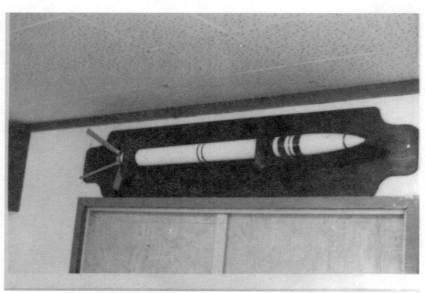

*• An inert "Willie Pete" marking rocket mounted over the doorway
at Nakhon Phanom Air Base, Thailand •*
(D.R. Lambert)

Both FACs and fighters used unguided rockets, from the basic 2.75-inch diameter folding fin aircraft rockets (FFAR) to five-inch diameter rockets. The various warheads available included:

- MK-1: High-explosive, impact detonating 10-pound warheads effective against personnel and unarmed vehicles.
- MK-5: Armor-piercing, impact detonating shaped-charge warheads effective against lightly armored vehicles.
- MK-151: High-explosive, impact detonating, anti-personnel warhead with a pearlite malleable iron casing designed to produce maximum fragmentation— although the M-151 could also be loaded with white phosphorous for target marking.

• M-156 warhead detonating after a FAC's target marking pass •
(Kansas Aviation Museum/Robert J. Pickett Collection)

- WDU-4: Shaped-charge warhead, dispersing anti-personnel miniature steel darts, or flechettes.
- M-156: White phosphorous incendiary, impact detonating warheads — standard target marking weapon for FACs.

Although FACs did not use or direct the use of air-to-air missiles or become involved often with the use of air-to-ground missiles, they were still expected to be familiar with the missiles commonly in use. The two most prevalent air-to-air missiles used by U.S. forces in Southeast Asia were the heat-seeking AIM-9 "Sidewinder" and the radar-guided AIM-7 "Sparrow," missiles still in use today although in later, much improved models. Air-to-ground missiles included the AGM-45 "Shrike" and AGM-78 "Standard Arm" anti-radiation missiles used by Wild Weasel aircraft to home-in on and destroy enemy radar sites. The AGM-62 "Walleye" electro-optically guided missiles were also used, today replaced in service by the AGM-65 "Maverick" used extensively in the 1991 Persian Gulf War.

Artillery adjustment and targeting was another mission assigned to FACs — with most artillery spotting duties accomplished by Army FACs from L-19/O-1 aircraft. Both ground-based and off-shore sea-based artillery were used extensively in both the Korean and Vietnam Wars. Typical artillery and naval guns with which a FAC had to be familiar included:

- Mortars: From 6- to 28-pound projectiles with ranges from one mile to over three miles and aircraft safe separation distances from 500 feet to 1,500 feet.
- Howitzers: 33- to 200-pounds projectiles with ranges from 7 miles to over 10 miles and aircraft safe separation distances from 1,500 to 2,000 feet.
- Naval Guns: 5- to 8-inch

• A fully loaded LAU-32A/A rocket launcher mounted on a USAF O-2A in South Vietnam •
(Kansas Aviation Museum/Robert J. Pickett Collection)

diameter barrels with 10- to 260-pound projectiles, ranges from 13 to 20 miles, and aircraft safe separation distances from 500 to 2,400 feet.

- Rocket Launchers: Five-inch diameter rockets similar to the aircraft-launched rockets with a range of 9,100 meters and an aircraft safe separation distance of 1,100 feet.

Mission Coordination

There were three general types of missions worked by FACs: preplanned, immediate, and pop-up. A preplanned mission was just what the term implies — a mission planned and ordered before either the fighters or the FAC launched from their home bases, with the targets and ordnance spelled-out in the daily air tasking orders. An immediate mission was requested through the Tactical Air Control System (TACS) via radio. Sometimes, a FAC found a "hot" target (such as troops on the move or an enemy storage facility) and initiated a request for "tac air" (tactical aircraft). At other times, an Army ground commander, finding himself in need of close air support, would initiate the request for an immediate air strike through Army channels or directly through an airborne FAC. Pop-ups, on the other hand, occurred when the TACS rerouted a flight of fighters, who may have had to abort a preplanned mission due to weather or other problems, into a FAC's working area — the FAC's job was then to find a suitable target quickly.

For preplanned missions, both the FAC and the fighters knew where they were going to be operating, what kind of target was involved, and at least a general idea of the type of defenses to expect. The daily orders specified the weapons to be carried by the fighters, weapons selected to be effective against the specific targets. The way things were supposed to work was for the FAC to fly to the target area, verify the targets, and then loiter until the fighters checked-in on the assigned frequency. If the mission was in support of troops on the ground, the FAC was responsible for communications and coordination with them as well as with the fighters, meaning he had at least two radios in use during a strike (VHF/FM to talk to the Army ground troops and UHF to talk to the fighters).

Immediate airstrikes occurred when the FAC was contacted by ground forces who needed close air support right away, when the FAC himself came across an unexpected or unreported target during his routine patrol, or when the TACS received information on a target from some other source and rerouted fighters to the area. "Immediates" required the FAC to move to the target area, determine the best direction and methods for the attack, and try to locate and define any ground-to-air threats. Fighters dispatched to handle "immediates" frequently were not carrying the best ordnance for the specific target, another reason that FACs had to understand the various weapons, their effects, and their use.

Pop-ups were similar to immediates in that the FAC had to make do with whatever ordnance the fighters were carrying when they checked-in. However, the fighters were usually turned over to the FAC with very little warning. This is why most FACs tried to keep track of a "back pocket" target or two just in case he was advised of inbound fighters at the last moment. Typically, fighters diverted for pop-ups would arrive with less "play time" (time available in the target based on fuel remaining and fuel needed to get back to base) than fighters tasked via preplanned or "immediate" — they may have already flown to a preplanned target area and been forced to abort that mission.

Once the fighters were in the target area, the FAC had to work quickly before the fighters ran low on fuel and had to return to base. He used landmarks and terrain features to focus the eyes of the fast-moving fighter pilots on the general target area, make sure they knew

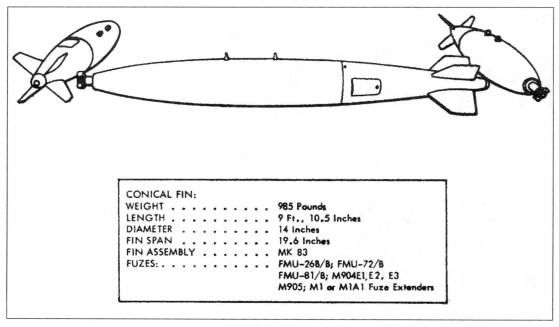

```
CONICAL FIN:
WEIGHT . . . . . . . . . . . 985 Pounds
LENGTH . . . . . . . . . . . 9 Ft., 10.5 Inches
DIAMETER . . . . . . . . . 14 Inches
FIN SPAN . . . . . . . . . . 19.6 Inches
FIN ASSEMBLY . . . . . . . MK 83
FUZES: . . . . . . . . . . . FMU-26B/B; FMU-72/B
                            FMU-81/B; M904E1, E2, E3
                            M905; M1 or M1A1 Fuze Extenders
```

• *MK-83 low drag bomb* •
(U.S. Air Force Handbook)

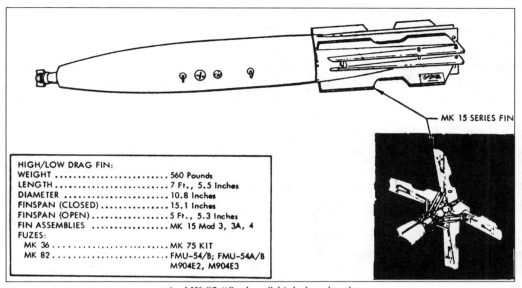

MK 15 SERIES FIN

```
HIGH/LOW DRAG FIN:
WEIGHT ...................... 560 Pounds
LENGTH ...................... 7 Ft., 5.5 Inches
DIAMETER .................... 10.8 Inches
FINSPAN (CLOSED) ............ 15.1 Inches
FINSPAN (OPEN) .............. 5 Ft., 5.3 Inches
FIN ASSEMBLIES .............. MK 15 Mod 3, 3A, 4
FUZES:
  MK 36 ..................... MK 75 KIT
  MK 82 ..................... FMU-54/B; FMU-54A/B
                             M904E2, M904E3
```

• An MK-82 "Snakeye" high drag bomb •
(U.S. Air Force Handbook)

where any friendly forces were located, and alert them to any known or suspected ground-to-air threats, particularly the crew-served weapons such as 23mm or 37mm anti-aircraft guns. (The following radio calls are intended for illustration purposes only.)

A typical initial check-in radio call from the inbound fighters to the FAC might be: "Covey 31, this is Blue Lead, 30 miles northeast of Pussy Mountain at 10,000 feet, flight of four F-4s."

The FAC's reply to the fighters might be: "Blue Lead, proceed to 75 miles off the 290-degree radial of the XYZ TACAN. Ready to copy your lineup." The orbit point ("75 miles off the 290-degree radial of the XYZ TACAN") would be in sight of the target and readily identified by the fighters — it could be defined by electronic coordinates, map coordinates, or a visual reference.

Blue Lead: "We've got wall-to-wall MK-82s and 200 rounds of 20 mike-mike. Fifteen minutes play time." ("Wall-to-wall MK-82s" meant a maximum load of 500-pounders, typically 24 bombs for an F-4. "20 mike-mike" was radio terminology for 20mm ammunition for the M-61 cannon. "Play time" indicated how much time the fighters could remain in the target area before fuel would dictate their departure.)

FAC, as the fighters arrive at the orbit point: "We have troops-in-contact along the east-west portion of a river, three klicks south of the saddleback mountain at your one o'clock. Friendlies are south of the riverbed. FAC is at your ten o'clock, four klicks, low. Threats include small arms up to 23mm. Plan your run-ins from west to east just north of the riverbed." ("Klick" was the radio term for kilometer.)

The flight lead had to acknowledge the position of the friendlies and the FAC, the known ground-to-air threats, and the attack restrictions.

The FAC's next call was to direct how he wanted the fighters to use their bombs. As an example, he might direct, "Blue Lead, set them up in pairs, instantaneous." (Translation: Drop the bombs two at a time with instantaneous fusing — typical if being used against troops that were not dug-in.) Once the general target area was agreed to and the fighters reported ready to attack, the FAC would roll-in to put a white phosphorous (Willie Pete) smoke marking rocket specifically where he wanted the fighters to drop their first bombs.

After pulling out of his marking run, the FAC had to check exactly where the Willie Pete had detonated and direct the fighters accordingly. "Blue Lead, hit my smoke." (If the smoke was exactly where the FAC had intended.) Or "Blue Lead, from my smoke — 50 meters west." Sometimes, this became difficult or even impractical when high winds caused the smoke to drift or disperse too quickly. Or when other activity in the area generated conflicting smoke or clouds of dust. Also, clouds could make it difficult for the fighters to spot the smoke prior to rolling in on the target. Frequently, FACs had to rely more on ground references or on some combination of ground references and marking smoke.

If friendly troops were in the area, the FAC had to coordinate thoroughly with them. He would call the ground commander to explain the planned attack parameters (direction and distance from friendlies). He also had to arrange for proper confirmation that the troops were sufficiently under cover ("heads down") before clearing the fighters to roll-in on their attack. When feasible, the ground commander would provide the fighters a visual signal (smoke, flares, signal mirrors, etc.) to ensure the pilots knew the exact location of the friendlies.

The fighters, having taken necessary spacing, would report the target, friendlies, FAC, and the FAC's smoke in sight and initiate their attack runs. If the FAC was certain each flight member had the target and smoke clearly in sight, he might call, "Blue Flight, cleared in hot." In which case, no further clearance was required. If there was any doubt as to the location of the target or if friendly troops were involved, the FAC usually withheld such clearance until each flight member was on his final dive and obviously aimed at the designated target, clearing each one individually. As the bombs of one fighter detonated, the FAC would issue appropriate corrections to the next flight member, such as, "Blue Three, from Two's smoke, six o'clock, 30 meters. Cleared hot."

When the target was destroyed or the fighters had dropped all of their bombs, the FAC might direct strafing runs against any light vehicles, storage facilities, or troops in the open. When the fighters had used all of their ordnance, each flight member or the leader (reporting for the flight as a whole) would report, "Off target, winchester." ("Winches-ter" was a code word meaning no more ordnance was available for the attack.) If the fighters ran low on fuel before using up their ordnance, they would report "bingo," meaning they had just enough fuel to return to base. The flight would then join-up, accomplish their post-attack checklists, and inspect each other for possible damage.

While the fighters were departing, the FAC evaluated the target to determine the extent of damage and how accurate the attack had been. If at all possible, the FAC called the fighters with his Battle Damage Assessment (BDA) before they left the area. A typical BDA might be: "Blue Flight, I'll give you a 50 over 90, with six vehicles destroyed and 20 KBA." ("50 over 90" was the bomb score — 50 percent of the target destroyed with 90 percent of the fighters' bombs on the target. "KBA" was shorthand for "killed by air.") If the fighters were in a hurry, the FAC might relay the BDA to them via radio through the TACS or by phone after returning to his base.

All of the above, from initial fighter check-in through several attack runs with various weapons (possibly even switching targets if the first one was obliterated) through the join-up and BDA report, might take place in as little as 10-15 minutes. During that time the slow-moving FAC would have to keep the target, all of the fighters, and the friendlies in sight, as well as keep track of the results of each fighter's attack run and watch for any enemy ground-to-air fire. Oh, yes, and he had to fly his airplane and possibly switch back-and-forth between radios to talk to the ground troops and the fighters.

Tactics

A FAC had to know his area of operation as intimately as possible. In Vietnam and Korea, that was usually accomplished by overflying the area daily until the FAC was able to recognize when "something was not quite right" or when something had changed. That "something" might not be obvious to somebody new to the area or to the crew of a fast-moving fighter overflying the area or even to the photo interpretation specialist reviewing the film from a photo reconnaissance mission. This need to really know the area meant that a new FAC required perhaps a month or more before he had gained sufficient familiarity to be truly effective.

Another problem with which FACs had to contend was the likelihood of enemy deception. Communist-led armies proved to be particularly prone to exposing their own civilian supporters to airstrikes whenever such actions suited their political or military objectives. In Vietnam, it was not uncommon for the Viet Cong to fire on United States or South Vietnamese aircraft or troops from within villages, hoping to draw return fire and gen-

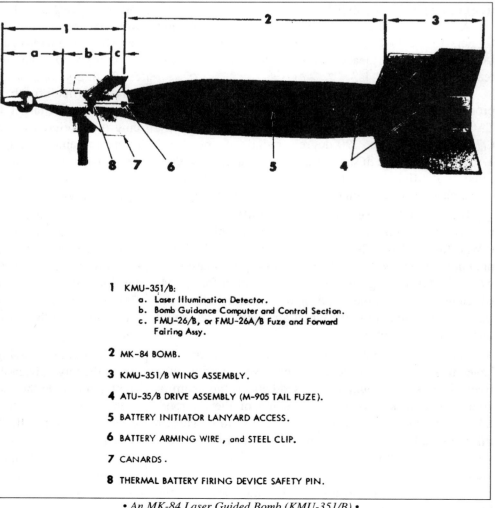

1 KMU-351/B:
   a. Laser Illumination Detector.
   b. Bomb Guidance Computer and Control Section.
   c. FMU-26/B, or FMU-26A/B Fuze and Forward Fairing Assy.

2 MK-84 BOMB.

3 KMU-351/B WING ASSEMBLY.

4 ATU-35/B DRIVE ASSEMBLY (M-905 TAIL FUZE).

5 BATTERY INITIATOR LANYARD ACCESS.

6 BATTERY ARMING WIRE, and STEEL CLIP.

7 CANARDS.

8 THERMAL BATTERY FIRING DEVICE SAFETY PIN.

• An MK-84 Laser Guided Bomb (KMU-351/B) •
(U.S. Air Force Handbook)

erate civilian casualties to be used for propaganda purposes. In addition, they frequently put their important military resources in population centers and used refugees or potential defectors to shield military operations.

Because of these tactics, FAC vigilance and familiarity with his area of operation became even more important. One recorded incident involved the Viet Cong forcing about 400 civilians into a contested area in sampans on a river and then blocking the river to keep them in place. The Viet Cong provided erroneous information through four different United States and South Vietnamese intelligence agencies that enemy forces were in the area. When a FAC responded to determine the validity of the report, the Viet Cong opened fire on him from within the group of sampans and then held the civilians at gunpoint until an air strike was launched and many of the civilians were killed or injured. The incident was falsely reported around the world as a flagrant violation by U.S. forces. The real story did not surface until much later.

The challenge for the FACs in those wars was twofold: first, fly low enough and often enough to be able to detect the signs of something amiss; and second, stay high enough and far enough away to avoid unnecessarily drawing enemy fire. In the predominantly unarmed — or very lightly armed — slow, and vulnerable aircraft used for FAC duties, drawing enemy fire could quickly prove catastrophic, even in areas with only small arms. O-1s and O-2s were both relatively easy targets for enemy troops with automatic weapons. It was not possible for the slow-moving FAC aircraft to get out of the way or gain altitude fast enough once somebody on the ground opened fire. Luckily, the aircraft were simple machines with few catastrophically vulnerable spots and were small targets. However, their best defense was always to stay above the range of small arms fire — usually at or above 3,500 feet AGL. When crew-served weapons (23mm or 37mm anti-aircraft guns) began showing up with more frequency in the areas covered by O-1 and O-2 FACs during the Vietnam War, altitude ceased to be a reliable defense.

FACs, at least the ones operating in Cessnas, were unable to operate deep inside North Vietnam due both to distance and the intense anti-aircraft threats, although some did operate "up North" just above the Demilitarized Zone and many flew missions in the southern portions of Laos along the Ho Chi Minh Trail against well-armed North Vietnamese Army regulars. For missions deeper into North Vietnam, "Fast FACs" were used — fighters like the two-seat version of the F-100 that could sprint into a target area, find the targets, mark them, and get the hell out — fast. ✠

L-19/O-1 Bird Dog

-chapter 7-

In August 1949, the U.S. Army and the U.S. Air Force announced a competitive procurement — the Army Observation Aircraft — for an all-metal, two-place, high-wing observation aircraft to replace the fabric-covered Piper L-4s and Stinson L-5s that had served admirably during and after World War II. The new aircraft needed to be ski- and float-capable and was to serve as a platform for ground observation, aerial search and rescue, visual and photographic reconnaissance, Forward Air Control (FAC) of fighter-bomber aircraft, cargo and personnel transport, control and adjustment of artillery fire, and pilot training. In addition, the aircraft had to be rugged, able to operate from unimproved forward airstrips, and be easy to maintain in the field. The official specification was released on 15 November 1949 and included a requirement for landing over a 50-foot obstacle in a total distance of less than 600 feet. A fly-off between competing contractors (Piper, Taylorcraft, Temco, and Cessna) was scheduled for March of 1950.

With several civilian projects underway and an engineering staff of only 18, Cessna's engineers decided to capitalize on existing designs to meet the planned fly-off date. They chose the basic wing design of the C-170 and the tail assembly of the C-195 (which the military had already purchased as the LC-126), and devoted their design efforts to creating the fuselage, landing gear, and powerplant installation. The landing-distance-over-an-obstacle requirement necessitated high-drag, high-lift flaps (unlike the plain or split flaps on other Cessnas of the day), manually operated to save weight. The solution was to modify the C-170's 45° slotted flap design to allow for 60° of extension, using an external hinge bracket with a pivot point below the wing (a configuration later seen on civilian Cessnas).

The six-cylinder 190-horsepower Continental O-470-11, with a 213-horsepower takeoff power rating, was selected, after modification by Continental to meet the Army design and performance requirements. A 90-inch McCauley two-blade, fixed-pitch, metal propeller with a very low pitch was installed. This allowed a high engine speed for short takeoffs and landings but reduced available power at cruise to avoid overspeeding the rated rpm. The carburetor delivered more fuel, under pressure, than the engine required and a fuel return line had to be installed. A unique fuel valve design was created that ensured adequate flow while returning excess fuel to the currently selected tank (a design subsequently used on other Cessnas).

The fuselage design was laid out on full-scale Mylar stretched out on six drafting tables bolted together. The Cessna Experimental Department built the first fuselage from laminated aluminum templates created from the original full-scale Mylar prints. Prototype construction began on 8 September 1949. The initial Model 305 rolled out of its Wichita womb a mere 90 days later.

The 1,400-pound aircraft (200 pounds over the specification weight) sported a semi-monocoque aluminum fuselage with the bulkheads and stringers made of aluminum alloy. The semi-cantilever wings, like those of the C-170 from which they had been borrowed, had dual spars, stressed aluminum skin, and single struts. The cockpit provided tandem seating for a pilot and observer in a fishbowl of plexiglass — windows all around plus six panels in the cabin roof. Flight controls were provided for both the pilot and the observer, although the observer's control stick

• *The original Cessna Model 305 engineering prototype (N41694)* •
(Kansas Aviation Museum/Robert J. Pickett Collection)

could be removed and stowed when not needed.

The new airplane first flew on 14 December 1949. After further factory test flights to determine the best takeoff and landing procedures for meeting the short-field requirements, the prototype (registration number N41694) was ferried to Wright Field in Dayton, Ohio, by Cessna's chief test pilot, Hank Waring. The fly-off evaluation was conducted between 6 April and 14 April, and the prototype Model 305 logged just under four hours during the evaluation. When the 305 proved it could meet or exceed all performance requirements, including the rigorous 600-foot landing over a 50-foot obstacle, its slight weight problem ceased to be an issue. The Army notified Cessna on 29 May 1950 that they had won the competition and would be issued a contract for 418 aircraft, to be designated L-19A.

• The first production L-19A delivered to the U.S. Army •
(U.S. Army Aviation Museum)

The Army requested delivery of the first production aircraft by September 1950, but that was delayed until December while Cessna acquired an approved type certificate from the Civil Aeronautics Administration (CAA — forerunner of today's Federal Aviation Administration), as the Army had mandated adherence to Civil Aeronautics Regulations rather than military standards. The CAA pilots put the new aircraft through its paces between 2 August and 26 October 1950.

Korean War Expedites the Bird dog

On 25 June 1950, North Korea invaded South Korea. When the United States joined with the United Nations in a "police action" to protect the South's sovereignty, the Army announced an accelerated need for its new observation aircraft. The Army budget for new aircraft soared from $2,000,000 before war broke out to $42,376,238 after hostilities began, enabling the Army to issue an initial L-19 contract for 418 aircraft (Army s/n 50-1327 through 50-1744). Cessna accepted the challenge and quickly built two more aircraft — a second prototype and an aircraft for the static load tests. The static tests were satisfactorily conducted in October and September, while Cessna was incorporating the agreed-upon modifications into the second prototype. This production-configured prototype was delivered

• General Mark Clark and Cessna President Dwane Wallace at the "Bird Dog" naming ceremony at the Cessna plant •
(Kansas Aviation Museum/Robert J. Pickett Collection)

• *A U.S. Army L-19A on a reconnaissance mission over Korea in 1951.*
Note the camera and observer in the rear window •
(U.S. Army Aviation Museum)

weather" trials in the snow and 20°F temperatures — where the cabin heater proved inadequate and starting even a pre-heated engine proved difficult. The skis had no appreciable effect on the flight characteristics and worked well in all snow conditions. Another crew flew south to New Orleans to test the float installation on the Bird Dog. In the warm, humid climate of Louisiana, engine cooling caused some minor problems and C-195 seaplane fins had to be added to the ends of the horizontal stabilizers to offset some directional instability. Spins, stalls, and recoveries in either configuration were never a problem.

Cessna also tested the L-19 with a constant-speed prop as well as a Hartzell two-speed one, but could not justify the added weight for the minimal performance gains.

to the Army in November for their own testing.

Following initial deliveries to the Aviation School at Fort Sill, Oklahoma, in December, the Army flight instructors had to learn completely new techniques in their transition from the lower-powered, flapless Piper L-4s to the comparatively high-powered L-19s with their 60° of flaps. Once they adapted to the steep, power-off glide to a three-point landing technique Cessna had used to achieve the required performance, the technique was quickly passed on to the students going through the training program. Their students were soon proving the Bird Dog's capabilities in the burgeoning war in Korea.

Initially, the Army established a 30-day flight training course at Fort Sill to requalify Reserve pilots recalled for active service in Korea. Once the 210 recalled Reservists were trained, the course was expanded to 29 weeks to train new pilots and, by the time the war ended, an additional 1,484 pilots had completed the course.

Meanwhile, Cessna's flight testing to certify the L-19 on skis and floats continued with one crew deploying to Iowa City, Iowa, to complete the "cold

The Bird Dog entered service in the Korean War on 16 February 1951, less than two months after initial deliveries and just in time to participate in the second liberation of Seoul. In the July 1951 issue of the company's magazine, *Cessquire,* Cessna announced a contest to name the new airplane. Cessna's Military Contracts manager, Derby Frye, asked General Mark W. Clark, Chief of Army Field Forces, to select the winning name from those submitted by Cessna

• *The Cessna Bird Dog final assembly facility during the Korean War.*
The aircraft closest to the door has its wings and empennage removed •
(U.S. Army Aviation Museum)

employees. In a 17 September ceremony at the Wichita plant, General Clark announced that the L-19 would henceforth be known as the Bird Dog. The winner, Jack Swayze, a member of the Preflight Department, was given a week's vacation with pay, transport for him and his family via Cessna 195 to a place of his choosing within 600 miles of Wichita, and $200 for expenses. A second employee, in the Engineering Department, submitted the same name, so the winner was determined by the toss of a coin.

By March 1951, 30 L-19s were serving with the Army in Korea. That same month, Army Chief of Staff General Collins flew in an L-19 from the parade grounds at Fort Myers, Virginia. In fact, the March issue of Cessquire reported that the general had "landed on

• *An aerial view of the Cessna factory at the height of L-19 production during the Korean War. All parked aircraft are L-19s* •
(Kansas Aviation Museum/Robert J. Pickett Collection)

and taken off from the yard of his residence quarters." He was suitably impressed with the performance of the new Army Aviation mount.

Additional L-19 contracts were issued as the war progressed, until nine more production lots had been purchased for a total of 2,068 L-19A aircraft with the following Army serial numbers:

- 51-4534 through 51-5109.
- 51-7286 through 51-7481, including a few for Canada.
- 51-11912 through 51-12911.
- 51-16428 through 51-16462.
- 51-16864 through 51-16973.
- 53-508 through 53-532.
- 53-2873 through 53-2878 for South Korea under the Military Assistance Program (MAP).
- 53-7698 through 53-7717.
- 53-7968 through 53-8067 for the French Army.

In a December 1951 letter to Cessna President Dwane Wallace, General Clark recalled his visit for the christening of the Bird Dog and added, "I have procured from General Van Fleet some reports on the plane's performance in combat in Korea. . .The Birddog (sic) has had a fine reception, both here and in Korea, among the men who are flying it."

By October 1954, Cessna deliveries of L-19s totaled 2,504 aircraft. Five aircraft were destined for service in the South Korean air force under the Military Assistance Program, and one (L-19-ACE, s/n 51-4754) was obtained by the British Army from the Canadian Army. Another 60 L-19As were delivered between 1951 and 1953 to the U.S. Navy for use by the Marine Corps — these were des-

• *A Canadian L-19A-CE flown by the British RAF out of Seoul, South Korea in 1952* •
(U.S. Army Aviation Museum)

• U.S. Army Precision Demonstration Team in the late 1950s •
(U.S. Army Aviation Museum)

ignated OE-1. Although the Korean War resulted in the production of more Bird Dogs than originally anticipated, the onset of wartime inflation reduced Cessna's expected profit margin for the fixed price L-19 contract.

In the late 1950s, the U.S. Army Precision Demonstration Team operated a four-ship of L-19A aircraft at airshows around the country. During the same time, the Colorado Army National Guard also flew a three-ship of L-19s for airshow demonstrations.

A major Bird Dog milestone for Cessna occurred in November 1957 when the 3000th L-19 aircraft was delivered to the U.S. Army.

In 1958, the Army took delivery of the first L-19E (Cessna Model 305C) with its beefed-up airframe, revised landing gear to eliminate an earlier tendency to "tuck under" on landing rollout, and some other minor improvements. Maximum gross weight was increased to 2,400 pounds. The last of this model was delivered to the Army in 1959, marking a temporary end of Bird Dog production. Designation for these aircraft was changed to O-1E in 1962. The O-1E was also built under license in Japan by Fuji Heavy Industries. Seven production lots of L-19E aircraft were delivered between 1958 and 1959:

- 56-2467 through 56-2696.
- 56-4034 through 56-4038 for Canada.
- 56-4161 through 56-4235.
- 57-1606 through 57-1609.
- 57-5983 through 57-6028.
- 57-6268 through 57-6277.

- 59-5928 through 59-5929.

But the Bird Dog production lines were not silent for long. Contracts for additional production runs of 70 L-19E (O-1E) aircraft in 1961 and 18 more in 1963 were issued (s/n 61-2955 through 61-3024 and 63-12741 through 63-12758), to bring total Bird Dog production for all models to 3,431, including nine deliveries for South Vietnam under the Military Assistance Program in 1963 (s/n 62-12280 through 62-12288). All 97 of these later Bird Dogs were delivered to the U.S. Army and USAF between June 1962 and May 1963.

During the early years of United States combat involvement in Vietnam, the Army recognized the need for an aircraft to use in the forward air control role to replace their OH-13 and OH-23 light helicopters, which were inefficient and unsuited to the hot and humid conditions common in Southeast Asia. The Army elected to acquire O-1F and O-1G aircraft on loan from the USAF. The O-1Fs were TO-1D aircraft modified to an O-1D configuration by deleting the dual controls and rear-seat instrument panel, and later modified again to O-1F status by adding underwing hardpoints and a VHF/FM radio to allow communication with Army ground commanders. Most of these O-1F aircraft were later returned to the USAF when the Army acquired the more capable OH-6 helicopters, although some continued in Army service until the United States withdrawal from Southeast Asia in 1973. Cessna's O-1 modification contracts continued from 1964 through 1968.

The USAF also acquired numerous O-1A aircraft and completed the same modifications described for the O-1F. These modified O-1A aircraft were designated O-1G.

The Inevitable Modifications

During its Korean War service, the little Bird Dog was called upon to carry most everything the Army could find. Rocket pods and bomb racks were mounted on its external wing hardpoints, as well as barrels of wire for laying telephone lines to forward areas and droppable oversized canvas bags to get supplies to those same areas. A camera mount was developed for installation in the observer's rear window. Cessna tested and certified the aircraft with whatever items the Army found to stick in or hang on the new "observation" aircraft.

Some weapons were deployed via more ad hoc methods. A 50-caliber M-60 machine gun was field-mounted under the wing of an L-19 during the Korean War, a bulky arrangement that must have done wonders for the plane's directional stability. An Air Force O-1 was modified during the Vietnam War with an M-60 protruding out of the left rear cockpit window, sort of an extremely small minigunship configuration. Rumor has it that at least one inventive L-19 aviator took a bazooka into battle, firing it out the window at the Communist troops below. Pilots, of course, carried smaller weapons routinely and, when the mood struck, fired handguns and machine guns and dropped grenades and napalm canisters out of the Bird Dog's windows.

During the Vietnam War, the U.S. Army came up with an interesting machine gun installation of its own. Alan R. O'Hollaran, an O-1 pilot assigned to the 184th Reconnaissance Airplane Company (callsign "Non-Stop") based at Phu-Loi, recalled that, after just getting pretty comfortable with the usual reconnaissance and artillery adjustment missions, he was "introduced to a rocket/machine gun configuration. The left wing carried the normal two rocket pods. The right had an M-60 machine gun hung across the rocket rails pointing toward the wing tip with a strange looking feed mechanism apparatus going through the rear window into the rear seat

• U.S. Army Precision Demonstration Team executes a break-away maneuver in the late 1950s •
(U.S. Army Aviation Museum)

where the ammunition was stored. The gun was fired by simply selecting the right inboard rocket position and pulling the trigger on the stick. I flew the aircraft that afternoon and shot up a box of M-60 ammunition. To hit anything the pilot had to maintain a continuous crab with the wing tip on the target, adjusting as necessary. I flew a few missions in this configuration and undoubtedly did little damage with the M-60."

AG Bird Dog • In spring, Korea was plagued with hordes of biting flies that made life miserable for the forward-based Army troops according to Dario Politella in his book "Operation Grasshopper." In April 1952 near Chipori, a 2nd Division aviator, Captain William Chaires, and a mechanic, PFC Lloyd Cook, rigged Chaires' L-19 with a crude spray rig — no more than a 20-gallon drum filled with the usual DDT-kerosene mixture and tubes running from a petcock on the drum to the two exhaust stacks, which were lengthened to prevent the bug spray from fouling the underside of the fuselage. The hot exhaust atomized the mixture into a suitable fog that drifted down over the area to kill the flies. His low-level spraying attracted quite a bit of attention from the troops on the ground, who at first thought his aircraft was on fire.

Not Quite Universal • In 1957, the Army tested the Universal Landing Gear (ULG) manufactured by the All American Engineering Company — a set of skis that mounted on the Bird Dog's main landing gear allowing the wheels to protrude slightly. In 111 hours of flight tests on two L-19s between 23 March 1956 and 11 January 1957, the ULG was tried out on snow, sod, water, sand, mud, plowed fields, and standard runways for a total of 450 landings. Flight characteristics were virtually unchanged from the normal Bird Dog, and maintenance and installation and removal posed no problems. However, only on sand was the ULG considered acceptable. On snow, skis were better. On mud, performance was unacceptable. The ULG performed well on water landings but required a special beaching area unnecessary with normal floats. The previously tested tandem main landing gear was better suited to use on freshly plowed fields. The Army's final report noted other problems such as "adjusta-

• The Colorado National Guard Bird Dog Demonstration team in the late 1950s •
(Kansas Aviation Museum/Robert J. Pickett Collection)

• *A U.S. Army L-19E from the first production lot of E-Models* •
(Cessna Aircraft)

bility of the ski assembly, lack of interchangability with other L-19 Airplanes, plowing effect of the skibow in soft ground and snow, accumulation of mud on top of the ski, excessive tailwheel drag, and inadequate handbook of instructions." They recommended continued use of the Whittaker Tandem Landing Gear for plowed field and mud operations and the Federal snow ski for snow landings.

Amphib Bird Dog • Also in 1957, the Army tested an L-19A with Edo Amphibious Floats in a variety of weather conditions operating from fresh and salt water and from paved, sod, and dirt airstrips. Twenty pilots completed a total of 50 hours of seaplane and 30 hours of landplane flying time with the aircraft. The final analysis concluded that "takeoff, landing, and ground-handling performance of the amphibious L-19 were comparable to the standard L-19 on land and the seaplane L-19 on water." Although the test team was pleased with the handling qualities of the floats, they did have some reservations that resulted in an unsatisfactory overall rating for the stock assembly in five areas:

• Gross Weight — L-19A allowable gross weight would have to be increased to 2,600 pounds with

these floats.
• Hydraulics — The "land wheels" required considerable hand pumping to extend and retract them.
• Wheels — Wheels and tires were too small for either adequate braking or ground flotation.
• Floats — Removal of compartment caps required a tool, and there were insufficient tiedown rings.
• Auxiliary Equipment — Crews needed a kit containing a bilge pump, some nylon line, an anchor, and a paddle.

The weight penalty reduced the maximum operating load factor, making the aircraft unsuitable "for performing tactical evasive maneuvers." The final test report recommended the floats "be considered suitable and adequate for utility category flight operation when the unsatisfactory conditions...are corrected and modified...provided the maximum allowable gross weight for amphibious operation of the L-19 is increased to 2600 pounds without major modifications."

Swivel Those Legs • In the mid-1960s, the USAF took delivery of several O-1s at Eglin AFB, Florida, that had been modified by Cessna with the Geisse crosswind

• USAF O-1F "Ronnie's Racer" in its revetment in South Vietnam with empty rocket tubes. The white square under "U.S. Air Force" is where the current armament load is written •
(Kansas Aviation Museum/Robert J. Pickett Collection)

to take a beating and still bring its pilots home safely occurred during the flight tests for its CAA certification. To achieve the required takeoff distance over that nasty 50-foot obstacle, Cessna had determined that an airspeed of just 5 mph over the best angle-of-climb speed had to be maintained. This resulted in a very steep climb angle, and CAA regulations required proof that the aircraft could safely recover from an engine failure during that climb immediately after takeoff. In his book "Cessna, Wings for the World," William Thompson relates that on one takeoff, the CAA inspector-pilot pulled the throttle back right after liftoff with Cessna test pilot Hank Waring at the controls. Waring's reactions were only a split-second late, but precious airspeed was lost before getting the nose down to a proper glide attitude. As a result, there was just not enough airspeed to complete the flare for landing. The resulting hard touchdown splayed the spring-steel landing gear such that the propeller and fuselage hit the concrete. The aircraft bounced as power was reapplied — airborne once more. Although the gear sprung back into normal position, the

landing gear. While taxiing, the main wheels castered freely, but while in flight, a coil spring centered the wheels. The original system, designed by Cessna engineer John Geisse, did reduce the frequency of ground loops, but only by increasing drag due to the bulkier wheel assemblies. Cessna proceeded to develop a similar system mounted almost completely inside the main gear axles, thus eliminating the drag problem. This internal system was tested at Eglin. Despite making the Bird Dog more docile when landing in a crosswind, the system was never widely employed on either USAF or Army aircraft.

Five Wheels • The Army also experimented with a tandem main landing gear configuration, with the hope that the extra set of tires would make operating from sandy, muddy, and snow-covered airstrips easier. One version was tested in 1954 at Fort Rucker, Alabama. The Army's Arctic Test Branch in Alaska tested another converted L-19 for winter operations in the mid-1950s. The Army did not adopt the idea.

Rugged Bird Dog

One of the first demonstrations of the ability of the L-19

• A M-60 machine gun mounted on the underwing hardpoints of an Army L-19A during the Korean War •
(U.S. Army Aviation Museum)

propeller tips had been shortened (luckily, losing equal pieces from each tip). The gear was slightly damaged but, following a propeller replacement, flight testing resumed the same day.

Army Bird Dogs in Korea

Bird Dogs participated in their first combat engagements during the second liberation of Seoul on 18 March 1951. Army aviators were quick to appreciate the added safety, improved performance, and enhanced comfort of the new airplane after the old, fabric-covered, heater-less L-4s, L-5s, and L-17s with which they had begun the war. One of the

• A USAF FAC inspects the side-firing M-60 machine gun installation on his O-1 •
(U.S. Army Aviation Museum)

new features on the L-19s that proved repeatedly to be a lifesaver was the shoulder harness that helped prevent the pilot and observer from being thrown around during the inevitable crashes resulting from combat flying. In the first 18 months of Korean combat, approximately 90 percent of all artillery fire had been directed from these "L-Birds" — most from the new L-19.

Night Flying • Night operation procedures and techniques were developed for Bird Dog operations during the first months of the aircraft's combat experience. Airstrips were typically illuminated by devices such as rows of cans filled with gasoline-soaked sand, set afire when needed. Another method was to use a standard searchlight pointed straight up for a homing beacon or aimed parallel with, and offset to one side of, the runway for landing reference. With the beam vertical, a spiraling descent could be safely made around the beam until at pattern altitude when the beam was lowered parallel with the ground.

In an after-action report following one of the first Bird Dog night combat sorties, Major Robert Hoffman reported, "Position lights were left on during the mission except when actually observing artillery firing and locating the target area. It was found that the white lights on the top and bottom of the fuselage are quite blinding. The bulbs of these two lights should be removed before a night mission is attempted." Major Hoffman went on to recommend that these night missions be planned only when conditions were ideal — moonlit nights, operating searchlights, good planning and communications, and a flight crew already familiar with the terrain and target area.

Harassment • Late in 1951, the first truce talks were held and rumors circulated that a cease-fire had been agreed-to by all parties. This proved premature and led to Allied ground troops being reluctant to fire on the Communists unless under direct attack. However, during this period of false truce, one L-19 pilot, Captain Ashby Snow, and his observer, Lieutenant Bill Dobbs, sprayed the harassing (and, no doubt, surprised) Communist forces from above with bullets from a carbine.

VIP Transport • During the winter of 1951-52, General James A. Van Fleet, Commanding Officer of the Eighth Army in Korea, used a fleet of L-19s for his personal transportation and that of visiting dignitaries over the width and breadth of the combat zone. Army s/n 50-1418 was his

• Flight tests of the airdrop package system on the L-19A in 1951 •
(U.S. Army Aviation Museum)

• Universal Landing Gear undergoing on-water tests on Lake Tholocco at Fort Rucker, Alabama in 1956 •
(U.S. Army Aviation Museum)

from Cardinal Spellman to General Matthew Ridgway, commander-in-chief of United Nations forces in their Bird Dogs.

But the unit's most distinguished passenger arrived in early 1953 when newly-elected President Dwight Eisenhower made good on his campaign promise to personally visit the war zone. While Army aviators flew the President and several staff and cabinet members around the front lines in a fleet of L-19s for morale-boosting visits with the troops, Air Force F-51 fighters circled overhead to preclude any enemy aircraft from getting close. For securi-

personal mount, usually flown by Captain Bruce Ihlenfeldt, who was assigned the duty after completing six months of combat duty. Dario Politella claims that it was during that winter that the legend of "Van Fleet weather" was born — a legend that sprang up among the Army avi-

ators and weathermen based on the observation that the general seemed to attract bad weather the way some combat pilots seemed to attract enemy fire. Van Fleet's insistence on meeting his commitments despite the weather resulted in Captain Ihlenfeldt nursing his Bird Dog through some of the worst weather in the Korean theater of operations — including weather that grounded the rest of the Army aviation fleet. During that same winter, Captain Ihlenfeldt and the other members of the Eighth Army Aviation Detachment found themselves shepherding VIPs

ty reasons, even the pilots were not informed of their route and itinerary until moments before takeoff. "Ike" was no stranger to Army Aviation, having briefly flown Piper L-4s in the Philippines in the early days of World War II and having used them regularly for inspection tours of the

• Edo amphibious float tests on Lake Tholocco, Fort Rucker, Alabama in 1957 •
(U.S. Army Aviation Museum)

• Getting ready to mount floats on a waiting L-19 in Fort Rucker, Alabama •
(U.S. Army Aviation Museum)

European front later in the war. He was, in fact, a champion of Army Aviation and appreciated the difficult job performed by the little observation aircraft. Throughout the President's brief tour of Korea, his assigned pilot was Lieutenant Colonel J. Elmore Swenson.

During the spring of 1951, General Matthew Ridgway, commander-in-chief of UN forces, was reported to have averaged two hours per day airborne in an L-19 overflying the front lines. On 8 May 1952, General Mark W. Clark replaced General Ridgway. His first inspection tour of his new command was made in an L-19 flown by Lieutenant Melrose Clark, a veteran of Piper L-4 dut during World War II who, despite his name, was no relation to the general.

Sink a Tank • And then there was the Korean tank sunk by a Bird Dog pilot. In late December of 1951, Lieutenant James Reed, while on a observation flight, spotted the tank driving across a frozen river and directed artillery fire against it. The artillery rounds shattered the ice and the tank sunk.

Cost-Effective • In the midst of efforts to hold down the costs of fighting the war, the Army elected to remind its aviators of the costs to the American taxpayers of buying and operating their equipment. As a result, every aircraft was labeled with its initial purchase price and its hourly operating cost. Army L-19s had stencils applied on the right side just aft of the cockpit door:

"Cost — $13,000."
"Cost per hour — $15."
The information seemed to have little effect on preventing boondoggle trips by the Army brass, so one crew chief added a comment line below the cost information: "Is this trip really necessary?"

Two KIA • L-19s were used for many missions over than artillery spotting and reconnaissance. They were frequently used to deliver supplies to forward-based ground troops by dropping the

• An L-19A with tandem main landing gear on the ramp at Chanute AFB, Illinois •
(U.S. Army Aviation Museum)

• U.S. Army's Arctic Test Branch experimental tandem-gear L-19A •
(U.S. Army Aviation Museum)

supplies from the air. Sometimes, the packages were wrapped and secured to the underwing weapons stations and jettisoned overhead. Other times, supplies were merely pushed out of the aircraft's open door. In one instance, an L-19 aviator accidentally threw a hefty box of C-rations overboard while still over enemy lines. Two North Korean soldiers were "killed in action" (KIA) when the box landed on them.

Close Encounter • Dario Politella documented the story of one Army aviator and his observer who had an all-too-close encounter with an unknown artillery shell in their L-19. Lieutenant William Bogert and Lieutenant Roy Bastine, flying along at 8,500 feet over enemy territory, were rocked violently by what they thought was flak. Bogert's grip on the controls was broken and he lost control of the aircraft for several seconds. On regaining control, he found the Bird Dog still flyable and went on to finish his mission. After landing an hour later, he and Bastine discovered a half-inch furrow creasing the right wing strut and dents along the right side of the fuselage. Somehow, the detonator never touched the airplane, or the outcome would have been less sanguine. There was no way to determine if the near-miss shell had been fired by the good guys or the bad guys.

Commie L-19 • One Army L-19, s/n 51-4794, ended up in North Korean hands where its pilot, a South Korean Army officer undergoing U.S. Army flight training at Kwangju, was briefly assigned as the official pilot for North Korean leader Nam II. On the morning of 3 December 1952, Lieutenant Kug Yong Am defected during a solo training flight — landing at Pyongyang. Kug, it was later determined, had a mother living in North Korea and had been recruited by a Communist agent working in the South. Three weeks later, before having a chance to fly Nam II in the L-19 or any other aircraft, Kug was reportedly assassinated.

Taking Prisoners • In February 1953, the Army Seventh Division commander, General Smith, let it be known that he wanted to capture some enemy troops for interrogation — something the Division had not done in several weeks. According to Dario Politella, an L-19 pilot came up with a plan to simulate being hit by ground fire, drop a dummy near enemy lines, and allow his airplane to "crash" just beyond a hill within friendly territory. When the enemy rushed out to capture the "downed flier," American troops, having sneaked into an ambush position, would likewise rush out and capture the North Koreans. The plot was made even more elaborate with smoke grenades strapped to the L-19's landing gear and a set of smoke pots (filled with used engine oil) waiting to create suitable smoke from the Bird Dog's "crash." The ambush patrol got into position before daybreak and waited in frigid temperatures all day until dusk when the trap was to be sprung.

The winds had kicked-up to 20 knots but the Army pilot launched his mission anyway, not wanting to disappoint the well-chilled patrol. When the L-19 drew the expected enemy ground fire, the pilot went into his rehearsed routine, popping the smoke grenades and bobbing and weaving as though hit. He tossed the dummy overboard and dove behind the preplanned hill, where ground troops ignited the engine oil. The Communist troops rushed out to retrieve the fallen "pilot," which had landed much farther from the ambush patrol than planned due to the wind. To slow down the advancing enemy and allow the ambushers to get into position, an artillery barrage was called-in — a barrage more accurate than usual that killed most of the enemy and scattered the survivors. No prisoners were taken.

Flame Throwers and Telephone Wire • In October of 1951, Army Captain George B. Daniels dropped two flame throwers by parachute from an L-19 to Army troops pinned down during an attack on enemy forces at Heartbreak Ridge. The flame throwers were immediately put to use. For his part, Captain Daniels was awarded the Distinguished Flying Cross. The citation read:

"Captain Daniels was advised that an infantry unit, engaged in an attack against a fanatically-defended, enemy-held hill (near Mundungnil) was desperately in need of flame throwers to dislodge the hostile troops from their elaborate fortifications.

Realizing the risk involved, he immediately loaded one of the necessary weapons aboard a light, unarmed aircraft (L-19) and flew to the scene of the fighting. Flying low over the battle area, well within range of enemy fire, Capt. Daniels made repeated passes over the terrain to find a suitable drop zone. After dropping the flame thrower, he returned to his base, loaded another weapon, flew over the same hazardous route and dropped it by parachute to the hard-pressed infantrymen.

The heroic achievement of Capt. Daniels enabled the friendly troops to dislodge the foe and to capture a hill of vital strategic importance with a minimum of casualties."

This award was followed on 27 October by a Silver Star, when Captain Daniels strung telephone wire from his L-19 to Army infantry under enemy attack. On this mission, Captain Daniels' observer was Signal Corps Captain Robert H. Bennet. To dispense the wire, the 2nd

• A flight of L-19A aircraft peel-off for landing over Korea in 1952 •
(U.S. Army Aviation Museum)

Division Signal Company put together a Rube Goldberg arrangement consisting of four canvas wire dispensers joined with salvaged metal culvert and hung from the wing hardpoints.

Blood • On 10 October 1951, another Bird Dog pilot, Captain Robert R. Harding, delivered plasma at night to an unlighted forward airstrip embedded in the midst of 1,500-foot hills. To prevent the six bottles of lifegiving fluid from getting shook up, crew chief Corporal Laurence F. Anderson rode along and held them. Although recommended for the Silver Star, Captain Harding was awarded instead a Bronze Oak Leaf Cluster to his previous Air Medal, while Corporal Anderson was awarded the Air Medal. The recommendation noted:

"During the day of 10 October 1951, the patient load was extremely heavy. During the evening, the number of seriously wounded rose alarmingly and so depleted the supply of blood. The material could not be resupplied by vehicle because the rough roads would cause it to hemolyze. In a desperate attempt to get this critical material to the clearing platoon, the airstrip was called and asked that the trip be made. Captain Harding volunteered to go. Captain Harding risked his life by attempting an extremely hazardous mission."

On Fire • On 28 December 1951, Lieutenant Melvin Goulding and his observer, Lieutenant Chester Huff, were flying an observation mission in northeast Korea when their Bird Dog was hit by ground fire and began to burn. Goulding was attempting to employ evasive techniques some three miles behind enemy lines. The plane shook as a 20mm shell ripped through the left wing and fuel tank, which promptly burst into flames. Goulding tried to keep the flames away from the cockpit by holding a right slip while heading for the friendly forces. Passing 6,000 feet, Goulding ordered a bailout and pulled the emergency release for the door. As Huff bailed out, his clothes were burning. Goulding held the stricken plane level until Huff was clear of the aircraft and his parachute had opened. Goulding then pushed his seat as far back as it would go, kicked the control stick forward and left, and dove out the door. Luckily, both men landed near the Korean Marine Division and were picked up and received emergency field treatment for their extensive burns. Both men were awarded the Silver Star for bravery.

Short Wing • Dario Plitella reported that at least one L-19 successfully landed with 12 feet of its right wing

• Brigadier General Wyman (left) and General Ridgeway (right) greet General Van Fleet (center) on his arrival by L-19 at a IX Corps conference at Tempest Airstrip, Korea, 1952 •
(U.S. Army Aviation Museum)

missing. On 24 February 1951, Captain Charles Posz and his observer, Lieutenant Ralph Clark were circling at 6,000 feet checking on an enemy position near Pyongyang, six miles behind the lines, when their Bird Dog was struck by anti-aircraft artillery fire. Clark managed to regain control by applying full left rudder and aileron and getting his speed up to 125 mph. At anything below 110 mph the plane stalled.

As Posz struggled back to friendly lines, he found he needed the extra muscle of his observer to hold the controls in that extreme position. Another L-19, flown by Lieutenant John Self, picked up the distress call, rejoined with Posz and Clark, and escorted them back for an attempt at a landing. Neither crewmember was willing to bailout, despite the hazards facing them, since it was not clear that control could be maintained once either of them released his pressure on the controls. After three attempts to land on a short forward Army airstrip, they realized that more runway was needed and elected to head for a nearby Air Force base at Chunchon with a longer runway. Posz brought the plane down at full throttle and 135 mph, taking almost all of the 4,600-foot runway to stop the Bird Dog — somewhat more than its design requirement of less than 600 feet. Both Posz and Clark were awarded the Distinguished Flying Cross.

Six days later, Captain Posz was awarded an Oak Leaf Cluster for his Distinguished Flying Cross for heroism in diverting enemy attention with repeated low-level passes, while friendly forces retrieved the trapped crews of two disabled tanks, without regard for his own safety in his unarmed aircraft.

Bird Dogs in Vietnam

In the early 1950s, the French Navy operated some L-19s out of Tan Son Nhut, South Vietnam. These were primarily used in a liaison and inter-base communications role.

On 1 July 1955, the South Vietnamese Air Force (VNAF) was created, and the French turned over their in-country aircraft to the VNAF. The aircraft involved consisted of two squadrons of L-19s, one squadron of C-47s, and a varied collection of other liaison and transport aircraft. The L-19s were based at Bien Hoa (1st Liaison Squadron) and Nha Trang (2nd Liaison Squadron). The 1st Liaison Squadron relocated to Da Nang in November. Later, fighter aircraft were added to the VNAF fleet.

The U.S. Military Assistance Advisory Group (MAAG) took responsibility for training VNAF personnel after the French departure. By 1961, additional USAF advisors were in-country to help train and counsel the fledgling and underequipped air force. These advisors consistently reported on the poor coordination and inadequate communications between the VNAF air and ground forces. With too few trained pilots and observers for the L-19s, forward air control was irregular at best, and FAC assignments were usually reserved for the VNAF's least capable pilots. Faced with the promise of severe reprimands for returning with a damaged aircraft or possibly jail for making an error directing an air strike, the pilots preferred to maintain high altitudes and mark targets well away from the ground troops. Despite these ineffective tactics, the Viet Cong were reluctant to risk an attack on a target if a FAC was spotted in the area. Although VNAF O-1s attempted to escort as many troop convoys as possible, their few numbers limited their success. The VNAF reconnaissance forces consisted of 2 camera-equipped C-45s and its L-19s for visual reconnaissance, although they were already transferring L-19 pilots to fighter units.

In December of 1961, U.S. forces, under the command of Brigadier General Rollen Anthis, joined with the South Vietnamese forces in conducting air mobile operations to shutdown a Viet Cong (VC) radio transmitter northeast of Saigon. Five U.S. Army helicopter companies and 16 USAF C-123s transported the ground troops. The VNAF provided the air cover with two AD-6D attack aircraft directed by a single L-19A. When the battle ended, the transmitter was silenced and there were two VC dead, one wounded, and 46 captured.

By the end of 1961, President Kennedy had authorized additional aircraft for the VNAF — three more squadrons including a third liaison squadron of L-19s. USAF Chief of Staff General Curtis LeMay established the 4400th Combat Crew Training Squadron (code named "Jungle Jim") at Eglin AFB, Florida, to train air commandos. A Jungle Jim detachment was deployed to South Vietnam to set-up the "Farm Gate" program at Bien Hoa with 151 personnel and a variety of obsolete aircraft.

Secretary of Defense Robert McNamara authorized three more U.S. squadrons to deploy to South Vietnam in March of 1962. A C-123 squadron, a squadron of USAF U-1A liaison aircraft, and an Army O-1A company were sent, with authorization to remain for no more than one year, at which time the aircraft were to be turned over to the VNAF. However, in July of 1963, another Army O-1A company was deployed to South Vietnam but its aircraft were dispersed among various Army corps advisors. In September, the USAF activated the 19th Tactical Air Support Squadron (TASS) at Bien Hoa, flying O-1s. USAF also established a FAC training detachment at Tan Son Nhut Air Base — instructors developed an extensive list of comparable English and Vietnamese words needed for voice communications in the air. By October, VNAF students were being trained in the United States at Hurlburt Field, after first attending a new eight-week English language school at the base.

In 1963, VNAF squadrons were renumbered. Three Liaison Squadrons were established, with the 110th and 114th (under the 41st Air Wing) based at Da Nang and the 112th (under the 23rd Tactical Wing) at Tan Son Nhut. All flew O-1s; the 114th also flew Cessna U-17s. The VNAF

• *Army technicians rig an airdrop package on the wing of an L-19A during the Korean War* •
(U.S. Army Aviation Museum)

Bird Dogs sported light gray on the upper wing surfaces to help the VNAF fighter-bombers spot the slow-moving FAC aircraft from above against the jungle foliage.

Later in the year, the United States began the build-up of advisors to South Vietnam in earnest. As part of that build-up (which included the "Dirty Thirty," a deployment of 30 USAF pilots to serve as copilots on VNAF C-47s, freeing VNAF pilots for strike fighter assignments), a USAF detachment was deployed to Nha Trang to establish a training center for O-1E Bird Dog pilots and maintenance personnel. As part of the Rules of Engagement, the American advisors were only allowed to participate in combat sorties if a South Vietnamese was on board. After the coup that overthrew the government of South Vietnamese President Diem in November of 1963, the air war heated up, particularly along the border with Cambodia. As a result, the United States began deploying more of its own aircraft and crews to South Vietnam as direct combatants. Between May and August of 1963, a total of 534 preplanned air strike requests from III Corps commanders went unfilled — 167 due to insufficient aircraft and 244 due to a lack of VNAF FACs. Army of the Republic of Vietnam (ARVN) commanders began calling on the readily available U.S. Army helicopter gunships for close air support.

On 19 March 1964, an O-1E from the 19th TASS, flown by a USAF pilot accompanied by a Vietnamese observer, allegedly strayed over the border where it was shot down by Cambodian Royal Khmer Aviation (RKA) T-28s. Both the pilot and observer were killed.

In 1964, the VNAF added the 116th Liaison Squadron based at Nha Trang, flying the O-1E. When an alleged incident off the coast of North Vietnam led Congress to approve the Gulf of Tonkin Resolution, American forces in Vietnam no longer had to negotiate the intricate labyrinth of rules caused by non-combatant advisors flying occasional combat missions. The United States provided more aircraft to the VNAF squadrons to increase their strength and to replace losses. Additional O-1E aircraft were provided until there were sufficient Bird Dogs to allow the VNAF to assign a FAC to each ARVN division.

It was about this time that the USAF asked the Army for 50 more O-1s for the build-up in South Vietnam. Dr. Jerry Robinson, now the Director of Aviation at Henderson State University and a Fort Rucker student pilot at the time, remembers that they "raided the Fort Rucker fleet for every old piece of junk airplane we could find (including a museum display airplane that had had

• Air drop of packages from an Army L-19A in Korea, 1952 •
(U.S. Army Aviation Museum)

the fuselage shortened by six inches) for 'hulls' to be reconditioned at the factory and sent to the Air Force for FAC use in Vietnam."

March of 1965 was a turning point for United States involvement in the war in Vietnam. Congress authorized General William Westmoreland to use U.S. aircraft any time the VNAF could not respond in a timely manner with appropriate support. The requirement for a VNAF crewmember aboard any U.S. aircraft committed to combat was also withdrawn. That same year, President Johnson authorized additional U.S. military advisors and initiated direct air strikes against North Vietnam. By the end of the year, the USAF had 500 aircraft in Southeast Asia and 21,000 personnel stationed at eight major bases throughout South Vietnam.

In 1967, the Cessna O-2 began to replace the USAF O-1 Bird Dogs in the USAF squadrons.

• A South Vietnamese L-19 •
(U.S. Army Aviation Museum)

By the time of the Tet Offensive in January 1968, Rockwell OV-10A aircraft were starting to replace both the USAF O-1s and O-2s in South Vietnam combat. In May and June of 1969, the NVA attacked Ben Het in South Vietnam. Army and USAF FACs, most of whom were flying O-1 and O-2 aircraft, flew 571 sorties and directed over 100 AC-47 and AC-119 gunship sorties and 1,828 fighter sorties to drive back the attackers. In 1970, VNAF combat sorties expanded rapidly, accounting for 37 percent of the 76,313 total flown by USAF and VNAF pilots.

In March of 1969, the United States began a covert bombing campaign in Cambodia in support of the Khmer government. This campaign continued until March of 1973 and involved O-1 FAC aircraft. The O-1 pilots requested strike aircraft support by providing target coordinates within South Vietnam. Once the fighters were airborne, the FACs gave them new coordinates for targets in Cambodia.

By 1972, the expanding VNAF possessed nine squadrons of O-1 aircraft (the 110th and 120th Liaison Squadrons at Da Nang, the 114th Liaison Squadron at Nha Trang, the 112th and 124th Liaison Squadrons at Bien Hoa, the 116th and 122nd Liaison Squadrons at Binh Thuy, the 118th Liaison Squadron at Pleiku, and the 12th School Squadron at Nha Trang). Total VNAF forces included nine tactical fighter wings, 40,000 personnel and 700 aircraft.

Right up to the end in 1975 when North Vietnam overran the South, the ubiquitous Bird Dog filled its role admirably in the modern combat arena. And it continued to prove its ability to do the job and bring its crew home safely, even after run-ins with enemy ground fire.

Aussie Bird Dog • In mid-1966, the First Australian Task Force, based at Vung Tau, was flying primarily helicopters and Cessna U-17 aircraft in its 161 Independent Reconnaissance Flight. Steve Eather reported in "Target Charlie" that the unit did, however, acquire a single O-1 on loan from the Army and flew it regularly in the FAC and "road recce" roles ("road recce" involved overflying the roads to check for enemy boobytraps and roadblocks). In September 1967, this loaned O-1, which continued to carry U.S. Army marking but with the Australian unit's kangaroo emblem on the tail, was destroyed in a landing accident in strong, gusty crosswinds. The U.S. Army quickly replaced the aircraft with another Bird Dog. This replacement aircraft was lost late in the war when 161 Flight's commanding officer, Major George Constable, was shot down near Bien Hoa while escorting a convoy of Australian Army vehicles — he was killed.

Arm Power • In March of 1970, Captains James Cronkhite and Dale Ward of the 21st Reconnaissance Airplane Company based at DaNang, while directing artillery for the 1st ARVN Division, were hit by a barrage of enemy fire. The artillery wounded Cronkhite and Ward and ripped up the bantam-weight O-1's empennage, severing the rudder cables. The Bird Dog snapped into a descending right spiral, heading for the enemy troop position below. Handicapped by a foot wound, Cronkhite was unable to wrestle the O-1 out of its precipitous descent with the rudders but, recalling a flight school tale about using arms as airfoils, he thrust his arm out the open left window. Ward did the same and the two of them generated enough drag on that side to right the aircraft and allow them to get away from the hostile area. Wounded, with no rudder control and only their left arms to maintain straight flight, they maneuvered for a landing at a nearby airstrip. During the rollout, the Bird Dog swerved into sand and flipped over. Neither pilot suffered any additional injuries.

Pop a Chute • In the early 1970s, a young USAF lieutenant O-1 pilot was flying regularly out of Da Nang, where everyone was accustomed to seeing the McDonnell Douglas F-4 Phantoms land and open their large drag chutes. This particular O-1 pilot, being a frustrated fighter pilot like most young FACs, rigged a special bag on the back of his little Bird Dog. In the bag, he carefully folded an 18-inch-square handkerchief. He loosely tied the bag shut and ran the securing string from the bag along the side of the fuselage up to the pilot's window on the left side of the aircraft. He then established a ritual of landing his O-1 about halfway down the runway, where he would open his side window, reach out, and pull the string. His very own "drag chute" would then blossom out behind him as he completed his landing rollout.

Camera Dog • Alan O'Hollaran recalled that the 182 Reconnaissance Airplane Company at Phu Loi also flew photographic reconnaissance missions using a strange configuration "with a camera pod on the left wing and two rocket pods on the right. This camera pod hanging from a Bird Dog looked like a 2,000-pound bomb minus the fins. The whole pod was large enough that two grown men could not wrap their arms around it yet it only contained four small cameras. The drag created on the left wing in flight was very noticeable and as the Bird Dog had a fixed rudder trim tab the pilot had to stand on one rudder pedal for the entire flight. This proved to be about as effective as the [sidefiring M-60 machine gun configuration] and after only three missions with camera pods, I never saw another one."

Air Force Crosses • At least five USAF Bird Dog pilots were awarded the Air Force Cross, second only to the Medal of Honor, for actions in Vietnam. In November of 1963, Captain Richard L. Whitesides was awarded the AF Cross posthumously for his actions in continuing to direct air strikes against enemy positions despite repeated anti-aircraft hits on his own aircraft. In March of 1965, Major William W. McAllister, while directing air strikes for two consecutive nights in darkness and deteriorating weather, was killed and awarded the AF Cross posthumously. In December 1965, Captain Delbert W. Fleener was wounded but continued

to fly cover until a downed pilot was successfully rescued — for his deeds he was awarded the AF Cross. An AF Cross was awarded to Captain Ramon A. Horinek in February of 1966 for directing air strikes from his O-1 and from the ground throughout a major battle. In November of 1967, Major Joseph B. Madden earned his AF Cross for continuing to direct badly needed air strikes from his damaged O-1.

Army O-1s used in Vietnam were either O-1Ds, which did not include racks for rocket pods, or O-1Gs, which did. The 220th Reconnaissance Airplane Company ("Catkillers") was based at Phu Bai in I Corps, 75 miles south of the Demilitarized Zone (DMZ). Initially, the 220th's 1st and 4th Flight Platoons were equipped with O-1Gs and the 2nd and 3rd Flight Platoons with O-1Ds. In 1970, the 220th's entire fleet was replaced with factory-rebuilt O-1G aircraft. The 220th's area of operation (AO) stretched from the A Shau Valley north up through the DMZ to the tri-borders where North and South Vietnam and Laos met.

Green Beret Dogs • After about four months in Vietnam, O'Hollaran was transferred to the 12th Special Forces, 5th Southern Operations Group at Quan-Loi. Their missions were intended to involve a cooperative arrangement with USAF FACs in O-2s flying high while the 12th pilots flew their Bird Dogs down low in support of reconnaissance missions in Laos and Cambodia. He noted, "All markings on our aircraft had been painted over with the exception of the tail number and a square white panel atop each wing which was a visual aid allowing the high bird to keep the low bird in sight." When

• *A U.S. Army O-1 on a combat mission over South Vietnam* •
(U.S. Army Aviation Museum)

O'Hollaran first arrived, their USAF counterparts were not yet on-station, so they initially worked high-low with all Army O-1s. The Special Forces maintained ARVN CH-34 heavy lift helicopters and U.S. Army Cobra gunship helicopters on standby at an airstrip just inside the Vietnam border.

On O'Hollaran's third mission, "a close friend drew the short straw that morning and was assigned as the low bird; I was his high cover. About an hour and a half into the mission he overflew an NVA base camp and drew a lot of fire. I saw the tracers coming out of the jungle and pieces flying off his aircraft. I initiated a climb to make radio contact with the rear and scramble our rotary-wing friends. After being assured they were launching I descended to join my friend who was leaving an unmistakable trail of black smoke. He managed to get 15 or 20 kilometers away from where he was hit before the engine seized and he executed a forced landing in an open field overgrown with elephant grass. Our helicopter friends were right on time. The Cobras arrived first, established a perimeter around the downed crew and started laying down fire. The ARVN was right behind them in the slower CH-34s and plucked my friend and his observer out of the elephant grass only 12 minutes after they landed. They weren't even scratched throughout this whole unforgettable experience."

According to O'Hollaran, another standard 12th mission was to launch "an aircraft at first light and again at last light to conduct radio relay and plot the positions of the several Long Range Reconnaissance Patrol Teams (LRRP Teams) the Special Forces Group had on the ground in Cambodia."

World War II Fighter • A 19-year-old Army O-1 pilot flying radio relay assisted an LRRP Team by calling in helicopters for an extraction. After a long, hot mission, he decided to climb to 9,500 feet for the return flight, where the air was much cooler. The Army O-1s at the time were not equipped with transponders and, when traffic control radar in South Vietnam picked up his aircraft cruising in

from Cambodia, they scrambled a two-ship of VNAF A-1E fighters. The A-1s intercepted the Bird Dog and slowed down, with their gear and flaps extended, to pull up alongside it. They motioned for the Bird Dog pilot to follow them, but he misinterpreted the signal as some kind of invitation to a slow-flying contest. He had never seen an A-1 before. He dropped 60° flaps and showed them how an O-1 can peg the airspeed indicator on zero. The VNAF pilots began to fire across his nose.

O'Hollaran had just launched for a high-low mission with a USAF O-2 FAC when he "heard the O-1 driver stutter on Guard that he was taking fire from World War II fighters. The FAC and I quickly realized what was going on, and the FAC summoned a pair of Air Force F-100s to the scene." Meanwhile, the Special Forces commander got wind of what was happening and sent out his UH-1 and a pair of Cobras to help the youngster. O'Hollaran said, "I've never before or since witnessed such an aerial circus. By now our Bird Dog driver was flying low-level down the Song-Ba River between the trees, and the A-1s were still firing ahead of him but now had F-100s hot in pursuit. This coupled with the three helicopters arriving at the scene made for some crowded airspace which the FAC and I chose to remain clear of."

Amazingly, everyone landed safely with nobody shot down and no mid-air collisions. O'Hollaran said, "It was beyond my comprehension how all those aircraft had taken part in this airshow without anyone taking any hits."

Cease Fire? • There is a 1969 story passed along to subsequent members of the 220th involving an O-1 pilot who became the Company authority on the AO that stretched from the DMZ north 20 miles into North Vietnam. He knew the area intimately and was usually the first to note subtle differences on the ground that might signify enemy activity or new fortifications. Let's assume his callsign was Catkiller 99. He was assigned to the 220th when President Richard Nixon ordered a hiatus on all bombing activity over North Vietnam as well as any other overflights. Now,

• A USAF O-1 being serviced for a combat mission over South Vietnam. Note the two white phosphorous rockets in the tubes under the wing • (U.S. Army Aviation Museum)

• Bill Gruber, flying one of nine Army O-1Ds assigned to 219 Reconnaissance Airplane Company, touches down on a PSP runway after completing the unit's 1000th combat flying hour in a single month in 1968 •
(U.S. Army Aviation Museum)

Catkiller 99 felt that the 20-mile deep portion of North Vietnam bordering the DMZ was his personal province and nobody, certainly not a mere President sitting in his Oval Office thousands of miles away, was going to tell him he couldn't overfly it if he wanted.

About five miles north of the DMZ, Catkiller 99 spotted an NVA truck driving up a road. He promptly loosed a pair of 2.75-inch FFARs and plopped them directly in the back of a truck. Before he had a chance to congratulate himself on such fine marksmanship, the truck exploded violently in a secondary explosion no doubt triggered by a load of ordnance. Catkiller 99's Bird Dog flew right through that explosion and fireball. A chunk of NVA truck flew up and impacted the leading edge of his left wing, leaving a sizable dent. Flying out the other side of the smoke and fire, Catkiller 99 was barely able to see through the coating of black ash and cinders that covered his aircraft and its windows.

Another Catkiller, seeing the impressive explosion from within the DMZ, radioed, "99, did you see that explosion up north?"

Catkiller 99, not wanting to find out what might happen to a mere captain who willingly violated the bombing halt, quickly replied, "Shut up."

Catkiller 99 now had to figure a way to disguise the soot and damage to his airplane before landing back at Phu Bai. He quietly diverted into an airstrip located within the historic Citadel at Hue City, acquired a bucket of water from the defunct Coca Cola plant, and washed his

dirty Bird Dog. As for the dent, he bought a freshly-killed chicken at the nearby market and thrashed the area around the dent with the dead bird.

On the five-minute flight back to Phu Bai, as he passed over a prominent reference point named the Three Sisters, he radioed, "Phu Bai Tower, Catkiller 99, Three Sisters for landing...Oops! Just took a pretty good bird strike."

The cover-up was now complete. Catkiller 99 had managed to knowingly violate the overflight restriction, violate the President's cease fire, and disguise the resulting damage to his own aircraft as a bird strike. (A pilot's inventiveness is only bounded by the amount of trouble he could be in if he doesn't think of something fast.)

Unarmed? • Captain Gerald DiGrezio was an O-1 pilot in the 220th in 1970-71 and had flown the O-1D for several months before converting to the reconditioned O-1G with its eight wing-mounted rocket tubes for 2.75-inch FFARs. DiGrezio recalls that they "were only to carry white phosphorous marking rounds but nobody ever obeyed that rule." Since the helicopter cavalry unit also based at Phu Bai routinely carried both 17-pound high explosive (HE) rockets and flechette rockets (an anti-personnel weapon that ejected a flurry of vicious barbed warheads, commonly referred to as nails) it did not take long before the O-1 pilots latched onto some of their ordnance. DeGrezio notes, "The favored mix among my platoon members was six 17-pounders outboard and two flechettes inboard. Suddenly, a pilot who had only had the unarmed D-model and marked targets by dropping smoke grenades out the window now had the ability to mark targets with gray smoke (exploding HE rounds)!"

Standard Army Bird Dog procedure called for a two-ship of FACs with one, the more experienced pilot, flying low and the newer guy, the Newbie, flying high to keep an eye on the low aircraft and learn the job and the area.

Knockout • While still flying the D-model, DiGrezio and his roommate (callsigns Catkiller 25 and Catkiller 35, respectively) were conducting a visual reconnaissance (VR) mission in the Rung Rung Valley armed only with smoke grenades that had to be hand-dropped out the win-

• An O-1 loaned to the Australian Army's 161 Independent Reconnaissance Flight by the U.S. Army •
(U.S. Army Aviation Museum)

dow. The pilots became fairly accomplished at accurately dropping the grenades from altitudes as high as 1,200 feet, frequently dropping as many as 20-25 per mission. While flying lead with Catkiller 35 trailing, DiGrezio spotted a uniformed North Vietnamese Army (NVA) soldier "choggieing" (a pace between a trot and a brisk walk) along a trail.

DiGrezio radioed, "35, got the guy choggieing down the trail up ahead?"

"Negative 25, no joy." (I do not see him.)

"He's coming up to the intersection of the trail and the small stream."

"Still don't have him, 25."

"Roger, I'll mark him with a smoke." At which, DiGrezio rolled in and dropped a 1.5-pound purple-smoke grenade (a "goofy grape") over the NVA soldier's head from about 700 feet. As he passed overhead and lost sight of the falling grenade, he radioed, "35, do you have a tally on my purple smoke?"

"Roger, I've got your goofy grape." A moment later, Catkiller 35 called out excitedly, "You hit him! You hit him! Jesus Christ, you hit him!"

DiGrezio whipped his Bird Dog around to check this out for himself. He remembers seeing the "smoke continuing to burn in the middle of the trail and two legs protruding from the undergrowth. I put the aircraft into a dive and as I passed over the legs sticking out of the bushes at approximately 100 [feet] AGL they started to disappear into the undergrowth as if someone was dragging the body into the bushes."

Old Nguyen • In September of 1970, DeGrezio (Catkiller 25) led a Newbie into the A Shau Valley from the north where they spotted another 220th two-ship following Route 922, an NVA infiltration route into the

South. Catkiller 35 (DeGrezio's roommate), leading the second two-ship announced he was going to make a run on "Old Nguyen" — an enemy gunner who had proven to be very effective and deadly with his big .30 caliber anti-aircraft artillery (AAA, or TripleA) piece. DiGrezio recalls, "If there was an enemy gunner who was particularly effective, there was a bounty on his head. Conversely, if there was an anti-aircraft gunner who was very ineffective, there were standing orders to leave him alone. The rationale was that if you killed the ineffective gunner, he may be replaced by an effective one!" Old Nguyen was very effective, but had proven equally elusive. Catkiller 35 was determined to find him and demonstrate the firepower of an angry Bird Dog. As DiGrezio and his observer listened, Catkiller 35 pushed the microphone button and narrated his attack:

"25, this is 35, yeah, Old Nguyen has been pretty bored, with nobody out to visit him lately. He has made good use of the down time by doing all the corrective maintenance to his heavy .30 cal. The weapon is in a detailed disassembly, with each part spotlessly clean and oiled. He hears my very faint engine sound in the distance, he knows I'm coming to see him, and starts to put the weapon back together.

"The weapon is back together now and he pulls the bolt back a couple of times and dry fires the weapon to check if everything is OK. He has just received a new supply of ammo that was brought down the Ho Chi Minh in either a truck or on a bicycle on a very perilous trip dodging B-52 strikes, F-4s and you name it. He opens one of the new ammo crates and takes out a shiny new band of linked .30 caliber ammo and locks and loads.

"He hears the sound of my engine getting louder and

swings the weapon in the direction that he knows I will be coming. The sound is getting louder and louder, he is aimed at a point just above the ridge line over which I will soon appear. Louder, louder, louder, he sees me, he has me in his sights and...

"Taking fire. Taking fire. Taking fire. Son of a bitch, he put a round right through my strut!"

DiGrezio, concerned for his buddy's safety in his newly modified O-1, radios, "35, are you OK?"

"Yeah, I'm OK. I took a hit, but I've got his position!"

"35," DiGrezio responded. "I'm on my way to your location. I've got six 17-pounders and 2 nails. Climb up to about 3,500 and mark his location for me."

"No, I'm not going to do it. He'll shoot your ass off."

For the next ten minutes, DiGrezio tried to coax Old Nguyen's position out of his roommate, but to no avail. Catkiller 35, determined to finish the job he had started, returned to the A Shau the following day and directed two flights of F-4 Phantoms loaded with low-drag 500-pound bombs against that AAA site. No one ever heard from Old Nguyen again.

Money on the Bar • Combat units always developed traditions to mark the progression of its members from green pilots to seasoned veterans — all, of course, leading up to that prized day when they flew their last mission and were transferred back to the States. In the 220th, according to DiGrezio, "Almost every tradition somehow involved drinking and putting money on the bar! Putting money on the bar allowed everyone in our club to drink until that money was gone." Everyone in the bar knew when there was "money on the bar" because the bartender would turn on the rotating beacon above the center of the bar, thus illuminating a cherished nude photo of Ann Margaret. There were three significant milestones necessitating that the pilot achieving them put his money on the bar:
- Cleared for solo combat missions
- First confirmed kill
- Lastly and most importantly, his going home party

Transition • When O'Hollaran was nearing the end of his Vietnam tour, the United States was in the process of pulling out of Vietnam entirely and had decided to leave most of the O-1s behind. As a result, O'Hollaran and

• *USAF O-1s in revetments in South Vietnam* •
(U.S. Army Aviation Museum)

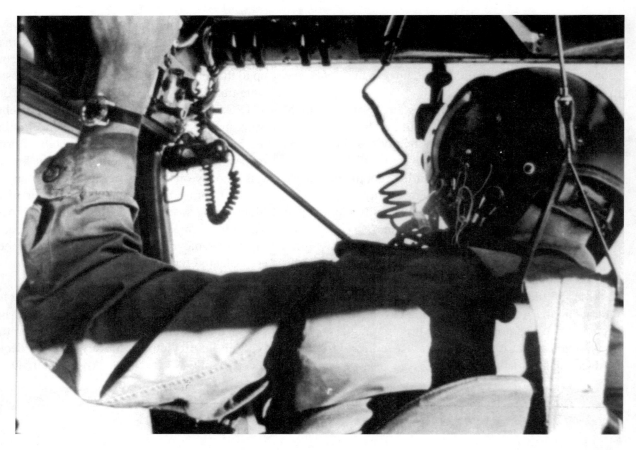

• *An Army O-1 pilot in flight over South Vietnam* •
(U.S. Army Aviation Museum)

many other experienced Army O-1 pilots were selected to move to Long Than North to help with transition training for the large number of Thai, South Vietnamese, and Cambodian pilots whose countries would soon be receiving the Bird Dogs. He recalled, "I had never seen so many Bird Dogs in one place at one time. The markings had all been changed to reflect the countries receiving these aircraft. . .I managed to survive three sets of VNAF students and finally received orders home."

Boats Sunk • In 1967, Cessquire reported that Rick Shoup, an O-1 pilot with the 199th Aviation Company stationed at Vinh Long, was awarded six Air Medals during his Vietnam service for sustaining bullet-hole damage to his aircraft during intense operations and for sinking four sampans on the rivers with rockets fired from his Bird Dog.

By the time the United States had pulled out of Southeast Asia in 1973, following signed agreements with the Communists and completion of a program called "Vietnamization," over 6,300,000 tons of bombs had been dropped on Southeast Asia, a large portion of which were the result of USAF and Army FACs directing air strikes against enemy positions. South Vietnam received the brunt of the bomb damage, with 3,900,000 tons.

Steve Canyon

In the 1960s, as the war in Southeast Asia heated up

and United States involvement escalated, the United States provided the Royal Laotian Air Force (RLAF) with some O-1E aircraft for use by airborne FAC personnel in their battle to expunge the North Vietnamese from Laos. Beginning in 1964, the USAF provided advisors on temporary duty as part of Project Cricket and Project Butterfly. Most of these advisors trained the Laotians to direct air strikes from the ground, some provided training for the Laotian pilots, and some participated openly, directing air strikes from aboard the RLAF O-1Es — air strikes involving USAF and U.S. Navy fighter-bombers as well as RLAF AT-28 aircraft (some of which were flown by Thai volunteers).

Ravens • The US government instituted Project 404 in October 1966 to track the Air Force and Army advisors who were serving on temporary duty assignments with the RLAF. This covert operation soon became an integral part of the war in Southeast Asia. Initially, the US provided the aircraft, the war material, and most of the air strike support for the RLAF. In 1960, RLAF aircraft numbered about 40, including 20 L-19s. In 1964, under the auspices of the "Water Pump" program, T-28D fighterbombers were added to the RLAF fleet with their pilots trained by the USAF's Detachment 6 at Udorn, Thailand. This operation was organized and run by Air America, the ostensibly civilian contract air service operated by the

•*The business office of an Army O-1 pilot in South Vietnam* •
(U.S. Army Aviation Museum)

Central Intelligence Agency (CIA). Soon, Air America was conducting its own air war with a conglomeration of aircraft from Helio Couriers to C-123s to O-1s.

This operation was later expanded into the RAVEN program, wherein USAF FACs flew both RLAF and USAF aircraft, primarily O-1s. In late 1964, the NVA began running supplies into South Vietnam through Laos, and the US initiated the "Barrel Roll" series of "armed reconnaissance" sorties over Laos. ("Armed reconnaissance" being a creative euphemism for searching out targets of opportunity and attacking them.) To gain maximum effectiveness, these "Barrel Roll" missions needed incountry forward air control. The CIA was tasked with providing the "civilian advisor" FACs for the "Barrell Roll" airtoground missions. The CIA recruited the first of these pilots pilots from the USAF ranks and assigned them the "Butterfly" callsign. Later, the program was redesignated the "Steve Canyon" program. Selected O-1 FACs with at least six months combat experience in South Vietnam were temporarily removed from the USAF roster and reassigned as civilians to work directly with RLAF forces ostensibly under the guidance of the American air attaché in Vientiane, Laos, but actually working for the CIA. To maintain the covert character of their operation, the unit's Bird Dogs were sold to the "Steve Canyon" volunteers for one dollar each. The callsign eventually assigned to these missions was "Raven" — taken from the Edgar Allen Poe poem.

Most Raven sorties were flown in O-1s, some in Cessna U-17s, and a few in RLAF T-28s. RLAF observers usually flew with the Ravens to coordinate with RLAF ground and air forces. All aircraft were painted overall light gray with the usual black antiglare panels and carried RLAF insignia. These Raven FACs usually flew with RLAF observers to facilitate communications with Laotian Army forces and to provide accurate target identification. Aircraft maintenance was performed by USAF mechanics. Neither the pilots nor the maintenance personnel were legitimately authorized to be serving in Laos and were thus in a "limbo" status — officially neither advisors, attachés, or combatants.

Up until 1966, four Raven FACs controlled all air strikes within Laos. For the next two years, six Ravens handled the escalating Laos air war. From then until the American withdrawal in 1973, there were never more than 22 Ravens in-country at any one time, although they were responsible for directing up to 1,000 air strikes per day against targets in the northern Laos region that was their exclusive responsibility.

The Ravens typically had to rely on archaic radios that made the necessary coordination difficult. Calling in an air strike required radio contact with the Laotian ground commanders and USAF Airborne Battle Command and Control Center (ABCCC) aircraft (C-47s or C-130s), as well as the USAF fighters flying in from bases in Thailand and South Vietnam. Effective communication was imperative, but the Ravens made do with what they had.

The Ravens were directed to bring their O-1s back to Udorn for maintenance every 100 flying hours, which they rarely did — in many cases, 100 hours would have been less than ten days of flying. Many times, to keep their Bird Dogs flying, they patched bullet holes with nothing more than 100-mph tape. Engine problems were routine due to dirt and rust contamination in their fuel. Aircraft were frequently grounded due to a shortage of spare parts.

Living conditions at the northern Raven outpost, Lima Site 85, were primitive in native huts with bunks on the porches, log fires for heat, open latrines, and showers fashioned from platform-mounted barrels and immersion heaters. Unlike their USAF counterparts in South Vietnam and Thailand, Ravens had to buy their own food and cook it themselves. Christopher Robbins has compiled the definitive history of the Ravens and their missions in his book "The Ravens" — the following few stories were taken from Robbins' book.

Don't Stop Now • When President Johnson ordered a temporary bombing halt over North Vietnam in November of 1968, there were large numbers of fighter aircraft with no targets. As a result, these sorties were turned over to the Ravens, even though the six Ravens in-country at the time were unable to manage so many aircraft. One of them directed 48 consecutive fighter sorties against a single target after expending just one WP marking rocket to mark it.

Bird Dogs on Attack • In the spring of 1969, lousy weather kept USAF fighters and most Ravens out of the air over Laos. One Raven, however, managed to fly through the mountains of northern Laos despite the low clouds. When he encountered a Royal Laotian Army company shouting for some air support, he could not convince any RLAF T-28s to risk the bad weather. He returned to base, loaded his O-1 with HE and WP rockets and flew his own air strikes, diving out of the clouds to fire the rockets at the enemy troops. He repeated the feat 15 times that day and eventually drove the NVA forces back.

When the Meo commander General Vang Pao requested air support and none was available, the Ravens loaded three O-1s with HE and flechette rockets, hand grenades, grenade launchers, and machine guns. Each aircraft had another Raven in the back seat. Through low clouds and mountains, the Bird Dog three-ship broke the NVA attack, killing 60 of them. Since formation flight and armed missions were forbidden, the air attaché in Vientiane wanted to court martial all of the participants, but the CIA and General Vang Pao convinced them that the men were heroes. Two of three front seat pilots were awarded Silver Stars, and the back seat pilots were awarded Distinguished Flying Crosses. The Raven-in-charge, who led the mission, received no award.

Raven High Flight • Another Raven achieved notoriety by regularly flying barrel rolls in his O-1 and orbiting above 12,000 feet to jump the inbound A-1 fighters when they arrived on-station for ground attack missions. Further, he liked to spin his Bird Dog from above 10,000 feet and pull out of the spin at 1,500 feet just in time to accurately mark the target. This particular Raven claimed an O-1 combat altitude record of 19,270 feet.

Ravens were involved in numerous covert rescue operations to recover aircrews downed during the "Barrel Roll" and "Steel Tiger" missions. Finally, on 22 December 1970, the U.S. Congress passed a resolution ending all further use of American forces in Laos and Cambodia. A total of 191 USAF pilots served as Raven FACs, 31 of them (16 percent) were killed in action in Laos.

Of the over six million tons of bombs dropped on Southeast Asia during the American involvement, Laos was riddled with 1,600,000 tons — an average of 17 tons per square mile of the small country, most dropped under the direction of the handful of Ravens.

Enemy Bird Dogs • A sad denouement to the employment of Bird Dogs in Laos came in May of 1977 when Bird Dogs, captured during the takeover of South Vietnam, were used by the newly-established communist Democratic Republic of Vietnam to direct air strikes by MiGs against the Hmong resistance fighters (who had fought valiantly for their homeland alongside the Ravens earlier in the war). These strikes apparently included extensive use of chemical weapons such as the notorious T-toxins. This systematic in-the-field testing on live subjects continued until at least 1982, a year in which it was estimated that more than 28,000 Hmong were killed by these T-toxins.

• Another way to return from a combat mission.
Note the large hole in the top of the vertical stabilizer and the damaged left wing strut •
(U.S. Army Aviation Museum)

Medal of Honor

On 24 February 1967, forward air controller Captain Hilliard A. Wilbanks was dispatched in his unarmed O-1 Bird Dog to assist in an operation against enemy forces attacking near Dalat, South Vietnam. Captain Wilbanks was assigned to the 21st TASS based at Nha Trang AFB.

While flying reconnaissance for a South Vietnamese Ranger Battalion, Captain Wilbanks discovered dug-in enemy troops on a pair of hilltops preparing to ambush the Rangers. He promptly requested helicopter gunships and alerted the Rangers advancing into the area. When the enemy realized their ambush was being compromised, they began a mortar, machine gun, and automatic weapon barrage. Captain Wilbanks took numerous hits as he tried to mark the enemy positions with WP marking rockets for the gunships.

To keep the enemy troops at bay until the gunships arrived, Wilbanks opened fire with the M-16 rifle he carried in his plane. Firing out of the side window of his O-1, Captain Wilbanks distracted the enemy troops and slowed their advance. Although the anti-aircraft fire increased, Wilbanks continued to pass directly over the enemy troops to distract them from the Rangers, inflicting many casualties with just his single M-16.

The outnumbered Rangers managed to withdraw as the attackers diverted their fire to Wilbanks' low-flying aircraft. Despite the numerous hits on his O-1, Captain Wilbanks continued to cover the withdrawal. On his final pass, however, he was severely wounded and crashed between the opposing forces. The Rangers managed to rescue Captain Wilbanks from the wreckage of his plane, but he died while being evacuated to a hospital.

For his heroic support of the Rangers, Captain Wilbanks was posthumously awarded the Medal of Honor. The presentation was made to his widow by Secretary of the Air Force Harold Brown at the Pentagon, Washington, DC on 24 January 1968. The citation accompanying the award ends:

"Captain Wilbanks' magnificent action saved numerous friendly personnel from certain injury or death. His unparalleled concern for his fellow man and his extraordinary heroism were in the highest traditions of the military service, and have reflected great credit upon himself and the U. S. Air Force."

The Bird Dog as a Trainer

In the early 1950s, before arriving at the Army

• An Army O-1 returns from a combat mission over South Vietnam. Note the empty rocket launcher tubes under the wings •
(U.S. Army Aviation Museum)

• *A USAF O-1 FAC overflying an Army convoy on a road in South Vietnam* •
(U.S. Army Aviation Museum)

Aviation School for their "graduate" training, all Army aviators-to-be underwent 17 weeks of flight training at a now-closed USAF base, Gary AFB, near San Marcos, Texas. After the USAF had taught them the basics and indoctrinated them with all those things one should never do with an airplane, the Army proceeded to train them just how to safely do many of those very things. At the Army Aviation School, fixed-wing training encompassed a progression of propeller-driven aircraft, from the L-19 to the L-20 (DeHavilland Beaver) to the L-23 (Beech Twin Bonanza). The first Army Aviation School was established at Fort Sill, Oklahoma, but was moved to Fort Rucker, Alabama, in the mid-1950s.

Fort Rucker's 65,000-acre reservation was dotted with about 50 potential landing sites, which were rarely more than several hundred feet of dirt or sod recessed in among the tall trees of the northern Alabama woods. All Army aviators had to learn to fly into and out of those sites. These were fields that justifiably could be called "unimproved landing sites" — with tall weeds and brush, even fallen logs and rocks just for added fun. Students also had to learn to land on and takeoff from narrow dirt roads (even around corners!). Just to keep the students honest

and test their judgement, the Army school threw in some "jokers" — unsuitable fields mixed in with the good ones ("good" being a relative term) — fields with too large rocks or holes or maybe too short for even the L-19 with its barn-door flaps.

O'Hollaran remembered a couple of specific fields that were more challenging than most. "One I remember very well had a steep enough slope that you felt as though you were going to fall sideways out of the seat on the strip. As I recall, it had about a 8-10 degree slope according to the attitude indicator at the center of the strip. It was a dirt (Alabama clay), strip which became very slick after a typical Alabama thunderstorm. Another that comes to mind was surrounded by 100-foot pines and not more than 1,000 feet wide at the widest point. It looked better suited as a landing zone for helicopter operations."

The Army's use of the Bird Dog as a pilot trainer led to a 1953 request to develop a modification designed specifically for that role. Ten L-19As were modified with appropriate instrumentation and designated TL-19A. In addition, Cessna modified the last 66 production aircraft into L-19A-IT aircraft equipped with constant-speed propellers, fully-equipped instrument panels, plus blind-

• *An Army Reserve TL-19A at Fort Worth, Texas in 1961.*
Note the rear cockpit instrument panel •
(U.S. Army Aviation Museum)

flying curtains and a swing-out instrument panel for rear seat instrument training. (The rear seat panel had to swing out to allow the pilot to get into and out of the rear cockpit.)

Another instrument training development was the TL-19D in 1956, with throttle-mounted microphone buttons, dual instrument panels, constant-speed propellers, and a 210-horsepower Continental O-470-15 engine. The airframe was beefed-up to allow a 2,400 pound gross weight, but with no underwing hardpoints. Cessna produced 310 of these variants between 1956 and 1957, which were redesignated TO-1D in 1962 (s/n 55-4649 through 55-2696 and 57-2772 through 57-2981). Some of these aircraft, without the rear-seat instrument panel, were designated O-1D and used in the Vietnam War.

In 1958, the Army evaluated a proposed TL-19E basic trainer configuration, under Engineering Change Proposal (ECP) 181, during a 14-day trial at Fort Rucker, Alabama. Cessna completed installation of the ECP 181 modifications on L-19A s/n 53-8005 on 13 October 1958 and the aircraft was turned over to the Army for testing. The modified aircraft was compared against L-19A s/n 50-1493, as modified by the Army Aviation Detachment at Camp Gary in 1957, to determine the suitability of the changes for formal training purposes. The specific modifications included in ECP 181 were:

- Replacement of L-19A landing gear with L-19E gear.
- Separate master cylinders for rear brakes.
- Provisions for boom microphones and TL-19D style throttle-mounted microphone and interphone buttons.
- Flap override capability for instructor.
- New linkage between front and rear throttles and more-accessible rear seat throttle quadrant.
- Cockpit mirror to allow the instructor "to observe the student's facial expressions."
- Modification of the rear control stick to ensure availability of full travel.
- Installation of a rear seat master magneto switch.
- Heftier engine mounts.
- Emergency front-seat release to improve instructor's escape capability.

These modifications increased the L-19A's gross weight by 22.5 pounds. The Cessna-modified aircraft was evaluated for 20 flying hours, both day and night, from both hard-surfaced and sod airstrips, in winds up to 15 knots, and on actual student training sorties in the Army Aviation course at Fort Rucker. The results of the tests were summarized in the formal report:

"As a result of the modifications, instructor pilot control of the aircraft is improved. The modifications will increase the effectiveness of the formal flight training program and assist in the accident prevention program."

The final recommendation was that "action be taken to implement ECP 181 for the retrofit kits and that the retrofit kits be provided for the Camp Gary and Rucker L-19A and L-19E training airplanes as soon as possible." The ECP 181 kits were approved for use on the L-19E but without the modified landing gear (these aircraft already incorporated the newer gear).

School For Boys • Jerry Robinson went through fixed-wing training in the L-19 at "Mother Rucker's School for Boys," as he called the Fort Rucker Army Aviation School, and was later a civilian contract instructor pilot at the school. He said it was obvious "the L-19 wasn't designed to be a trainer." In flight, the long and limber landing gear, needed to ensure ground clearance for the 90-inch propeller, "hung down in such a way that the wheels had considerable camber, and if you made a 'squeaker' of a landing, one wheel would lose its camber before the other, with the result that the airplane would dart sideways with a mind of its own." This interesting tendency was complicated by the reduced aft fuselage and tail area (resulting from cutting down the aft fuselage to get those required 360° windows), meaning there was less area than needed to provide sufficient directional stability during the landing rollout. And finally, those 60° flaps "caused the rudder to be almost completely blanked by the flaps, and the result was a 'Dog that would bite,'" Robinson said.

O'Hollaran recalled his first day at Fort Rucker. "The Instructor Commander briefed us that there are two kinds of Bird Dog pilots: (a) old Bird Dog pilots who have already groundlooped a Bird Dog, and if they continue to fly them will surely do so again, and (b) new Bird Dog pilots who will never be real Bird Dog Pilots until they have experienced their first groundloop."

Rudders and Flaps • The early L-19 trainers still had the folding rudder pedals in the back and mechanical flaps operable only from the front seat. This was less than optimum from an instructor's viewpoint. The rudder pedals, Robinson said, "would also fold flat without warning at just the most inopportune time when giving dual in the airplane, resulting in the instructor having no rudder control." With those 60° Bird Dog flaps fully extended, student go-arounds from a botched landing attempt could become exciting. Robinson said, "If the student got rattled and didn't retract the flaps, the instructor couldn't get them up from the back seat." With the "somewhat limited" hot day, full flap climb performance, instructor vigilance and skill were important.

These two instructional deficiencies were later corrected. Non-folding rear seat rudder pedals with separate brake master cylinders were installed in all of the Fort Rucker trainers. However, Robinson noted, the instructor could not "do anything about the student who locked the brakes. Whoever pushed hardest (whoever was scaredest!) had the brakes." (The brakes were the old floating disk type and susceptible to locking up.) The mechanical flaps were replaced with electric flaps, designed so the rear flap switch had priority.

Lockup • Robinson recalled an episode with a student who had been doing well — lulling him into a relaxed complacency instructors do well to avoid at all costs. On one landing, the student "got a good touchdown and immediately started a swerve to the right. I grabbed the stick to make sure it was all the way back, and 'helped' him with left rudder and a bunch of brake, while passing along some commentary about his flying skills. Despite all our efforts, the airplane continued to the right and, because of the heavy braking, lifted the tail off the runway. We came to a stop cocked about 45° to the centerline, with less landing roll than I'd ever seen. When I looked out the window, the right wheel was smoking, and the brake disc was cherry red. Maintenance came out and fixed the brake, which had locked up, apparently just as we touched down."

Over Gross, Now What? • All of the trainer versions of the L-19/O-1 operated by the Army Aviation School at Fort Rucker carried a placard on the instrument panel: "This airplane with full fuel, two pilots, and parachutes is 254 pounds over maximum gross weight." There was no indication as to what one should do about it, however.

Bird Dog Speed? • Robinson remembered the TO-1D instrument trainers fondly. These aircraft had folding rear instrument panels, full IFR instrumentation, constant speed propellers, and rear seat curtains to allow the student to practice "blind flying." The instructor flew from the front seat while the student practiced instrument flying in the back. He recalled that the TO-1D "was about 25 knots faster, and what a sweet airplane it was!"

Around and Around She Goes • To instill a certain respect, if not outright fear, for the Bird Dog's proclivity for swapping ends on the runway — groundlooping — the U.S. Army Aviation School's training department at Fort Rucker, using one of the school's most worn-out Bird Dogs, filmed an instructor intentionally groundlooping. Robinson recalled that the story behind the film was that the hapless instructor chosen to star in the epic tried maybe 20 times before steeling his nerves enough to let the aircraft actually whip beyond the point of no return. The cameras kept running through every attempt, since they had no way of knowing when the momentous event would really happen. That truckload of film was later edited into the 10-minute "what not to do" training film. Robinson said, "I'll bet one of his students could have gotten it done in one pass." He described the movie this way:

"The film shows, in very slow motion, an L-19 in wheel landing attitude start to swerve, shows the outboard tire roll under, followed by the landing gear leg tearing

• An Army TL-19D, s/n 55-4719, at Fort Hood, Texas in 1956 •
(U.S. Army Aviation Museum)

• *Army Aviation School L-19s on the ramp at Lowe Army Air Field, Fort Rucker, Alabama in 1960 waiting for the weather to clear* •
(U.S. Army Aviation Museum)

touchdown and after landing roll until positive directional control was established. The flare was quite positive, resulting in a (ideally) tail-wheel first touchdown with the mains about 4-6 inches in the air. This resulted in a rather firm (read 'hard') plop-down which spread those long, limber main gear legs out and took the camber out of the wheels. Then the stick was held securely back and directional control was maintained with rudder and, quite often, a lot of brake. Heavy emphasis was placed on control position during takeoff, landing, and ground operations, as deflected ailerons were quite effective in helping to maintain directional control."

out of the fuselage, and the plane spinning around on one wing tip and the belly. Everyone had to watch the film a minimum number of times (I forget how many), and sign a log book each time he watched it. We were impressed."

Three-point • Beginning in 1964, the Army stopped teaching the L-19 wheel landing technique at Fort Rucker. This was the result of too many wheel landing accidents with the Bird Dog. Wheel landings, in a tailwheel airplane, required touching down on the two main wheels only and then slowing down before lowering the tailwheel — as opposed to a three-point landing on all three at once or a tailwheel-first landing (yielding the slowest possible touchdown speed). During a wheel landing in the L-19 with full flaps extended, there was a brief interlude wherein airflow over the rudder was blocked by the wing, meaning the pilot was little more than a passenger during that time. The long springike main landing gear could easily "spring" at the wrong moment as a student tried to force those main wheels onto the ground, resulting in a progressively worsening "porpoise" — during which the aircraft bounced from main wheels to tailwheel and back as the distraught pilot applied corrections — always just out of phase with the action due to pilot reaction time. The almost inevitable result was that the propeller struck the ground, which destroyed the propeller and, many times, the crankshaft.

Jerry Robinson described the standard Fort Rucker Bird Dog landing technique in the following words:

"The aircraft [was] flown down short final with power set at about 50 rpm above idle, and left there through the

Fuel Selector Valve Handle — Fullest Tank? • Improper fuel system management was a common student error when flying the L-19. It was easy to turn the fuel selector, intending to switch feed tanks, but not get it in the detent — stopping fuel flow to the engine until the selector was properly seated in the detent. Robinson once initiated a practice forced landing with a student by placing the selector in an intermediate position. While running the checklist, the student touched the selector but did not check it properly. When Robinson told him to climb back to altitude — the engine would not start and the aircraft would not climb. Robinson told him to run through the checklist again. He did — with the same result. Four tries later, the student still had not physically checked that the selector was in the detent. Another student, on a solo night cross-country sortie, radioed back that he was lost and running out of gas. He was so low on fuel he had already jettisoned the cabin door — ready to bail out. His instructor calmly asked him over the radio how much fuel was in each tank. The student's response was "Oh" as he switched to the other, full, tank. His return to base was uneventful although, Robinson noted, "He reported later that it was a little windy in the cockpit with the door missing."

Belly Landing • In another example of the ruggedness of the L-19 and its landing gear (despite its spindly appearance), Robinson recounted the following story:

"A solo student rounded out high, pushed the nose over, hit hard on the main gear, and rebounded into the air. From then on, his elevator and throttle action was exactly 180° out of phase with what he should have been doing, and he

• *This is the aftermath of an Army L-19 groundloop accident at Fort Rucker, Alabama* •
(U.S. Army Aviation Museum)

got into the wildest pilot induced oscillation I've ever seen. Each time the airplane contacted the runway, the main gear absorbed enormous amounts of energy and recoiled it back into the system, each bounce getting bigger. Finally, in a BFO (Blinding Flash of the Obvious), he applied power and went around. We walked out onto the runway where his last bounce occurred, and found the shattered lens of the belly rotating beacon, which was mounted between the main gear legs. Incredibly, the prop did not strike the runway. Apparently, it was exactly parallel to the ground when the airplane came down hard, and the only damage to the airplane was the broken rotating beacon."

Different Fronts — Same Bird Dog

Bird Dogs not only performed their essential duties in the Korean and Vietnam Wars, but around the world in conflicts large and small.

On 21 January 1971, NVA troops raided the Pochentong air base of the Khmer Air Force (KAF), destroying most of their aircraft. To resupply the KAF, the United States set-up "Project Flycatcher" — providing a variety of replacement aircraft including Cessna T-41A, A-37B, and O-1 aircraft. By June of 1974, when "Flycatcher" was terminated, some 160 aircraft had been transferred to the KAF.

The war in Southeast Asia was by no means over when North Vietnam overran the South and formed the typically misnamed Democratic Republic of Vietnam. Following a genocidal war against the Cambodian people, Vietnam renamed the country Kampuchea and installed a puppet government — the People's Republic of Kampuchea. Several disparate groups continued to resist the new regime (National Army of Democratic Kampuchea, Khmer People's National Liberation Front, and the National Sihanoukist Army), but none of them possessed air power. However, Thailand was forced to maintain a vigilant air surveillance along its common border with Kampuchea, flying almost daily observation sorties in Royal Thai Air Force (RTAF) L-19s, A-37s, and Northrop F-5s. In January of 1987, while ostensibly pursuing rebel forces, Kampuchean aircraft shot down an RTAF L-19.

The French Army employed perhaps ten L-19s from

the mid-1950s through the mid-'80s in the Aviation Légère de l'Armée de Terre (ALAT, Army Light Aviation) in the French First Army for liaison and observation duties. At least two of these were deployed to Chad between 1981 and 1985 during the French involvement in that fighting. The L-19s assigned to Chad were outfitted with makeshift heat shields around the exhausts to disguise the infrared signature and make it more difficult for the rebels to use their Soviet-made SA-7 heat-seeking, surface-to-air missiles against them.

The Indian Army spread its fleet of L-19A and L-19E aircraft around the country at various bases. These aircraft were painted in an overall olive drab color with white s/n on the vertical stabilizer.

France, Chile, and Canada all acquired their Bird Dogs through direct purchases from Cessna, while other countries were provided with the aircraft through the Military Assistance Program, including aircraft for the Italian Army and the Nationalist Chinese Army (Taiwan).

High Flight — Bird Dog Style

In 1955, two Army lieutenants assigned to Fort Kobbe, Panama Canal Zone, were given a unique task. Lieutenants John Dome and Thomas Long were directed to fly a Bird Dog to the high plateau region of the Andes Mountains to determine whether the aircraft could be used safely for low-level reconnaissance of the plains, where the average elevation was 13,500 feet — before taking off!

They used the 13,000-foot runway at La Paz using the slight downward slope available when launching to the west and the opposite upward slope landing to the east, regardless of winds. Their Bird Dog was loaded with 85 pounds of radio gear (hey, these were 1950s-vintage radios!), partial fuel, survival necessities, oxygen apparatus, and two pilots. Takeoff required leaning the mixture for peak rpm during the engine runup — resulting in a maximum rpm of 2000 just before brake release and 2,250 at their planned takeoff speed of 60 mph indicated airspeed.

They experimented with various flap settings between 0° and 45°. The 45° setting allowed them to get airborne

• It is, however, possible to land too hard for even the indestructible Bird Dog •
(U.S. Army Aviation Museum)

at 60, but the aircraft would not accelerate beyond that speed, despite the deceptively fast ground speed in the rarified atmosphere. With 30°, the aircraft felt more stable as it lifted off and they were able to retract the flaps and accelerate to 70 in a steady, albeit slow, climb. Liftoff and climbout were both acceptable with flaps retracted, but control during the takeoff roll was deemed marginal. Likewise, various landing configurations were tried. Dome and Long noted that the "aircraft had a tendency to 'fall through' four or five feet during the two three-point landings" with either 45° or 60° of flaps deployed. At 30°, 45°, or 60° flap settings the landings were normal, but the median setting of 45° provided the best control. All approaches were made at 80 mph.

Cruise speed of 70 mph was obtained at 2,200 rpm with the aircraft attitude more tail-low than at lower altitudes, although the two Army pilots discovered that, by extending the flaps until the trailing edges were about four inches down with the flap handle blocked in place, the airspeed increased to 72 and the tail came up to a more normal level flight attitude. When performing stalls at 14,500 feet, they noticed that the "normal 'whistling' of the Bird Dog approaching a stall was not audible, and the rate of fall after the stall was alarmingly rapid." Normal stall recovery procedures broke the stall but not the descent — cautious control inputs were required, along with immediate flap retraction.

Were these two stouthearted aviators able to contour-fly in the rarified Andean atmosphere? Not quite.

Lieutenant Dome noted in his report:

"We flew it down a straight, level road with the flaps completely retracted. While holding an indicated airspeed of 100 mph, we tried a slight pull-up to simulate an obstacle in the flight path. The airspeed immediately fell to 80 mph, and full power was added. Since the airspeed continued falling to 60 mph, the contour flying phase of this test was considered to be too dangerous to continue."

Dome also mentioned that, if a downdraft caught them during climbout, they quickly found themselves sucked into an 800 foot-per-minute descent with full throttle and an airspeed of only 60 mph. The two aviators recommended that, if it were deemed necessary to repeat the experience, the Bird Dog be equipped with a supercharged engine, constant-speed propeller, and electric flaps. And get rid of all unnecessary equipment to keep the weight down. (Electric flaps were later installed on all Army L-19s under a Standard Configuration and Modification Program — SCAMP.)

A Little Extra Drag

Lieutenant Jack Kalmbach was stationed at Fairbanks, Alaska, in the mid-1950s when he discovered just how much drag a Bird Dog can have hanging from it and still fly. It was winter and Kalmbach and another pilot ferried some passengers in a pair of L-19s to Stevens Village where they landed on a snowy, frozen river. After unloading his passengers, Kalmbach watched his comrade takeoff before beginning his own

• *French First Army L-19 in Chad in 1984, with heat shielded exhaust (just forward of the landing gear) to protect the plane from the rebels' heat-seeking SA-7 missiles* •
(French Army)

• *A Nationalist Chinese Army L-19* •
(U.S. Army Aviation Museum)

takeoff run. Shortly after liftoff, his aircraft slammed into a left descending bank that took all the right aileron and rudder he could apply just to get back to level flight. He had to hold that full right rudder to stay there. He soon discovered that the Bird Dog would not climb despite producing full engine power, but he still had no idea what had gone wrong. His flying buddy circled back to check Kalmbach's plane — and found the left ski hanging straight down.

Kalmbach chose to fly to Ladd Air Force Base in case he needed the assistance of their full-service crash and rescue team. He flew past the Ladd tower, and the operations officer on duty observed the errant ski hanging down and cocked to the rear at about a 45° angle. Kalmbach shutdown the engine on final to reduce the fire danger and landed on the right main gear and the tailwheel about four feet short of the runway — he had not quite forecast the full effect of all that drag on his powerless bird. When the left wing came down, the aircraft groundlooped but remained upright — and Lieutenant Kalmbach exited the stricken Bird Dog at a high rate of speed. Once more, a Bird Dog had suffered a potentially deadly malfunction and, yet, flew on to deliver its pilot safely home.

The O-1 Missile

Imagine an O-1E Bird Dog pilot flying to a designated geographical point and then keeping the vertical needle on his Course Deviation Indicator (CDI) centered to follow a defined navigational course until intercepting a specific glidepath, when the horizontal CDI needle would provide guidance down to a minimum safe altitude — at which point the pilot breaks off the descent and returns for another try. What's that you say? Sounds like just another instrument training sortie, flying multiple Instrument Landing System (ILS) approaches?

Not quite.

The aircraft in question was, indeed, a garden-variety Army O-1E until, in 1959, the Army's Artillery and Missile School at Fort Sill, Oklahoma, modified it. What the Artillery and Missile School needed was some way to train the personnel who were destined to operate the Lacrosse surface-to-surface missile, while keeping the costs down. Use of the actual Lacrosse missile had proven prohibitively expensive, so an alternative was needed. And that's how the O-1 Missile Simulator came to be.

A stock Army O-1E was modified with the following equipment:

• *A photo of the Italian Army L-19s* •
(Kansas Aviation Museum/Robert J. Pickett Collection)

- 100-ampere generator
- Safety circuit breaker
- Equipment rack in lieu of the rear seat to hold:
  - Transponder
  - Radio beacon
  - Motor generator
  - Special guidance components
  - Junction box to connect the new equipment to the aircraft's electrical system

The radio beacon was used to allow the Lacrosse ground guidance equipment to track the O-1, which then uplinked appropriate guidance commands via the transponder. The onboard guidance gear translated the commands and displayed them on the pilot's CDI.

The missile crew would start the training scenario by radioing an appropriate altitude and heading for the pilot to fly to arrive at a specific Initial Point (IP). Once the aircraft was over the IP, a yellow light on the instrument panel alerted the pilot to expect heading steering commands from the ground. All the pilot had to do was fly the CDI's vertical needle using the same course interception and maintenance techniques as for any other navigation signal. Fifteen seconds from the descent point required to replicate the downward portion of the Lacrosse trajectory,

a green light lit up on the panel, followed by movement of the horizontal CDI needle. The pilot followed those commands as if he were flying an ILS approach for landing. Airspeed control was critical, and a minimum safe descent altitude was prescribed for each sortie. At this altitude, a red light indicated that the onboard equipment had received the missile warhead arming command. The pilot pulled out of the dive and returned to the IP for another run.

With two missile control centers working a single O-1, the alternate control center was ready with new coordinates by the time the pilot was on his way back to the IP. Working in this manner, each control center was able to accomplish two runs per hour — and witness the results in real-time.

As always, the Army's Bird Dog was ready and able to support the ground commanders, whether in combat or in training.

Operation Gold Road

April of 1954 provided the Army with an opportunity to prove the practicality of L-19 support for an infantry company on the move through dense jungle conditions. "Operation Gold Road" involved 72 soldiers from the

23rd Infantry Division, a trek through the Panamanian jungle from Madden Airfield in the Canal Zone to Porto Bello, Panama, and one L-19 aircraft. The trial required the L-19 to drop required rations and supplies to the troops every day, despite the dense foliage and 100- to 175-foot trees that screened the company from the over-flying aircraft. Paradrops were not used because of economic considerations — the parachutes would have to be left behind as the troops already were traveling with 70-pound packs. Instead, the packages were lashed together with metal bands and fastened to the two underwing bomb racks, allowing up to eight cases of C-rations to be dropped per sortie. Every drop was recovered by the troops on the ground and only 30 percent of the packages broke open.

The Panama jungle test participants determined that the best drop zone selection was an area of dense underbrush, which seemed to cushion the drops. Second choice was to drop bundles into large pools of water. They were not able to successfully drop water supplies but did find that the aircraft crew was usually able to identify suitable water and direct the men on the ground to it.

Turbine Bird Dogs

At least four different turbine engine installations have been tested and flown on L-19 aircraft, both in the United States and abroad. The best-known experiment was conducted in 1952 and 1953 with a Boeing-designed engine. At Boeing's request, the Army loaned aircraft s/n 52-1804 for installation of the 210-shaft-horsepower 502-8XT-50-1 engine. This engine featured a free turbine that permitted the installation of a fixed-pitch propeller, a McCauley metal prop with a 12° blade angle. The engine was installed by Cessna engineers aided by a couple of Boeing engineers. First flight of the aircraft, designated the XL-19B by the Army, was completed on 5 November 1952 by Cessna test pilot Hank Waring. Recurring problems with the fuel governor resulted in 19 forced landings after engine flame-outs, although the problems were eventually corrected. Power, and thus airspeed, control on final with the turbine engine was not as good as with the piston engine (due to the comparatively slow acceleration of the turbine), and fuel consumption was significantly higher, particularly at the low altitudes and slow speeds the airplane's mission demanded.

Altitude Record • After numerous successful XL-19B test flights, Boeing suggested a high-altitude record attempt. Cessna stripped the aircraft of radios, battery, and starter to reduce weight and chose their lightest test pilot, Ralph Price, for the mission. Price underwent the high-altitude flight training course developed and conducted by Boeing for their pilots. With official observers standing by and an airborne barograph sealed and installed in 52-1804 on the scheduled day, Price reported in with a severe head cold, ruling out any high flights for him. In his place, 195-pound Bill Thompson climbed into the cockpit on 16 July 1953 and coaxed the little modified Bird Dog to 37,063 feet for a world's record in its weight class.

According to Thompson in "Cessna, Wings for the World," the flight was not without incident. Due to a snagged oxygen hose, Thompson succumbed to the early symptoms of hypoxia (oxygen starvation) passing through 20,000 feet until he located and corrected the problem. The engine flamed-out at 37,063 feet and smoke filled the cockpit, creating an unpleasant prospect with the -65°F outside air temperature. However, the smoke soon dissipated, and Thompson began the long, quiet glide down to the Cessna field at Wichita, racing a building thunderstorm for landing right-of-way. After a 45-minute descent, Thompson touched down on the

• Army Pilot (Captain George Rice) strapping on snowshoes after landing his ski-equipped L-19 near Fort Richardson, Alaska in 1961 •
(Kansas Aviation Museum / Robert J. Pickett Collection)

runway and coasted to the hangar, where the assembled test and certification personnel were surprised to find the cold-soaked aluminum too cold to touch with a bare hand, despite the +100°F temperatures on the ground.

Later that year, the XL-19B team was awarded the Louis Bleriot Medal at a Washington, D.C. awards banquet. The new altitude record exceeded the previous record by 6,860 feet.

Prototype Crash • The XL-19B was destroyed and the crew, Ralph Price and an Army officer, were injured during a demonstration of the aircraft's combat evasive capability in a steep descending spiral. A high-pressure fuel line ruptured, pumping remaining fuel overboard. The aircraft hooked the top of a wire fence and slammed into the ground.

Two other Army L-19As (s/n 52-6311 and 52-6312) were modified with another turbine engine in 1953. This engine was a French engine developed by Turbomeca and built in the United States under license by Continental — the 260-shaft-horsepower XT51-T-1 Arouste II. This engine was a fixed-shaft design that needed a constant-speed propeller with the ability to flatten to a low 5° blade angle. Cessna engineers again installed the modification, and Cessna test pilot Ralph Price flew the inaugural flight of the XL-19C on 1 September 1953.

• *Cessna/Boeing XL-19B demonstrating its steep climbout capability* •
(U.S. Army Aviation Museum)

Excitement • If control of power and airspeed on the XL-19B was less than desirable, control of the XL-19C could be downright exciting, although Cessna tried innumerable combinations of governor and fuel control settings to alleviate the problems. Easing the throttle to flight idle on final led to a sudden increase in drag, due to the flat 5°-6° angle on the prop blades, and a potential short landing. The pilot would then have to wait several seconds for the engine to wind-up again and produce power for a go-around. However, the XL-19C did establish an L-19 speed record of 182 mph on Cessna's closed course. Both of the XL-19C aircraft were later returned to L-19A configuration and put back into the Army inventory.

One More Time • A third turbine-engine variant of the durable L-19 Bird Dog was tested in 1959. An Army L-19A, s/n 51-7391, was delivered to the Army Aviation Board on December of 1958, and another Boeing engine, the 502-10G (originally designed for use in RP-77 drones), was installed. Following evaluation test flights, the Aviation Board noted that, although the high-altitude limit was better and the engine was easier to operate and maintain, the aircraft was objectionably noisy in flight and burned excessive amounts of jet fuel, significantly reducing both range and loiter time. In the board's 16 October 1959 report to the Commanding General of U.S. Continental Army Command, Colonel Jack Marinelli noted that "slow power response and high minimum propeller idle rpm materially reduce the capability for short field landings over a barrier." The Aviation Board also made the following recommendations for any future turboprop L-19 trials:

- Improve the power response
- Install a constant-speed propeller
- Provide a minimum prop idle speed of 450-550 rpm
- Reduce fuel consumption to improve range and endurance
- Route exhaust to reduce heat and fumes during taxiing
- Develop a compact oxygen system for the crew

Italian Turbo • There was one other turbine-powered L-19, developed for the Italian Army Light Aviation units. The Italian Army had been operating L-19Es for some time when, in 1969, Siai-Marchetti designed the SM-1019 version, powered by a 317-shaft-horsepower Allison 250-B15G engine, later upgraded to the 400-horsepower Allison 250-B17, with a three-blade Hartzell constant-speed propeller. The Italian Army purchased 100 of these SM-1019s. Despite the significant increase in power, the attendant increase in fuel consumption required carrying over 800 pounds of fuel, resulting in a normal takeoff gross weight of 2,865 pounds, almost 500 pounds more than its lower-powered cousins. With more power cou-

• *Cessna test pilot Bill Thompson (fifth from left) with the XL-19B after his record-setting flight* •
(U.S. Army Aviation Museum)

pled to more weight, the takeoff and landing performance was actually somewhat worse than the original. And the problems of power control on final persisted.

Marine Bird Dogs

Of the initial production run of L-19A aircraft in 1951-1954, 60 were delivered to the Marine Corps, designated OE-1, and assigned to VMO-6 of the Marine Air Group in the Pacific, with many serving in Korea. These aircraft were assigned Navy Bureau Numbers (BuNo) 133782-133816 and 136887-136911. The first OE-1s were delivered to Korea in May 1951, replacing VMO-6's Stinson OY-1s. The Marine Bird Dogs were soon flying supplies, medical evacuation missions, and artillery-spotting missions.

On 23 April 1952, Chinese troops hit the dug-in Marines in the Hwachon Reservoir area with a "human wave" attack. Allied close air support was called-in on the morning of the 24th to soften the attackers' positions along Horseshoe Ridge and provide cover for a Marine withdrawal ordered by Eighth Army. VMO-6 used its OY-1 and OE-1 aircraft to identify targets for the Army and Marine artillery and for the attacking fighter-bombers, resulting in minimal losses despite the overwhelming opposition. Throughout the war, VMO-6's Bird Dogs continued to spot for artillery and provide observa-

tion coverage of enemy activity.

He-e-ere's Ed • In March of 1953, Captain Ed McMahon (later to gain fame as Johnny Carson's sidekick on the "Tonight Show") was checked out in a Bird Dog of VMO-6 and flew his first combat mission the following day, eventually racking up 85 missions in the OE-1. If not for bad weather, he likely would have logged the last Marine Corps mission before the armistice in July of 1953. Although the war ended, the Bird Dogs of VMO-6 continued to fly surveillance missions to enforce the "No Crossing" line just south of the demilitarized zone.

Bird Dog Hot Rod • To accommodate the bigger fuel tanks and the heftier gross weight, Cessna switched from the original C-170 wing design to the C-180 wing (maintaining the same 36-foot span). The new wings and fuel tanks, however, necessitated a reduction in maximum flap travel from the 60° of the L-19A/OE-1 to only 40°, resulting in some increase in minimum landing distance. The larger engine also caused some instability, which necessitated a more powerful rudder. Cessna chose to change from the rounded planforms of the L-19/OE-1 empennage to more squared-off horizontal and vertical stabilizers, again much like that used on the C-180. A dorsal fin was also added to improve stability and control. The fuselage was redesigned, lengthening it by six inches.

The prototype OE-2 (Cessna Model 321) carried registration number N41767 and first flew on 19 August 1954 with Cessna test pilot Bob Crawshaw at the controls. Flight test verified a top speed of 180 mph and a service ceiling of 26,000 ft., despite a 220-pound increae in gross weight over previous L-19s.

Deliveries of the first OE-2s began in mid-1955, with 25 aircraft produced in 1955 (BuNo 14078-14102) and two more produced in 1959 (BuNo 148250 and 148251). The Marines were pleased with the results but no further orders were placed. Unfortunately, the Congressional approach to budget cutting in the late 1950s involved a "slash-and-burn" attack on the defense budget, and the Marines could not come up with the funds for their more expensive version of the L-19. All OE-2s were redesignated O-1C in 1962.

• A comparison of a standard L-19A nose (right) and an XL-19B nose (left) •
(U.S. Army Aviation Museum)

As part of the Marine acceptance requirements, the CAA-certified OE-2 was required to meet the Naval Structural Flight Demonstration tests. A production aircraft (BuNo 140078) was loaned to Cessna for completion of these tests and some antenna radiation pattern and stores delivery test.

Based on their experience in Korean combat, the Marines determined that an aircraft with more power would be better suited for frontline combat employment. In October of 1954, they contracted with Cessna for the development of the OE-2, incorporating:

• Armor plating around the pilot
• Flak curtains for the cockpit
• Electrically operated flaps
• Circuit breakers instead of fuses
• Red night-lighting for the instrument panel
• Beefier 260-horsepower supercharged Continental TSO-470-2 engine
• Constant-speed propeller
• Increased gross weight (2,650 pounds)
• Larger fuel tanks for longer range

To accommodate the bigger fuel tanks and the heftier stores delivery tests. To satisfy the structural tests, Cessna had to demonstrate the structural integrity of the aircraft throughout the certified flight envelope using full control deflections. Landings also had to be demonstrated with a 10 feet-per-second sink rate at touchdown in all potential landing configurations — including at full gross weight plus wing-mounted stores. After all these attempts to "break" the airplane were finished, there was no damage and not even one rivet had popped. A real testimony to the structural integrity of Cessna design!

In 1959, two L-19E aircraft were acquired by the Navy, assigned BuNos 144663 and 144664, and designated OE-1 (changed to O-1B in 1962). And in 1968, the Marines acquired eight O-1G aircraft, assigning them BuNos 156678-156685.

During the Vietnam War, the U.S. Marine Corps' operated OE-1 and OE-2 aircraft as liaison, support, observation, and FAC aircraft.

Boundary Layer Control

In 1954, Cessna's Research Department, working with the University of Wichita, was contracted by the Office of Naval Research and the Department of the Army to install and test a Boundary Layer Control (BLC) system on an Army L-19A. In September, the modified aircraft (Cessna Model C-319A) was demonstrated at the Dayton Air Show in Ohio. The BLC L-19 was airborne in less distance, climbed steeper, approached at a steeper angle, and used less runway for landing than the standard L-19 that flew alongside it for the demonstration.

The advantages of BLC had been known for decades and several experimenters had tried various methods to achieve it, although few of the techniques were able to be applied outside of the laboratory. A notable exception was the German Arado system developed early in World War II, which used a combination of blowing air over the deployed wing flaps and sucking air through slots or holes in the surface of the wing.

Two problems are created by the ultra-thin layer of air that just skims the surface of an aircraft's wing in flight. These air particles actually adhere to the wing surface as a result of the viscosity of the air itself and exhibit no relative motion between themselves and the wing surface. This lack of particle motion and the particles' adhering qualities create a form of aerodynamic drag called skin friction drag. This boundary layer of air tends to be thicker and more turbulent at the trailing edge of the wing, causing problems with the effectiveness of the flaps and ailerons mounted along the wing's trailing edge. The primary goals of controlling this boundary layer of air are to reduce high-speed drag by decreasing the air layer and smoothing the flow of air across the wing and to increase low-speed lift by reducing the turbulence and delaying the separation of air flow over the deployed flaps.

Cessna installed a version of the German Arado BLC system on L-19A (s/n 51-11972) that included a pair of hydraulic-motor-driven axial fans (one in each wing) deriving power from a pilot-controlled engine-mounted hydraulic pump. The hydraulic lines were routed within the wing struts. To provide adequate hydraulic power for the fans, the engine had to be operated at full rpm when the BLC system was on, requiring a very low propeller pitch (6°) and similar engine control problems as found on the turboprop XL-19C. The fans sucked air from the perforated upper wing surface and injected it over the flaps via a slot between the trailing edge of the wing and the leading edge of the flaps. One of the original problems with BLC was the lack of lightweight power sources that would not drain needed engine power to provide the BLC air flow. In the mid-1950s, research into missile and jet engine starter power units provided the necessary power sources.

Cessna modified the flaps into a split configuration (the inboard sections deflected an incredible 75° while the outboard sections were limited to 45° of deflection). Air was drawn in by the fans over the inboard flaps and blown out over the outboard flaps and ailerons (which were drooped 15°). The aircraft had a nasty tendency to roll-off vigorously to the right as the wing stalled — due to slight differences in the performance of the two wing-mounted fans. The maiden flight was completed on 10 November 1953 by Cessna test pilot Bob Cranshaw.

For the Cessna-modified L-19A, BLC resulted in a 36 percent reduction in takeoff roll and a 38 percent reduction in landing roll (and, again, a 25 percent reduction in distance required to clear a 50-foot obstacle) compared to the standard L-19A. Total distance required to clear a 50-foot obstacle, on either takeoff or landing, was reduced by 25 percent. In addition, the aircraft was able to fly controllably at significantly lower indicated airspeeds. However, a lower limit was reached when available elevator power proved insufficient to control pitch at the greatly reduced aerodynamic efficiencies at very slow speeds. Alex Petroff, Cessna's Director of Research in 1954, noted in a September of 1955 "Army Aviation Digest" article that "as forward speed goes down still further, say to 10 mph, there is still a real problem." His suggested solutions were to apply BLC to the horizontal tail surfaces and to use an autopilot system that could react faster than a human pilot with larger control deflections. The stall speed with BLC was 32 mph, compared to 43 mph without BLC (and 47 mph for the standard Bird Dog with 60° flaps deployed). With the Bird Dog at 75 mph with BLC working and the flaps fully deployed, the rate of descent was about 1,000 feet-per-minute. In the same configuration but without BLC, the aircraft dropped at 7,000 feet-per-minute!

The BLC-modified L-19A was later turned over to the Aero Physics Laboratory at Mississippi State University (MSU) for further test flights and analysis. MSU had completed earlier BLC experiments on a Schweizer TG3-A sailplane and an Army Piper L-21. Unlike the earlier installations, the L-19's BLC system allowed full blowing and suction power independent of the engine speed. To permit safe flight at the BLC aircraft's reduced speeds, MSU enlarged and altered the shape of the vertical stabilizer and rudder and modified the wing flaps. MSU also installed a hydraulic pump that was able to power the fans without the necessity of running the engine at full power.

• *The first XL-19C with Cessna test pilot Ralph Price at the controls* •
(U.S. Army Aviation Museum)

One of the problems encountered was that the suction perforations in the wing surface tended to clog a bit when flown in the rain. This temporary blockage resulted typically in a 10 percent reduction in the effectiveness of the suction system and led to an accumulation of about two pints of water inside the wing per hour of exposure. To delay air flow separation at the leading edge of the wing during the high angle-of-attack (AOA) flight made possible by the BLC system, the geometry of the L-19's leading edge was modified by increasing the leading edge radius and drooping the leading edge slightly. The configuration of the leading edge of the wing flaps was modified to reduce the gap between it and the trailing edge of the joining wing, thus ensuring smooth and continuous air flow from the wing down across the flap. This reduced, to some extent, the "blanking" effect of the flaps on the horizontal stabilizer at high AOA.

Finally, MSU researchers determined that the conventional landing gear of the L-19 limited the ability of the pilot to rotate on takeoff and achieve the high lift inherent in the BLC design. Therefore, the L-19 was modified into a tricycle landing gear configuration by turning the main landing gear legs 180° and replacing the original tail wheel with a nose gear assembly from a Piper Tri-Pacer.

During the 400 hours of flight tests, MSU test pilots determined that the aircraft could safely be flown as slow as 29 mph and complete a landing roll-out in about 150 feet from touchdown. The aircraft was virtually unstallable.

Carrier Landings

In 1975, as the fall of South Vietnam to the communist invaders from the North became obvious, Vietnamese personnel began using desperate means to escape — particularly those military personnel who had worked closely with American forces and had actively led the fight against the NVA and Viet Cong. VNAF officers fled in whatever aircraft they could commandeer, and others launched to sea in whatever flimsy, and not usually seaworthy, craft they had. The expression "Boat People" soon became part of the language as these people became an international problem. In the midst of the chaos, one VNAF pilot gambled not only with his own life but with the lives of his entire family as well.

On 29 April 1975, the deck of the aircraft carrier USS Midway was packed with its own aircraft plus the HH-53 helicopters of the USAF's 21st Special Operations and 40th Aerospace Rescue and Recovery Squadrons. The Midway's commander, Captain Lawrence Chambers, was

• *The Boundary Layer Control L-19A experimental aircraft after conversion to tricycle landing gear by Mississippi State University's Aero Physics Lab* •
(U.S. Army Aviation Museum)

• *Major Ly touching down on the deck of the USS Midway on 30 April 1975* •
(National Museum of Naval Aviation)

ordered to execute Operation "Frequent Wind" — the evacuation of Saigon.

The first evacuee to land on board was South Vietnam's Vice President, General Nguyen Cao Ky, in a VNAF UH-1 helicopter. Shortly afterward, the Midway began launching the USAF HH-53s to predetermined landing zones in Saigon, setting up a shuttle service that lasted through the night and into the following day. For these USAF pilots, that night marked their first night carrier landing — all were completed without incident and hundreds of evacuees were brought on board the Midway.

April 30th proved to be even more hectic. Not only was the Midway launching and recovering the USAF helicopters but some 60 VNAF and Air America helicopters came and went all morning, including UH-1 Hueys overflowing with up to 50 people. Then, at 1100 hours, Midway lookouts reported to Captain Chambers that an O-1A was approaching the carrier. The Midway deck was covered with helicopters most of whose crews had been transferred off the ship. Chambers' dilemma was com-

pounded by not having the proper support equipment to move the helicopters around to make room for a novice to attempt to land an aircraft without a tailhook.

Chambers' crew attempted to contact the aircraft on emergency frequencies but the pilot continued to circle overhead with his landing lights turned on. When a spotter reported that there were at least four people in the two-place aircraft, all thoughts of forcing the pilot to ditch alongside were abandoned — it was unlikely the passengers of the overloaded Bird Dog could survive the ditching and safely egress before the plane sunk.

After three tries, the Bird Dog pilot, Major Bung Ly, managed to drop a note from a low pass over the deck:

"Can you move the helicopter to the other side, I can land on your runway, I can fly one hour more, we have enough time to move. Please rescue me! Major Bung (Ly), wife and 5 child."

Captain Chambers directed that the arresting wires be removed and that any helicopters that could not be safely and quickly relocated should be pushed over the side! To

• *Major Ly inspects his weatherbeaten O-1 with a couple of USS Midway crewmen* •
(National Museum of Naval Aviation)

get the job done, he called for volunteers. Soon virtually every able-bodied seaman on board, regardless of rank or duty, was out on deck providing the manpower to get the job done. With a 500-foot ceiling, five miles visibility, light rain, and 15 knots of surface wind, Chambers ordered his Chief Engineer to build-up steam to get 25 knots speed into the wind. Warnings about the dangerous downdraft created behind a steaming carrier were transmitted in the blind to Major Ly in both English and Vietnamese. To further complicate the situation, another five UH-1s landed and cluttered the deck. Without hesitation, Chambers ordered them scuttled. Time was running out.

Captain Chambers recalled in an article in the Fall 1993 issue of the national Museum of Aviation History's "Foundation" magazine that "the aircraft cleared the ramp and touched down on center line at the normal touchdown point. Had he been equipped with a tailhook he could have bagged a number three wire. He bounced once and came to a stop abeam of the island, amid a wildly cheering, arms-waving flight deck crew."

Major Ly was escorted to the bridge where Captain Chambers congratulated him on his outstanding airmanship and his bravery in risking everything on a gamble beyond the point of no return without knowing for certain a carrier would be where he needed it. The crew of the USS Midway was so impressed, and admired Major Ly so much, that they established a fund to help him and his family get settled in the United States.

Captain Chambers retired as a Rear Admiral and joined Unisys Corporation of Reston, Virginia. Major Ly and his family live in Orlando, Florida, where he works at the Polynesian Hotel at Disney World.

Marines Do It, Too • The above episode was not the only instance of Bird Dogs landing on aircraft carriers. Several Marine OE-1 (O-1B) aircraft stationed at Okinawa flew out to, and landed on, the anchored USS Ranger in the mid-1960s. In this case, at least, the carrier was expecting them.

Where Are They Now?

As the active duty Army relinquished its Bird Dogs, many continued to serve for years in the National Guard and Army Reserves. All are now retired and many examples are available on the civilian used plane market. There is no challenge to finding a flyable L-19/O-1, except perhaps to your financial health. Considering the aircraft's relatively slow cruising speed, one is unlikely to buy a Bird Dog on the basis of practicality or cost-effectiveness. But for flying fun and for a relatively inexpensive introduction to the world of warbirds, you can't beat the old Bird Dog. Parts are readily available, you can get in and out of most anywhere, and you will have a certified, honest-to-god warbird. A perusal of recent issues of "Trade-A-Plane" turned up at least a half-dozen airplanes in each issue. Prices ranged from a low of $54,000 to a high of $94,900 (for a recently completed restoration), seeming to settle around the $60,000 figure.

At least a dozen examples of the ubiquitous Bird Dog, in both flyable and static-only display condition, can be found in museum collections across the United States:

- *U.S. Army Aviation Museum*, Fort Rucker, Dothan, Alabama
- *Maxwell Aircraft Museum*, Montgomery, Alabama
- *Hurlburt Field Air Park*, Fort Walton Beach, Florida
- *National Museum of Naval Aviation*, Pensacola, Florida
- *Valiant Air Command*, Titusville, Florida
- *Museum of Aviation*, Warner Robbins, Georgia
- *Kalamazoo Aviation History Museum*, Kalamazoo, Michigan
- *U.S. Air Force Museum*, Dayton, Ohio
- *Fort Sill Museum*, Fort Sill, Oklahoma
- *45th Infantry Division Museum*, Oklahoma City, Oklahoma
- *Oregon Air & Space Museum*, Eugene, Oregon
- *U.S. Army Transportation Museum*, Fort Eustis, Virginia ✛

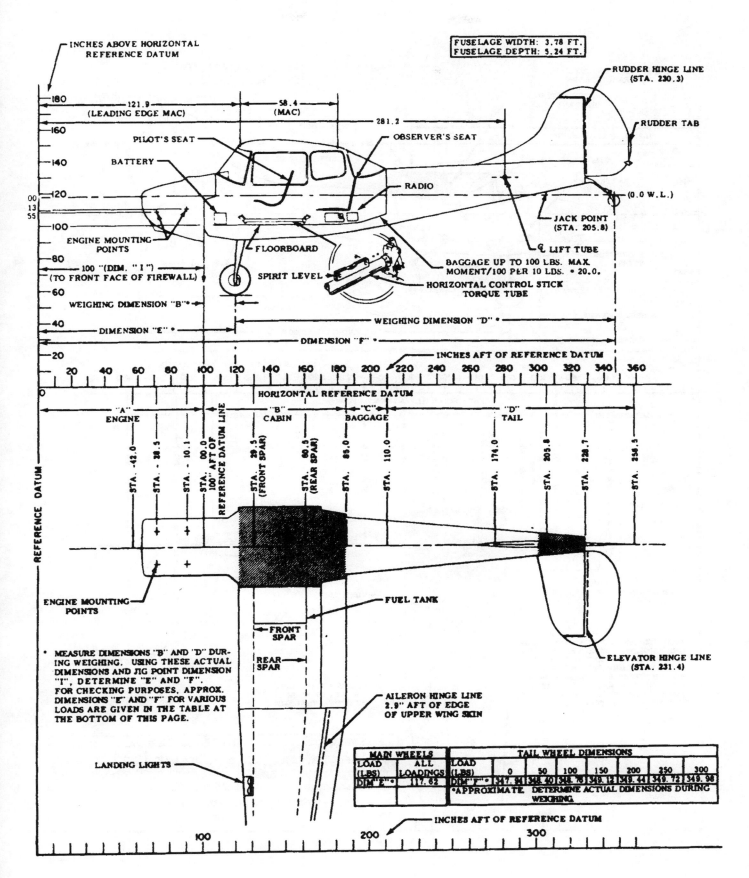

• *An aircraft diagram — L-19E and TL-19E* •
(Army Flight Manual)

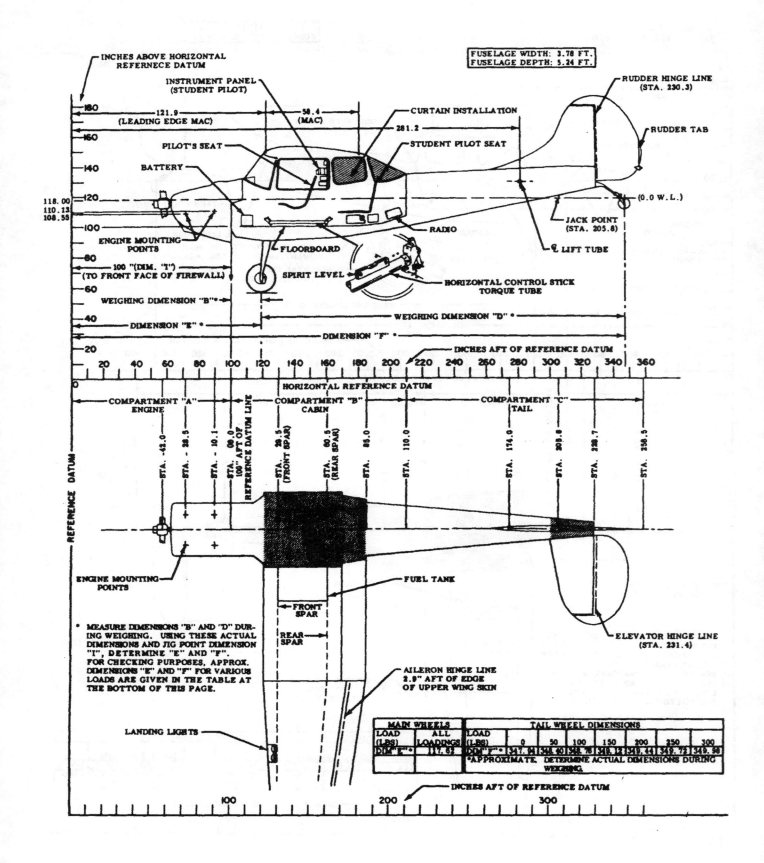

• *An aircraft diagram — TL-19D* •
(Army Flight Manual)

Specifications

Wingspan . . . . 36 ft.
Length . . . . 25 ft.
Height . . . . 7 ft. 6 in.
Maximum Gross Weight
       L-19A, TL-19A . . . . 2,100 lbs.
       L-19D, TL-19E . . . . 2,165 lbs.
       TL-19D . . . . 2,400 lbs.
Engines . . . . 213 horsepower, 6 cylinder, air-cooled, Continental
       L-19A, TL-19A, L-19E, TL-19E O-470-11
       TL-19D O-470-15
Propellers
       L-19A, TL-19A, L-19E, TL-19E . . . . McCauley fixed-pitch, 2 blade, 90 inch, metal
       TL-19D . . . . McCauley, constant-speed, 2 blade, 90 inch, metal
Fuel Capacity . . . . 43 U.S. gallons
Takeoff Ground Roll
       L-19A, TL-19A . . . . 355 ft.
       L-19E, TL-19E . . . . 380 ft.
       TL-19D . . . . 375 ft.
       Seaplane Configuration . . . . 590 ft.
Takeoff Distance Over 50-foot Obstacle
       L-19A, TL-19A . . . . 580 ft.
       L-19E, TL-19E . . . . 634 ft.
       TL-19D . . . . 772 ft.
       Seaplane Configuration . . . . 1,660 ft.
Rate of Climb
       L-19A, TL-19A . . . . 1,290 fpm
       L-19E, TL-19E . . . . 1,230 fpm
       TL-19D . . . . 1,140 fpm
       Seaplane Configuration . . . . 960 fpm
Normal Climb IAS
       L-19A, TL-19A, L-19E, TL19E . . . . 80 mph
       TL-19 . . . . 90 mph
Best Rate of Climb IAS
       L-19A, TL-19A, L-19E, TL19E . . . . 65 mph
       TL-19 . . . . 83 mph
Landing Ground Roll
       L-19A, TL-19A . . . . 260 ft.
       L-19E, TL-19E . . . . 305 ft.
       TL-19D . . . . 250 ft.
       Seaplane Configuration . . . . 560 ft.
Landing Distance Over 50-foot Obstacle
       L-19A, TL-19A . . . . 550 ft.
       L-19E, TL-19E . . . . 605 ft.
       TL-19D . . . . 580 ft.
       Seaplane Configuration . . . . 1,200 ft.
Landing Approach IAS
       L-19A, TL-19A . . . . 67 mph
       L-19E, TL-19E . . . . 71 mph
       TL-19D . . . . 75 mph
       Seaplane Configuration . . . . 78 mph

Specifications continue on next page

Specifications

Maximum Cruise (L-19A, TL-19A, L-19E, TL-19E)
- TAS . . . . 117 mph
- Altitude . . . . 10,000 ft.
- Fuel Flow . . . . 7.8 GPH
- Range (No Reserves) . . . . 491 statute miles

Maximum Cruise (TL-19D)
- TAS . . . . 150 mph
- Altitude . . . . Sea level
- Fuel Flow . . . . 14.2 GPH
- Range (No Reserves) . . . . 649 statute miles

Maximum Range Cruise (L-19A, TL-19A, L-19E, TL-19E)
- TAS . . . . 105 mph
- Altitude . . . . 15,000 ft.
- Fuel Flow . . . . 6.4 GPH
- Range (No Reserves) . . . . 690 statute miles

Maximum Range Cruise (TL-19D)
- TAS . . . . 122 mph
- Altitude . . . . 15,000 ft.
- Fuel Flow . . . . 6.7 GPH
- Range (No Reserves) . . . . 764 statute miles

Maximum Cruise (Seaplane)
- TAS . . . . 112 mph
- Altitude . . . . Sea level
- Fuel Flow . . . . 9.8 GPH
- Range (No Reserves) . . . . 546 statute miles

Maximum Range Cruise (Seaplane)
- TAS . . . . 89 mph
- Altitude . . . . Sea level
- Fuel Flow . . . . 6.3 GPH
- Range (No Reserves) . . . . 590 statute miles

Maximum glide
- IAS. . . . . 75 mph
- Glide Ratio. 7.5:1

Maximum IAS (Flaps Up)
- L-19A, TL-19A . . . . 179 mph
- L-19E, TL-19E, TL-19D . . . . 190 mph

Maximum IAS (Flaps Down, All Aircraft) . . . . 100 mph

Maximum IAS (Front Side Window Open)
- L-19A, TL-19A, L-19E, TL-19E . . . . 120 mph
- TL-19D . . . . 131 mph

Maneuvering IAS
- L-19A, TL-19A . . . . 119 mph
- L-19E, TL-19E. . . . . 134 mph
- TL-19D . . . . 131 mph

Stall Speed (No Flaps)
- L-19A, TL-19A, L-19E, TL-19E . . . . 59 mph
- TL-19D . . . . 56 mph

Stall Speed (Full Flaps)
- L-19A, TL-19A, L-19E, TL-19E . . . . 54 mph
- TL-19D . . . . 51 mph

Model Differences

	L-19A		L-19E	TL-19A	TL-19E	TL-19D
	50-1327 to 53-8067	53-8068 +				
Wing Flaps	Manual	Elect	Elect	Elect	Elect	Elect
Rear Rudder Pedals	Hinged	Hinged	Hinged	Fixed	Fixed	Hinged
CB Panel	LRH Inst Panel & RH Volt Reg Cover	LRH Inst Panel & RH Volt Reg Cover	LLH Side Under Pilot's Window	LRH Inst Panel & RH Volt Reg Cover	LLH Side Under Pilot's Window	LLH Side Under Pilot's Window
Propeller	Fixed-Pitch	Fixed-Pitch	Fixed-Pitch	Fixed-Pitch	Fixed-Pitch	Constant-Speed
Lower Rotating Beacon	Some	Yes	Yes	Some	Yes	Yes
Rear Brake Master Cylinders	No	No	No	Yes	Yes	No
Radio/Intercom Switches on Throttle	No (Radio only on stick)	No (Radio only on stick)	No (Radio only on stick)	Yes	Yes	Yes
Cabin Air Control Lever Labels	"Ram Air" & "Heat"	"Ram Air" & "Heat"	"Ram Air" & "Heat"	"Ram Air" & "Heat"	"Ram Air" & "Heat"	"Ram Air" & "Alt Air"
Emerg. Magneto Switch (Ceiling Rear Seat)	No	No	No	Yes	Yes	No
Rear View Mirror	No	No	No	Yes	Yes	No
Drop Shackle Emergency Salvo Switch	Yes	Yes	Yes	Yes	Yes	No
Aux. Fuel Pump Switch	LRH Instrument Panel	LRH Instrument Panel	LLH Side Under Pilot's Window	LRH Instrument Panel	LLH Side Under Pilot's Window	LLH Side Under Pilot's Window
Battery Switch	LRH Instrument Panel	LRH Instrument Panel	LLH Side Under Pilot's Window	LRH Instrument Panel	LLH Side Under Pilot's Window	LLH Side Under Pilot's Window
Generator Switch	LRH Instrument Panel	LRH Instrument Panel	LLH Side Under Pilot's Window	LRH Instrument Panel	LLH Side Under Pilot's Window	LLH Side Under Pilot's Window
Landing Light Switch	Inst. Panel	Inst. Panel	LH Switch & CB Panel	Inst. Panel	LH Switch & CB Panel	LH Switch & CB Panel
Switch Guard Bar	No	No	Yes	No	Yes	Yes
Battery Generator Gangload Bar	Yes	Yes	No	Yes	No	No
Rear Seat Elevator Trim Wheel	Yes	Yes	No	No	No	Yes
Provisions for Front Seat Survival Kit	Yes	Yes	No	No	No	Yes
Adjustable Rear Seat	Some (-IT)	Some (-IT)	No	No	No	Yes
Air Vents	4 (3 on -IT)	4 (3 on -IT)	3	3	3	4
Master Drop Load Shackle Release Switch on Stick	Yes	Yes	Yes	Yes	Yes	No
Drop Load Switch Panel (4 Shackle System) LH Wing Root	Yes	Yes	Yes	Yes	Yes	No
Removable Rear Seat Blind Flight Curtains	-IT Only	-IT Only	No	No	No	Yes
Underwing Hardpoints	Yes	Yes	Yes	Yes	Yes	No

U-3 Blue Canoe

-chapter 8-

When Cessna introduced its Model 310 light twin aircraft in 1954, it was arguably the sexiest twin-engine aircraft on the market. It was fast, good-looking, and offered the comfort needed by business executives looking to move up from the cabin-class singles like Cessna's own Model 195. Cessna test pilot Hank Waring completed the maiden flight of the first prototype Model 310 on 3 January 1953, and the FAA certified the aircraft in March of 1954. Cessna delivered the first 310s in April. In 1955, Cessna's commercial aircraft sales increased almost 50 percent over the previous year, an increase attributed primarily to the new twin. Commercial sales almost doubled in 1956, and again the Model 310 was a pacesetter. By the time the last Cessna 310R was delivered in 1981, Cessna had produced nearly 5,500 of the sleek, fast, sturdy twins. The aircraft achieved a certain popular recognition when the successful '50s weekly television series, "Sky King," chose the 310 as the aeronautical co-star Songbird. In fact, there were three different aircraft used over the several years the show was produced — a civilianized UC-78 Bobcat (Songbird), a 1958 Cessna 310B (Songbird II), and a 1960 310D (Songbird III).

• *The second USAF L-27A, s/n 57-5847, later redesignated the U-3A* •
(Kansas Aviation Museum/Robert J. Pickett Collection)

Following the 310's excellent acceptance and outstanding performance in the civilian market, the USAF selected it for administrative, liaison, and light cargo duties as a utility transport. In 1957, the USAF ordered 80 Model 310A aircraft to replace aging Beech C-45s, designating them the L-27A (s/n 57-5846 through 57-5925). All 80 were delivered in 1957, and the USAF followed up the next year with a second order for 80 more L-27A aircraft (s/n 58-2107 through 58-2186).

A final contract was issued in 1960 for 35 Model 310E (L-27B) aircraft (s/n 60-6047 through 60-6081). The average fly-away cost of an L-27 under these military contracts was $56,000. All L-27A and L-27B aircraft accommodated a pilot plus four passengers — one in the right front seat and three in the rear bench seat. Although equipped with full dual controls, U-3s were most often flown by a single pilot. In 1962, the L-27A was redesignated as the U-3A, the L-27B as the U-3B.

The original U-3A aircraft were powered by six-cylinder Continental O-470-M engines producing 240 horsepower at 2600 rpm. Maximum gross weight was limited to 4,830 pounds. The U-3B aircraft were powered by fuel-injected six-cylinder Continental IO-470-D engines producing 260 horsepower at 2625 rpm. Maximum gross weight for the U-3B was 4,990 pounds. Besides the engines, the main differences between the two models were the addition of wing de-icing and propeller anti-icing equipment, more sophisticated radio and navigation equipment, an aft-swept vertical tail, and a third side window on each side on the later model. Many of the earlier U-3A versions were later modified to incorporate the U-3B's all-weather gear.

The USAF distinctive blue paint scheme for the U-3 in its utility transport role quickly led to the unofficial, but universally recognized, nickname of "Blue Canoe." In 1960, 25 L-27A Blue Canoes were transferred to the U.S. Army. Later, the Army acquired 13 U-3Bs from the USAF. In the late '50s, the U.S. Navy acquired eight U-3As from the USAF and two from the Army, assigning them BuNos 159073, 159074, 528176, 575849, 575891, 575916, 582111, 582123, 582131, and 582176. In the early '60s, the Navy acquired two more U-3Bs from the Army, assigning them BuNos 606047 and 606068. Despite the application of service-unique paint schemes on the Army and Navy aircraft, the U-3A/B will be known forever as the Blue Canoe.

In all three services, the U-3 fulfilled its staff and administrative support duties around the world. Typically, one or two aircraft were assigned to a base for pilot proficiency flights and for transporting personnel between bases. Many saw service as testbeds for new avionics equipment and as survey aircraft for military navigational routes.

USAF U-3s served in Southeast Asia from the beginning of the Vietnam War. Two U-3B aircraft arrived in the theater in May of 1963 to support the Farm Gate aerial reconnaissance program by transporting film, photographs, and intelligence reports, gathered and prepared by the USAF RB-57E, RF-101, and RB-26 aircraft, to combat units throughout South Vietnam.

The "Me-Too"

A unique and relatively unknown use of the U-3 was as chase plane and introductory trainer for the Lockheed U-2 high-altitude reconnaissance aircraft. The U-2 was essentially a powered glider produced only in a single-seat version, and every pilot's first flight was a solo flight in what was recognized as one of the most difficult airplane in anyone's inventory to land properly. The 100th

• *A U-3A, s/n 57-5904, after being repainted for the Army in white over brown* •
(Kansas Aviation Museum/Robert J. Pickett Collection)

• *The first USAF L-27B, s/n 60-6047, redesignated the U-3B in 1962* •
(Cessna Aircraft Company)

Strategic Reconnaissance Wing, Davis-Monthan AFB, Arizona, conducted a search for an existing dual-control aircraft that could replicate U-2 airspeeds and glide paths to permit some lead-in training before a pilot was turned loose in a U-2. After carefully evaluating all the available aircraft, the U-3A was chosen, based in part on its dual control yokes that allowed similar hands-on techniques to the hefty control yoke/column found in the U-2. According to Fred McNeill, who was a U-3 chase pilot for several years, the straight tail U-3A was selected rather than the swept tail U-3B because the swept tail version was too unstable at the slow speeds needed to chase or simulate U-2 approaches.

These U-3A chase planes had turn rates, descent profiles, and traffic pattern airspeeds very similar to those of the U-2, or "U-Bird," as the spy plane was nicknamed. Airspeed control in the U-2 was critical both in its descent profile and its rigid "T-Speeds" (required airspeed when crossing the runway threshold that varied depending on landing weight). When flying in formation on a chase mission, the U-2 and U-3 became known as the U-2 and the "Me-Too." The U-3 was able to intercept a descending U-2 at 15,000-18,000 feet at 160-180 KIAS, stay on

• *The New Mexico National Guard roadrunner emblem painted on both sides of the fuselage of the U-3B pictured below* •
(Kansas Aviation Museum/Robert J. Pickett Collection)

its wing through the descent and traffic pattern, and slow to a typical U-2 "T-Speed" of 65-70 KIAS (75-80 mph, about 10-15 mph above the U-3's stall speed and 15-20 mph below its minimum single-engine control speed). The chase U-3 always flew on the U-2's right wing and

• *The first U-3B, s/n 60-6047, in a later incarnation with the New Mexico National Guard in Santa Fe* •
(Kansas Aviation Museum/Robert J. Pickett Collection)

• A U-3B, s/n 60-6052, in the unique colors of the Montana Air National Guard. The Air National Guard Minuteman emblem is on the tail •
(Kansas Aviation Museum/Robert J. Pickett Collection)

• A USAF U-3A like the ones used by the 100th SRW to chase the U-2 •
(Kansas Aviation Museum/Robert J. Pickett Collection)

• A U-3A tucked in tight with a 100th SRW U-2 over Tucson, AZ, in November of 1972. The U-2 still has wing "pogos" installed •
(Fred McNeill)

the ground and usually allowed to fall away on takeoff) remained secured for the entire flight to preclude inadvertent scraping of those long wings.

The U-3 chase pilot took off and climbed to 15,000 feet to wait for the U-2 first-solo pilot. After they had joined up, the U-3 followed the new U-2 pilot through some approach-to-stall exercises and observed while the student pumped fuel from the heavy wing to the light wing to trim the aircraft properly for traffic pattern work (the older U-2's 103-foot wet wing required manual fuel transfer to trim the aircraft laterally prior to landing). Then, after the U-3 chase pilot had calibrated his airspeed indicator against the U-2's airspeed indicator, the two aircraft (U-2 and "Me-Too") descended into the traffic pattern. The U-3 followed the U-2 through the traditional three traffic patterns and landings (breaking off the chase at ten feet and rejoining after the U-2's touch-and-go). This entire process was called the "Dragon Lady Checkout." Successful completion cleared the new U-2 pilot for solo training to learn the intricacies of strategic reconnaissance missions in an aircraft capable of extreme high altitude flight for extended periods (above 70,000 feet for up to 12-16 hours at a time).

discontinued the chase at ten feet above the runway — when a souped-up Ford El Camino with a 454 cubic-inch engine would sprint onto the runway and chase the "U-Bird" all the way to touchdown, calling out height above the runway (such as "three feet. . .two feet. . .one foot, hold it off, hold it off."). For the U-2, a full stall landing was imperative.

The pilot's eye-to-ground height in the U-3 was almost identical to that in the U-2, making it a useful pre-solo trainer. The U-3 in its "Me-Too" persona was used in what became known as the "Dragon Lady Pattern" to prepare new U-2 pilots for the real thing. The U-3 instructor managed the throttles to ensure proper simulation of U-2 glide and "float" characteristics. Fred McNeill says the student was required to "level-off at one foot over the numbers and hold it there for the entire length of the 12,500-foot runway." The U-3 with the proper power settings responded much like a U-2 with power-off. When the student was able to complete the exercise successfully, and repeat it satisfactorily, the instructor landed the U-3 and taxied up to a waiting U-2. The student hopped out of the U-3A and into the U-2. For this first flight, the removable wingtip "pogo" landing gear (designed to support the wings on

• The 100th SRW U-3A chases the 100th SRW U-2 through descent to traqffic pattern. Note the U-3's wingtip tank and top of engine nacelle •
(Fred NcNeil)

There were only two U-3A aircraft assigned to the 100th SRW and usually no more than three U-3A chase pilots at any one time. They were, however, indispensable both for that initial training and for routine chase missions to assist pilots fatigued after long-duration solo flights or during in-flight emergencies. Fred McNeill remembered the program well since his last flight in the USAF was flying the U-3 on a U-2 chase mission.

• A USAF U-3B is bracketed by a pair of USAF T-37Bs •
(Kansas Aviation Museum/Robert J. Pickett Collection)

Foreign Sales

Several foreign services purchased variants of the Cessna 310 for similar duties. In 1961, Thailand bought two 310F models — one for personal and VIP transportation for the Prime Minister of Thailand (Marshal Sarit Thanarat) and another for the Royal Thai Police Force. That same year, two 310Fs were delivered to Kuala Lumpur for use by the Prime Minister of the Malaya States.

In early 1975, the government of Zaire purchased 15 Model 310R aircraft for use by the Zaire Air Force for multi-engine training and liaison duties. The first aircraft

• The U.S. Air Force Museum's U-3A, s/n 58-2124 •
(U.S. Air Force Museum)

was delivered in January at a ceremony attended by Colonel Kikunda, Chief of the Zaire Air Force; General Fallu, Zaire military attaché to the United States; Dwane Wallace, Cessna's Chairman of the Board; and Russ Meyer, Executive Vice President. Besides the usual military duties, the Zaire Air Force 310s were used to support the country's widespread mining, construction, and road building operations.

Mustering Out the "Blue Canoe"

Gradually, military U-3s were turned over to Army and Air National Guard units, and some were used for administrative duties by USAF officers assigned as liaison officers to Civil Air Patrol wings around the country. The Air Force Museum at Wright-Patterson AFB near Dayton, Ohio, has a U-3A from the second contract lot (s/n 58-2124) on display. This aircraft had been transferred to the Army and later to the Indiana National Guard before being turned over to the museum. The Museum repainted it in the USAF blue and white scheme.

Other museums reported to have U-3 aircraft on display include:

- *Pima Air & Space Museum*, Tucson, Arizona
- *Castle Air Museum*, Atwater, California
- *Travis Air Force Museum*, Vacaville, California
- *Lowry Heritage Museum*, Denver, Colorado
- *Museum of Aviation*, Warner Robbins, Georgia
- *Grissom Air Park*, Bunker Hill, Indiana
- *Liberal Air Museum*, Liberal, Kansas
- *45th Infantry Division, Museum*, Oklahoma City, OK
- *South Dakota Air & Space Museum*, Rapid City, South Dakota
- *Hill Aerospace Museum*, Ogden, Utah

Although there are numerous 310/U-3 aircraft flying in the United States, it can be difficult to determine whether a particular aircraft was ever actually flown by the military, given the fact that the aircraft were purchased off-the-shelf with the only real differences from the corresponding civilian models being the use of military radio and navigational equipment. Some 310 owners have taken to painting non-U-3 Cessna 310s in the distinctive USAF "Blue Canoe" paint scheme. ✦

• A nicely restored U-3A on display at the 1994 Labor Day airshow in Mineral Wells, Texas •
(Walt Shiel)

U-3A

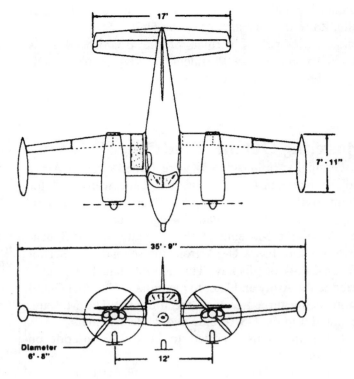

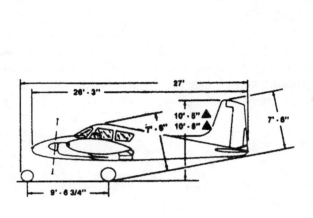

• A three-view drawing of the U-3A. •
(Air Force Flight Manual)

U-3B

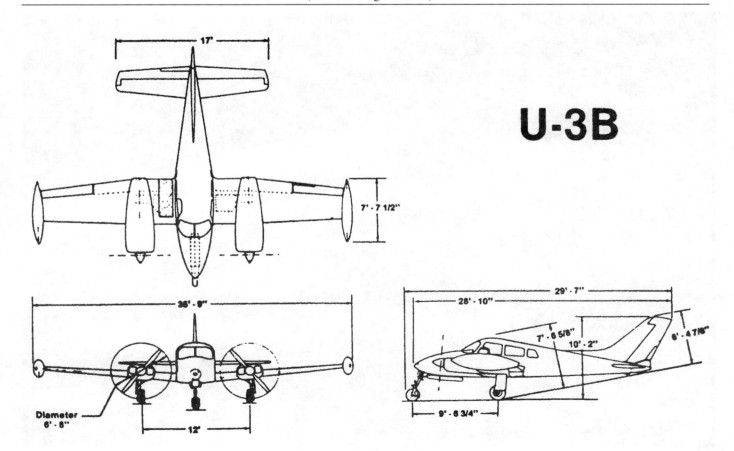

• A three-view drawing of the U-3B •
(Air Force Flight Manual)

Specifications

	U-3A	U-3B
Wingspan	35 ft. 9 in.	35 ft. 9 in.
Length	27 ft.	29 ft. 7 in.
Height	10 ft. 5 in. (early)	10 ft. 2 in.
	10 ft. 8 in. (late)	
Engines	O-470-M	IO-470-D
Horsepower	240 hp	260 hp
Maximum Engine Speed	2,600 rpm	2,625 rpm
Maximum Gross Weight		
Takeoff	4,830 lbs.	4,990 lbs.
Landing	4,600 lbs.	4,750 lbs.
Empty Weight	3,145 lbs.	3,330 lbs.
	3,200 lbs (modified)	
Fuel Capacity, U.S. gallons		
Mains	102	102
Tips	31	31
Total Usable	120	120
Cruise TAS		
Maximum	200 mph	210 mph
65% Power @ 10,000 feet	175 mph	184 mph
Total Cruise Fuel Flow		
65% Power @ 10,000 feet	23.4 gph	24.2 gph
Takeoff Ground Roll	1,450 ft.	1,300 ft.
Normal Liftoff IAS	95 mph	95 mph
Minimum Control IAS		
Single Engine	95 mph	95 mph
Landing Ground Roll	900 ft.	950 ft.
Best Rate of Climb		
Two Engines	1600 fpm	1700 fpm
Single Engine	340 fpm	400 fpm
Maximum IAS		
Flaps U-p	248 mph	252 mph
15°Flaps	160 mph	160 mph
45° Flaps	140 mph	140 mph
Window Open	130 mph	130 mph
Landing Light Extended	140 mph	140 mph
Stall IAS		
Flaps Up	80 mph	82 mph
45° Flaps	65 mph	73 mph
Maneuvering IAS	164 mph	167 mph
Best Glide IAS	107 mph	107 mph
Glide Ratio	12.7:1	12.7:1
G Limits		
Gear Up	+3.8/-1.5	+3.8/-1.5
Gear Down	+2.0	+2.0

T-37 Tweety Bird

-chapter 9-

On 15 April 1952, the United States Air Force (USAF) announced a competition for its first-ever primary jet trainer. The Request for Proposals was titled Trainer Experimental, and the requested aircraft was dubbed the TX. The new aircraft was to bridge the performance gap between the prop-driven trainers (North American T-28 Trojan and Beech T-34 Mentor) and the Lockheed T-33 Shooting Star advanced jet trainer. The USAF decided that a lower-performance jet trainer was needed for the primary phase of pilot training.

The new trainer aircraft was to be designed from the ground up as a flying classroom with the emphasis on ease of instruction. Simplicity, durability, and ruggedness were to be as important as performance. The USAF intentionally kept the design requirements to a minimum to allow maximum flexibility for the designers. These requirements included:

- Good low-speed handling characteristics.
- Good high-altitude maneuverability.
- Service ceiling above 30,000 feet.
- Fuel for 20 landings within a two-hour lesson.
- Maximum final approach speed of 113 KIAS.
- Maximum empty weight of 4,000 pounds.
- The ability to takeoff and land over a 50-foot obstacle in less than 4,000 feet.

The USAF expected its new trainer to exhibit handling characteristics similar to those of the current jet fighters (remember, this was in 1952) as well as the ability to provide an introduction to high altitude flight. Beyond the basic design parameters, the USAF let the

• *First prototype TX, with the "TX-001" label before being officially named the XT-37* •
(Kansas Aviation Museum/Robert J. Pickett Collection)

responding design teams specify exactly how the new trainer should look and fly. In the fall of 1952, eight manufacturers submitted a total of fifteen designs.

Cessna's advanced design team was still basking in the praise from their successful Army L-19 project when they were tasked with developing the winning proposal for the TX program. They soon settled on a game plan centered around a single proposed design with no contract options or alternative designs. The final Cessna proposal — the twin-jet Model 318 with side-by-side seating — was turned over to the USAF at Wright-Patterson AFB in Dayton, Ohio, barely six months after the original USAF announcement. Both the seating arrangement and redundant engines seemed to be contrary to what the USAF evaluators were expecting — all the trainers of the era, both jet-engined and propeller-driven, had only one engine and used tandem seating. Cessna's management felt they had a better idea.

The Model 318 sat low to the ground, a feature that required a lot of duckwalking during preflight inspections but minimized the need for maintenance stands and ladders. Designated the T-37 by the USAF, the Model 318 was declared the winner in December of 1952. The Cessna jet trainer's design included:

- Low wing with 3° dihedral and double aluminum spars.
- Wide-tread landing gear for ground handling stability.
- Side-by-side ejection seats capable of safe ejection at altitudes down to 100 feet and airspeeds as slow as 100 KIAS.
- Jettisonable clamshell canopy.
- Miniscule turbojets in thickened wing roots.
- Conventional, mechanical flight controls.
- Hydraulically actuated high-lift, slotted flaps.
- Hydraulically actuated speedbrake.
- Electric aileron, elevator, and rudder trim tabs.

USAF's First Primary Jet Trainer

Although other jet trainers had been developed as of 1953 — notably Lockheed's T-33 Shooting Star — none had been developed from concept to production specifically as a trainer. Even the ubiquitous T-33 had been an evolution of the P-80/F-80 series of fighters. In addition, the T-37 would be the first military jet to be designed, developed, and produced by one of the premier manufacturers of light, reciprocating-engine airplanes. The aircraft design, performance, and "feel" were all influenced by a desire to ease the transition from the existing prop-driven trainers to jets.

The Air Force was becoming an all-jet service with aircraft ranging from the slick B-47 bomber to the jet fighters (F-86, F-89, etc.). If there was one common trait among these aircraft it was the "dark corner" in their flight envelopes, a chronic problem for these early high-performance jet aircraft. The jet had a tendency to snap out of control into the aptly named "post-stall gyration" when the pilot inadvertently exceeded the critical angle-of-attack. Even the T-33 advanced trainer, despite its straightforward design and overall benign handling, had its share of ego-busting and potentially dangerous "surprises" within its flight envelope.

Having experienced higher than desired accident rates for the high-performance jets due to those "dark corners," the USAF dictated that their new primary jet trainer be spinnable with a well-defined and predictable recovery. Flight tests of the T-37 prototypes showed the aircraft to be, indeed, spinnable. However, the spin characteristics were not sufficiently predictable, and the recovery was less than optimum. Cessna's solution was to install the spin strakes along either side of the T-37's blunt nose. There has been a recurring rumor that these strakes were installed to force the aircraft to spin — not true. They were installed to ensure predictability in the spin and recovery.

On to Production

With the USAF contract in hand, Cessna quickly had to hire enough personnel to turn what had thus far been a paperwork exercise into a flying airplane. The first challenge was to produce the three required flight test prototype aircraft. Two dozen, mostly young, engineers were quickly hired and put to work. One of them was Bruce Peterman, who is now Senior Vice President of Aircraft Development at Cessna. Peterman recalls:

"Someone figured out that the average experience for each of the T-37 engineers was about two and a half years, but the leaders were experienced, and what we might have lacked in experience we made up in enthusiasm and determination. We had our slide rules and information sources and standard references. The process was basically what it is today, except that we did what we had to do without the benefit of a mountain of analytical data now available at the touch of a key."

Another position that needed to be filled was a suitable flight test pilot for the project. Cessna had test pilots, but none of them were experienced in jet aircraft. Management found the solution in Bob Hagan, a member of the engineering staff responsible for aircraft weight-and-balance calculations. Hagan had flown the Republic F-84 Thunderjet while serving in the USAF and had flown combat missions in both World War II and the Korean War. Early in 1954, he was reassigned as a test pilot and sent to Edwards AFB, California, to complete a test pilot training course. Hagan was closely involved in all phases of the development of the T-37 prototypes.

The first XT-37 prototypes (serial numbers 54-716 through 54-718) had an empty gross weight of 5,000 pounds and were powered by a pair of Turbomeca

• *First XT-37, s/n 54-716, in flight with Cessna test pilot Bob Hagan at the controls. This aircraft has a flight test probe on the left wingtip and does not yet have the "spin strakes" on the nose* •
(Kansas Aviation Museum/Robert J. Pickett Collection)

Marboré turbojets, christened XJ69-T-9 and built under license in the United States by Continental. Each engine generated a whopping 920 pounds of static thrust. The fuselage was a semi-monocoque design of all metal construction. Low and high speed wind tunnel tests were completed at Wichita State University and Cornell University during the design and development process, and spin tests were completed in the Wright Aeronautical Laboratories' vertical wind tunnel at Wright-Patterson AFB.

All the detailed paperwork, construction, and testing were validated when Bob Hagan took off in 54-716 from the Wichita Municipal Airport shortly after one o'clock on the afternoon of 12 October 1954 on the XT-37's maiden flight. The flight lasted one hour and five minutes. At 15,000 feet, Hagan joined-up with his two chase planes — a Cessna 310 and a USAF T-33. After landing, Hagan reported, "I think it's going to be a real sweet airplane." Cessna quickly followed 54-716 with roll-out of the

remaining two prototypes. Number two (54-717) first flew on 6 January 1955, and 54-718 completed its inaugural flight on 3 May 1955. Cessna also produced a static loads test aircraft (54-2731) under a separate contract. Over 1,000 test flights were flown on the three prototypes by both Cessna and USAF pilots at Wichita, Kansas; Wright-Patterson AFB, Ohio; and Edwards AFB, California. On its 205th test flight, the original prototype XT-37 (54-716) crashed during spin testing. Flight tests demonstrated the following performance:

- Top speed — 393 mph (at 35,000 feet).
- Stall speed — 92 mph (flaps up), 77 mph (flaps down).
- Service ceiling — 39,800 feet (both engines), 19,200 feet (single engine).
- Maximum range — 935 statute miles (with 30-minute reserve). (More on range later!)
- Maximum climb rate — 3,000 feet-per-minute.

Cessna made changes on the prototypes during the flight

• *Second pre-production T-37A, s/n 54-2730. Note the angular dorsal fin, angled rudder lower edge, "spin strakes" on the nose, taller rudder, shorter span of the horizontal stabilizer, and new ventral fin compared to the XT-37* •
(Kansas Aviation Museum/Robert J. Pickett Collection)

test program to rectify deficiencies and to improve the stall and spin characteristics. These changes included:

- Lengthened fuselage and rudder for stability.
- Upswept wingtip undersurfaces for a milder stall.
- Reduced horizontal stabilizer span.
- Cabin ventilation air scoop ahead of the windscreen for improved cabin ventilation.
- Dual ventilating air intakes on the nose cone for electronic equipment carried in the nose section.
- Enlarged engine inlets.
- "Spin strakes" added along either side of the nose.
- Stall warning spoilers added above the engine pods.
- Shortened pitot tube.
- Longer, deeper, and more angular dorsal fin.
- Added ventral fin.
- Taller vertical tail and rudder with a longer rudder horn and an angled, rather than straight, lower edge.
- Landing lights moved from the nose to the wings.

Several other modifications were tried out on the prototypes but were not included in the final version of the aircraft. These unincorporated modifications included vortex generators and aerodynamic spoilers on the wings,

automatic deploying wing leading edge slats, and extended wing leading edges. At the conclusion of the flight test program, the design baseline was established and the resulting design was designated the T-37A.

The USAF ordered 11 pre-production T-37As (serial numbers 54-2729 through 54-2739), with all of the above modifications incorporated. The first pre-production airplane, serial number 54-2729, was rolled out of the Prospect Plant on the west side of Wichita (renamed the Military Aircraft Division in April of 1957) on 3 September 1955. The official acceptance flight test of 54-2729 was completed on 27 September, and the aircraft was delivered to the USAF in June of 1956. These original T-37A aircraft boasted an empty weight of 3,870 pounds and a maximum gross weight of 6,400 pounds. Although the engines cranked out only 920 pounds of thrust apiece, the little jet was able to takeoff and land over a 50-foot obstacle in less than 2,500 feet (but not with a student pilot at the controls!). The second pre-production aircraft, s/n 54-2730, was turned over to the Air Force Flight Test Center (AFFTC) at Edwards AFB, California, in October 1956 for its USAF flight test validation.

The new trainer quickly impressed USAF maintenance personnel with its ease of maintenance, ready access to all components, and low overall maintenance requirements. In fact, it was possible to completely change-out a T-37 engine in 30 minutes total labor time with nothing more exotic than a small portable overhead crane.

Meanwhile, Cessna and the USAF began a publicity campaign for the new trainer. From 1955 through 1961, Captain Robert Fogg was assigned to the Cessna plant as the USAF's Chief of Flight Test and Acceptance. Captain Fogg toured with the new aircraft around the United States, South America, and Europe, showing off the talents of the Air Force's newest trainer in airshows. In 1959 alone, Fogg and the T-37 performed in Guatemala in January, Colombia in April, and at the Paris Air Salon in June. He also performed at T-37 delivery ceremonies at Reese AFB in Lubbock, Texas — a performance carried on the NBC "Today" TV show. Frequently, he performed on the same program as the Air Force Thunderbirds or the Navy Blue Angels. Fogg would perform most of the same maneuvers — but without exceeding the airfield boundaries (something the hot jets of that day could not hope to emulate). He usually finished his routine with an inverted pass just a few feet above the runway. The crowds loved it, frequently declaring that the "little airplane was the best." In October of 1962, following Captain Fogg's excellent series of demonstration flight performances, the Air Force Thunderbirds considered acquiring the T-37B to replace their F-100 Super Sabres. However, they elected instead to transition to the McDonnell Douglas F-4C Phantom (despite a very brief, and unsuccessful, use of the Republic F-105 Thunderchief).

Captain Fogg's trip to Colombia in 1959 resulted in massive publicity and media attention for Cessna's new aircraft. Fogg and the T-37 dazzled the crowds at the Columbia National Aviation Week festivities in Bogota. Over 150,000 Colombians turned out and Fogg flew the commander of the Colombian Air Force, General Alberto Pauwels, and retired 68-year-old Colombian Army

• Second T-37A, s/n 54-2730, on the famous Rogers Dry Lake runway at Edwards AFB, California, 19 October 1956 •
(U.S. Air Force)

• *The right nose compartment, housing the communication and navigation equipment, opens with only two lathces* •
(Walt Shiel)

• *Left aft nose compartment open, exposing air conditioning and electrical power gear. To the left (forward) is the battery compartment* •
(Walt Shiel)

Colonel Carlos Doya (also Colombia's first licensed pilot) on orientation flights. After returning from his first-ever jet flight, Doya declared, "It was the greatest thrill I've had since I received my pilot's license in the '20s."

The T-37 flight training program was initially set-up as a civilian contract operation. The first aircraft were delivered to contract schools at Bainbridge AFB, Georgia, and James Connally AFB, Florida. In preparation for the first students, a cadre of civilian flight instructors was checked-out in the new jets by USAF instructors at Waco, Texas, in late 1957.

A test class of student pilots was trained in the initial T-37A aircraft in early 1958 under "Project Pam" at Bainbridge AFB. In March, Second Lieutenant Thomas W. Beaghan became the first student to solo in the new jet. The second T-37A class at Bainbridge AFB started training in November of 1958 and became part of the evaluation program for the eventual "All-Through Jet" training syllabus under USAF's Project All-Jet. In January of 1959, Second Lieutenant Gene McGinnis became the first USAF student to solo in a jet trainer without ever having received training in a propeller-driven aircraft. McGinnis' total dual instruction time before his initial solo was ten hours and one minute.

Shortly after its integration into the USAF jet fleet, the little T-37 began "endearing" itself to pilots and maintenance personnel with the ear-piercing whine and squeal generated by the combination of its engine inlet and 21,730 rpm centrifugal flow compressor section. When first heard — from a distance — the sound might cause one to think of a flock of canaries all singing at once. Up close, it is hardly as charming. After a few months on a T-37 flightline, one finds the sound annoying. After a year, it is a major irritant that has caused hearing loss in the high-pitch region among many T-37 instructor pilots and maintenance personnel. The particularly piercing quality of the sound and its decibel level required the use of special hearing protectors for pilots and ground crew alike — these were quickly dubbed "Mickey Mouse Ears." In fact, maintenance personnel, who spent long hours on the flightline exposed to the Tweet's audible torment, were required to wear both the standard foam ear plugs and the "Mickey Mouse Ears." As a result of the airplane's noisy personality, nicknames were created every time the airplane cranked up. Some of the more popular were:

- Tweety Bird
- Tweet
- Squeak
- Sixty-six-hundred-pound dog whistle
- The only machine made by man capable of turning JP-4 (military jet fuel) directly into noise
- Baby Jet
- Slowest jet in the Air Force

The one that stuck, however, was Tweety Bird. The diminutive jet was never christened officially by the USAF, but everyone called it the Tweety Bird or Tweet — as everyone still does to this day.

As a trainer, the T-37 quickly validated Cessna's design. Its safety record was unsurpassed. The Tweet achieved a new standard for military jets with an operational readiness rate of 98 percent. Its acquisition and operating costs were the lowest on record. The side-by-side seating allowed instructors to monitor their students in flight in a manner never before seen in a primary military trainer. The little jet's maneuverability and stability throughout its flight envelope made it a perfect introduction to military jet aviation for new students. Its broad performance envelope ideally prepared students for the next step in their training — the T-33 and, later, the supersonic Northrop T-38 Talon.

A total of 534 A-models were produced, the original 11 plus the following serial numbers:

- 55-2883 through 55-2972 and 55-4302 through 55-4321.
- 56-3464 through 56-3590.
- 57-2230 through 57-2352.
- 58-1861 through 58-1977.
- 59-241 through 59-285.

The 200th T-37A was produced in July of 1958 and the 300th one in February of 1959, when the production rate hit 15 aircraft per month. However, the production rate soon soared and, at its peak, Cessna was cranking out one T-37 every 11 hours and 12 minutes during the eight-hour working day. With this greatly expanded production, the last T-37A rolled out onto the flightline at Wichita in October of 1959.

In April of 1959, Cessna and the USAF agreed on a configuration update for the T-37, and on 6 November 1959, the first T-37B (59-286) was introduced into the USAF fleet. This evolution of the Tweet, which Cessna called the Model 318B, included upgrading the aircraft to 1,025-pound-thrust Continental/Teledyne J69-T-25 engines, which were virtually the same size as the original J69-T-9. The new engine provided better reliability, increased longevity, less maintenance, and a fully automatic altitude compensating fuel control, along with its higher performance. In addition, new instrumentation was incorporated in the B-model — including a VOR navigation receiver, military-standard UHF radio transceiver, and a redesigned instrument panel layout.

Nine follow-on contracts were awarded, bringing the total T-37B production to 552 aircraft between 1959 and 1968. The prototypes and the initial production A-model aircraft were produced at the Prospect Plant, but the bulk of the T-37 aircraft were built at the Wallace Plant. The following B-Model lots and USAF serial numbers were produced:

- 59-286 through 59-390
- 60-071 through 60-200
- 61-459 through 61-473, 61-2494 through 61-2508, and 61-2915 through 61-2919.
- 62-5950 through 62-5956.
- 64-13409 through 64-13466.
- 65-10823 through 65-10826.
- 66-7960 through 66-8006.

• *A Continental J69-T-25 ready for installation, seen from the intake end* •
(Walt Shiel)

• Looking down the left engine inlet at an installed J69-T-25 •
(Walt Shiel)

- 67-14730 through 67-14768 and 67-22240 through 67-22262.
- 68-7981 through 68-8084.

Once the initial USAF delivery requirements were filled, production was reduced to four aircraft per month, where it was maintained until the start of production of the A-37 (a ground attack version of the T-37). In mid-1967, the 1000th T-37 (67-14745) was delivered to the USAF. Cessna delivered the last T-37B in 1968. All T-37s were assigned Cessna constructor numbers between 40,000 and 44,999.

In 1959, Cessna was awarded a $3.5 million contract to deliver T-37s to Peru for the Peruvian Air Force's planned all-jet pilot training program. Cessna and the USAF worked diligently to garner more overseas sales — such as the orientation plant tours and T-37 flights given to visiting Chilean Air Force officers in April of 1960. In the summer of 1961 as the first Peruvian T-37s were being delivered, Cessna received a second $5 million contract for delivery of T-37s to a variety of foreign countries under the Military Assistance Program (MAP).

Almost all A-models were eventually returned to Cessna for conversion to B-model standards (some had been lost to accidents and others were assigned to non-training duties and were not included in the conversion plans). The conversion program at Cessna was named Project Turnaround. Duane Moore, then Military Aircraft Division Production Manager, took on the task of scheduling the massive upgrade program. The first T-37A entered the modification line at Cessna in April of 1959, and the last converted T-37B rolled off that line in July of 1960 — sixteen months to convert 521 aircraft and install new engines. The rate of conversions was intentionally kept low for the first several months and then increased dramatically for the last half of the project. Moore was counting on the "learning curve" for his engineers and technicians, meaning they were expected to be able to complete the jobs faster the more they had done. It worked, and Cessna held to their planned schedule. All A-model aircraft with the following exceptions were converted to B-model specifications under Cessna's "Project Turnaround:" 54-2731, 54-4302, 54-4304, 56-3495, 56-3502, 56-3510 through 56-3513, 56-3525, 56-3528, 56-3485, and 57-2271.

Syllabus Changes

Under Project All-Jet between 1961 and 1964, the T-37 training syllabus included 130 flying hours before the student pilot graduated to the Lockheed T-33 for advanced training. Although the T-37 was easy to fly and ideal for instructional purposes, it was still expensive to operate and maintain compared to propeller-driven trainers. Its pure turbojet engines burned a healthy 154 gallons of jet fuel per hour at its normal cruise speed of 300 KTAS. So, although several thousand USAF pilots were first introduced to military aviation in a jet during that three-year span, in 1964 the USAF purchased Cessna T-41s (a militarized Cessna Model 172) for 30 hours of primary training and reduced the T-37 syllabus to 90 flying hours.

• T-37B, s/n 67-14745 (the 1000th T-37 produced), tucked in tight for the camera. Note the B-model's UHF blade antenna on belly and upper rotating beacon just aft of cockpit •
(Kansas Aviation Museum/Robert J. Pickett Collection)

• *1000th T-37, s/n 67-14745. Circles along leading edge of each wing mark the refueling caps.*
Red line across top of fuselage aft of cockpit marks location of engine turbine wheels •
(Cessna Aircraft)

And then along came the full-motion-base simulators in the 1970s. Prior to their introduction, Air Training Command (ATC) ground training had included fixed-base Link trainers with no visual displays. All the needles and instruments responded to control inputs, and instrument navigation and approaches could be practiced and reviewed afterwards on a plot board display. The first "real" simulators used terrain modeling boards, consisting of handcrafted landscapes like the ones created by model train aficionados. A tiny camera was mounted on a traveling boom, which tracked the course flown by the simulator pilot, to provide visual feedback to the cathode ray tube displays in the cockpits. Cockpits were mounted on large hydraulic actuators to provide six-degrees-of-freedom motion. One of the big selling points was a potential to save money previously spent on fuel (this was during the OPEC scares), so ATC slashed in-aircraft instrument sorties. Performance on instrument checkrides promptly deteriorated. Getting the budget for those lost flying hours back from Congress proved much more difficult than giving it up.

The simulators were later upgraded with computer generated imagery to replace the terrain boards. This was a major improvement, and eliminated some of the idio-syncrasies of the older terrain boards, such as: fluctuating image quality, the possibility to fly off the "edge of the world," and the possibility of running the camera into the "ground." In the terrain board simulators, whenever the student was close to the "ground," the instructor kept a finger poised above the simulator's FREEZE button — if the camera crashed, the instructor might have to pay for it — and those early miniature cameras cost around $25,000. Once the USAF realized simulator hours could not replace, but only augment, aircraft hours for student pilots, they had to fight with Congress annually to reinstate flying hours in the syllabus — one or two hours at a time over a period of several years — to correct the results of overzealous initial expectations. Today's T-37 syllabus is once again just under 90 flying hours.

Not Really a Joke

Student pilots' initial reactions to the Cessna T-37 Tweet were mixed and evidenced a certain love-hate relationship. The damn thing was so small! And it was noisy. And, in the summer, it was hot. And damned if all the wives and girlfriends didn't come right out and call it cute. Cute, for chrissakes! (Before anyone chastises me for my chauvinistic attitudes — I am well aware that there

• *Student and instructor mounting their Tweet for a training sortie, both wearing the regulation "Mickey Mouse ears." The white taxi light (left) and red passing light (right) are visible on either side of pilot tube* •
(Air Force)

• A T-37B two-ship in their all-white, late-1970 paint schemes •
(Air Force)

are now female student pilots and instructors, but way back when I first entered the mysterious, magical world of military aviation and saw my first Tweet — Well, let's just go along with Bob Dylan and say, "The times they are a'changin'.")

What jet fighter pilot-to-be wanted to fly a cute airplane? Be that as it may, we all learned at the outset that this diminutive airplane was plenty challenging and, all jokes aside, a helluva lot of fun to fly. However, the love-hate affair was evidenced in many ways. For example, in most of the pilot training class yearbooks from Webb AFB in Big Spring, Texas (don't bother with the map — the base no longer exists), the section dealing with T-37 experiences begins with this little gem:

"Cessna's joke on the Air Force turned out to be a true awakening for us. We were flying with the military now, and their professionalism and expertise convinced us that, although there were many setbacks and hardships to be endured before we reached our silver goals, flying was definitely the only way to travel. As a result of their perseverance and the Tweet's forgivingness, we discovered for ourselves what the man had in mind when he wrote about those surly bonds."

And, of course, somebody simply had to create a Tweet-specific version of the classic "High Flight" poem.

This following edition evokes memories perhaps unique to the erstwhile Webb AFB but the sentiment holds for everywhere men (and now women) have flown the T-37:

Low Flight
(with apologies to John Gillespie Magee, Jr.)
Oh, I have slipped the squirrely bonds of earth
And buzzed the base on zero lift and overstressed wings;
Toward the tower I've dived and joined the fumbling mirth
Of Webb Approach Control and done a hundred things
I'd dare not dual — boomed and bounced and spun
Above the sunlit Dry Lakes. Hov'ring there,
I've chased the Sandhill Cranes along, and forced
My faltering craft through restricted halls of air.
Down, down, beneath the radar's searching view
I've hugged the wind-swept hills with smiling face
Where never Jones nor even Shaver flew.
Leaving now for my South East Asia post I see
A chance to leave this God-forsaken place,
Thrust out my hand, and flip the bird to ATC.

Flight Controls

The T-37's flight control system is basic and conventional: all primary flight controls (ailerons, elevators, and rudder) are operated via cables, pulleys, bellcranks, and

• *T-37A banking away. Flap hinges are clearly visible on
underside of wing* •
(Kansas Aviation Museum/Robert J. Pickett Collection)

push-pull rods; secondary flight controls (left aileron trim tab, left elevator trim tab, and rudder trim tab) are electrically operated from the cockpit.

Ailerons are effective from stall speed to structural limiting airspeed, and the elevators provide adequate pitch control throughout the normal operational envelope, although they become quite sensitive at higher speeds and can lead to overcontrol and over-G in high-speed maneuvering. Rudders (combined with aileron inputs) allow safe and accurate heading control right down to the stall, even with one engine failed. However, the aircraft nose does exhibit a tendency to "hunt" in landing configuration at final approach airspeeds. This "hunting" requires constant pilot attention to maintain assigned headings during instrument approaches. For a trainer aircraft, this is not all bad — once a student achieves consistent heading control

while flying instruments in the Tweet, that student will never forget those hard-won techniques.

Dual throttles are provided on the student's left and on the center console to the instructor's left. A friction lock is provided for both sets of throttles so they can be adjusted to prevent creeping during flight. Each right engine throttle includes a microphone push-button and a sliding speedbrake switch, both of which are activated by the pilot's thumb. To shut-off the engines, the instructor's throttles must be lifted over a detent into the "Idle Cut-Off" position. The student's throttles cannot be used to shutdown the engines.

Emergency Fuel Shutoff T-Handles are located in the top center of the instrument panel. Each T-Handle has an integral engine overheat and warning light and controls a DC-electric shutoff valve between the respective boost pump and engine fuel control. The light in each T-Handle will flash for an overheat condition and illuminate steadily for a fire condition in the respective engine nacelle. These T-Handles provide another way for a devious instructor pilot to befuddle a student.

The standard military stick grips include a weapons release trigger that is nonfunctional on the T-37. During their first flight, I would warn my students to never touch that trigger because it would shut down the engines. They always gave me an "aw, come on" look. While taxiing back from one of their early flights, I would surreptitiously pull the T-Handle circuit breaker, which conveniently was located just forward of my left knee on the bottom of the panel. I would then find a way to distract the student into looking off to his left. While he did, I reached up and pulled the T-Handles (which no longer worked with the circuit breaker pulled) — one at a time with sufficient delay to be sure there was no malfunction that might cause the engines to quit. Later, as we turned into the parking area, the student was always intent on following the crew chief's hand signals to be sure the Tweet was stopped right on the yellow line. I would tell the student to hold down the trigger as he parked, and would then reset the circuit breaker (it takes up to 10 seconds for the engines to quit using the T-Handles). A few seconds later, shortly after the skeptical student had stopped the airplane — the engines would wind down into silence. They always knew it could not be the trigger but could never figure out how I had done it. Eventually, I would tell them, but not before they had tried futilely to figure it out.

Elevator and aileron trim tabs are operating by a standard military "coolie hat" trim switch mounted on top of the control stick. Since the trim is electrical, its failure modes can be benign (failed in last position) or more exciting ("runaway trim" — wherein the actuating motor runs the trim to one extreme or the other of its limits). In fact, one of the standard training requirements is for the student to demonstrate his ability to control the aircraft with the trim in a "runaway" condition.

One young second lieutenant instructor pilot (who shall remain anonymous so as not to embarrass the author), on returning from the practice area at about 2,000 feet AGL, had forgotten to administer that particular student torture. He took the airplane (to offer his student "a rest"), ran the trim full nose down (good idea...with the ground so close), pulled the trim circuit breaker (low on the instructor's panel), and said, "You've got the aircraft."

The student took the controls, felt the stick lunge forward in his right hand under the influence of that full nose-down trim setting, and promptly let go of it with a shocked "Ahh!" Our young instructor was flabbergasted at just how fast Mother Earth filled the windscreen as his T-37 attempted an imitation of a West Texas oil drill bit. With the aid of some native skill, a surge of adrenaline,

• *Student's side of T-37B cockpit. Fuel shutoff T-handles (clear with center red buttons) are just under glareshield lip at top of center engine-instrument stack* •
(Walt Shiel)

and a particularly watchful guardian angel, our intrepid aviator saved the day — although not without first getting an "up close and personal" aerial look at a local radio tower. He also learned a valuable lesson: Always expect your student to do the most unexpected, and possibly the stupidest, thing you can think of.

Thrust Attenuators and Speedbrake

Like most military jets, the T-37 had a speedbrake — on the Tweet it was a large slab of aluminum hinged at the forward edge extending into the lower slipstream just aft of the nosewheel well. Activated by a sliding thumbswitch on each right-engine throttle, it had two positions: full open or full closed. There was no cockpit indicator, which has allowed many an instructor to fool the more gullible among his students. The speedbrake's real purpose was to control airspeed in high-speed dives, increase descent rates during letdowns from high altitudes, and to enforce higher throttle settings and increase the approach angle in the traffic pattern. The pilot's flight manual (Technical Order 1T-37B-1, the "Dash One") noted, "The speedbrake is designed to give only a minimum pitching moment change...Extension of the speedbrake causes a noticeable buffet which decreases in intensity as airspeed is reduced." This "noticeable buffet" could be used to create "clear air turbulence" during a student's first flight in the Tweet — in the hands of a suitably devious instructor, that is.

While cruising along with a student, who was usually still ill-at-ease in his parachute and helmet and mask and sitting on an ejection seat under a fishbowl canopy, the instructor, flying the airplane, might say, "See that up ahead?"

"What, sir?" replied the somewhat stressed-out student.

"That patch of clear air turbulence. Don't you see it?"

"No, sir." The young fledgling aviator would squint

• *T-37A with the speedbrake extended* •
(Kansas Aviaiton Museum/Robert J. Pickett Collection)

and try hard to see this unfamiliar phenomenon.

"We're about to go through it — there!" With that, the instructor fanned the speedbrake switch, letting the speedbrake extend just slightly before retracting it again. The resulting "noticeable buffet" rumbled through the airframe for a second or so while the speedbrake cycled.

If accomplished two or three times on the student's first flight, most of them figured out what was going on. But there was always that one-in-ten who thought this was for real and returned to the flight room talking about it. The student's classmates were generally quick to explain just how gullible he had been.

The most frequent "legitimate" use of the speedbrake was in the traffic pattern where it is extended for all normal patterns just after rolling into the pitchout, or "break," as the throttles were retarded to about 60 percent rpm. With the speedbrake thus extended and either throttle below 70 percent rpm, small trapezoidal thrust attenuators extended into the exhaust stream from inboard, effectively reducing thrust by about 10 percent rpm. This combination ensured that the student pilot kept the engines at a high-enough rpm for a safe go-around.

Thrust attenuators? For engines producing a mere 1,025 pounds of thrust under ideal test-stand conditions? Yes, because those old cast iron turbojet engines spooled-up oh-so-slowly. If a go-around was necessary, merely retracting the speedbrake (which also retracts the thrust attenuators) created an immediate 10 percent rpm gain on top of eliminating the speedbrake's drag.

With practice, a student learned to hear the thrust attenuators cycling in-and-out as he played the throttles around that magic 70-percent-rpm point through the final turn and down the final approach to the runway. By doing so, precise airspeed control was possible without large power adjustments — or the accompanying risk of initiating a go-around while waiting, and praying, for those heavy compressors to wind up and generate some needed thrust.

Spoilers

The T-37 design also included automatically deployed spoilers. These were not intended to enhance roll control or to "dump" lift à la gliders but were designed to provide stall warning when the flaps were extended. With the horizontal stabilizer located halfway up the vertical stabilizer, turbulent airflow off the wings in a landing-configuration stall tended not to strike the tail until the wing had completely stalled. This produced an undesirable, very sudden, very sharp stall break with little or no warning. The spoilers were designed to correct this lack of native aerodynamic stall warning.

The true stalling characteristics could be observed simply by pulling the spoiler circuit breaker (just in front of the instructor's left knee, low on the panel). If the aircraft was not well-coordinated at the moment of the stall, it tended to snap into a spin. I usually demonstrated this nasty little habit to my students before their first solo and to new instructors who had not seen it previously. During slow flight practice, they were instructed to see just how slow they could fly and sustain level flight. When the stall occurred, the nose would snap downward precipitously. Recovery was straightforward and an incipient spin easily prevented, unless the pilot was slow to respond. Once learned, it was a lesson long remembered, although not one required by the syllabus — or even officially condoned.

The spoilers were flush-mounted on top of the engine nacelles on either side and were hydraulically actuated when the flaps were extended 25 percent or more with the airspeed within four to ten knots of stall speed (a transducer mounted in the lower left wingtip senses angle-of-attack). The result when they were extended was a pronounced buffet felt through the stick, giving plenty of warning of an impending stall.

Instrumentation

The original T-37 panel reflected the state-of-the-art for non-radar-equipped military aircraft — state-of-the-art for the early 1950s, that is. In the top center of the left-hand side of the instrument panel, directly in front of the student, sat the J-2 heading indicator. This was bracketed by an attitude indicator (either the ancient "black ball" J-8 or the more up-to-date black-and-white MM-3) and an airspeed indicator. It was common in the 1950s to have the heading indicator dominate the panel. The Tweet's cockpit was wide and the instructor had no primary flight instruments beyond airspeed, altimeter, and turn-and-slip — instructors learned to fly instruments cross-cockpit and compensate for the resulting parallax when reading the attitude indicator, CDI, RMI, or J-2. Engine instruments and radios, at least, were down the center of the panel where both student and instructor could read or reach them. In the 1970s, a standby attitude indicator was added to the instructor's cluster.

All T-37Bs were equipped with a single UHF radio and one VOR receiver. In the 1970s, transponders and DME equipment were added, but until then we regularly flew "hard" IFR in Tweets with nothing more than a single nav/comm and no transponder. After I had accumulated several hundred hours as a lieutenant T-37 instructor (with many of those hours in IMC), I read a Flying magazine article defining single-nav/comm IFR as strictly an emergency procedure. My comrades got quite a laugh when I read the article aloud in the flight briefing room.

The T-37's lack of navigational gear could sometimes lead to embarrassment. On one flight into McConnell AFB (Wichita, Kansas), the Approach Controller began vectoring us for our approach into the base, where the ceiling was about 500-feet overcast with one-mile visibility.

The controller's first words were, "Rod 990, is your transponder inoperative?"

"Negative transponder, sir," I replied.

After having us make an identifying turn, he picked us out on his scope and told us to "expect the ILS."

I responded, "Negative ILS."

"Roger. Rod 990, report two-zero DME from Wichita VOR."

"Negative DME."

To which the frustrated controller responded, "All right, Rod 990, exactly what DO you have?"

"One VOR, sir," I informed him.

There was an exaggerated pause followed by: "Then expect radar vectors to PAR final."

By his tone of voice, you would have thought I was somehow personally responsible for the equipment Uncle Sam Provided me.

Fuel

The T-37 fuel system consisted of three fuel tanks (one in each wing and one in the fuselage). Each wing tank held 721.5 pounds (111 gallons) of usable fuel and incorporated six interconnected cells to minimize sloshing, lateral center-of-gravity shifts, and inaccurate gauging. Fuel flowed from the wings to the fuselage via a DC-electric proportioner pump which turned on whenever the fuselage tank fuel quantity dropped below approximately 380 pounds. This proportioner pump maintained a balanced fuel transfer for both wing tanks. In the event of electrical or system failure, fuel could flow by gravity feed from the wing tanks to the fuselage tank. From the fuselage tank, which held 565.5 pounds (87 gallons) of usable fuel, a DC centrifugal boost pump (controlled by a cockpit switch) supplied low-pressure fuel to both engines simultaneously.

In addition, each engine included an engine-driven, three-element pump (one centrifugal boost pump and two gear-driven elements). Each gear-driven element could supply the total engine fuel requirements. The centrifugal

• T-37 thrust attenuator extended into the engine's exhaust •
(Kansas Aviation Museum/Robert J. Pickett Collection)

element was a backup for the fuselage tank boost pump, again to allow operation in case of electrical or other system malfunction. A fuel control unit regulated fuel flow to the engine via starting fuel solenoid valve, a speed governing element, and an acceleration control.

Fuel quantity was displayed on a single, large, round dial indicating total fuel on-board. To determine fuel in each wing tank, a manual switch had to be held in either the left or right position until the gauge settled. Fuel balance had to be maintained within 160 pounds or the mission was aborted. This became an oft-repeated and critical checklist item during flight since it was the only way to detect trapped fuel in a wing tank or improper operation of the proportioner pump. Checking fuel balance was critical prior to entering any kind of intentional spins, for which fuel balance had to be within 70 pounds with total fuel less than 1400 pounds. It took several seconds for the fuel gauge to settle on a reading, so T-37 students became adept at flying while holding that switch to check fuel in the wing tanks. And, of course, that was the moment when a high-priority radio call was most likely to require an answer.

• *T-37B cruising above the plains* •
(Kansas Aviation Museum/Robert J. Pickett Collection)

Two-thousand-pounds (309 gallons) of fuel may sound like quite a bit, but the best advice I ever received as a new T-37 instructor was from my first flight commander who admonished me, "If you will just mentally consider yourself to be in a minimum fuel condition as soon as the landing gear first stows in the wheel wells, you'll be okay." After a few practical lessons, I realized just how true that warning was. Lessons such as deciding to have the student try "just one more" traffic pattern when he seemed to be on the verge of an aeronautical revelatory experience — only to be forced to break out of said pattern and reenter with the fuel gauges reading precariously low. This led to a different sort of aeronautical revelation than what I had planned!

Local flights in the T-37 typically lasted between 1.1 and 1.4 hours, depending on how much time was spent in the traffic pattern. As with most jets, fuel consumption increased dramatically at lower altitudes. Cross-country flights might stretch to 1.5 or 1.6 hours, with enough cruise time spent above 20,000 feet. Regulations mandat-

ed a minimum of 200 pounds of fuel on final touchdown (350 pounds for students flying solo).

When the fuel level in the fuselage tank dropped below approximately 380 pounds (58.5 gallons), a red Fuel Low Level Warning Light came on. When the system was operating on gravity feed, an amber light illuminated in the cockpit. This Gravity Feed Light had a tendency to flicker as the wing tanks depleted the last few gallons in them, and the Fuel Low Level Warning Light also flickered as the fuel level in the fuselage tank depleted to near the 380-pound level of the low level switch. This flickering of warning lights would usually quickly draw the pilot's attention to the fuel gauge quickly.

I have a few 1.7 sorties in my logbook and one (only one!) 1.8 sortie — from which I landed with the Gravity Feed Light (indicating dry wing tanks) and Fuel Low Level Warning Light both illuminated steadily. The fuel gauge itself was notoriously inaccurate below about 200-pounds. At least one T-37 has flamed-out with over 100-pounds showing on the fuel quantity gauge. The "Pucker Factor" increases significantly with Gravity Feed and Fuel Low Level lights illuminated unless you are on short final with the field in sight. On my 1.8-hour sortie, those two lights came on while we were still on an extended radar downwind and more minutes than I cared to contemplate from a landing. I shut down one engine while taxiing in to avoid the embarrassment of having to request a tow to parking. Cessna and the USAF published range figures for the T-37B of 932 statute miles, but my experience was that those numbers were grossly unrealistic unless the aircraft was flown at 35,000 feet at maximum range cruise speed, an idle power descent was used at recommended glide speed, and a single straight-in approach to a full-stop landing was made. Although cruise altitudes above 30,000 feet were routine in the early days of T-37 use, the unpressurized cockpit later resulted in a USAF operational restriction of 25,000 feet (true of all USAF unpressurized aircraft). Using a 25,000-foot cruise at a normal cruise power setting (usually yielding a cruise speed of 300 KTAS), a normal letdown, and at least a few extra traffic patterns and landings (this was, after all, a trainer), a reasonable maximum range of around 425 nautical miles (490 statute miles) was achievable. However, I rarely flight planned for anything over 400 nautical miles. Remember that warning from my first flight commander? He was right.

Spins

To test and validate the spin and spin recovery characteristics of the T-37, Cessna approved an exhaustive spin flight test program in April 1957 under Engineering Test Request 375, titled "Aggravated Spins — Quantitative Evaluation of Fixes." (An aggravated spin is a stabilized, high rotation rate spin, usually resulting from a botched recovery attempt.) The aircraft for the flight tests were fitted with a dual spin recovery parachute assembly. The directions provided to the flight test department were to "conduct spins with control manipulations and fuel loadings established by [a previous] test...with the following aircraft modifications:
1. Up elevator travel extended
2. Aft stick travel extended
3. Four-inch wide nose strakes
4. Three-inch wide nose strakes
5. Forward vertical fins
6. Larger ventral fins
7. Ventral fin removed."

Two T-37A aircraft were used for the tests (56-3467 and 56-3469), completing a total of 59 test flights and 53.5 flying hours between March and November of 1957. In July, USAF test pilots conducted an additional five spin test flights as part of the evaluation. A total of 198 spins were accomplished by the Cessna pilots, and an unrecorded number by the USAF pilots. According to the flight test report, "The effect of fuel unbalance and accelerated entry on the spin and recovery were proven not to be the factors inducing an aggravated spin. However, these factors may make it easier to enter a spin, cause the initial turns to be faster, and delay the spin recovery somewhat." The report also noted that, with the four-inch nose strakes, "the aircraft demonstrated a mild 'pitch-up' approaching the stall and especially during accelerated stalls." As a result, the report recommended retaining the original, somewhat smaller and tapered, nose strakes.

Prior to this flight test program, T-37A 56-3468 had sustained damage to the rear wing spar during spin testing (and the first prototype had crashed during initial spin testing). During the 1957 spin testing, aircraft 56-3467 was also damaged during a USAF flight — and in almost exactly the same manner as the earlier aircraft, under almost identical conditions. The right-hand rear wing spar of both aircraft was deformed during the maneuvers. The specific conditions included two pilots on board, high total fuel quantity, and repeated aggravated spins. In a later test, aircraft 56-3467 sustained similar damage on its left wing. These instances of spin-induced damage resulted in a flight restriction of a maximum of 1,000 pounds of total fuel and a maximum of 100 pounds of fuel imbalance between the wing tanks for entering and recovering from intentional spins.

After all the spins had been completed and the data analyzed, the USAF pilots were still not satisfied that the aircraft's spin and recovery were as stable and predictable as they wanted. The test report noted, "All in all, no fix was found which was acceptable to the aircraft user." As a compromise, a detailed description of the T-37 spin characteristics and recommended recovery procedure was developed and added to the "Dash One."

The new "Dash One" spin section included the following:
- At the stall, the airplane tugs at the stick and a moderate amount of force will be required to hold the stick full back with ailerons neutral.
- Using a 3-G pullout, the maximum airspeed will usually not exceed 220 KIAS.
- Approximately 2,500 to 3,000 feet of altitude is lost during the spin recovery and 3-G pullout.
- A large amount of lateral fuel unbalance will cause an oscillatory spin. With this condition, the rotation rate may increase to magnitudes where recovery may be difficult or impossible, unless controls are used properly and in a very positive manner.

The first published spin recovery procedure, established as a result of this test program, consisted of four steps:
1. Abruptly apply full opposite rudder and hold.
2. One-half turn later, rapidly "pop" the stick to the forward stop.
3. When the nose starts down, bring the stick back slightly from the forward stop.
4. As the rotation stops, neutralize the controls.

The procedure then went on to describe different recovery procedures for accelerated spins, landing configuration spins, inverted spins, and aggravated spins. Intentional aggravated spins were prohibited due to the likelihood of severe wing spar damage.

Following a rash of spin-related accidents and several fatalities, ATC requested that the AFFTC at Edwards AFB conduct another in-depth spin evaluation of the T-37B. This "T-37B Qualitative Spin Evaluation" (as opposed to the earlier "quantitative" test) was accomplished between 13 September and 20 October 1961, with Major Walter F. Daniel and Captain William J. Knight participating in all flights, although seven other AFFTC pilots, two ATC pilots, and one Cessna pilot also participated. The objective for this second spin test program was to "conduct a qualitative analysis of the Flight Manual procedures and, if possible, determine if a simplified spin recovery procedure could be developed." The test pilots completed 18 flights in 22.5 flying hours for a total of 270 spins (including erect, inverted, and accelerated spins with various entry load factors from -1G to +2.5G and at varying fuel loads) to arrive at the following recommendation:

"The Flight Manual recovery procedures are valid but not considered optimum. A single recovery technique which is considered to be the best spin recovery procedure under any spin condition was developed. The AFFTC recommended procedure is considered optimum because: one single procedure will recover from all spin modes under all conditions; after the first recovery step has been made, the aircraft cannot spin in any mode except erect normal; confusion as to which rudder to apply in an inverted spin is eliminated; and a minimum of altitude is lost during recovery."

The test pilots tried every possible combination of flight control inputs, sequences, input rates, and amount of control deflection, allowing the spins to progress for between ½ and 11 turns for the erect spins and between ¼ and five turns for the inverted spins before applying recovery procedures. They determined that the existing Flight Manual procedures worked — but required the pilot to determine immediately the type of spin and

• *Pair of T-37s "going vertical"* •
(Kansas Aviation Museum/Robert J. Pickett Collection)

then to correctly apply to recovery procedure for that condition. Also, the existing recovery procedures did not result in the most expeditious recoveries, in some conditions taking up to ten seconds and 2,500 feet of altitude to complete the recovery. The report notes, "However, further tests disclosed that there was a single recovery procedure which would effect positive recovery from all three types of spins under all conditions. Over 100 recoveries were made from all types of spins using this one procedure."

Although the AFFTC pilots did develop a single recovery procedure, they noted that it was not a "cureall." In fact, the two participating ATC pilots did not agree that the resulting single recovery procedure should be adopted for all types of spins — they preferred to retain the existing recovery procedure for intentional inverted spins as it resulted in a smoother recovery. The AFFTC recommendation was, nonetheless, to adopt the single recovery procedure for all conditions since it "does minimize the areas in which a pilot might become confused." They listed four advantages to the new recovery procedure:

- It would recover the T-37 from all spin modes under all conditions.
- After the first step, the T-37 could not spin in any mode except erect normal (i.e., a "known" condition).
- It eliminated possible confusion as to which rudder to apply in an inverted spin.
- It resulted in a minimum loss of altitude.

A final comment was provided in the flight test report that highlights the most important aspect of T-37 spin recoveries:

"One of the major reasons for missing a recovery is not waiting long enough after the recovery controls have been initiated. This is primarily caused by the pilot failing to count turns during recovery."

Despite the dissenting opinions of its own pilots, ATC adopted the new procedure and the revised description of the T-37 spin and recovery characteristics for inclusion in the T-37 "Dash One." This one procedure was to become indelibly etched in the mind of every T-37 pilot from that moment on as the "Single Spin Recovery" (this old Tweet instructor can still recite it verbatim without having to think about it). T-37 instructor pilots were exposed to the other various recovery techniques annually during a dedicated spin orientation flight conducted by a designated T-37 flight examiner. Although it was considered important for every instructor to appreciate the variations, their success was not guaranteed. On the other hand, the aggressive and abrupt "Single Spin Recovery" worked — every time, if done correctly.

Single Spin Recovery

1. Throttles - Idle
2. Rudder and Ailerons - Neutral
3. Stick - Abruptly Full Aft and Hold
4. Rudder - Abruptly Apply Full Rudder Opposite Spin Direction (Opposite Turn Needle) and Hold
5. Stick - Abruptly Full Forward One Turn After Applying Rudder
6. Controls - Neutral After Spinning Stops and Recover From Dive

The repeated use of the word "abruptly" was very intentional — the T-37 was designed to spin and would not recover with neutralized controls. It might recover if controls were eased in anti-spin directions, although there was no guarantee. The T-37 had three defined spin modes: erect normal, erect accelerated, and inverted. Inverted was difficult to analyze but easy to stop — the third step would "pop" the aircraft into an upright stall but if maintained too long would transition the aircraft into an erect spin (no problem, just continue with the rest of the procedure). Once opposite rudder was applied, the rudder began to acquire limited effectiveness — one full turn was needed for maximum rudder effectiveness. Upon initial rudder input, the nose would pitch further down and the spin rate would increase. Most students, worrying about disorientation, would count "one thousand one, one thousand two, one thousand three" rather than use the preferred method — a ground reference). The aircraft transitioned from the spin to a near-vertical dive (sometimes beyond). An immediate pull-out was required!

There were a lot of cautions and warnings in the Dash One, but they all boiled down to one fact: if you did not follow the "Single Spin Recovery" exactly as written, the usually innocuous Tweet might continue to spin earthward at 120 knots vertical speed with the nose 45° below the horizon.

Over the years, numerous Tweets have done just that — spun right into the ground. Pilots have been killed, ejecting from their spinning Tweets as the minimum safe altitude for ejection slipped past. What happened? Poor recovery technique! (And a delayed decision to eject — but that's another story.) When I was a T-41 student, one of the base's T-37s spun in, and our airborne T-41s were directed to search for the wreckage. One of my classmates and his instructor found the aircraft in a West Texas arroyo. The aircraft had spun all the way to earth without the crew attempting ejection until the last moment — when it was too late. Our class, as well as the classes in T-37 training at the time, lost several students the following day due to "self-initiated elimination" — in other words, they quit. It was just a bit too sobering for them. Later, one of my fellow instructors and his student ejected from a spinning Tweet after allegedly attempting "10 or 20" spin recoveries — which means none of those attempts were given a reasonable chance of success with "abrupt" and properly held recovery controls.

Although accidents continued and instructors bitched, one fact remained: if performed as written and if recovery controls were applied properly, the T-37 would always recover from a spin, erect or inverted, gear-up or gear-down. Period. Case closed.

The T-37 "Dash One" provided an excellent description of spin entry:

"Spin entry is not violent, but will vary depending on the pitch attitude. . .(the higher the pitch attitude, the slower the spin entry) and with gross weight (the higher the gross weight, the slower the entry)...The first turn of the spin is more like a roll with the nose dropping below the horizon in the first half and then above the horizon in the last half. Succeeding turns will cause the nose to progressively drop below the horizon and finally stabilize at -40° to -45° pitch attitude...The left spin is more oscillatory...the altitude loss is approximately 550 feet per turn, completing a full turn in approximately three seconds."

The "Dash One" defines an accelerated spin and makes it clear this requires positive, and abnormal, pilot action:

"The accelerated spin is caused by placing the elevator control in some position other than full back stick. The highest stabilized rotation rate occurs with the stick full forward and rudder opposite the direction of rotation. This maneuver is difficult to perform as the controls must be moved abnormally slow, requiring a minimum of four seconds to full deflection...lateral accelerations will be felt and the aircraft will whip as the rate of rotation increases."

Inverted spins could occur either from an inverted stall (maybe at the top of a botched Immelmann) or after an erect spin recovery when the controls were held in the recovery positions for too long. The "Dash One" noted that the inverted spin "can be accelerated by allowing the controls to free float or by holding the rudder in the direction of rotation and moving the stick aft."

Recovery characteristics were straightforward. From an erect spin, the nose would drop sharply as forward stick was applied and the rotation would stop within one-fourth to three-fourths of a turn. If the aircraft was in a landing configuration when the spin was entered (something never practiced and unlikely if the pilot applied good spin prevention techniques at the first indication of rotation during a stall — but something that, nonetheless, has happened), gear and flap retraction had to be accomplished as soon as possible after the rotation stopped to avoid overspeeding them.

I well remember my first T-37 spin as a student. While climbing to spin entry altitude (above 20,000 feet) my instructor recited a speech about how the Single Spin Recovery always works and about how doing spins and

• *A T-37B in its late-1980s white-over-dark blue paint scheme and bird-proof windscreen* •
(U.S. Air Force)

recoveries would build confidence in my skills and in the aircraft itself. He put the jet into a spin and began talking his way through the steps of the Single Spin Recovery in the sing-song manner of one who has done this umpteen times and finds it boring. As he reached the next-to-last step, he sang out, "Stick — Abruptly full forward one turn after rudder. . .Damn! We'll start over. Throttles idle, rudder and ailerons neutral. . ."

I was not impressed, and the demonstration did little to instill confidence, even though the second attempt was successful. It was also apparent that my instructor was not really following the Dash One advice about abruptly applying and about holding the controls until the aircraft showed signs of recovering. My instructor had attempted to "finesse" the recovery by using less than abrupt control inputs and by bouncing the stick off the forward stop rather than waiting for the nose to pitch down. Most of the time, such techniques work — but not 100 percent of the time. Aggressive control inputs always worked but they tended to upset some students. But it was probably less upsetting than watching one's instructor repeat the procedure after failing on the first attempt!

There was one other "Note" of interest in the Tweet "Dash One" concerning spins: "The T-37 will spin with neutral rudder if held for a prolonged time in a full aft stick stall." Remember, the Tweet was designed to spin. The author always thought spinning the Tweet was fun — others did not. He always applied the "Single Spin Recovery" as abruptly and aggressively as it was intended — others did not. Could there have been a connection?

As a T-37 instructor, I always emphasized applying

the spin recoveries the way the AFFTC test pilots recommended. My students never had a problem with failed recoveries. Sometimes, a slight negative G was encountered during the recovery, but the students always knew the airplane was going to snap out of its spin. This was especially important when working with apprehensive students, such as those whose hyperventilation was evident by the loud, rapid breathing coming through the intercom.

One student hyperventilated excessively and promptly locked his elbow straight as he jammed the stick full forward during the spin recovery. Unfortunately, I (being still a relatively inexperienced Second Lieutenant instructor pilot) had failed to properly tighten and lock my restraining harness and had floated just a bit off the seat as the aircraft transitioned into inverted flight and into an inverted spin. I was unable to grab the full-forward stick. I yelled for the student to let go of it, knowing it would float aft just a bit when he did. His only response was more loud, rapid breathing. Finally, in desperation I managed to smack the student across his upturned elbow and break his grip on the stick. I was then able to seize the stick, pull it full aft, and complete the recovery. I was more careful about my harness after that episode!

Bird Strikes

Throughout the first dozen years of its service life, the little T-37 seemed prone to being attacked by birds almost its own size. There were many examples of bird strikes, and many of those strikes shattered, or at least penetrated, the windscreen. Injuries to the occupants were common when a bird arrived unannounced inside the cockpit, and there were several instances of pilots or student pilots being killed. The problem was that the Tweet spent a lot of time at 1,000 feet or less while students practiced traffic patterns and landings — and altitude block the birds also seemed to prefer.

In one case, an instructor pilot was killed by a large bird that came through the windscreen on the right side, leaving the student flying solo with a dead instructor and with bird remains splattered all over the cockpit. It was the student's first sortie in the Tweet. With radio assistance from instructors on the ground, the student managed to land the airplane.

The upshot of all these incidents and accidents was that ATC issued a contract in 1971 for development of a windscreen that could withstand the impact of a five pound bird at 200 KIAS. The result was a much thicker, laminated windscreen with a special coating. ATC quickly scheduled the entire fleet for modification, with the Webb AFB, Texas, maintenance unit selected to do the work. I was stationed at Webb AFB at the time as a T-37 instructor, and our squadron received the very first of the new windscreens in the winter of 1971. One of the first problems we noticed was the significant visual distortion evident as the aircraft descended close to the ground — like when trying to land! The problem was bad enough that ATC issued an edict that no students could fly the modified aircraft solo, pending further research.

But that was not the only problem with the new "safety" windscreens. One cool, overcast, humid day, another instructor and I took off with our students in a pair of the modified aircraft for a local sortie in the traffic pattern. As we flew down the outside downwind (a ground track that paralleled the runway but several miles offset to the west), we passed through a small rain shower. Instantly, our windscreens fogged over — on the inside as well as the outside! That "special coating" was certainly special. The defroster successfully cleared the inside of the windscreen, but the outside remained fogged. I landed first, looking out of the side of the canopy while sighting across the leading edge of that big wing. I flew a tight final turn, rolling out just over the overrun, allowing me to maintain a bank to help keep the runway in sight as long as possible. I could just make out the right edge of the runway when I rolled wings level, kicked the airplane's nose straight, and plopped it down. It wasn't real pretty, but it was safe.

After this episode, ATC restricted the aircraft further to non-rainy days as well as dual flights only. Eventually, a solution was developed that minimized the forward visual distortion and corrected the fogging problem. I guess it never rained on the original test pilots for that modification.

Performance

The Tweet is stableand easy to fly, with low-end jet performance suitable for a student transitioning from the familiar shirtsleeve environment of the Cessna T-41 into the jet fighter-like world of ejection seats, oxygen masks, and bubble canopies. Although the students were more than a little excited about their first jet sortie, most of them experienced a bit of understandable apprehension as they strapped a parachute on their back for the first time, climbed into the small cockpit, cinched up all the straps, put on that new helmet, fastened the oxygen mask tight on their face, lowered the dark visor, removed and stowed the safing pins for the ejection seat, and then watched as the big canopy lowered and was locked down. Their breathing rate usually increased at each milestone step in the checklist, and the instructor's job was to reassure them and point out how much fun they were about to have. Most adapted quickly to the new environment.

The T-37 takeoff ritual was to pump-up the brake pressure once aligned with the runway centerline and hold

• *Tweet ejection seats from the instructor's side of the cockpit, with inertia reel shoulder harnesses dangling. Backpack parachutes provide cushoning from the metal seat backs. Yellow lever at bottom of picture is canopy locking lever (in locked position to disable canopy motor)* •
(Walt Shiel)

them firmly while running the engines up to 100 percent rpm. After verifying that all engine instruments showed normal readings and that no warning or caution lights had come on, the brakes were released. Acceleration was typical of a non-afterburning jet — sluggish until the aircraft had rolled a ways, then acceleration increased steadily. The nosewheel was lifted off the runway at 65 KIAS (higher if a strong crosswind was blowing), and normal liftoff speed was 90 KIAS. Initial climbout was not dazzling for a jet, but did improve significantly after the landing gear was retracted at 100 KIAS (retraction took approximately 10 seconds), followed quickly by the flaps at 110 KIAS. Climbout was then held to 500-1000 feet per minute until reaching 200 KIAS. This marked the beginning of the "tech order climb," which required reducing the airspeed 2 knots for every thousand feet of altitude (thus, at 10,000 feet, the indicated airspeed should be 180 KIAS). The initial climb rate was 3,000 feet-per-minute and decreased to around 1,500-1,800 feet-per-minute approaching 25,000 feet.

Maximum altitude was limited to 25,000 feet by USAF regulations since the T-37B was unpressurized. Actual service ceiling was 39,200 feet with both engines running — 20,100 feet on only one engine. For cross country flights, the Tweet routinely cruised between FL200 and FL250 where fuel flows and true airspeeds optimized range. There were complicated charts in the back of the "Dash One" to determine true airspeed and fuel flows but, at least up in the flight levels (above 18,000 feet), a good rule of thumb has always been to plan on 300 KTAS and 1000 pounds-per-hour of fuel consumption. After applying forecast winds to the distance, the answer would be within a tolerable accuracy of those acquired with a sharp pencil and the charts.

Power-off stall speed for a clean configuration (landing gear and flaps retracted) at maximum gross weight in 1-G level flight was 86 KIAS; power-off with gear and full flaps is 72 KIAS at maximum gross weight and 60 KIAS at minimum fuel landing weight. A clean configuration stall was announced early by a heavy aerodynamic buffeting felt through the stick about four knots above the stall speed. If the aircraft was stalled at high speeds by pulling more than the stalling angle-of-attack (i.e., excessive G forces are applied), noticeable buffeting occurred about eight knots above the stall speed. In a landing configuration stall with more than 25° of flap extension, stall warning was provided by the spoilers. If the spoilers were inoperative, there was no advance stall warning in that configuration and, unlike in the clean stall, the aircraft usually tried to roll-off to the left or right. Stall recoveries were straightforward — push the stick forward quickly and apply power.

The T-37's maximum limiting airspeed was 382 KIAS or 0.70 Mach, whichever occurred first. This critical, or limit, Mach number resulted in a lower maximum indicated airspeed at higher altitudes. In fact, the 0.70 limit Mach number was only valid in one-G flight and was lower at higher load factors (G's). Approaching this limiting airspeed, the aircraft suffered from some reduced directional stability, particularly with the speedbrake extended — readily observed by the tendency of the nose to "hunt" laterally. If the aircraft was allowed to exceed the critical Mach number in a dive (which was the only way to exceed it!), the aircraft exhibited a "tuck under," with the dive angle increasing and a lot of back pressure on the stick required to pull-out of the dive. In addition, as the airspeed built above critical Mach there was heavy aerodynamic buffeting. Recovery from such conditions took a lot of vertical room — a five-G pull-out from a vertical dive initiated at critical Mach number from 10,000 feet took about 6,000 feet before level flight was again achieved, and a lot more than that at any speed above critical Mach.

Landing Gear

Initial approach for the standard military 360° overhead pattern was flown at 200 KIAS, downwind at 120 KIAS minimum, final turn at 110 KIAS, and final approach at 100 KIAS. The standard ATC procedure was to fly the initial approach until about one-third of the way down the runway, roll into 60° of bank while reducing the throttles to 60 percent ("idle and up an inch" was the rule of thumb). After a 180° turn to the downwind leg, power was adjusted to maintain 120 KIAS minimum as the landing gear and flaps were lowered. The landing gear was lowered when below 150 KIAS, the flaps below 135 KIAS. The final turn (a 180° descending turn from downwind to final) was flown at 110 KIAS minimum, final approach at a minimum of 100 KIAS (110 KIAS for a no-flap landing). Touchdown was at 75-80 KIAS, higher in a stiff crosswind. The flare to touchdown was gentle and easily controlled, with no excessive pitch sensitivities. Final approach and touchdown in a crosswind required transitioning to a wing-low method before touchdown.

The T-37 was stable during crosswind landings, and its published maximum crosswind component was 18 knots. Landing with the maximum crosswind required touching down at 100 KIAS (to ensure adequate rudder authority was available to keep the aircraft tracking straight) with no flaps extended (to prevent touching down on the nosewheel first). However, I have landed the Tweet with steady crosswinds of up to 25 knots, gusting to 35 knots. It wasn't exactly fun, but it could be done safely — although it was something to avoid if at all possible.

One of the idiosyncrasies of the Tweet's side-by-side seating arrangement was that flying a right-hand final turn was different than flying a left-hand final turn. In a right-hand pattern, the student was looking across the cockpit throughout the final turn, making it easy to crosscheck airspeed and altitude with a quick glance. In a left-hand pattern, the student had to actually turn his head to crosscheck those same instruments. Due to these differences, every T-37 training base maintained an auxiliary airfield with a traffic pattern planned to always require the opposite direction pattern from the home base. This allowed the student to practice both traffic patterns on a single mission, maximizing training.

There was a standard Tweet litany that had to be recited on downwind during the process of configuring the aircraft for landing: "Handle, horn, lights, light, pressure." This was meant to be a confirmation that the landing gear handle was down, the landing gear warning horn had ceased blaring, the three green landing gear down indicator lights were on, the red landing gear warning light was no longer flashing, and the hydraulic pressure was in the normal range. Of course, such litanies are frequently recited as though the words alone ensure the actions have occurred. More than one student rolled into the final turn, having recited the appropriate refrain, but with the gear and flaps still retracted. In fact, instructors have been known to do so, which is why a short-final recheck was

normal practice: check that the landing gear was down and locked and that the hydraulic pressure was in the normal range.

The landing gear warning horn's intentionally raucous "BE-EEP. . .BE-EEP. . .BE-EEP" can make it difficult to administer instruction or just to converse. Instructors frequently depressed the silencing button so they could dispense critical information to the student on downwind while the gear was in transit. This sometimes became a bad habit. Back in the early 1970s, two instructor pilots flew their T-37 into Tinker AFB at Oklahoma City on a lovely afternoon. They were enjoying the day and were involved in typical "male-bonding" discussions as they alternated flying the traffic patterns and touch-and-go landings. While on downwind, the instructor not flying silenced the landing gear warning horn to eliminate interruptions to their sparkling repartée. Unfortunately, their conversation was apparently more interesting than the all-too-familiar checklist items, and they skidded to a stop on Tinker's long runway with nothing extended except the speedbrake. After the accident investigation had been completed, ATC reiterated that the use of the silencing button should be judiciously applied.

From the portable control tower we used to manage

• *Portrait of a T-37 from the trail formation position* •
(U.S. Air Force)

local T-37 traffic, I once watched a student on his first solo, who seemed intent on landing without benefit of wheels. One of the unique T-37 features is the red passing light mounted in the nose to the left of the pitot tube — it flashed when the gear was down-and-locked, it was on steadily when the gear was not down. This student rolled into the final turn and reported, "Rod 99 [BE-EEP], solo, [BE-EEP], final [BE-EEP] turn, gear [BE-EEP] check." The controller (at an ATC base, controllers of local traffic were experienced instructor pilots) directed him to recheck his landing gear, but the student could not hear the radio call over that loud horn. Once the student rolled out on final with his passing light shining steadily, the controller ordered him to initiate a go-around — several times. The student blithely ignored the warnings and flew lower and lower toward the runway. When the student reached short final, the controller directed me (serving as his assistant controller) to fire a red flare — which arced, flaming and smoke, across the student's flightpath. This, luckily, did get the student's attention, and he made his go-around safely. On his next approach, the student had his landing gear down. It was too late, he had already failed that mission.

Of course, some pilots could get in trouble even when landing with the gear down. During Pilot Instructor Training (PIT), would-be instructor pilots are paired for what are termed "team sorties," on which they are supposed to take turns practicing their instructional techniques. A few years back, two PIT student lieutenants took off from Randolph AFB at San Antonio, headed for Mathis Field at San Angelo. Mathis is a civilian airport where a local contractor provides fuel and other services for transient military aircraft. Goodfellow AFB, with its long-closed runway, is a mere five miles across town. Towering weeds pushed up through broad cracks in what used to be a concrete runway. Sizable yellow X's covered the runway to indicate that this was a closed runway. When flying the VOR approach to Runway 21 at Mathis Field, one flew close to Goodfellow's runway. The two lieutenants in question spotted a large runway and proceeded to land on it. They were first amazed at the sorry condition of the runway — then amazed that an Air Force Security Police car was chasing them down that runway with its lights flashing. Rather than having to explain their erroneous ways, the two aviators executed a quick 180° turn on the broken, overgrown runway, and blasted off again, leaving the cops in a cloud of West Texas dust. They sprinted the five miles to Mathis and landed, hoping to refuel before being found out. However, the phone in the operations office at Mathis Field was already ringing when they walked in to file their return flight plan to Randolph AFB. Of such antics, legends were made.

Maneuvers

ATC T-37 regulations mandated a minimum of 5,000 feet AGL for dual aerobatics (8,000 feet AGL solo). Spin training had to be conducted above 18,000 feet AGL. Over-the-top maneuvers required 240-250 KIAS (260-270 KIAS for an Immelmann) and three-to-four Gs for the pull-up. These maneuvers could all be completed within a 3,000 foot vertical block, making the T-37 an enjoyable mount for aerobatics. The T-37's big, thick wing created noticeable adverse yaw at slow speeds, requiring good rudder coordination at the top of an Immelmann to keep the nose on the reference point.

There were eight designated prohibited maneuvers for the T-37: vertical stalls, snap rolls, spins with more than 70 pounds fuel imbalance, intentionally fishtailing the aircraft by repeated rudder reversals, flying maneuvers by using the trim switch alone, trimming in a dive within 20 knots of limiting airspeed, practicing maneuvers with one engine actually shutdown (rather than simulating a shutdown using idle power), and inverted flight for more than 30 seconds (due to fuel limitations). Although snap rolls were prohibited, this did not mean that they were never done. However, I know of only one pilot who accomplished, with the help of his student, a snap roll in the final turn of a traffic pattern and flew out of it safely.

The young lieutenant instructor was flying at the Webb AFB auxiliary training airfield near Sweetwater (the radio call sign for the auxiliary's instructor pilot/traffic controller was "Peckerwood") with a student who was having a lot of trouble getting from downwind to final approach without overshooting final. As the student rolled into the final turn for his fourth attempt, the aircraft was clearly about to overshoot again. ATC T-37s were restricted to 45° of bank in the final turn. Lieutenant Instructor said, "Don't let it overshoot." Student banked up to 45°, but it was not enough, so he added some inside rudder while using opposite aileron to keep the aircraft from overbanking. Instructor, now frustrated, yelled, "Don't overshoot!"

The embarrassed student decided to show his instructor what he was made of and hauled back on the stick, promptly stalling the airplane. With a boot-full of rudder in one direction and a handful of aileron in the other, the stalled Tweet performed a perfect descending snap roll — from about 700 feet AGL! The Peckerwood controller leaped to his feet, expecting to see a fireball and hear an explosion as the aircraft dropped below the ubiquitous mesquite trees (mesquite being rather short trees!). Within a few seconds, the die-hard Tweet staggered up out of a gigantic cloud of dust and flew away. The controller assumed they were heading back to Webb AFB to land and report the unusual stress the aircraft had just endured. After 30 minutes or so with no phone call asking him what he had witnessed, the controller called the squadron

• *Four-ship of T-37s overflying Randolph AFB, Texas, 1982. AETC headquarters is the white "tower building" just below the lead arircraft's nose* •
(U.S. Air Force)

operations officer and inquired. The snap-rollers were still practicing touch-and-go landings after having stopped in a training area to try a few spins and some acrobatics! They were quickly directed to land and taxi back to the chocks.

Formation training in the T-37 introduced the student to a new and even more demanding phase of military flying. The normal formation position (referred to as "fingertip" position) put the wingman on a 30° line off the lead aircraft, stacked slightly lower than lead, and with about three-to-five feet between wingtips. The Tweet's long wingspan and minimal excess thrust forced the wingman to anticipate well and work hard to maintain proper position when lead was maneuvering. When lead turned away, it could seem like a long climb to hold position and could require all the power available to get there. Conversely, a turn into the wingman might require almost idle power and an aggressive application of forward stick to hold position.

The current Specialized Undergraduate Pilot Training (SUPT) syllabus includes only two-ship formation training in the T-37, but the EuroNATO Joint Jet Pilot Training (ENJJPT) program conducted at Sheppard AFB (Wichita Falls, Texas) also provides four-ship formation in its T-37 syllabus.

And the Tweet Goes On...

The May 1995 "Air Force Almanac" issue of Air Force Magazine listed 494 T-37B aircraft on the active USAF roster, with an average age of 31.7 years. The only older aircraft still in service are a single remaining NT-33 (a flight test asset soon to be retired), a single C-131, and six Rockwell T-39s (averaging 33.5 years of age). When first delivered, all T-37s sported bare aluminum exteriors with appropriate USAF markings. In the late 1970s, ATC experimented with a variety of paint schemes on T-37s assigned to Randolph AFB in an attempt to find a scheme that made it easier to spot the tiny jets through various poor visibility conditions, including the summertime haze. The final solution was an all-white paint job with black anti-glare paint on the top of the nose section ahead of the cockpit. In the late 1980s, all T-37s were again repainted to the present more dramatic scheme of white over dark blue.

Between June of 1969 and December of 1970,

• *A flock of Tweety Birds waiting for the weather to improve* •
(Walt Shiel)

Cessna's Military Twin Division conducted an exhaustive fatigue life testing program on the T-37B — 24,000 hours of tests lasting 18 months. The testing goal was to determine the actual service life that USAF could expect from the airplane and to define what was needed to extend the Tweet's original estimated life of between 5,000 and 10,000 flying hours to the new goal of 15,000 flying hours. According to John Huffman, then supervisor of the structural fatigue department, "We loaded the test aircraft with the same loads and in the proper sequence that it would encounter while flying in the field."

In fact, Huffman and his crew applied almost 530,000 load cycles spread over 26 different load levels to a T-37B loaned directly from ATC's fleet. Approximately 3,400 data points were recorded at 50 specific locations on the airframe, requiring over 18,000 feet of recorder paper. In the end, Cessna put the aircraft through the equivalinet of four complete 30-year lifetimes of use. The engineers evaluated the accumulated data and the damage showing up on the test aircraft and identified several critical fatigue areas that were not then being monitored. Cessna recommended three specific structural

• *A Reese AFB T-37B on static display at a summer airshow. The canopy is open slightly to prevent excessive heat build-up* •
(Walt Shiel)

modifications, which were approved by the USAF, to allow the T-37B fleet to achieve the target 15,000-hour life. Huffman noted, "By finding and correcting these critical areas prior to the occurrence of fleet problems in the field, you might say that we, literally, kept ATC flying."

While these "fixes" were being incorporated, ATC imposed a few maneuvering restrictions on the T-37B fleet. Aircraft not yet repaired were limited to a maximum speed of 300 KIAS, a maximum five-G load factor, and no more than 30° of bank when flying in close trail formation. It was a big

• Unusual all-grey paint scheme of a T-37B assigned to the Air Force Material Command for flight test support duties •
(Kansas Aviation Museum/Robert J. Pickett Collection)

relief to all the instructors when those restrictions were lifted. We were like kids turned loose with a new toy — everybody was out doing 6.5-G loops and pushing the jet right up to its maximum of 382 KIAS (or 0.7 Mach, whichever came first). Great fun for a while — until some jets were over-G'ed due to the overexuberance of a few pilots.

In August of 1989, with many T-37s approaching that magic 15,000 hour limit, Sabreliner Corporation was awarded a contract to design and produce Service Life Extension Program (SLEP) kits to replace durability-crit-

ical structural components and extend the operating life of the T-37 fleet beyond the year 2000, when the Joint Primary Aircraft Training System (JPATS) is scheduled to provide a replacement for USAF T-37s and Navy T-34s. The result of these structural upgrades was to allow the aircraft to be flown a full 18,000 hours — double its original design life!

ENJJPT

The ENJJPT program at Sheppard AFB differs from the SUPT conducted at the four other Air Education and

• A hangared T-37B with protective engine inlet covers installed •
(Walt Shiel)

• Brigadier General Borardus S. Cairns christening the Army T-37A "Pinta" at Ozark Army Airfield, July 1957 •
(U.S. Army Aviation Museum)

four-ship formation, additional low-level navigation, and some "fluid maneuvering" two-ship formation (sort of an introduction to dogfighting) — sorties not provided in the SUPT syllabus. As a result, the ENJJPT T-37 syllabus specifies 107 hours of flying time rather than SUPT's 90 hours. Another difference is that ENJJPT does not use the motion-base simulators used by the rest of AETC — retaining, instead, the original Link trainers (with upgraded capabilities).

Because of the uniqueness of their training program, ENJJPT operates its own Pilot Instructor Training (PIT) course right at Sheppard AFB.

Jets for the Army

As soon as the USAF was created in 1948, the Army began coveting go-fast machines — jets in particular. Finally, in September of 1956, the U.S. Army initiated Project Long Arm to investigate the feasibility of operating its own high-performance aircraft and to define the organization, techniques, and procedures required to employ them to meet Army reconnaissance, observation, and artillery fire control requirements. The Higher Performance Army Observation Aircraft (HPAOA) unit was established under the command of Lieutenant Colonel Jack W. Ruby with nine officers, one warrant officer, and 33 enlisted personnel. The Army wanted an

Training Command (AETC) bases in style as well as content. One of the most notable aspects of the 89th Flying Training Squadron (FTS) facility at Sheppard AFB is the number of foreign instructors and students. In fact, ten countries other than the United States contribute students and/or instructors. The supervisory and command positions rotate among the participating countries' personnel.

The 89th FTS, the ENJJPT T-37 squadron, has the capacity to train over 300 students per year, although in 1994 they trained only 200, with 110 in training at any one time. Every country sending students must send a proportionate number of instructors. Canada, Greece, Portugal, and Turkey provide ENJJPT instructors but no students. Denmark, Germany, Italy, the Netherlands, Norway, the United Kingdom, and the United States provide both instructors and students. The United States provides about half of the total student and instructor pilot force with Germany providing the next largest contingent.

Germany originally owned 47 T-37s, which were used at Williams AFB, Arizona, as part of the German pilot training program. In the mid-1960s, this program moved to Sheppard AFB, Texas, and eventually became the ENJJPT program. Germany still owns 34 of the 89th FTS's 90 T-37s.

The ENJJPT T-37 syllabus includes

• Some of the Project Long Arm officers in front of the "Santa Maria," s/n 56-3464 •
(U.S. Army Aviation Museum)

• *All three Army Project Long Arm T-37A aircraft* •
(Kansas Aviation Museum/Robert J. Pickett Collection)

aircraft with easy field maintenance and an ability to operate from unimproved air strips near the front lines. It, therefore, had to be small, robust, and uncomplicated. The USAF's T-37 seemed ideal, so the Army talked the USAF out of some aircraft for evaluation. Three A-models with the original J69-T-9 engines (serial numbers 56-3464, 56-3465, and 56-3466) were delivered to the Army Aviation School at Fort Rucker, Alabama, for evaluation. They were christened by Brigadier General Bogardus S. Cairns, commanding general of Fort Rucker, at Ozark Army Airfield in July of 1957 as the Niña, the Pinta, and the Santa Maria.

Test operations were conducted at Fort Rucker; Fort Sill, Oklahoma; Fort Knox, Kentucky; and Fort Benning, Georgia. Final operational evaluation was conducted during corps-sized maneuvers (Operation "Grand Bayou") in April 1959. Project Long Arm was the Army's first opportunity to operate jet aircraft and, according to a statement issued by Brigadier General Carl I. Hutton at the time, "The success of this test will determine to a large measure whether or not the Army will be allowed to operate high speed, high performance aircraft in the future." At the conclusion of the Army tests, the three T-37s were returned to the USAF inventory, after completing 218

missions and 360 flying hours.

The Army conducted day and night tests at altitudes from 50 feet to 25,000 feet, including tests to determine the practicality of night artillery fire adjustment from the air. The night artillery adjustment missions, for safety reasons, were conducted at 25,000 feet and up to 15 miles away from the targets. Comparison flights were made with the same observers in Army L-19 aircraft.

Since the Army was never authorized to operate jet aircraft other than during these tests, does that indicate the tests were less than successful? No. The Army was very pleased with the evaluation and went on to evaluate the Northrop N-156 (later to become a mainstay in both the USAF and foreign air forces as the T-38/F-5 series), the Italian Fiat G.91, and the Douglas A-4D. However, the USAF protested Army ownership of high performance, and particularly jet, aircraft — claiming that realm as theirs alone (I guess they were willing to accept Navy jets, what with all those aircraft carriers). The Army did use this experience later as a springboard for acquiring the twin-turboprop Grumman OV-1 Mohawk as a reconnaissance and gunship platform.

Nonetheless, the USAF won the bigger battle and, to this day, the Army relies on USAF jets for high-speed close air support (CAS) of Army units. The debate has recently flared again, with some high-ranking USAF officers proposing to shift the Grumman A-10 Thunderbolt II ("Warthog") aircraft to the Army along with the entire CAS mission, although equally high-ranking Army officers are now resisting the whole idea. Who knows? The Army may yet get its wish to operate jets, albeit 40 years late.

The C-Model

In 1961, Cessna used a T-37B, serial number 62-5951, as the prototype for a new model. The concept resulted from USAF-expressed interest in a small, cheap combat aircraft for counterinsurgency operations against fast, well-armed guerrilla forces. The aircraft was intended primarily for export to foreign air forces that could not afford, and probably did not need, the current front-line fighters. The USAF considered armed models of the T-6 and the T-28, as well as an updated F-51, while Cessna pushed its armed T-37. To allow carriage of the external stores, Cessna increased the structural strength of the wing spars.

This new design included jettisonable 65-gallon wingtip fuel tanks and a single weapons hardpoint under each wing. The wingtip tanks boosted maximum range to more than 900 nautical miles. These tanks included a boost pump to transfer fuel from the tip tanks to the corresponding wing tanks.

For weapons delivery, the new aircraft incorporated a K-14C computing gunsight and an AN/N-6 16mm gun camera, plus provisions for a variety of cameras in the aft lower access bay (such as the KA-20 or KB-10A reconnaissance cameras or the HC-217 cartographic camera). With the same 1,025-pound thrust engines and increased gross weight of 8,700 pounds, the aircraft's top speed was slightly more than 10 percent slower than the T-37B. After flight testing, the USAF designated the new aircraft the T-37C, intended exclusively for export. On each pylon, the C-model could carry either a rocket pod, a gun pod, a bomb of up to 250 pounds, or even an AIM-9 Sidewinder air-to-air missile. In fact, Cessna offered "combination .50 caliber machine guns/2.75 inch rocket armament training pods" for production installation. These jettisonable pods, manufactured by General Electric, could carry 360 rounds of .50-caliber ammunition, four 2.75-inch rockets, and even eight 3-pound practice bombs, simultaneously.

As part of the flight testing of the C-model, another qualitative spin test program was conducted on one of the first production T-37C aircraft, serial number 62-5975, at Edwards AFB in May of 1963. The aircraft was flown with and without the tip tanks — nine flights, eleven flying hours, and 38 spins. The report concluded that the "T-

• The Project Long Arm team in front of the three T-37As at Fort Rucker, Alabama, 1957 •
(U.S. Army Aviation Museum)

• Pakistan Air Force T-37C, s/n 77664, 4 September 1977 •
(Kansas Aviation Museum/Robert J. Pickett Collection)

37C will recover from normal erect and accelerated spins with empty (5 percent residual fuel) tip tanks when symmetrically loaded with 1,300 to 1,000 pounds of internal fuel utilizing the T.O. 1T-37B-1 spin recovery procedures. . .Fuel transfers from the wing tanks to the tips during spins." The final recommendation, however, is that "the T-37C not be intentionally spun with tip tanks installed." In addition, the project test pilots recommended a slightly modified spin recovery procedure for the new model Tweet's Flight Manual.

Although the original concept was to provide limited ground attack capability, the aircraft was really only suitable as a ground attack training aircraft to provide an introduction to the tactics and techniques. A total of 273 T-37C aircraft were built, and all were sold to foreign countries under the MAP program. The last T-37C was shipped to Pakistan in July of 1977.

The T-37C prototype aircraft, serial number 62-5951, later became the YAT-37D light attack aircraft prototype. It was retired to the U.S. Air Force Museum on 14 December 1964. Less than two years later, in August of 1966, it was returned to service for the final

Country	T-37B		T-37C	
Brazil	0		65	(30 later sold to South Korea, 12 to Paraguay)
Burma	0		12	
Cambodia (Kampuchea)	4	(later destroyed)	0	
Chile	20		12	
Columbia	4		10	
Greece	8		24	
Jordan	15		0	
Pakistan	24		39	
Paraguay	0		12	(from Brazil)
Peru	32		0	
Portugal	0		30	
South Korea	0		55	(30 from Brazil)
South Vietnam	24		0	
Thailand	10		6	
Turkey	0		50	
Subtotals	141		273	

TOTAL 414

• *Peruvian Air Force T-37C at the Cessna plant in Wichita* •
(Kansas Aviation Museum. Robert J. Pickett Collection)

design testing of the A-37 being developed for use in the Vietnam War. After four years of flight test duties, 62-5951 was again retired to the Air Force Museum in July of 1970. The aircraft was flown on its last flight by Cessna test pilot Jim LeSueur, who had also flown its initial test flight as the T-37C prototype. It was the only aircraft to have been retired to the Museum twice.

Everyman's Tweet

Besides West Germany's stateside Tweets (back when there was a Berlin wall), T-37s were exported to a slew of other foreign countries via the MAP program (see table on page 167).

After the Tweet

On 20 September 1956, Cessna completed Summary Data Report Number 3001 titled "Design Proposal of a Personnel Utility Land-Based Class VU — Twin Jet — Four-Place Airplane." This proposal was the first to build

upon the early success of the T-37A and was intended to be sold to the military for personnel transport and proficiency flying missions. In fact, the wings, aft fuselage, empennage, engines and engine nacelles, landing gear, and flight controls were all listed as T-37A components that would be used directly on the Model 405. The major differences between the basic USAF trainer and the new model were to be its four-place, fully pressurized cabin and additional wingtip fuel tanks for greater range. Maximum gross weight was expected to be 8,380 pounds, which, when coupled with the original 920-pound-thrust J69-T-9 engines, was certain to result in lower top speeds and climb rates. No performance figures were offered in this initial proposal. The Model 405's dimensions, however, were described as being only slightly greater than those of the T-37: 1.67 feet longer, 1.3 feet taller (to the top of the vertical tail), and a 1.37 foot greater wingspan.

In September of 1959, Cessna unveiled a further variant of the T-37 with a two-foot longer fuselage and a pressurized four-place cockpit — the Model 407. Passenger

• *The eight T-37C aircraft of the Portuguese Air Force demonstration team, "Asas de Portugal" (Wings of Portugal).*
Tip tanks were removed and a smoke system installed •
(Kansas Aviation Museum/Robert J. Pickett Collection)

entry and exit was via a door on the right side of the fuselage rather than via the clamshell canopy on the T-37 and the proposed Model 405. The one-and-only prototype made several successful flights. Cessna attempted to interest the USAF in the Model 407 as a military liaison aircraft, but they selected the North American T-39 instead (which, in turn, borrowed heavily from North American's own F-86 Sabre design). The two prototype Cessnas claimed a normal cruise speed of 465 mph, a range of up to 1,590 statute miles, a service ceiling of 46,400 feet, and a maximum gross weight (for the four-seat Model 407) of 9,300 pounds. Continental 356-9 jet engines, next-generation versions of the T-37's J69s, provided 1,400 pounds of thrust apiece. A mock-up of the new aircraft was displayed to military officials between 29 September and 2 October in Washington, DC, and 13-15 October at Wright-Patterson AFB in Dayton, Ohio.

Cessna's president, Dwane Wallace, said at the time, "To achieve minimum cost and maximum utility, we drew upon the experience of T-37 trainer development, and 200,000 hours of T-37 service utilization as a basis for 407 design." Besides military applications, Wallace foresaw a commercial potential and, in a statement that seems in retrospect to hint at the Model 500/Citation series to come, added, "The Model 407 could foreseeably be the forerunner of a modern commercial fleet in the next five to ten years." A subsequent five-seat prototype, the Model 407A, was also flown but it never sold.

When the U.S. Navy announced a competitive procurement for a new Tandem Navy Trainer (TNT), Cessna proposed a tandem-seat T-37 using a variant of the J-85 engine, but again lost — this time to the Rockwell T-2 Buckeye. Building on the preliminary design work for the TNT, Cessna proposed a tandem two-seat Vertical Takeoff and Landing trainer to the USAF, employing large underwing engine pods containing three jet engines each for vertical thrust in addition to a standard pair of J-85s for horizontal flight.

In the 1980s, Cessna lost a USAF competition for a T-37 replacement, the USAF's Next Generation Trainer program. Cessna's entry was basically an updated, re-engined T-37 with a high-mounted T-tail. Fairchild Aircraft, however, won the contract with its ill-fated T-46, which was later cancelled and never proceeded beyond the flight test stage.

After the cancellation of the T-46, Cessna again proposed two possible T-37 variants to fill the gap: a low-cost update and airframe strengthening to stretch-out the

• *Chilean Air Force T-37B, s/n J-386 (USAF s/n 59-0258), at McConnell AFB in Wichita, Kansas, awaiting delivery, 6 April 1974* •
(Kansas Aviation Museum/Robert J. Pickett Collection)

life of the current T-37; and a more extensive new-production variant dubbed the T-48. The proposed T-48 was to use the T-46's more fuel-efficient Garrett F-109-GA-100 turbofan engines producing 1,350 pounds-thrust each. The T-48 would also have incorporated modern avionics and cockpit displays, as well as a pressurized cockpit. Although a prototype T-48 was almost created, using a T-37B airframe, the project was dropped when Congress refused to allocate funds.

Cessna's most recent attempt to replace its own T-37 in the USAF inventory occurred through the competition for the Joint Primary Aircraft Training System. Cessna competed against six other contenders, but Beechcraft eventually won the competition.

Where are They Now?

On 14 October 1994, Cessna hosted a special birthday celebration — to honor the T-37 Tweety Bird on the 40th anniversary of its maiden flight. A reception and dinner were held at the Cessna Citation Customer Center at Wichita's Mid-Continent Airport. USAF Major General Joe Engle, former astronaut and space shuttle commander, was the guest speaker. The center of attention, however, was the little T-37B in its dark blue-and-white AETC

tuxedo. A major milestone — 40 years of service — had been achieved, but it was certain to be exceeded by many years before the last AETC T-37 would retire. The following day, Cessna hosted an Open House at its Wichita facilities.

But that was not the last achievement for that particular little Tweet. In December, a team of volunteers from the Kansas Aviation Museum in Wichita and an escort from the Sedgewick County Sheriff's Department braved 12° weather for over four hours on a Saturday morning to move the aircraft to its final resting place — an honored spot outside the Museum's facility at old Wichita Municipal Airport. A Chevy pickup towed the aircraft while the volunteers guarded its wingtips and tail. Others carefully removed and replaced street signs to make way for the aircraft's 33.8-foot wingspan. Just before dawn, the team cleared the last hurdle as they angled the aircraft through the Museum's gate one wing at a time. It had been a long trip from the Cessna plant to ATC flight training duties to the Air Force's desert aircraft "boneyard" near Tucson to the Cessna plant again for restoration and, finally, to the Museum. The aircraft had to be towed rather than flown because the restoration team had installed fake engines for static display purposes.

• *Last four Brazillian Air Force T-37C aircraft being prepared for ferrying to Brazil, 20 June 1970* •
(Kansas Aviation Museum. Robert J. Pickett Collection)

• First USAF T-37A is delivered to USAF officers Major Ray W. Rogers (left) and Major Roscoe L. Crownrich (center) while Captain Harold W. Stoneberger, USAF plant representative at the Cessna Factory, watches •
(Kansas Aviation Museum/Robert J. Pickett Collection)

During the peak of the Vietnam War, ATC operated T-37s out of 10 pilot training bases from Williams AFB, Arizona, to Moody AFB, Georgia, plus the PIT aircraft at Perrin AFB. In 1995, however, the remaining T-37s were operated by AETC at only six total bases: Randolph AFB, San Antonio, Texas (where T-37 PIT is conducted); Columbus AFB, Columbus, Mississippi; Laughlin AFB, Del Rio, Texas; Reese AFB, Lubbock, Texas; Vance AFB, Enid, Oklahoma; and Sheppard AFB, Wichita Falls, Texas. In addition, some aircraft were based in four-plane units at three Air Combat Command bases with C/KC/RC-135 units to upgrade and maintain the proficiency of unit copilots under the Accelerated Copilot Enrichment (ACE) program. A few T-37s are operated by the Air Force Material Command to support flight test activities.

Besides the USAF's 494 T-37B aircraft still flying, several hundred are still performing admirably in the service of foreign air forces. Some, however, have turned up in the open marketplace and at least two have been purchased by civilian operators for restoration to flying status. Edward Wachs of Madison Valley Aircraft in Ennis, Montana, bought two 1966 T-37C aircraft in an open auction from the Brazilian Air Force. They are well on their way to full restoration. Others will surely follow as T-37s are retired and replaced with more modern training aircraft.

There are a number of T-37s in museum collections around the United States, including:

*   *U.S. Army Aviation Museum*, Fort Rucker, Alabama.
*   *Pima Air and Space Museum*, Tucson, Arizona.
*   *Travis Air Force Museum*, Vaccaville, California.
*   *Florida Military Aviation Museum*, Clearwater, Florida.
*   *Museum of Aviation at Warner Robbins*, Georgia.
*   *U.S. Air Force Museum*, Dayton, Ohio.
*   *History and Traditions Museum*, San Antonio, Texas.
*   *Hill Aerospace Museum*, Ogden, Utah. +

TURBOFAN T-37

• Cessna's prototype T-37 with Garrett turbofan engines, later called the T-48 •
(Kansas Aviation Museum. Robert J. Pickett Collection)

*• USAF Second Lieutenant Thomas W. Beaghan standing beside the T-37A in which
he had just soloed, the first student to do so. Bainbridge AFB, Georgia, March 1958 •*
(Kansas Aviation Museum/ Robert J. Pickett Collection)

• One of Project Long Arm's T-37A aircraft, s/n 56-3465, on outside display at the Army Aviation Museum •
(U.S. Army Aviation Museum)

• Peruvian T-37C flightline •
(Kansas Aviation Museum/Robert J. Pickett Collection)

• Air Force Museum's T-37B, s/n 57-2289. This plane was originally a T-37A •
(U.S. Air Force Museum)

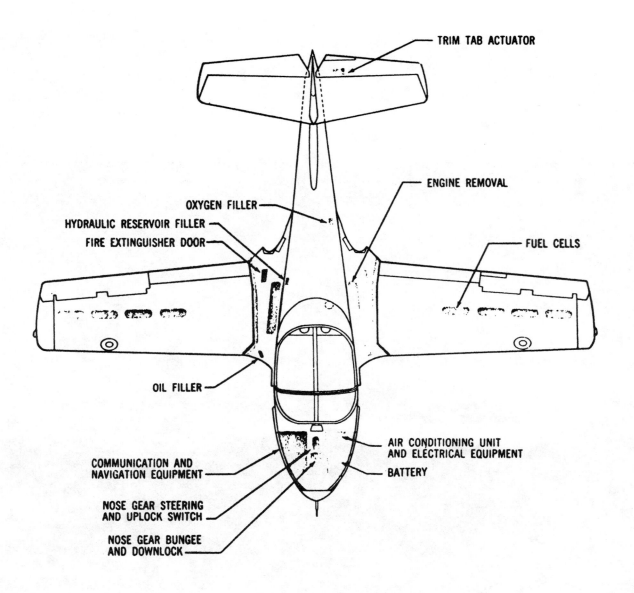

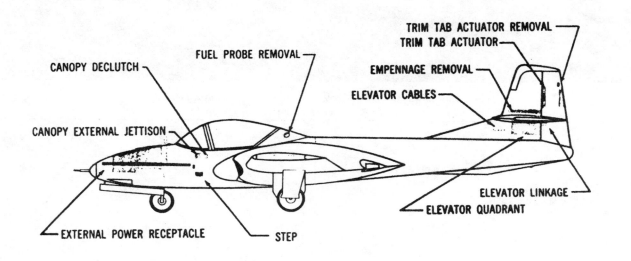

• Depiction of access for routine T-37B maintenance tasks •
(Kansas Aviation Museum/Robert J. Pickett Collection)

Specifications

T-37B

Wingspan	33.80 ft.
Length	29.30 ft.
Height	9.20 ft.
Wheel Base	7.75 ft.
Wheel Tread	14.00 ft.
Engines	Continental J69-T-25 turbojets, 1,025 pounds static thrust each
Gross Weight	
Normal (Two pilots, Full Fuel)	6,575 lbs.
Maximum Allowable	6,800 lbs.
Fuel Capacity	
Fuselage Tank	87 U.S. gallons
Wing Tanks (2)	111 U.S. gallons each
Total	309 U.S. gallons (2,008.5 pounds)
Minimum Single Engine Speed	100 KIAS
Maximum Glide Speed	125 KIAS
Glide Ratio	13.4:1
Maximum Allowable Speed	382 KIAS or 0.70 Mach
G Limits	+6.67/-2.67
Stall Speed (Power Off)	
6,400 Pounds, Flaps Up	86 KIAS
6,400 Pounds, Full Flaps	72 KIAS
4,400 Pounds, Flaps Up	71 KIAS
4,400 Pounds, Full Flaps	60 KIAS
Stall Speed (85% Power)	
6,400 Pounds, Flaps Up	82 KIAS
6,400 Pounds, Full Flaps	68 KIAS
4,400 Pounds, Flaps Up	67 KIAS
4,400 Pounds, Full Flaps	56 KIAS
Takeoff Ground Roll	1,700 feet
Takeoff Distance Over 50 Foot Obstacle	2,500 feet
Normal Liftoff Speed	90 KIAS
Rate of Climb, Two Engines	3,000 fpm
Rate of Climb, Single Engine	750 fpm
Normal Cruise	
Airspeed	295 KTAS
Fuel Flow	850 PPH
Range (no reserves)	500 nautical miles
Maximum Cruise	
Airspeed	325 KTAS
Fuel Flow	1000 PPH
Range (No Reserves)	470 nautical miles
Landing Ground Roll	1,500 ft.
Landing Distance Over 50 Foot Obstacle	2,900 ft.

A-37
Dragonfly

-chapter 10-

In the early 1960s, the USAF determined that a new light attack aircraft was needed for the counterinsurgency (COIN) operations prevalent in the myriad of Third World nations that could not afford to purchase and operate, and in reality did not have a military requirement for, the current generation of high performance fighter aircraft.

In 1962, the original T-37C prototype aircraft (62-5951) and a subsequently modified T-37B (62-5950) were evaluated by the USAF as armed COIN aircraft at Eglin AFB, Florida, at the Special Air Warfare Center. These prototype aircraft still carried the same 1,025-pound-thrust Continental J69-T-25 engines used in the basic T-37B, although the aircraft gross weight was increased

to 8,700-pounds. The USAF objective was to develop a lightweight, easily maintained attack fighter with excellent short-field performance. It was soon clear that these first prototypes needed more power to achieve the latter objective.

In 1963, the USAF Aeronautical Systems Division at Wright-Patterson AFB near Dayton, Ohio, issued a bcontract to Cessna for two YAT-37D prototypes for evaluation. To meet the six-month delivery schedule, Cessna used the prototypes previously evaluated at Eglin AFB as the airframes for the new prototypes. The biggest challenges were the 10,500-pound gross weight and the speed and short-field performance requirements. To meet these

• *A-37B in formation with its trainer precursor, the T-37B* •
(Kansas Aviation Museum/Robert J. Pickett Collection)

• *YAT-37D prototype, s/n 62-5951, salvoing the rockets from a 14-shot pod under its left wing* •
(Kansas Aviation Museum/Robert J. Pickett Collection)

- Mk 20 Mod 4 gun sight mounted in front of the pilot.
- Gun camera mounted on the top of the instrument panel just left of the windscreen center rail.
- Wingtip mounted 95-gallon external fuel tanks.
- Larger wheels and tires for use on unimproved runways.
- Special avionics package for communication, navigation, and target acquisition.

goals, Cessna had to find a new engine—one small enough to fit in the existing engine nacelles. The chosen engine was the General Electric J85-J2/5, a derivative of the J85-GE-5 used in the USAF's new supersonic T-38 jet trainer. In the T-38, the J85 produced 2,050 pounds of thrust (2,900 pounds in afterburner), but space and simplicity dictated the use of a non-afterburning engine in the YAT-37D. With some modifications, the new engines were certified at 2,400 pounds of thrust apiece—more than doubling the aircraft's available power. The engine inlets had to be slightly enlarged to accept the bigger J85 engines.

In just six months, both aircraft were re-engined and the airframes and wings were beefed-up to accommodate the required 10,500-pound gross weight. Other changes made for the new aircraft included:

- Three underwing hardpoints and pylons on each wing with provisions for a variety of weapons as well as external, 100-gallon, jettisonable fuel tanks.
- Armor plating (7/32-inch steel) on the cockpit floor and behind the seats for protection against ground fire from up to 30 caliber weapons.
- Self-sealing fuel tanks able to sustain penetration by up to 30 caliber weapons.
- Vortex generators located on top of the wings just forward of the ailerons.
- General Electric GAU-2B/A 7.62mm Minigun mounted in the nose compartment with 1,500 rounds of ammunition.

Although Cessna test pilots flew the prototypes a few times during development to ensure proper engine integration, the first flight of the completely modified YAT-37D (serial number 62-5951) was completed on 22 October 1963 by Cessna engineering test pilot James LeSueur. This flight was to demonstrate aircraft performance with both the new engines and simulated external stores. LeSueur reported that the aircraft "performed well in all maneuvers."

Initial flight testing of the first prototype was conducted at Edwards AFB, California, by both Cessna and USAF test pilots. At the same time, a North American YAT-28E COIN prototype was being tested and evaluated by the USAF. Once the YAT-37D's airworthiness and per-

• *YA-37A prototype, s/n 62-5951, now on display at the Air Force Museum* •
(U.S. Air Force Museum)

formance had been validated, flight testing activities centered on Eglin AFB, Florida, and its Special Air Warfare Center. The second prototype (serial number 62-5950) underwent extensive weapons evaluation and COIN operations testing in 1964. The Cessna candidate was clearly superior to the modified T-28 in performance and capability. The prototypes did not lead to a production contract, and on 14 December 1964 one of the prototypes (serial number 62-5951) was retired to the US Air Force Museum in Dayton, Ohio.

Within two years, however, the USAF again became interested in the proposed Cessna attack jet as a replacement for its aging Douglas A-1E Skyraiders, which were performing well in the escalating war in Vietnam but were also sustaining heavy combat losses. The retired YAT-37D prototype (62-5951) was pulled from the Air Force Museum in August 1966 to be used as the prototype for a new version — the YA-37A. The aircraft was refurbished to fully flightworthy condition and a fourth external weapons pylon was added under each wing. The maximum gross weight of the aircraft increased to 12,000 pounds, which allowed a maximum ordnance load of 4,855 pounds with only one pilot on board. After four years of A-37 flight test duties, 62-5951 was again retired to the US Air Force Museum in July 1970, flown from Cessna's Wichita plant to the Museum in Dayton, Ohio, by Jim LeSeuer, who had also flown the aircraft on its maiden flight as the prototype T-37C in 1961.

Meanwhile, the USAF issued a contract to Cessna for the delivery of 39 AT-37D aircraft to be tested in combat in South Vietnam under operation Combat Dragon. The aircraft were soon redesignated A-37A and assigned sequential serial numbers 67-14503 through 67-14541. In order to produce the aircraft in the short time allowed

• *USAF pilots strap in for the first flight of an A-37A in South Vietnam, at Bien Hoa Air Base, September 1967 (604th Special Operations Squadron, 3rd Tactical fighter Wing)* •
(Kansas Aviation Museum/Robert J. Pickett Collection)

under the contract, Cessna converted 39 new T-37Bs already in production into A-37As (Cessna Model 318D). The aircraft soon received its official name of Dragonfly.

Twenty-five of the new aircraft were assigned to the 604th Air Commando Squadron (later the 604th Special Operations Squadron) of the 3rd Tactical Fighter Wing (TFW) at Bien Hoa Air Base, South Vietnam, in August 1967 to evaluate them for close air support, escort, and armed reconnaissance use. In the aircraft's first 3,000 combat sorties, no A-37A aircraft were lost to hostile fire. Combat Dragon ended in December 1967, after completing 5,000 sorties in five months—an average of 40 sorties per month per aircraft. All 39 of the original A-37A aircraft were later withdrawn from service to be rebuilt into an improved A-37B configuration.

According to John Macartney, who was the Weapons Officer for the 3rd TFW at Bien Hoa in 1968, the Wing's battle damage records showed that the "A-37s took proportionately less hits from ground fire than [the wing's faster] F-100s, despite the fact that the [F-100s] flew ordnance delivery at up to 400 KIAS while the A-37s delivered at 300 to 350 KIAS." He said this was most likely a result of the A-37's smaller size. Macartney, who flew 10 combat missions during Combat Dragon in the right seat of the unit's A-37A aircraft, noted, "The A-37 had so much power relative to the T-37 that you had to yank BACK on the throttles immediately after takeoff to keep from exceeding the gear limit speed. As soon as the gear was up and locked, you put on the power again for climbout."

USAF Colonel Heath Bottomly, the officer in charge of the Combat Dragon evaluation program, gave a briefing to Cessna management shortly after the completion of

• *A-37A clearly showing its three underwing stores stations* •
(Kansas Aviation Museum/Robert J. Pickett Collection)

Combat Dragon. Colonel Bottomly noted that the A-37:

- Would perform without question on air missions in permissive locations (target areas with no enemy air force opposition).
- Demonstrated very short turnaround times between missions.
- Was economical to operate and acquire (initial purchase price was about $340,000 apiece).
- Proved to be highly reliable and easy to maintain, typically making 200 landings on one set of tires.
- Allowed pilot training time to be reduced to as little as two weeks, due to the aircraft's simplicity and to pilot familiarity with the T-37 version.
- Was highly survivable and difficult for enemy gunners to hit due to its maneuverability and slim silhouette.

Improved Dragonfly

The Combat Dragon evaluation identified several areas for improvement, which led to the development of the A-37B Dragonfly (Cessna Model 318E) and a USAF $3.6-million contract to Cessna for 127 aircraft with deliveries beginning in May 1968. These were all totally new aircraft, not modified T-37s, and the contract called for the structure to be strengthened once more to a maximum gross weight of 14,000-pounds.

Although many of the B-Model improvements stemmed from the results of Combat Dragon, the USAF had actually signed a Letter Contract with Cessna on 24 January 1967 for "the production of 57 A-37B aircraft and 1 Mobile Training Set." In the resulting 7 June 1967 Cessna Project Activation Memo, the specific contract

• *Combat Dragon insignia used by the 604th Air Commando Squadron, Bien Hoa, South Vietnam, 1967* •
(Kansas Aviation Museum)

requirements included:

- Production of 55 A-37B aircraft with USAF serial numbers 67-14777 through 67-14822 and 67-22483 through 67-22491.
- Instrumentation of the prototype A-37B (serial number 67-14823), instrumented for Category I flight tests.
- Instrumentation of the first production A-37B (serial number 67-14776) for USAF Category II flight tests.
- Refurbishment and updating of the AT-37A prototype (serial number 62-5950) to A-37B

• *A-37A loaded and parked in a revetment at Bien Hoa illustrates the low profile that made it a difficult target for enemy gunners* •
(Kansas Aviation Museum/Empire News Service)

• Cessna's A-37B assembly line in October of 1967 •
(Kansas Aviation Museum/Robert J. Pickett Collection)

- Nose-mounted probe-and-drogue in-flight refueling system.
- Enlarged landing gear, wheels, and high flotation tires (with larger and slightly bulging main gear doors).
- Explosion-suppressing foam in the self-sealing fuel tanks.
- Redesigned instrument panel to improve cross-cockpit flying from the right seat.
- Further wing strengthening to increase the maximum structural load limit to six Gs (from the A-37A's five-G limit).
- Deletion of the A-37A's wing vortex generators.
- Layered nylon flak curtains around the cockpit.
- Improved cockpit air conditioning system.
- Additional avionics equipment — UHF and VHF/FM radios, IFF/SIF system, and TACAN and ADF navigation receivers.
- CA-503 fixed reticle optical gunsight.
- KS-27C 16mm gun camera mounted in the nose just to the left of the taxi light.

configuration, instrumented for contractor Category I flight tests.

When the final formal contract was issued for the initial production of A-37B aircraft an additional 70 aircraft were ordered (serial numbers 687911 through 687980).

The new B-Models included an in-flight refueling capability, and an increased gross weight of 15,000 pounds was allowed after completion of in-flight refueling. Deficiencies reported during the Combat Dragon trials included excessive control loads with external ordnance at the required delivery airspeed of around 400 KIAS, lack of flight control redundancy, and an asymmetrical thrust condition when cruising on one engine.

To correct these and other deficiencies and, in general, to improve the new model, Cessna implemented the following improvements in the A-37B:

- Two-step engine start sequence (to replace the five-step procedure required in the T-37B and A-37A).
- New engine model (General Electric J85-GE-17A) producing 2,850 pounds of thrust.
- Revised engine installation to cant them downward and outboard to counter single-engine asymmetric thrust.
- Force-sensitive aileron boost tabs to reduce stick forces at high airspeeds.
- Redundant elevator control cable runs (with the cables separated as far as possible in the A-37's narrow tail section).
- Automatic engine inlet deicing, using hot bleed air from the engine.
- Relocation of the gun camera (from inside the cockpit to the nose centerline beside the gun).
- Switch-selectable rate-of-fire capability for the minigun (variable from 3,000 to 6,000 rounds per minute).

• A-37 undergoing inflight refueling tests with a KC-135 •
(Kansas Aviation Museum/Robert J. Pickett Collection)

• *GE GAU-2B/A 7.62mm minigun installatIon
in the nose of an A-37A* •
(Kansas Aviation Museum/Robert J. Pickett Collection)

• *Cockpit of an A-37A. Gunsight and armament panel are on top of
instrument panel. Gun camera can be seen forward of armament
panel (it was relocated to the nose compartment on the A-37B)* •
(Kansas Aviation Museum/Empire News Service)

• *A-37B, s/n 67-14807, from the
first B-model production lot on the
Salina, Kansas, gunnery range. The
most outboard underwing stores station on each wing is empty* •
(Kansas Aviation Museum/Robert J.
Pickett Collection)

• *A-37B, s/n 69-6361, with a full load (the two inboard tanks on each wing are fuel tanks). The refueling probe and external plumbing down the nose centerline and around the cockpit can be seen clearly* •
(Cessna Aircraft Company)

• *Combat Dragon A-37A on final at Bien Hoa after a mission. Note that the only remaining external stores are fuel tanks* •
(Kansas Aviation Museum/
Empire News Service)

- KB-18 panoramic strike camera mounted on the aircraft belly just aft of the trailing edge of the wings.
- 90-gallon wingtip fuel tanks.

The in-flight refueling system made the A-37B unique in the USAF inventory—it was the only USAF fixed-wing aircraft to use that system rather than the standard boom-and-receptacle method, although the system was commonly used on Navy aircraft. From the nose-mounted probe, external fuel tubing routed fuel down the center of the top of the nose section to the base of the windshield where it split into separate tubing runs to fuel tanks in either wing. The tubing was routed internally from above the engine inlets and fed fuel to the external underwing fuel tanks, wingtip fuel tanks, and internal wing fuel tanks. In addition, the in-flight refueling system allowed the aircraft to be refueled using the single-point pressure refueling system, with a single-point refueling adapter. For in-flight refueling, all internal and external tanks could be filled with the exception of the fuselage tank. In-flight refueling, or single-point pressure refueling on the ground, of internal and wingtip tanks took three to four minutes (to fill a pair of underwing external fuel tanks required an extra minute).

A-37 pilots developed a technique to dramatically increase their loiter time over targets with minimal impact on performance. They routinely shut down one engine at

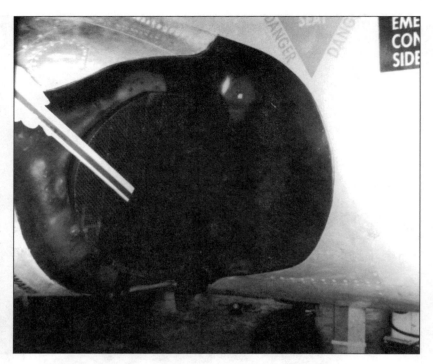

• A-37 engine inlet with the inlet screen in the up position, covering the inlet •
(Kansas Aviation Museum/Robert J. Pickett Collection)

cruise altitude to conserve fuel — with only a 10-knot penalty in cruise speed. The second engine was restarted prior to ingress to the target area and, again, prior to letdown for landing. This technique was feasible in the A-37 due to the excess thrust available at normal cruise speeds with the larger engines. Not only was this procedure regularly used, it was condoned by the pilot's flight manual with a specific normal (as opposed to emergency) procedure for "Single Engine Cruise." The excess thrust that made this practical also resulted in an impressive performance that led to the A-37 Dragonfly's unofficial nickname of "Super Tweet" (derived from its trainer sibling's nicknames of Tweety Bird or Tweet).

Like the T-37, the A-37's cockpit was not pressurized and, therefore, was restricted to a maximum operating altitude of 25,000 feet by USAF regulation, although its actual service ceiling was 41,765 feet. With all of the above improvements, the A-37B weighed almost twice what the T-37B weighed. It was capable of carrying up to 5,880 pounds of ordnance and external stores — close to the T-37B's gross weight of 6,575 pounds! Including fuel weight, the aircraft's total expendable load was 9,527 pounds.

In all, 577 A-37Bs were delivered, including the original 39 A-models which were later rebuilt to B-model configuration. The following serial numbers were assigned to subsequent production aircraft:

• Close-up of the underside of the right wing of an A-37 with a 20mm gun pod mounted on the inboard weapons pylon •
(Kansas Aviation Museum/Robert J. Pickett Collection)

- 68-7911 through 68-7980 and 68-10777 through 68-10827.
- 69-6334 through 69-6446.
- 70-1277 through 70-1312.
- 71-790 through 71-854, 71-858 through 71-873, and 71-1409 through 71-1416.
- 73-1056 through 73-1115 and 73-1654 through 73-1658.
- 74-998 through 74-1013 and 74-1694 through 74-1723.
- 75-374 through 75-385, 75-410 through 75-417, 75-424 through 75-441, and 75-669 through 75-680.

Beginning with the 69-series production, a redesigned and strengthened wing was incorporated. Earlier aircraft were later modified with the same wing. Aircraft with serial numbers in the 71-series and later were produced with improved landing gear with faster extension times. This allowed for a gear-down limiting airspeed of 170 KIAS (versus 150 KIAS for earlier aircraft) — earlier aircraft were later modified with the newer landing gear system.

In the early 1970s, the A-37s were retrofitted with the same bird-proof windscreen developed for the T-37 fleet. I suspect they were installed on the A-3s only after all of the windscreen's initial design problems were worked out

• An A-37 with an array of possible weapons loads. Belts of 7.62mm ammo are at the front. White honeycombed tubes are 7- and 14-tube rocket launchers •
(Kansas Aviation Museum/Robert J. Pickett Collection)

on the T-37. Some of these problems included visual distortion and a tendency to fog over in light rain.

Dragonfly Systems

Most of the basic systems on the A-37 (such as hydraulics, electrical, etc.) were the same as those found on the T-37. There were some important differences brought about by the aircraft's combat persona as well as by the demands of the more powerful engines.

One of the most noticeable visual additions to the A-37, not found on its T-37 relative, was the hinged engine inlet screen provided for each engine. These were deemed necessary due to the significant suction generated by the larger engines and their proximity to the ground. The screens prevented the engines from sucking dirt and debris off the ground and ingesting it. The screens had two positions — stowed (folded back against the underside of the engine nacelle) and up (completely covering the inlet). Screen position was switch-selectable by the pilot, who could also select an "auto" position — reverting control of inlet screen position to a squat switch on the right main landing gear.

The internal fuel system for the A-37B was similar to that of the T-37B, with six interconnected cells in each wing and a single fuselage tank. However, the A-37 also included a

• A-37 engine inlet with the inlet screen in the down position, folded back underneath the inlet lip •
(Kansas Aviation Museum/Robert J. Pickett Collection)

• A USAF A-37 in desert camouflage paint scheme •
(Kansas Aviation Museum/Robert J. Pickett Collection)

CONTROL STICK GRIP

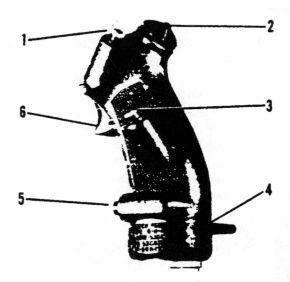

1. **BOMB/ROCKET BUTTON**
2. **ELEVATOR AND AILERON TRIM SWITCH**
3. **YAW DAMPER DISCONNECT SWITCH**
4. **HANDREST**
5. **NOSE WHEEL STEERING BUTTON**
6. **TRIGGER**

• A-37 pilot's control stick grip •
(Air Force Flight Manual)

pair of 90-gallon wingtip tanks, plus provisions for installing droppable 100-gallon fuel tanks on the two most inboard pylons of each wing. With full internal, full tip, and four full pylon fuel tanks, the A-37B could carry a maximum fuel load of 846.7 gallons (5,503.5 pounds) — in an aircraft with an empty weight of 6,254 pounds (6,616 pounds with the minigun, one pilot, and other miscellaneous gear)! And then you could hang weapons on the remaining four pylons and add 1,500 rounds of ammunition for the minigun to bring the total gross weight up to the aircraft's design limit of 14,000 pounds, more than double its empty weight.

Refueling on the ground could be accomplished either "over the wing" through the fuel tank caps located on the outboard leading edge of each wing for internal fuel and the filler caps on each tip tank (pylon fuel tanks also had filler caps), or pressure refueling with a single point ground refueling adapter connected to the aerial refueling probe (although some export models were delivered without an aerial refueling probe). If using the aerial refueling probe, either on the ground or in flight with a tanker aircraft, all fuel tanks could be filled, including tip and pylon tanks.

Although both the A-37 and the T-37 had thrust attenuators, designed to force higher throttle settings during landing approaches, those on the A-37 were considerably larger. This made sense when the higher-thrust engines were considered, although the A-37's J85 engines required only a few seconds to spool-up from idle thrust to full military power (unlike the T-37's slow-winding J69s). An interesting note in T.O. 1A-37B-1 (the "Dash One" or pilot's manual for the A-37B) was that the thrust attenuators "may also be used to reduce taxi speed." Now, that was something the T-37, with its puny J69s, never needed!

Starting with production of aircraft 68-7975, Cessna added slot lip spoilers just forward of the leading edge of the wing flaps (earlier aircraft were retrofitted with the slot lip spoiler system). These hydraulically-actuated slot lip spoilers, according to the Dash One, "provide a marked increase in roll rates at all gross weights and airspeeds," thus correcting one of the deficiencies noted during the Combat Dragon evaluation. The slot lip spoilers remained retracted when the ailerons were in the neutral position or when a corresponding aileron was deflected downward (recall that an aircraft rolls away from a downward deflected aileron). However, when an aileron was deflected upward, the corresponding slot lip spoiler raised — with the amount of deflection proportional to the amount of aileron deflection. This deflection served to reduce lift further on the downward moving wing, consequently increasing the roll rate. Since the slot lip spoilers were actuated through hydraulic servo-actuators that provided no feedback to the pilot, aileron stick forces were not affected.

Other flight control system changes from the basic T-37 system included an adjustable bob weight located under the cockpit floor just forward of the copilot's control stick. It was designed to harmonize the aileron and elevator stick forces throughout the complete range of aircraft gross weights and external stores configurations.

Cessna also added aileron boost tabs. These were force-sensitive tabs on the ailerons connected to the aileron control system through preloaded torsion bars. When aileron aerodynamic forces exceeded the torsion bar preload, the torsion bar flexed and activated a push rod to deflect the boost tab — thus increasing aileron deflection without increasing stick forces.

The A-37 design included a yaw damper system to increase the aircraft's stability about the yaw axis. The yaw damper servo was driven by a computer and actuated by a pneumatic system of bellows fed by engine bleed air. Use of the rudder pedals overrode the yaw damper, which was activated by the pilot with an On/Off switch located on the instrument panel.

And, of course, another major difference between the T-37 and the A-37 was the pilot's stick grip itself. Although they looked the same, all of the various switches worked on the A-37, whereas on the T-37 only the trim switch and the nosewheel steering button worked. On the A-37, the trigger, naturally, controlled the minigun. The bomb/rocket button, obviously, released the bombs or launched the rockets. (Although neither the trigger nor the bomb/rocket button could operate anything unless the Master Armament Switch was placed in the On position.) The remaining button was used to disengage the yaw damper system quickly, and the yaw damper remained disengaged until the On/Off switch was recycled to the On position.

The A-37 was also better equipped to fly in rain and icing conditions than its little brother, the T-37. Cessna installed a rain removal system using a pressurized rain repellent which dispensed 10cc at a time onto the windshield through eight nozzles and was activated by a push button on the air conditioning control panel. An anti-ice system, also activated by an On/Off switch on the air conditioning panel, distributed hot engine bleed air through

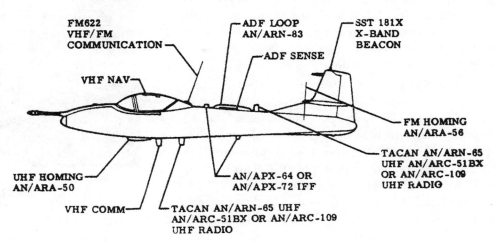

ANTENNA LOCATIONS

• A-37B antenna locations and associated radio nomenclatures •
(Air Force Flight Manual)

ducts in the engine's compressor front frame, inlet guide vanes, engine nose dome and struts, and the forward inlet duct nacelles.

Radio equipment varied depending on the contract lot and which modifications had been incorporated. Generally, all aircraft had a pilot and copilot intercom system, a UHF communications radio, a VHF/FM communications radio with homing capability, TACAN navigation system, IFF/SIF and X-Band transponders, and LF/ADF receiver. Provisions were made for installation of the KY-28 secure voice communication system (scrambler and descrambler). Some aircraft included a UHF/ADF capability, VHF/AM communications radio, and/or a VOR navigation system.

The A-37 takeoff and climb airspeeds were higher than those of the T-37, and varied considerably depending on aircraft gross weight. Normal takeoff at maximum

• A-37B during underwing fuel tank separation test •
(Kansas Aviation Museum/Robert J. Pickett Collection)

gross weight was about 130 KIAS with initial rotation 20-30 KIAS below that. A normal climb speed schedule required accelerating to about 250 KIAS with no external stores (about 200 KIAS with the maximum number of external stores) and then reducing the climb speed by 23 KIAS for each 1,000 feet of altitude during the climb. With both engines operating and no external stores, the Dragonfly's cruise speeds were in the 400+ KTAS range at 25,000 feet (about 35 percent higher than the T-37's normal cruise). However, fuel flows under those same conditions also increased by a factor of about three — from the Tweet's 1,000 pounds-per-hour to the Super Tweet's 3,000 pounds-per-hour of JP-4. This was why the A-37 had to have all those extra fuel tanks.

A-37 traffic pattern airspeeds were very nearly the same as those of the T-37 — 105 KIAS minimum on final versus 100 KIAS for the T-37 (although the A-37 pilot had to add five knots extra for every 1,000 pounds of aircraft weight above 7,500 pounds). Best glide speed for the A-37 (in the event of a dual-engine flameout, with all external stores jettisoned) was 140 KIAS versus 125 KIAS for the trainer model, and approximately 1.8 miles could be flown for every 5,000 feet of altitude versus 2.2 miles per 5,000 feet for the trainer.

Off to Vietnam

Of the total A-37B production run, 254 were provided to the South Vietnamese Air Force (VNAF) to replace their old Douglas A-1 Skyraiders and to complement their new Northrop F-5 Tigers. In January 1968, the VNAF 524th Fighter Squadron (FS) stood down its A-1s. Eighteen of its pilots, plus a cadre of maintenance technicians flew to Wichita where they were trained on existing

• *A-37 pilot in his business office ready to go to work* •
(Kansas Aviation Museum/Empire News Service)

T-37Bs while their A-37s were being manufactured. In May, the USAF dispatched a mobile training detachment to Nha Trang to continue training the maintenance personnel of the 524th. By summer, A-37Bs had replaced the A-1s of the VNAF 524th FS at Nha Trang. However, the Viet Cong Tet Offensive of January 1969 delayed final conversion training, and the 524th did not achieve full operational status until March.

The diminutive A-37 ideally fitted the average Vietnamese pilot, both in size and performance. The 524th was soon achieving outstanding bombing results, despite the aircrews' lack of jet aircraft experience. US and Vietnamese officials jointly decided to replace the VNAF's remaining A-1s with the new aircraft. By May 1969, 54 A-37B aircraft had been delivered to the VNAF 516th, 520th, and 524th Fighter Squadrons, while overall VNAF strength increased by 5,000 personnel to 29,000 total. The last of these first three VNAF A-37 squadrons was declared combat ready in July 1969. Eventually, 10 VNAF squadrons were equipped with the Dragonfly (with the last unit, the 548th FS, becoming combat ready in January 1973), making it the most common combat aircraft in the VNAF inventory:

- Da Nang — 516th FS, 528th FS, 550th FS.
- Nha Trang — 524th FS.
- Phan Rang — 520th FS, 534th FS, 548th FS.
- Binh Thuy — 526th FS, 546th FS.
- Phu Cat and Pleiku — 532nd FS.

The USAF also operated its own A-37 squadrons under the 3rd TFW (the 604th, 8th, and 90th Special Operations Squadrons)

• *A-37A "loaded for bear" with (left to right) cluster bomb unit, napalm cannister, fuel tank, and M-117 750-pound bomb on its right wing* •
(Kansas Aviation Museum/Empire News Service)

with most of the aircraft based at Bien Hoa, Pleiku, and Tan Son Nhut. Following U.S. disengagement from combat in the Vietnam War in 1973, the U.S. began preparing the VNAF for combat self-sufficiency. The first phase of this program was Project Enhance, intended to replace VNAF combat losses and improve some of its support capabilities. Among the aircraft transferred to the VNAF under Project Enhance were 36 A-37B aircraft. Shortly afterwards, Project Enhance Plus was initiated, which added another 54 Dragonflies to the VNAF roster.

• VNAF A-37B, 68-7921, taxiing out of revetments for a combat mission in May of 1970 •
(Kansas Aviation Museum/Robert J. Pickett Collection)

Although the A-37 proved to be an effective and accurate bomb delivery platform, the little 7.62mm Minigun was only marginally effective against anything other than troops in open fields. Even the heavy vegetation prevalent throughout much of South Vietnam reduced its combat effectiveness significantly. FACs appreciated the loiter time and accuracy of the aircraft as an attacker but were frequently frustrated by the ineffectiveness of that little gun — essentially the same weapon mounted on the Rockwell OV-10 FAC aircraft!

Some of the initial A-37B production aircraft were assigned to the 24th Special Operations Wing in the Panama Canal Zone in late 1969.

Infrared Countermeasures

About 1970, the NVA introduced the shoulder-fired, heat-seeking SA-7 Grail surface-to-air missiles into the war in South Vietnam. This significantly changed the nature of the close air support missions and necessitated some aircraft adaptations. The VNAF and USAF A-37B aircraft were modified with an infrared countermeasures (IRCM) system that allowed the pilot to dispense an MJU-3/B countermeasure flare from an underwing dispenser. To use the system, the Dragonfly had to use one or two of its external weapons stations (one could be hung on each wing), thus reducing the ordnance that could be delivered on a single sortie. The pilot had to select, via a cockpit switch, the dispenser on either the left or right wing and then press a button to release a flare once he had sighted an SA-7 launch. To preclude having to relinquish an external stores station for the IRCM system, an improved IRCM system was retrofitted into the aircraft in 1972, allowing release of up to 16 ALA-17 decoy flares from an ALE-20 flare dispenser mounted on the underside of the fuselage just aft of the trailing edge of the wing, replacing the KB-18 strike camera. The new system also provided the pilot with a "flares remaining" display.

Despite the implementation of the IRCM system in VNAF A-37B aircraft, the VNAF was unable to satisfactorily counter the SA-7 threat. A-37s continued flying ground attack sorties against tank and troop concentrations, but their effectiveness was dramat-

• USAF A-37A loaded and ready for combat in its Bien Hoa revetment in 1967 •
(Kansas Aviation Museum/Empire News Service)

ically decreased as the pilots raised their attack altitudes to ever higher altitudes.

Landing on Fumes

When then-Major Fred McNeill served as an O-2 FAC in the Central Highlands of II Corps during 1972, he operated out of Pleiku into Cambodia, Laos, and even extreme southern North Vietnam. In the spring of 1972, he was tasked to direct an airstrike in support of an ARVN firebase on a mountaintop northwest of Kontum. The ARVN had deployed a reconnaissance patrol, composed of about 100 ARVN troops and 20 U.S. Army advisors, along an extremely rocky and absolutely barren ridgeline that stretched south from the firebase. Once well away from their base, they began taking intense fire from an entire company of NVA regulars that were scaling the sides of the ridge from both directions. When McNeill received the orders for a dawn close air support mission, the only available tactical aircraft was a pair of A-37Bs from Bien Hoa — Kontum was at the limit of their combat range. The squadron commander, Colonel Weed, and his wingman agreed to fly the mission, and McNeill asked them to bring all the napalm they could carry (about four 750-pound canisters). McNeill arrived in the target area at first light and contacted the pinned-down patrol. They were completely surrounded with no way to dig in or find cover on the rocky ridge. Casualties were already running to 30 percent and they were about to be overrun completely. The rules of engagement prohibited dropping napalm within 100 meters of friendly troops unless the troops were safely dug in. However, the patrol leader insisted that McNeill direct the napalm attack — they were going to die anyway if he did not. To be sure there was no misunderstanding or later recriminations, McNeill recorded the approval and the patrol leader's name on the tape recorder that was standard equipment on all combat aircraft in that war.

As the A-37s reported overhead and readied for the attack, with no excess fuel for subsequent attacks, McNeill briefed them carefully and told one of them to drop on the north side of the ridge and the other on the south side of the ridge. McNeill placed one marking rocket on each side of the ridge to mark the point where he wanted them to start laying down the napalm. He gave final attack directions to Colonel Weed and his wingman and then gave them a post-attack heading for a direct route to Pleiku, the nearest suitable airfield. The Army radio operator keyed his microphone to say something just as the napalm from the A-37s began to explode. As the initial explosions died out, McNeill could hear the troops whooping and hollering — the napalm had been laid precisely on target without hitting a single ARVN or U.S. Army soldier. The NVA immediately broke contact and pulled back — after losing up to 300 of their troops to the napalm. The A-37s zoomed away and took up their heading for Pleiku with their fuel state dwindling. When McNeill landed back at Pleiku, he discovered that Colonel Weed's wingman had ran out of fuel on the runway and had to be towed to a parking spot for refueling. That night in the Pleiku bar, neither of those Dragonfly pilots was able to buy his own beer — every Pleiku pilot was too impressed with their performance that day!

Ode to a Dragonfly

During its combat operations in the Vietnam War, the Cessna A-37B Dragonfly sparked the poetic soul of at least one USAF aviator, Captain Oliver A. Maier — an A-37B pilot with the 3rd TFW at Bien Hoa. Captain Maeir wrote the following poem and sent it to the people at Cessna who had made the aircraft:

From a kiddy park, they say you were taken;
    to fight in Vietnam? We must be mistaken!
You are quite small, this is true. . .
    coming in assorted colors, green or blue.
Plus being so light, so simple and quick,
    small wonder they think you must be some trick.
But a fierce fighting fire burns deep in your soul,
    defeating the enemy is your primary goal.
Having one-third of your weight in ordnance,
    you don't give Charlie much of a chance.
The bombs, rockets and nape you hold under your wings
    can demonstrate to Charlie some terrible things.
One little nose gun is all that you carry
    but its 6,000 per minute make his life very hairy.
One engine shut down, less fuel you burn,

• A photo taken over the shoulder of the "jammer" driver as he positions a CBU for loading on the right wing of a Bien Hoa A-37 •
(Kansas Aviation Museum/Empire News Service)

allowing you to loiter, while others return.
Over the target on one engine you can wait,
   persuading Charlie to decide his fate.
If they attack Ranch Hand, outpost or convoy,
   all your precision you will quickly employ
To stop the enemy, repulse the attack,
   and make him think twice about coming back.
Two comm radios, two nav radios too,
   allow you to proceed when the sky isn't blue.
Low ceilings, bad vis. . .you maneuver so fast,
   keeping the target throughout every pass.
Charlie doesn't like you, this we know,
   the bullet holes in you, this surely must show.
Back from the target, your mealtime is small,
   then return to the enemy to give them your all.
No A/B, no drag-chute, not supersonic, I'm sorry.
   It's for your big brothers to get all the glory.
Yes, from a kiddy park they implied you came,
   but you're a determined fighter just the same.
Even though your parent hurt only the ear,
   you've given Charlie his life to fear.
So here's to you, O Little Dragonfly,
   you've proven you're a fighter, hold your head high!

After reading Captain Maier's epic poem, Cessna
employee Shirley Spence penned a response to the captain:

Dear Captain, we thank you
For your oh so kind words
You make "from a kiddy park"
Sound so absurd.
You told of fierce fighting,
Of the nose gun and such
And how it doesn't give Charlie
Time to think much.

Yes, we here at Cessna
Are proud of this plane
And Little Dragon Fly seems
An appropriate name.
But this plane's effectiveness
Without pilot, is nil
Your skills are what make Charlie
Run for the hills.
Yes, we plane-builders are proud
Of the work that we do
And of our men in Vietnam, well. . .
We're proud of you too.

POW Dragonflies

The spring of 1975 saw the beginning of the final
North Vietnamese assault on South Vietnam. On 9 March,
the NVA launched a massive assault on the important
Central Highlands city of Ban Me Thuot, with relentless
artillery, mortar, and rocket attacks. Although the VNAF
flew more than 200 combat sorties in that battle, no aircraft were lost. However, 15 VNAF aircraft were
destroyed on the ground, including three A-37Bs
destroyed by 122mm rockets on 11 March. By 14 March,
the city and surrounding area were taken over by NVA
forces. On 28 March, the South Vietnamese 1st Air
Division was forced to evacuate with 130 aircraft from Da
Nang Air Base in the face of the NVA onslaught —
although 180 aircraft and associated ordnance were abandoned (among them 33 A-37Bs). By 30 March, most of
the major South Vietnamese towns and airfields were in
communist hands.

By mid-April, there was no doubt that the NVA forces
were soon to completely overrun South Vietnam. As the
NVA tightened the noose around Phu Cat, VNAF maintenance personnel fought back the attackers from the base
perimeter as their pilots refueled and armed
their own A-37Bs. Nonetheless, the base soon
fell to the communists. Bien Hoa fell on 15
April after perhaps a dozen A-37s were
destroyed by NVA rockets. Adding insult to
the heavy losses being sustained by the VNAF,
a trio of A-37B Dragonflies bombed the airfield at Tan Son Nhut on 28 April — using aircraft that had been captured by the advancing
NVA forces. The pilots for these captured aircraft were either (depending on which sources
one chooses to believe) VNAF defectors, captured VNAF pilots trying to protect their fam-
ilies from communist retribution, or North
Vietnamese Air Force (NVAF) pilots trained
by VNAF defector Captain Nguyen Thanh
Trung.

As North Vietnam completely overran the
South, they captured hundreds of aircraft,

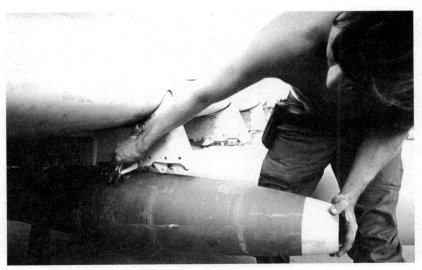

*• An armament technician secures an MK-82 bomb
under the wing of a Bien Hoa A-37 •*
(Kansas Aviation Museum/Empire News Service)

I. THỐNG KÊ CÁC THIẾT BỊ CHỦ YẾU

Số thứ tự	TÊN CÁC THIẾT BỊ	Số lượng	KÝ HIỆU	SỐ SẢN XUẤT	THỜI HẠN BẢO ĐẢM		
					Số giờ	Số năm	Ngày hết bảo đảm
1	Động cơ số 1		J85-17A	GE-E-248282	24	00g	0
	Bộ quạt nến			Không hồ sơ			
	Bánh xe truớc bên 1			Không hồ sơ			
	Bánh xe truớc bên 2			Không hồ sơ			
2	Động cơ số 2		J85-17A	GE-E-248675	24	00g	
	Bộ quạt nến			Không hồ sơ			
	Bánh xe truớc bên 1			Không hồ sơ			
	Bánh xe truớc bên 2			Không hồ sơ			
3	Bộ khí nhập		4432-1	u u	600g		
4	Ống dầu đỏ		9900070-1	u u	1000g/3năm		
5	Bộ điều áp dưỡng-khí		14590-34	u u	18 thg		
6	Bộ điều áp dưỡng-khí		14590-34	u u	18 thg		
7	Trục cuốn		1000-17	50490	60 thg	2	
8	Trục cuốn		1000-45	50482	60 thg	2	
9	Hạt nổ M5A1		8593686	0335	60 thg	5	
10	Hạt nổ M5A1		8593686	0289	60 thg	5	
11	Hạt nổ M3A2		8595821-1	Không biết	60 thg	6	

621 → Trong phiếu công nghệ

• *A page from the flight log of a Vietnamese A-37B now belonging to Australian David Lowy •*
(Stephen Crocker)

including 95 of the VNAF A-37B aircraft — the remaining 92 aircraft were flown out of the country, many to neighboring Thailand. Of these, some were eventually passed on to other countries in the region (16 to Thailand, 27 to South Korea, and 15 to Cambodia) or returned to the United States for deployment with Air National Guard and Air Force Reserve units. Other A-37 aircraft captured by the NVA were later used during the Vietnamese invasion of Cambodia — which meant that both sides were using the same aircraft for some of their combat sorties. In addition, Thailand flew regular overflights of the contested areas in a variety of aircraft, including its own A-37Bs.

Dragonfly for FACs

Most of the USAF A-37s returned from South Vietnam were transferred to the Air National Guard and Air Force Reserves when the United States withdrew from Vietnam. At least 130 of these were later redesignated as OA-37Bs and used as Forward Air Control aircraft to replace the Cessna O-2s and Rockwell OV-10s deployed in Korea, Europe, and Panama, as well as with the Air National Guard and the Air Force Reserve. The aircraft served in South Korea with the 5th Tactical Control Group of the Pacific Air Force and in the Panama Canal Zone with the 24th Composite Wing. In its FAC role, the OA-37B never saw combat, and all the aircraft had been retired by 1990. The OA-37B was supplanted by the better armored and more awesomely armed OA-10A "Warthog."

• *A close-up of the nose of a 434 TFW A-37B at Richards-Gegaur AFB, Missouri, August 1979, showing the unit's Dragonfly emblem •*
(Kansas Aviation Museum/Robert J. Pickett Collection)

• An A-37B of the New York Air National Guard's 174 TFG,
"The Boys From Syracuse," s/n 73-1108 •
(Kansas Aviation Museum/Robert J. Pickett Collection)

Other Dragonfly Exports

Between 1971 and 1974, the U.S. government ran Project Flycatcher to aid the Khmer communist resistance in Laos. Under this program, 15 A-37Bs were provided to the Khmer Air Force, which flew them out of Pochentong.

Cessna produced an additional 110 A-37B aircraft after the United States involvement in the Vietnamese War ended. These aircraft were all exported under the MAP to South and Central American countries. Additional A-37s were later provided to MAP countries as they were removed from active USAF service. It proved to be an ideal aircraft for operation by countries with limited defense budgets and smaller, less technologically advanced air forces. Some of these exported aircraft had the refueling probe removed or replaced with a shorter probe for use as a single-point ground refueling system.

In addition, in the 1970s Ethiopia placed orders for 12 A-37Bs, which were subsequently embargoed and never delivered.

In February 1984, the Nicaraguan Contra rebels attacked Nicaraguan Army positions with air support from an A-37B and five helicopters of the Fuerza Aerea Hondurena (Honduran Air Force).

In El Salvador on 27 January 1982, rebels attacked the main airfield at Ilopango and destroyed 19 aircraft, but the United States quickly replaced the losses with 27 replacement aircraft (including eight A-37Bs). A rebel near-takeover of the town of Berlin, El Salvador, was thwarted when the Fuerza Aerea Sandinista (FAS) strafed rebel positions with a flight of A-37s backed up by a battalion of Army troops. Dragonflies were also instrumental in stopping major rebel attacks in the summer of 1983 in the area near the nation's capitol. The FAS flew 227 airstrike missions, most flown by A-37s. The following March, the United States provided 10 more A-37B aircraft to the FAS.

Another, much more limited, use of A-37 aircraft took place in Guatemala on 8 August 1983 when extremists within the armed forces overthrew President Montt and repeatedly overflew the capitol to demonstrate their strength and willingness to use whatever force was necessary.

On 3 February 1986, rebels captured the town of Morales, Colombia, but were quickly driven out by government forces, including numerous airstrikes by Colombian A-37B aircraft.

And the Inevitable Modifications

Cessna, like most other aircraft manufacturers, kept looking for possible modifications and follow-on designs to its successful and profitable designs, like the A-37 Dragonfly. After having attempted to win various T-37 follow-on contracts (such as the Tandem Navy Trainer and the USAF Next Generation Trainer), Cessna proposed a variation on their TNT design to compete for a U.S.

A-37 Deliveries to South and Central America		
Country	Quantity	Year
Chile	34	1974-75
Columbia	26	1980 - including 12 for anti-drug efforts
Ecuador	12	1975
El Salvador	21	1983-84 - including 3 replacements in 1991
Guatemala	13	1969 and 1973
Honduras	15	1974-75
Peru	36	1974-75 - including last production A-37B, also the very last of the A/T-37 series
Uruguay	12	1975
Total	**169**	

• *An A-37B, captured by North Vietnam in 1975 and now belonging to Australian David Lowy, at the start of its 1994 restoration* •
(Stephen Crocker)

Navy VTOL (vertical takeoff and landing) trainer — a unique design that added three "lift engines" on a pod on each wing to provide the necessary vertical thrust.

Using the TNT design as a point of departure, Cessna proposed an A-37D. This design used the TNT's tandem fuselage but with a fuel tank in place of the rear seat. The gun system was to be mounted on the fuselage centerline in the nose, with provisions for an external centerline gun pod.

About the same time, Cessna used its design experience on the TNT proposal again — this time for a USAF STOL (short takeoff and landing) aircraft for the close air support mission. This effort was dubbed the AT-37E/STOL and incorporated more powerful engines, increased wingspan, and thrust

• *Cessna's AX candidate design* •
(Kansas Aviation Museum)

reversers, but used the T-37's side-by-side cockpit layout.

Flush with its A-37 achievements, Cessna joined the competition in the 1970s for the Attack Experimental (AX) contract. The Cessna design was not a derivative of the A-37 program but did build on lessons learned from it. The AX competitive flyoff contracts went, however, to the Northrop A-9 and the Fairchild A-10 — with the A-10 eventually winning the production contract.

• *A group of Dragonflies badly in need of care and attention in the "boneyard" at Davis-Monthan AFB, Arizona* •
(Kansas Aviation Museum/Robert J. Pickett Collection)

Where Have All the Dragonflies Gone?

Many A-37s are still being flown in active service by the air forces of various foreign nations, mostly in South and Central America. The Royal Thai Air Force operates a single squadron of A-37Bs. The forcibly unified, communist Vietnam has retired its captured A-37s, replacing them primarily with the Sukhoi Su-7 — with many of them since sold to private warbird operators.

There is only one A-37B still flying in the USAF, and it is no longer flying operational sorties. The aircraft belongs to the Air Force Flight Test Center at Edwards AFB, California, and is being used for spin training in the Air Force Test Pilot School curriculum.

Several of the ex-Vietnamese Dragonflies are being flown regularly by private owners in Australia. At this writing, the Lone Star Flight Museum in Galveston, Texas, operated the only privately owned flying A-37B in the United States — although a few others were being restored to flyable condition by private individuals and aviation museums. A flyable A-37 was turned over to the American Wings Air Museum in Minnesota from the USAF, but its condition necessitated considerable refurbishment before being taken on the airshow circuit.

Museums around the United States that claim to have Cessna A-37 Dragonflies on display include:

- *Museum of Aviation*, Warner Robbins, Georgia (A-37A).
- *US Air Force Museum*, Dayton, Ohio (YA-37A).
- *Lone Star Flight Museum*, Galveston, Texas (A-37B).
- *Sheppard AFB Air Park*, Wichita Falls, Texas (YA-37A). ☩

• *David Lowy and Stephen Cocker taxi out in the now fully restored ex-Vietnamese A-37B* •
(Stephen Crocker)

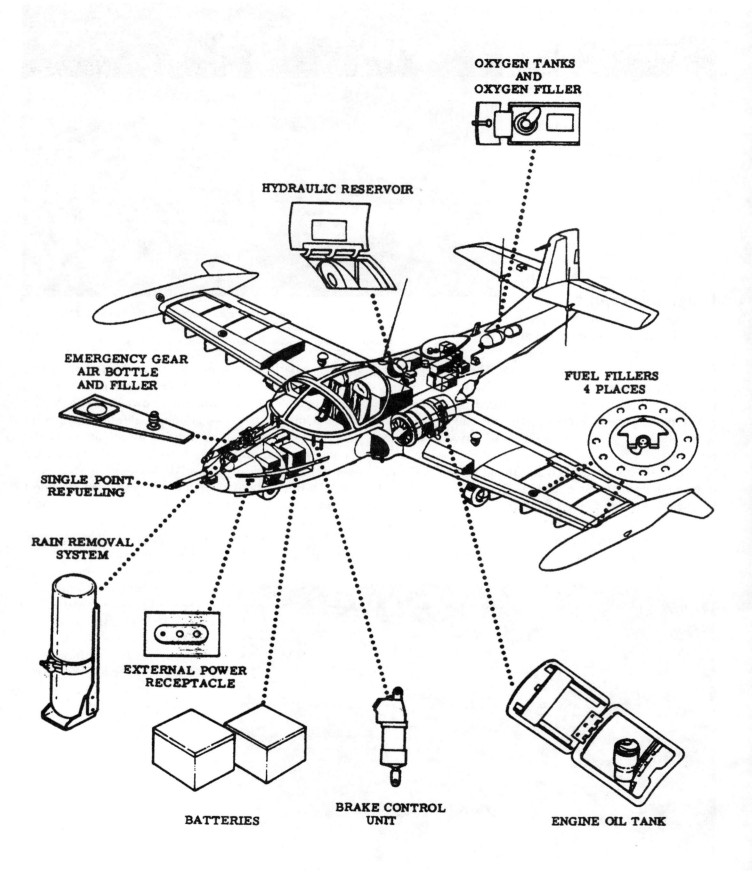

OXYGEN TANKS
AND
OXYGEN FILLER

HYDRAULIC RESERVOIR

EMERGENCY GEAR
AIR BOTTLE
AND FILLER

FUEL FILLERS
4 PLACES

SINGLE POINT
REFUELING

RAIN REMOVAL
SYSTEM

EXTERNAL POWER
RECEPTACLE

BATTERIES

BRAKE CONTROL
UNIT

ENGINE OIL TANK

• *The A-37B internal arrangement and servicing diagram* •
(U.S. Air Force Flight Manual)

Specifications

A-37B

Wingspan with tip tanks . . . . 38.34 ft.
Length
        With Aerial Refueling Boom . . . . 31.83 ft.
        Without Aerial Refueling Boom . . . . 29.28 ft.
Height . . . . 9.47 ft.
Wheel Base . . . . 7.83 ft.
Wheel Tread . . . . 13.66 ft.
Engines General Electric J85-17A turbojets,
. . . . 2,850 pounds static thrust each
Weight
        Empty . . . . 6,254 lbs.
        Normal With Internal & Tip Tank Fuel . . . . 9,689.5 lbs.
        Maximum Allowable . . . . 14,000 lbs.
. . . . 15,000 pounds inflight after aerial refueling
Fuel Capacity
        Fuselage Tank . . . . 79 U.S. gallons
        Wing Tanks (2) . . . . 99.25 U.S. gallons each
        Wingtip Tanks (2) . . . . 90 U.S. gallons each
        Pylon Tanks (4) . . . . 97.3 U.S. gallons each
        Total (no pylon tanks) . . . . 457.5 U.S. gallons (2,973.5 lbs.)
        Total (4 pylon tanks) . . . . 846.7 U.S. gallons (5,503.5 lbs.)
Minimum Single Engine Speed . . . . 105 KIAS
Maximum Glide Speed . . . . 140 KIAS
Glide Ratio 10.9:1
Maximum Allowable Speed . . . . 415 KIAS or 0.70 Mach
G Limits . . . . +6/-2.4
Stall Speed (Power Off)
        14,000 Pounds, Flaps Up . . . . 127 KIAS
        14,000 Pounds, Full Flaps . . . . 106 KIAS
        6,00 Pounds, Flaps Up . . . . 83 KIAS
        6,000 Pounds, Full Flaps . . . . 70 KIAS
Stall Speed (85% Power)
        14,000 Pounds, Flaps Up . . . . 124 KIAS
        14,000 Pounds, Full Flaps . . . . 103 KIAS
        6,000 Pounds, Flaps Up . . . . 80 KIAS
        6,000 Pounds, Full Flaps . . . . 67 KIAS
Takeoff Ground Roll . . . . 2,800 ft.
Takeoff Distance Over 50-Foot Obstacle . . . . 3,900 ft.
Normal Liftoff Speed . . . . 130 KIAS
Normal Cruise, No External Stores
        Airspeed . . . . 265 KTAS
        Fuel Flow . . . . 1,700 PPH
        Range (No Reserves) . . . . 390 nm
Normal Cruise, Single Engine
        Airspeed . . . . 250 KTAS
        Fuel Flow . . . . 1,200 PPH
Maximum Cruise, no external stores
        Airspeed . . . . 420 KTAS
        Fuel Flow . . . . 3,300 PPH
        Range (no reserves) . . . . 325 nm
Landing Ground Roll . . . . 1,800 ft.
Landing Distance over 50-foot obstacle . . . . 3,500 ft.

O-2 "Fighting Skymaster"

-chapter 11-

In 1962, Cessna developed the prototype of a unique twin-engined aircraft aimed at the business traveler who was looking for the enhanced safety of a twin, but without the asymmetric engine-out control problems typically associated with twins. Cessna's solution was to mount one engine on the nose in single-engine aircraft style and the other directly behind the four-place cabin — thus, from the pilot's perspective, the two engines rotated in opposite directions and virtually eliminated the effects of engine torque. In an engine-out situation, the pilot would have no more control problems than with a typical single-engine aircraft. To maintain simplicity, Cessna elected to install fixed tricycle landing gear and strut-braced wings, making it the first such twin in recent aviation history. To accommodate the rear-facing aft engine, a twin tail boom configuration was designed with the rear engine's propeller spinning between the booms.

The new aircraft was dubbed the Model 336. The first of two prototypes flew in 1962, and the 336 hit the market in 1964. Some 200 Model 336s were sold that year, and Cessna decided the market was ready for an aircraft with such an unusual configuration. However, in 1965, the Model 337 replaced the 336 in the Cessna line-up. The new model, named the Skymaster, sported an increased wing incidence, retractable landing gear, and a number of cosmetic changes. The aircraft's handling was typical Cessna — with reasonable aileron control and somewhat heavy pitch control, but able to handle turbulence with aplomb. The airplane's unique looks resulted in several less than complimentary nicknames, from "Push Me, Pull You" to "Mixmaster." Although safety was the Skymaster's raison d'être, its accident rates proved dismal when compared to normal light twin-engine aircraft. This was despite the lack of a "critical engine" as in most twins and the fact that, with one failed engine, the 337 was basically a normal single-engine aircraft.

Skymaster production continued through the 1980 H-II model, with 2,058 civilian 336s and 337s produced by Cessna in the United States and another 84 produced by Reims Aviation in France. Engines throughout remained the 210-horsepower Continental IO-360 (except for some of the turbocharged models after 1973, which used an uprated 225-horsepower TSIO-360). Although climb and cruise perfor-

• An O-2B from the right side. The large loudspeaker is visible where the baggage compartment door would normally be located (under the rearmost side window). Note that the extra right-side lower windows of the A-Model are not installed on the B model •
(Kansas Aviation Museum/Robert J. Pickett Collection)

mance were about average among light twins, Skymasters were capable of taking off and landing in somewhat shorter fields than most other light twins.

As an interesting aside, the 336/337 was the only specific general aviation aircraft model to be banned from an airport in the United Kingdom. Although certified by the UK's CAA, all 336/337 aircraft were banned from the Elstree Aerodrome north of London due to noise. It was the only general aviation aircraft banned at that airport!

Skymaster Battle Wagons

In 1966, USAF realized it needed a replacement for its O-1 Bird Dogs in Vietnam. Although Rockwell Corporation was working on a dedicated counterinsurgency and forward air control (FAC) aircraft, the OV-10, the USAF wanted something cheaper to replace its O-1s — and they wanted it quickly. Hoping to get lucky, the USAF started a program to evaluate off-the-shelf civilian aircraft to fill the gap between the unarmed O-1 and the lightly armed OV-10, which was still a couple of years from active combat service.

One of the aircraft that immediately sparked official interest was Cessna's new Model 337 Skymaster. It pro-vided twin-engine safety but with the high-wing visibility necessary for visual surveillance of combat activity on the ground. Early in 1966, personnel from USAF's Tactical Air Warfare Center (TAWC) at Eglin AFB, Florida, participated in a Cessna-conducted demonstration of the 337's capabilities (the TAWC had previously evaluated a modified Cessna Model 206 for similar missions). Cessna had modified a normal production Skymaster with two external stores stations under each wing. Cessna's Don Simon noted in an internal 12 May memo, "To a man, [the USAF pilots] have been enthusiastic about the aircraft and General Pritchard [TAWC Commander] has established this as a top priority program."

TAWC pilots provided Cessna a list of questions about the feasibility of modifying this businessman's airplane for a classified military application. The following questions and Cessna's responses were also listed in Simon's 12 May memo. (On the attached memo routing slip Bob Lair noted: "They are buying the airplane.")

Q. Could high flotation tires be used?

A. Yes, 8.00 tires were feasible but only in a nonre-tractable mode — in fact, these had been optional on the Model 336.

• The unique O-2/C-337 configuration is obvious in this photo. Note the extra windows in the cockpit ceiling, as these are not found in the civilian model •
(John Wiley)

Q. Would feathering of the rear engine be required to allow dropping anything out of the baggage door?

A. This would require flight testing at Eglin.

Q. Could an escape hatch or disposal tube be installed through the floorboard — for example, for the dropping of smoke bombs?

A. Yes, using the present camera viewfinder hole modified from trapezoidal to rectangular shape.)

Q. Could a smoke generator be installed, such as by dispersing oil into the engine exhaust?

A. Yes, using some available T-37 components.

Q. Could the armament panel for the wing pylons be modified with additional switches for more selective dropping of external stores?

A. Yes, but only with a manual capability.

Q. Could control sticks and tandem seating be installed?

A. Yes, but the redesign would require an extra 18 to 24 months.

Q. Could electric elevator trim be installed?

A. Yes, this was optional equipment on the 337.

Q. Could flap travel be increased?

A. No, due to structural interferences.

Q. Could additional plexiglass be installed in the ceiling above the pilot's head and in the lower portion of the right-hand door?

A. Yes, within structural limitations.

Q. Could a squat switch be installed in the landing gear system to prevent activating the armament system until the gear was retracted?

A. Yes.

Q. What about slimming the fuselage into some sort of tandem configuration?

A. No, this would entail a major redesign.

With most of the feasible modifications incorporated, the aircraft was purchased and designated the O-2A.

1800 Watts of Attack Power

While the TAWC evaluated the 337 as a FAC platform, the Commander of Air Force Systems Command appointed General Gordon Seville to form a team to

• An O-2 dispensing leaflets from the baggage door. This photo accompanied an October of 1967 Headquarters 7th Air Force news release which read:
"O-2B Super Skymaster Pilots Fight a War Without Bullets: Psychological warfare leaflets fill the air during an O-2B Super Skymaster mission. The O-2 is used by 'C' Flight, 9th Air Commando Squadron, at Nha Trang Air Base for psy-war missions from Bong Son to Phan Thiet." •
(U.S. Air Force)

determine the feasibility of using an "available commercial aircraft for a highly classified, special air warfare requirement," according to an internal Cessna memo written by Derby Frye, vice president of the Military Division. Frye went on to announce that a pair of captains from AFSC Headquarters "will visit us Monday AM, May 9, to evaluate the flight characteristics and general adaptation of the Model 337 to meet the mission requirements." He asked that the 337 they had been using for the Eglin evaluation be scheduled for the upcoming AFSC evaluation. This "highly classified" mission turned out to be psychological operations (or psy-ops) warfare wherein the aircraft would be used to drop leaflets over enemy-held territory or blast anti-Communist propaganda over on-board loudspeakers to the enemy troops and local citizens who sympathized with these factions. The two AFSC pilots had additional questions, such as:

Q. Do the booms have sufficient space for a backup control system to the tail surfaces?

A. This idea was later scrapped as any damage to a tail boom would likely damage both sets of control cables.

Q. If an engine or a fuel line is knocked out due to ground fire, will the balance of the system continue to operate?

A. It should, since the left and right portions of the basic C-337 fuel system are separate, unless crossfeed is manually selected.

Q. Is the gross weight limited due to the structure or due to available horsepower?

A. Structure seemed to be the primary limiting factor, and the USAF elected to keep the standard 210-horsepower Continental engines.

The special sound system later incorporated on the

aircraft purchased for this mission, designated the O-2B, consisted of a University Sound Model SA-1800C Supersound loudspeaker system (with three 600-watt amplifiers and highly directional speakers) and a Sony TC-800 reel-to-reel tape recorder. The 1800-watt sound system's broadcasts could be heard up to ten nautical miles under optimum environmental conditions and could be heard on the ground when broadcasting from altitudes up to 10,000 feet. Although the amplifier used the aircraft's 28-volt DC electrical power, the tape recorder required a set of eight "D-cell" flashlight batteries (the pilot's flight manual, T.O. Il-2A-1 or "Dash One," recommended always carrying a spare set of batteries). The system allowed for playback of prerecorded messages via the tape recorder (which could be removed for off-aircraft recording purposes), as well as the broadcast of live messages through the loudspeaker and amplifier system using a noise-cancelling microphone. Long cables were provided so the tape recorder itself could be placed on the copilot's seat for operation by the pilot alone. The Supersound system weighed about 200 pounds and fit into a space 28 inches wide, 15 inches deep, and 12 inches tall.

The leaflet dispensing system was not a permanently installed item. The dispenser chute itself was provided as loose equipment. Two removable covers, one on the floorboard just aft of the copilot's seat and the other located directly below on the aircraft's belly, had to be removed so the dispenser chute could be installed. The dispenser extended into the slipstream below the aircraft, allowing the leaflets to be dispersed. It was important to replace the covers when the chute was removed to prevent sucking front engine exhaust gases into the cabin.

Although still producing the 210 horsepower, the O-2B's front engine was an IO-360C. This version of the engine was identical to the IO-3600 except for a dual accessory drive section to operate both the standard hydraulic pump as well as an additional engine-driven vacuum pump. The O-2B retained the IO-360D for the rear engine. The vacuum pump provided power for the B-Model's heading and attitude indicators, while the A-Model's indicators were electrically driven.

The O-2B also had the standard civilian combination magneto/starter rotary switches rather than the A-Model's more military set of four separate magneto toggle switches and pair of starter buttons. On the O-2B, the electrical switches were standard civilian rocker types — on the O-2A, military style toggle switches were used. Although the A-Model's pilot's control wheel included a micro-

• A 9th Air Commando Squadron O-2B dispensing leaflets from the belly-mounted chute that can be seen protruding from under the rear fuselage. The photo was snapped near Nha Trang in 1967 •
(Kansas Aviation Museum/Empire News Service)

phone button (with "Intercom" and "Transmit" positions), trigger button (for external stores release), and an electric elevator trim tab switch, the B-Model's included only the microphone button. On the B-Model, the amber landing gear indicator light illuminated to indicate the gear was up and locked, while on the A-Model the same light illuminated only when the gear was in transition between up and down. Many of the engine instruments were different for the two models as well, such as:

- Dual tachometer gauge mounted on the right panel on the O-2B, on the left panel on the O-2A.
- B-Model used a split FRONT/REAR manifold pressure gauge, while the A-Model used a pair of concentric pointers.
- B-Model used a split FRONT/REAR fuel flow gauge, and the A-Model used a pair of concentric pointers.
- B-Model had separate pairs of gauges for oil pressure and temperature, and cylinder head temperature. The A-Model had a single pair of combination gauges (one for each engine).
- Only the B-Model had a suction gauge and a flight hour recorder on the panel.
- The O-2B did not have the O-2A's accelerometer (G meter) on the panel.

Despite the fact that all airspeed and operating limitations were the same for both models of the O-2, the O-2B was restricted to 4,200 pounds maximum gross weight, while the O-2A's gross weight limit was 4,850 pounds (with all weight in excess of 4,400 pounds carried on the underwing pylons). Ferry flights, with reduced G limits, were authorized for A-Models at up to 4,600 pounds. Maximum landing weight for both models was restricted to 4,400 pounds.

USAF Orders 337s

While the USAF was considering purchase of the Model 337, the Marines also contacted Cessna and asked how soon they could deliver 55 Model 337s for some unspecified application (most likely to replace their own OE-1s and OE-2s). Cessna's Bob Lair responded that Cessna could produce eight aircraft per month beginning in June 1967, depending on the specifics of the Marine configuration. The Marines never proceeded with this project, apparently deciding instead to wait for the production OV-10.

In early December of 1966, two officers from the Pentagon's research and development organization toured Cessna's plant and the Model 337 assembly line to discuss the possibility of producing a tandem military version of the C-337, tentatively designated the O-2C — with armor plating, more powerful engines, day/night TV capability, possible side-firing weapons, laser rangefinder equip-

ment, self-sealing fuel tanks, and external microphones for detecting the location of ground fire.

On 29 December 1966, while O-2C talks were still ongoing, the USAF placed an initial order for 145 O-2A aircraft (serial numbers 67-21295 through 67-21439) for the FAC mission and an additional order for 31 O-2B aircraft (serial numbers 67-21440 through 67-21470) for the psy-ops mission. The flyaway price of an O-2A in that contract was $92,000. As the B-model did not require underwing hardpoints and deliveries were wanted as soon as possible, the USAF elected to purchase 31 already built but not yet sold civilian Model 337s and have them modified with the necessary sound system, leaflet dispenser, and associated electronics. The O-2B retained the civilian propeller spinners, which were not installed on the A-model aircraft. Only the O-2A aircraft had the extra overhead and right side windows, which were designed to improve the FAC's ability to monitor simultaneously troops on the ground and fighter aircraft above.

O-2B deliveries began 31 March 1967 and were destined for the 9th Air Commando Squadron (later redesignated as the 9th Special Operations Squadron) based at Ton Son Nhut and Nha Trang, South Vietnam. A-model deliveries began one month later, destined for the following Tactical Air Support Squadrons (TASS) in Southeast Asia:

- 19th TASS, Bien Hoa, South Vietnam.
- 20th TASS, Pleiku, South Vietnam.
- 21st TASS, Tan Son Nhut and Phu Cat, South Vietnam.
- 22nd TASS, Da Nang, South Vietnam.
- 23rd TASS, Nakhon Phanom and Ubon, Thailand.

Subsequent orders for O-2A aircraft brought the total delivered to 501 (plus the 31 O-2Bs). These additional A-Models were purchased in three lots, with the following serial numbers:

- 68-6857 through 68-6903, 68-10828 through 68-10872, 68-10962 through 68-11070, and 68-11122 through 68-11173.
- 69-7601 through 69-7669.
- 70-1409 through 70-1442.

Equipment

All O-2As were delivered with two underwing weapons hardpoints on each wing, a rear engine smoke generation system, an armament system with a weapons release trigger mounted on the control wheel, a CA-505 non-computing optical gunsight, provisions for a floor-mounted vertical KB-18A strike camera, and a radio equipment rack mounted in the aft baggage compartment. Voice communication equipment consisted of an array of transmitters and receivers with control heads mounted on the instrument panel to the pilot's right and included:

- Interphone system for intra-cockpit communications.
- AN/ARC-164 UHF transceiver.
- Wilcox Model 807 VHF/AM transceiver.
- Two Magnavox FM-622 VHF/FM transceivers.

In addition, a military AN/APX-64 or AN/APX-72 Identification Friend or Foe/Selective Identification Feature (IFF/SIF) transponder system, a Motorola SST-181X X-Band radar identification beacon, and a KY-28 speech scrambler (used with the number two VHF/FM radio) were installed. For navigation, an AN/ARN-52 TACAN navigation system and an AN/ARN-83 LF/ADF navigation receiver were provided. On later aircraft, a Low Frequency/Single Sideband (LF/SSB) radio was added, and the KY-28 was revised to be operable on all communications radios except the LF/SSB unit. Direction finding capability was possible on all communications radios with the exception of the LF/SSB, providing azimuth information to one of the RMI card needles.

For the O-2B psy-ops aircraft, radio equipment did not include the second VHF/FM (primarily used for air-to-ground communication with Army ground units) or the X-Band radar beacon. Due to the power requirements of the psy-ops broadcast gear, the VHF/AM, LF/ADF, TACAN, and IFF/SIF equipment were automatically disabled whenever the loudspeaker system was operating.

To control which incoming radio transmissions and which navigation identification signals were routed to the pilot's headset, an Interphone-Audio System Control Panel was used comprised of nine switches with push-off/pull-on and rotary volume control. To control outgoing transmissions, a single five-position rotary switch was provided on the panel. One of the many challenges every new FAC faced was learning when to activate the appropriate switches to ensure receiving all necessary radio and navigation information and then recognizing who was transmitting on which radio so he could respond on the

• An early O-2A, s/n 67-21331, now on display at the Air Force Museum. Note the small rectangular pilot's side window •
(U.S. Air Force Museum)

proper frequency. After gaining some experience, a FAC could usually identify the source of a radio call by the sound quality of the incoming message and quickly punch-off any interfering radios, if necessary. However, even highly experienced FACs occasionally neglected to select the correct position of the Microphone Selector Switch and transmitted a message on the wrong radio. A FAC had to communicate almost simultaneously with Army ground commanders on VHF/FM, airborne fighters on UHF, and command post personnel on either the VHF/AM, the second VHF/FM, or on a separate UHF frequency. Radio management in the midst of a busy airstrike merely added one more item to the FAC's already intense workload.

One of the early complaints from FACs putting the first O-2As through their paces in combat was the small window on the pilot's side. The original configuration used the standard civilian side window, a rather small rectangular window which was difficult to use to spot targets below on the left. If the FAC rolled into a steep left bank to allow better downward visibility, he could not look out away from the aircraft very far and could not look back over his left shoulder at all due to the small size of the window. Cessna soon corrected this with a much larger window that extended farther down as well as upward in front of the leading edge of the wing. This was a big improvement, and all but the earliest delivered O-2s included the new window.

Although every O-2A was delivered with the CA-505 non-computing optical gunsight, once out of training most of the FAC pilots used it less and less as they gained more and more experience. Since it was a non-computing sight, the pilot had to determine the appropriate settings for the sight from a voluminous set of tables in the O-2A "Aircrew Weapons Delivery Manual (Non-Nuclear)."

• An O-2 in its revetment at Pleiku Air Base, Vietnam, in 1972. Note the much larger pilot's side window, and the empty rocket pods •
(Fred McNeill)

(Seriously, "Non-Nuclear" is in the title!) This involved determining the target elevation, headwind or tailwind, cross-wind, release altitude, dive angle, and true airspeed at release. Then, with a sharp pencil, trace across the rows and down the columns until the proper sight depression or elevation setting was found. This setting was defined in "mils" — one mil being one milliradian, or 1/1000 of a radian (17.45 mils = 1 degree of arc). The entire calculation assumed no bank angle, no sideslip, and a steady state dive — conditions unlikely to be achieved in the heat of combat while trying to get a marking rocket on a target for the inbound, fast-moving fighters whose fuel was rapidly being depleted. Besides, the result was based on the assumption that the bomb racks and rocket pods were all carefully and properly aligned with the sight ("boresighted" in military parlance) — not necessarily a valid assumption for the O-2.

In reality, a grease pencil mark on the plexiglass and a little "Kentucky windage" were just about as accurate. Everybody learned the "right way," but soon realized it was no better than the TLAR (That Looks About Right) method. In fact, then-Lieutenant Darrell Lambert, now a Lockheed Martin engineer, recalls that during his initial O-2 training, "You'd see the instructor sitting in the right seat [with no sight] and he'd take his grease pencil and put a little mark right there on the windscreen and then he'd demonstrate and hit right where it was supposed to. It

• A pair of O-2As from the 22nd TASS, Da Nang, traveling from a refueling stop at Dong Ha to missions just across the DMZ in North Vietnam in September of 1967 •
(Kansas Aviation Museum/Empire News Service)

didn't take us long to figure out the sight wasn't that important."

Flight Testing the "Oscar Deuce"

At the same time the O-2A contract was issued, a 200-hour flight test program was authorized via Air Force Flight Test Center (AFFTC) Project Directive 67-25 to evaluate O-2 systems and aircraft performance, including qualitative and quantitative evaluation of stability and control. Two aircraft (67-21296 and 67-21299) were delivered to the AFFTC at Edwards AFB, California, to "determine the functional reliability and systems compatibility of the O-2A aircraft, and to obtain quantitative data on aircraft performance." Aircraft 67-21296 was used for

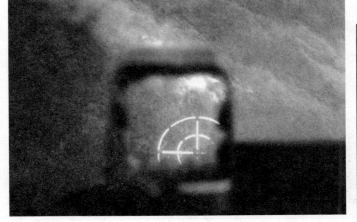

• A view through an O-2A's CA-505 gun sight. The outer segmented circle diameter is 200 mils, and the inner circle is 100 mils •
(Fred McNeill)

the systems testing with 108 hours of tests completed between 1 July and 1 September 1967. No discrepancies were discovered, and the aircraft was returned to Cessna on 3 September.

Cessna installed the necessary flight test instrumentation in the performance evaluation aircraft, 67-21299, and delivered it to Edwards AFB on 2 August 1967. Testing was delayed until 23 August to allow complete calibration of the instrumentation. A total of 100 hours of performance tests were completed between 23 August 1967 and 31 March 1968. Flight testing included:

- Sawtooth climb and descent profiles.
- Heavyweight takeoffs from a hard surface runway.
- High altitude takeoffs and landings from Long Valley Airport in the mountains northwest of Edwards AFB.
- Lightweight takeoffs and landings without external weapons stores.
- One- and two-engine continuous climb tests without external weapons stores.

During the flight tests on 67-21299, the aircraft sustained damage to the landing gear during a hard landing (the nose gear collapsed) and was grounded for repairs for two weeks. Otherwise, the aircraft passed all tests with no problems and no major discrepancies. While the flight tests were being conducted, the first operational O-2A and O-2B aircraft were delivered to Hurlburt Field in Florida for training purposes and, almost simultaneously, to the TASS units in South Vietnam to replace their Bird Dogs.

Ground Attack in an O-2

The O-2A had been tested and certified for carrying a pair of SUU-11A/A 7.62mm minigun pods on the inboard weapons pylons. The first O-2A pilots in South Vietnam, in fact, used the miniguns in combat. Pilot bravado soon led to the FACs taking on enemy ground forces while waiting for fighter aircraft to arrive with heavier, and more effective, weapons. When an unarmored and slow O-2 squared off against a crew-served AAA weapon like a 23mm, even with those "mighty" miniguns aboard, the O-2 invariably lost. Unfortunately, many O-2As sustained needless hits while pressing attacks, and several pilots were shot down. Pacific Air Force (PACAF) headquarters quickly outlawed the minigun pods and removed them

• *An O-2A with minigun pods on inboard pylons, and empty rocket pods on outboard pylons* •
(Kansas Aviation Museum/Robert J. Pickett Collection)

from the theater entirely. From that point on, USAF FACs, whether flying the old O-1s or the new O-2s, were prohibited from carrying any armament except white phosphorous ("Willie Pete") smoke marking rockets.

When Lambert first arrived at Nakhon Phanom Air Base (NKP), Thailand, each FAC was issued an M-16 to carry with him on missions. Most of them would carry three or four clips of ammunition in their helmet bags. When the fighters had gone home and the FAC had some fuel left, he might find some enemy troops (maybe trying to fill-in the bomb craters on the roads), poke his M-16 out the open right window, and open fire. Likewise, then Lieutenant John Wiley, now a pilot for US Air, recalls they tried various techniques for firing the M-16 out the window. They found that if it was fired upright through the small vent window, the shells were ejected into the instrument panel and cracked a lot of instrument glass. If the weapon was held inverted, the shells flew into the back and bounced around in the radio rack assembly. To prevent the shell casings from being ejected into the cockpit, the gun was held far enough out the right side window to ensure they were ejected outside. Unfortunately, those spent casings tended to strike the rear propeller and put nicks in it, causing bad vibrations.

The maintenance technicians were replacing a lot of rear propellers, which were not being bought in sufficient numbers to cover this unexpected damage. After several months, the squadron commander at NKP ordered that no more M-16s could be carried — besides the propeller supply problem, he did not want his FACs flying that low

• *USAF mechanics work on an O-2A in its revetment at Binh Thuy, 1967* •
(Kansas Aviation Museum/Empire News Service)

or trying to fight the battles on their own. After that, they were only allowed to carry their service-issue .38 revolvers. Not to be completely foiled by petty regulations, many FACs took to shooting at the enemy soldiers with that little .38 sticking out the small vent window on the pilot's side!

During 1970, the 23rd TASS FACs discovered the NVA was moving supplies down a river that wended its way down from Tchepone and more-or-less paralleled Route Nine. The enemy had stretched cables across the river and just floated the supplies downstream. The FACs often went out searching for those cables and any supplies that might be on the river during the day. Occasionally, there were no fighters available and, since the river rafts tended to be lightly defended, the FAC would just fire some "Willie Pete" rockets at the barges. White phosphorous burned very hot and was capable of exploding the oil drums or burning through the cables and releasing the supplies to float away uncontrolled.

Over the "Big Pond" in a Duck

Most of the original contract O-2s were ferried to South Vietnam, according to a 1967 USAF press release, "directly from the plant in Wichita to the theater of operations by civilian pilots under Air Force contract." The contractor was World Aviation Services, Inc., of Newton, Kansas, who hired pilots meeting certain criteria: 3,000 hours total flying time; 1,000 hours multi-engine flying time; and at least three previous ocean crossing flights. Each pilot was given a qualification check ride to prove he could fly the airplane satisfactorily and then had to pass a written test covering O-2 systems operations and malfunctions. They were given some survival training and introduced to the survival gear they would be carrying — an inflatable life raft packed with a variety of gear from canned water and water purification pills to first aid items to minimal fishing gear.

Final indoctrination for the long flight consisted of familiarization with the special equipment needed to span the vast open stretches of the Pacific Ocean. This included:

- Two 90-gallon fuel tanks in the rear seat area
- 60-gallon fuel tank and five-gallon oil tank, with pump and selector valve, instead of the right seat
- HF radio
- Self-contained ADF receiver

• *Lieutenant John Wiley, Rake 24, is armed and ready to go to war. He's carrying a CAR-15 (which replaced the bulkier M-16s) with tape over the barrel to keep dirt out. The white square on the side of the engine cowling is where the armament technicians note the current load. In this case, it reads "WP Rockets"* •
(John Wiley)

The extra equipment added almost 2,000 pounds to the O-2's gross weight and made getting into the airplane a gymnastic challenge, the pilot sliding in over the top of the 60-gallon tank. Each flight of four was led by a World Aviation Services staff pilot, and all pilots were supplied with necessary charts, guides, and even traveler's checks. Each pilot carried a Poopy Suit — an immersion suit similar to a diver's dry suit designed to keep a pilot dry and warm in the cold ocean waters after a ditching, while waiting for the escorting USAF Grumman HU-16 Albatross amphibious rescue aircraft to pick him up. From Wichita, the formations proceeded to San Francisco where they were given extensive briefings by USAF meteorologists before beginning the long haul over water. On takeoff, the over-gross aircraft lumbered much farther down the long runway, lifting off at 95 MPH or more. The 2,450-mile flight from San Francisco to Honolulu required a little more than 14 hours of cramped flying time. The next legs were shorter — from Honolulu to Wake Island, then on to Guam in the Marianas Islands and then to the Philippines, where a local Cessna dealer removed the extra oil tank and replaced the three extra fuel tanks with a single smaller one. The pilots were then given an extensive briefing on the multitude of restrictions necessitated by their last leg from the Philippines into the war zone for the delivery of the aircraft to the USAF at Nha Trang, South Vietnam. Some 200 O-2s were ferried from Wichita to South Vietnam by civilian pilots — it was the least expensive and most efficient means of getting the aircraft quickly to where they were most needed.

The Route to Combat

When a FAC-to-be received his assignment, his next stop was Eglin AFB, Florida, and its auxiliary base, Hurlburt Field. In 1968, the O-2s actually flew out of a more remote base, Holly Field, where facilities were more "modest." Holly Field consisted mostly of old World War II-era Quonset huts and trailers. The Flight Operations office was in a trailer, and routine maintenance was conducted in inflatable maintenance hangars (although major maintenance was handled back at Hurlburt Field). Both the O-1 and O-2 pilots were trained at Holly Field, as well as the Helio Courier U-10 pilots. Navy AT-28s roamed the area and frequently "bounced" the FACs-in-training while they were learning low-level map-reading and visu-

• *Smoke from a "Willie Pete" billows up out of dense jungle in II Corps, 1972* •
(Fred McNeill)

al reconnaissance (VR) techniques. In Florida, the FACs learned the basics of shooting rockets and controlling fighters, although the fighters were usually AT-33s, A-1Es, or AT-28s, rather than the jets they routinely would have to control once arriving in South Vietnam.

The route to Vietnam involved a stay in the Philippines to attend Jungle Survival School — "Snake School." After learning the dos and don'ts of jungle living, the FACs were shipped to Bien Hoa for some in-theater indoctrination. They flew a few sorties with instructors during which they had their exposure to combat operations in the Cessna Super Skymaster. From there, they were sent to their permanent base of assignment. John Wiley remembers arriving at Long Than North where his commander showed up with an O-2, put Wiley's bags in the back, and left on a mission — solo. Wiley had to ride the 30 miles to their forward location in a Jeep driven by a crew chief. Those 30 miles took almost an hour and a half. Welcome to the war, Lieutenant Wiley.

True O-2 Tales

Forward Air Controllers (FACs) flying O-2s saw action throughout the theater of operations during the Vietnam War. Flying from bases in South Vietnam and Thailand, they flew reconnaissance missions and directed air strikes against targets in South Vietnam, Laos, Cambodia, and even the southern portion of North Vietnam. Most of these FACs were frustrated fighter pilots who chose lightplane cockpits rather than cargo aircraft flight decks to get as close to the shooting war as possible. They probably had no idea just how "up close and personal" the war was to become for them. Most felt, at least, they could fire a few marking rockets at the bad guys and direct the real fighters to drop bombs and strafe. As a result, the tales of FAC exploits are legion (as illustrated in the earlier L-19/O-1 chapter). The O-2 generated its own stories.

Bombard 'Em With BS • Some of the most frustrated O-2 pilots were those assigned to the B-model, or "Bullshit Bomber." There they were in a war zone not only flying an off-the-shelf civilian airplane — they didn't even have the wherewithal to do any visible damage! Most of them kept a tape recording of the popular song "Snoopy and the Red Baron," which they would broadcast (at full volume) as they entered the traffic pattern. Everyone on the base knew when an O-2B had arrived.

One O-2B pilot found a way to wake up the troops at his home base. This particular pilot had been more than a

• *A close-up view of an O-2B. The leaflet dispenser and loudspeaker are in plain view. The psy-ops system operator can be seen through the rear window* •
(Kansas Aviation Museum/Empire News Service)

little chagrined upon receiving his assignment to the B-model after completion of O-2 training — with no way to participate in the air-to-ground war! Armed with a recording of an F-4 taking off in full afterburner and the trusty 1,800-watt sound system of his "Bullshit Bomber," he got everyone's attention at small forward airstrips with his "F-4 in afterburner" recording blaring at full volume while taking off in his relatively quiet O-2B. I guess no one expected to hear an F-4 takeoff from a short forward airstrip.

The O-2B's primary mission was to broadcast recorded messages and scatter leaflets from the leaflet dispenser, in attempts to coerce defection or instill dissent among the Viet Cong or the populace who supported them. Sometimes, they paired up with local well-known village leaders and overflew areas targeted for upcoming airstrikes. The village leader broadcasted warnings and directed the people to evacuate before the bombs began to fall.

I'm Supposed to Drop These Bombs? • Then there's the tale of the most junior pilot in an Air National Guard fighter unit deployed to Vietnam. Seems the young lieutenant aviator had a reputation for always bringing his ordnance back home to be downloaded — due to mal-functions, losing sight of the target in bad weather, or having his lead destroy the target on the first pass. After his flight aborted a scramble airborne due to weather, the lieutenant reported he was airborne, armed, and available. An O-2 FAC, having just requested a strike on a single (as in only one) ammunition resupply truck, vectored the lieutenant to the target area. Lieutenant Hotshot reported a positive identification of the target, but the FAC reminded him of the "friendly fire" regulation requiring every target be marked. Lieutenant Hotshot orbited above while the FAC rolled in and put a "Willie Pete" smoke rocket directly into the back of the ammo-laden truck — destroying it in a great conflagration. The FAC was credited with the "kill," while Lieutenant Hotshot once again returned to his base with all his ordnance intact on what turned out to be his last mission of the war.

Just Do It Again • One USAF Academy graduate, as a lieutenant FAC in the O-2, drew the fire of an enemy 37mm antiaircraft gun and called for some fighters to silence it. When the fighters showed up, he dove on the 37mm and fired a "Willie Pete" rocket just as the 37mm decided to get the FAC out of their hair. The sound of the 37mm caused the lieutenant to pull back on the yoke with more than his usual gusto. Both wingtips folded upwards,

• An O-2A over the Mekong Delta, South Vietnam, in September of 1967 •
(Kansas Aviation Museum/Empire News Service)

a fact he did not discover until returning to base. After an inspection, the maintenance officer called in the Cessna technical representative who examined the aircraft, measured the wingtip deflections, and sent the data back to the Cessna engineers. Cessna determined the aircraft was still structurally sound and flyable, but the only way to reverse the warped tips would be to repeat the maneuver — inverted this time! Deciding that was not an acceptable procedure, the squadron demoted the aircraft to flying mail pickup sorties for the remainder of the war.

Runaway • A common practice for a rocket pass was to pull the nose up 30 degrees or so, kick in full rudder to swing the nose down toward the target, and cut the power to idle. Aim. Fire. Pull-up, and add power. Sometimes, the governor on one of the propellers would malfunction and the propeller would accelerate to full RPM (a "runaway" prop). Proper corrective action is to throttle that engine back and attempt to reduce the RPM so the governor would again control the RPM. If you did not reduce power, an engine failure could result. Darrell Lambert, a FAC with the 23rd TASS at Nakhon Phanom (NKP), pulled out of a rocket pass, added full power, and had the front propeller run away. In front of him soared a typically craggy Laotian mountain. A power reduction did not seem appropriate since he needed to get some altitude fast. "That was the only time I ever jettisoned both rocket pods," he said. Once clear of the mountain (but just barely!), he reduced power on that front engine and coaxed the propeller to recover.

Maintenance of the Trail • The 23rd TASS FACs working out of NKP covered the area from the Laotian Plain of Jars down to the northern Cambodian border, including the Ho Chi Minh Trail. The Rules of

• *Lieutenant Darrell Lambert's flight suit patch recognizing his 100th mission flown over Laos in support of Operation "Steel Tiger" in 1969. He also has a patch recognizing his 200th mission* •
(Walt Shiel)

Engagement (ROE — militaryese for the dos and don'ts of combat) over Laos required a target had to be within 200 yards of a discernable road. Lambert recalled it wasn't long before the NVA figured that out. Although roads and bridges were destroyed, supplies were getting through somehow. The NVA simply moved 500 yards away from the known roads and built new ones, keeping them hidden under the dense jungle canopy. Only when Intelligence found the new roads, or a FAC spotted the dust from construction or vehicles, could they try to stop them. Soon the area surrounding the Ho Chi Minh Trail was turned into barren sand where there had been lush tropical vegetation — the result of thousands of tons of bombs. Lambert recalls, "You could leave there at six o'clock in the evening with humongous bomb craters. You'd think there was no way in hell they could rebuild. But you'd come back the next morning and there was a brand new road like they had used a bulldozer. But you knew they hadn't."

In fact, Lambert recalled directing air

• *Lieutenant Darrell Lambert is ready to go to work from Nakhon Phanom in 1969. He has a full load of "Willie Pete" rockets* •
(Darrell Lambert)

strikes against roads in front of supply caves and spotting enemy troops through his binoculars "filling up the bomb craters on the road as the fighters were dropping bombs right on them." The enemy's determination and persistence in the face of massive air strikes made it difficult to slow, let alone stop the flow of supplies down the Ho Chi Minh Trail.

First Time • The NVA used a variety of antiaircraft artillery along the Trail, from 23mm to 100mm, and Lambert remembered clearly the first time he was fired on by an NVA 37mm gun. He was flying with the right window open to listen for small arms fire down below, while waiting for his next set of fighters to arrive, when he heard a pop-poppop and a whooshing noise. When he saw the red fireball hurtle past, he realized somebody was shooting at him. He could even smell the "putrid, phosphorous smell. . .you'll never forget it once you've smelled it!" With his heart pounding, Lambert began to jink hard and "the stall warning horn is on because I can't get any more airspeed — I had to stay at altitude." He said that was his first realization that the enemy was actually willing to kill him to keep him from calling in the fighters.

Almost Made It • NKP was not directly in a combat zone, so it was a safe haven from the threat of mortar attacks and such. Unfortunately, the radar approach final course sometimes strayed out over the river into Laos. Some of the 23rd TASS O-2s took hits on their extended final approach and did not know it until the crew chief pointed it out to them. One FAC stopped in the chocks before noticing the fuel dripping from the wing from a vertical shot that had passed completely through the wing.

Smoke On • Not all the excitement was caused by the enemy. All O-2's were delivered originally with rear engine smoke generators. Pilots had to check the oil sump supply on every preflight. The smoke was used to make an aerial mark to help the fighters find the FAC. Lambert remembers one day when the smoke system malfunctioned while he was taxiing in after a mission. With the smoke trailing behind him, he had no idea what was going on as fire trucks began to chase him. NKP Tower had called them thinking he was on fire.

We Know You're There • Flying the Ho Chi Minh Trail out of NKP frequently required O-2 FACs to direct the dropping of electronic sensors along the Trail to create Secretary of Defense Robert McNamara's infamous electronic wall to detect any and all enemy movement. The unit that monitored these sensors, a highly classified unit code named Task Force Alpha, worked out of a separate guarded facility at NKP. Task Force Alpha personnel would provide coordinates for the FAC, demanding as close to pinpoint accuracy as possible. The FAC flew into Laos, positively identified the location, and called for the fighters. Lambert says, "You put down the smoke and then the fighters would come in at 500 feet or less on a

• *Lieutenant Lambert, Nail 66, in the "front office" of his O-2A, somewhere over Laos in 1969* •
(Darrell Lambert)

• *The remains of an O-2 that crashed in the final turn at Nakhon Phanom on a night sortie in 1969. The pilots, Major Richard Swift and Lieutenant Johnny Campbell, were killed* •
(Darrell Lambert)

• *Taking off in an O-2 from the PSP runway at Nakhon Phanom* •
(Darrell Lambert)

• A pair of 23rd TASS FACs, Captain Razin and Major Jennero, prepare for
their last combat sortie from Nakhon Phanom in 1969 •
(Darrell Lambert)

delivery and the sensors would come off at a preset inter-
val." Task Force Alpha could then electronically monitor
any activity in the vicinity of the dropped sensors, relay-
ing the information back to 7th Air Force headquarters,
who then determined how many NVA vehicles or troops
had passed through the area the previous night.

Observers • FACs throughout the theater frequently
flew with observers, sometimes indigenous military personnel who knew the area and could communicate better
with their own Army forces, and sometimes with USAF
photographers who came along to ensure good photos of
specific targets. Because of the number of special missions (Laotian troops in contact, night sorties, friendly
road teams needing support, sensor drops, etc.), the 23rd
TASS pilots flew solo only half of the time. Lambert flew
frequently with Laotian observers when operating over
the Trail, sometimes with U.S. Army Green Beret
observers, and sometimes with both when Laotian road
teams were on the ground. Besides having somebody with
whom to share the dangers, there was a second advantage
to having another crewmember — when a FAC was particularly effective or accurate, the observer would make
sure the pilot's superiors knew about it.

I've Got It! • John Wiley, an O-2 FAC assigned to the
19th TASS at Long Tanh North in II Corps, flew frequently with Royal Thai Army Volunteer Force (RTAVF)
pilots. The USAF FACs were supposed to be teaching the
Thais how to FAC and how to fly the O-2 (the RTAVF had
O-1s at the time). Language was always a problem, even
though the Thai pilots supposedly knew English. Once
things got tense, many of the RTAVF pilots forgot their
English and their basic piloting skills and simply froze on
the controls. On one sortie, Wiley was letting an RTAVF

pilot fly the O-2, the aircraft was in a sideslip, the
propellers were out of synch, and they were getting
slow with the stall warning horn blaring away.
Wiley asked, "Do you know how slow we are?"
"Yes, sir!"
"Do you know we are in a slip?"
"Yes, sir!"
"Do you know we are about to stall and maybe
spin?"
"Yes, sir!"
With the aircraft on the verge of out-of-control and
the RTAVF pilot not making any attempts to cor-
rect the situation, Wiley ordered, "I've got the air-
plane!"
"Yes, sir!" Which was apparently the only English
he could remember.

Yes, Sir, Elephants • Then-Major Fred McNeill,
an O-2 FAC with the 700-pilot 20th TASS at Pleiku
and the first FAC to fly missions inside Cambodia
(now an adjunct professor of law at the Uniersity of
Phoenix), recalled the day he scared up a pack of
elephants that, during previous debriefings, he had told the
Intelligence officers were being used to transport supplies.
The Intelligence folks had not believed his stories,
although he had been certain he saw the tracks of the elephants. One day, he and a South Vietnam observer were
flying over a small village near Pleiku at 10,000 feet (to
get above a dense cloud of smoke caused by locals burning off their rice fields). McNeill shutdown both engines
(so nobody would hear him coming), rolled inverted, and
dove straight down on the village. When he restarted the
engines in the dive, they emitted a tremendous "bra-a-a-
at!" sound that spooked the elephants in the village. As the
animals scattered, McNeill's observer snapped a few photographs. Despite the photos, they still had a hard time
convincing the Intelligence officers there really were elephants down there.

• Major Charoon, commanding officer of the Royal Thai Army
Volunteer Force (RTAVF) pilots at Long Thanh North, and
Lieutenant Verra, another RTAVF pilot •
(John Wiley)

Nighttime FACs • Night missions were difficult. With rugged terrain in many areas, few ground lights for reference or navigation, and hostile forces hiding in the dark jungle below, it was a job usually reserved for two somewhat specialized units. Standard procedure was to fly with a navigator or another FAC in the right seat using a starlight scope. This required a checkout sortie for the pilot, on which he flew in the right seat with the starlight scope to learn its operation and limitations. To use the starlight scope from the right seat, the observer had to stick his head out the open window and scan down below. Lambert remembered his night checkout sortie:

"Those things [the starlight scopes] back then were heavy and cumbersome. Of course, you'd have the wind coming at you and water in your eyes but the damned things worked pretty good. You had one mission and you'd fly along and press on the [foot-operated intercom] toggle switch with your left foot and say 'Come 5 degrees left, come 5 degrees right' because the road was wandering. You were trying to follow the road and find the trucks."

Fred McNeill recalled working out tactics to use on night sorties, missions for which he and the other FACs in

• Major McNeill is marshalled into a parking spot by a USAF crew chief at Pleiku in 1972•
(Fred McNeill)

the 20th TASS were tasked only infrequently during his 1971-72 tour. They operated with two FACs, one flying and the other using the starlight scope, and turned off all cockpit lights to preclude interference with the highly sensitive night vision equipment. The procedure they developed to ensure accurate target marking was to find the target area, drop a parachute retarded flare, then roll inverted and attempt to split-S below the floating flare as quickly as possible. From a position just below the flare, they could checkout the target under its five-million-candlepower glow, find the specific target, and fire "Willie Pete" marking rockets at it for the fighters. McNeill remembered vividly his first, possibly overly aggressive, attempt at the maneuver: "I miscalculated and rolled-out with the flare filling the windshield directly ahead. I lost my night vision completely for the next 30 minutes or so."

For night missions, the aircraft were typically loaded with a pod of seven "Willie Pete" marking rockets on one wing and a rack with four or six flares ("logs") on the other wing. The plan was to bracket the target with flares, which burned brightly for almost an hour, and then call in the attackers. The FACs working out of NKP frequently worked with the Royal Australian Air Force (RAAF) English Electric Canberras (license-built in Australia) — code named "Yellow Bird." After rendezvous with the

• This photo shows the floor on the copilot/observer side. The button on the floor in front of the left rudder pedal is the intercom switch. The instrument on the bottom of the center pedestal is the KY-28 scrambler control head •
(Darrell Lambert)

Canberras at night, the FAC would turn on his navigation and position lights (referred to as "going Christmas tree") so as not to get run over during the attack. Using the marking flares for references, he would give directions such as "one-third of the distance from the east log."

Although most of the O-2s were painted in the standard light grey color with white on the top of the wings (to allow the fighters more easily to spot, and thus avoid, them), some were painted solid black with red identification markings, such as the 23rd TASS's aircraft assigned to Ubon. These aircraft even sported black cones around the rotating beacons on the tips of their vertical stabilizers — to allow the fighters above to see the beacons at night while masking the lights from the enemy troops on the ground. The FACs from NKP had to log a specific number of combat hours before they could rotate down to Ubon to fly night missions in those black O-2s. Daytime operations entailed patrolling large areas of Laos almost into South Vietnam, whereas night operations were flown mostly over identifiable roads.

• The empennage of a black 23rd TASS O-2 stationed at Ubon for night sorties. The rotating beacon on top of the right vertical stabilizer has a black cone around it •
(Darrell Lambert)

The black-painted O-2s used for night missions out of Ubon required longer takeoff runs than the other aircraft. Apparently, the extra paint added quite a few pounds. For night FAC missions, the O-2s were loaded with either flares on both wings or flares on one wing with WP rockets on the other. Soon, the squadron began experimenting with ways to increase the number of flares carried since they were the most effective target markers at night. One experiment was to hang a standard fighter-type Triple Ejector Rack (TER) on one wing, which allowed carrying three flares on the one station. However, the whole TER assembly with flares was a lot heavier than any loads planned for by Cessna. Besides

looking ungainly, the added weight caused the aircraft to lean noticeably toward the heavy side during taxi and was difficult to manage on takeoff. They finally decided the increased payload just was not worth the extra weight and in-flight drag — or the risks.

The Lineup and Play Time • One of the challenges facing the mostly young FAC corps was learning to work fast and with multiple sets of fighters. Although they were usually given one or two preplanned targets and preplanned fighter flights before takeoff, they usually had time to find targets on their own and call for additional fighters as needed. Also, it was not uncommon for fighters to check-in unannounced if their originally planned mission had been canceled. The fighters would check-in with the FAC as they let down into the target area. One of the FAC's first questions was always, "How much play time?" (Meaning, how long can you work in the target area before you get low on fuel and have to go home?) For most of the fighters, typical "play time" was 10 to 15 minutes from check-in to departure for home base.

Lambert once worked a preplanned flight of Republic

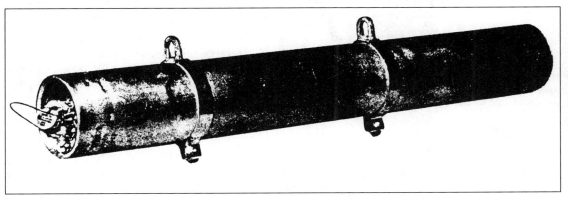

• An MK-24 flare typically used on night FAC missions •
(Air Force Flight Manual)

F-105 Thunderchiefs against one target while finding a second target for a pop-up flight of F-4 Phantoms. This meant keeping the two flights separated visually to preclude conflicts during their attacks, marking both targets and providing attack corrections as needed to both flights, while maintaining a scan for enemy ground fire. Quick thinking and calmness were necessary.

At initial check-in, the lead fighter would describe the lineup (how many of what kinds of aircraft) and their ordnance (how many of what kinds of droppable weapons and how many rounds of ammunition available for strafing). The FAC had to know the capabilities of the various weapons and what kinds of weapons were effective against what kinds of targets. Many FACs carried a chart in the back of their checklist with the various types of weapons and their effects. For instance, there was little point to laying down a lot of CBUs (cluster bombs) or napalm if you wanted to take out a road or a bridge. For that, normal high-explosive bombs were preferred. A

FAC also had to know what kind of fuzing to ask the fighters to select — immediate or delayed. Immediate fuzing might be effective against vehicles and bridges, but a delayed fuzing (allowing the bombs to dig-in before detonation) was better against bunkers and particularly the many caves and tunnels used by the NVA and Viet Cong.

100 Over What? • Once the attack was completed, the FAC had to give a score and a Battle Damage Assessment (BDA) to the flight lead. The score was expressed as a percentage of bombs on target and a percentage of the target destroyed or damaged. Something like "100 over 50" — meaning 100 percent of the bombs hit the target and 50 percent of the target was destroyed. Lambert remembered that, since numbers two and four in a flight of fighters were usually the least experienced combat pilots, they frequently had the worst scores until they grew accustomed to combat. As a result, he sometimes had to provide a score like, "Everybody got their bombs on target on that last pass except Number Four, so I'm giving you an 80 over 40 today."

Aussie Bombing • The Royal Australian Air Force (RAAF) Canberra crews, with a bombardier perched in the aircraft's nose section, always used a level delivery and carried four to six 1,000-pound bombs. During the day, the FAC would mark the target and get out of the way. The Canberras set-up their flat runins from four or five miles out, dropped the bombs, and then swung around in a wide racetrack for the next pass. Due to a combination of aircraft capability, pilot proficiency, and effective tactics, the Yellow Birds were respected by the FACs

• A sample of a leaflet (Safe Conduct Pass) dropped by O-2B aircraft in Vietnam. The message on the front of the leaflet is in English and two Asian languages, the message on the back is in Vietnamese •
(USAF)

for the accuracy of their bombing.

Winchester • Once the fighters had dropped their bombs and used up their ammo, they would call "Winchester," meaning they had no more ordnance left. As the fighters regrouped and climbed up to altitude to hold "high and dry," the FAC flew back over the target to assess the actual damage. When possible, he radioed the BDA to the flight lead before low fuel necessitated their departure. A typical BDA might include, "Four trucks destroyed and 10 KBA (Killed By Air)."

The problem with the "Winchester" radio call was that the enemy, despite a problematic command of English, quickly learned its meaning and waited for the FAC to come down close for the BDA so they could open fire on him. Lambert said, "It didn't take us long to coordinate with the fighters to say, 'hold your last round and when you come off your last run call *Winchester, High and Dry.* As soon as the FAC goes in for the BDA and they open up, you're cleared in hot.' When they did and the fighters rolled back in and dropped again, that got their attention!"

Blue Sixteen • One day, just south of Tchepone Pass in Laos during the monsoon season, the Direct Air Support Center (DASC) called Lambert on the radio and asked if he could take a pop-up flight whose primary target had been scrubbed after takeoff due to bad weather. Lambert said he had some trucks on the move in need of attention. When the fighters checked-in on the FAC's frequency, Lambert was surprised to hear: "Blue Lead ... Two ... Three ... Four ... Five ..." — with the last position calling out "Sixteen." He had 16 Navy A-7s in a single flight! Lambert worked fast and furiously to get everybody into the target area and get the targets marked — the three trucks were smoldering ruins that day after 16 loads of bombs were dropped on them.

On the Ropes • Flying sorties from NKP into Laos meant assisting with helicopter pickups for the Laotian and Green Beret road teams. The FAC would mark the pickup point for the helicopters, who then swooped in and extracted the teams. After Lambert marked the pickup point one day for a large contingent that required several helicopters, the road team began taking fire from the

advancing NVA troops. Some of the helicopters landed and picked up their loads normally, but when the last ones came up out of the trees in a rush to get away from the ground fire, they were trailing long ropes and "at intervals there were three guys attached to the rope and away they went with those guys just hanging on."

Alternate Gear Extension • As a standard part of the parachute assembly, FACs carried a tree-lowering device. If, after a bailout, he found himself caught hanging from the tall jungle trees, it could be used to lower himself to the ground safely. One of the O-2's idiosyncrasies is the way the main landing gear folds back before being retracted into the fuselage — this somewhat comical mechanical activity resembles the way a duck slowly tucks its legs back against its body after taking off. This retraction scheme is why the O-2 earned the nickname of the Duck. One young over-eager FAC discovered his main landing gear would drop down out of the fuselage but would not rotate far enough forward to lock into place for landing. He tried to lean out through the open door but could not reach the right main gear to pull it into position. Which is when he remembered his tree-lowering device and its long lanyard. He managed to lasso the right main gear but then lost his grip on the lanyard. The rope was sucked out of the door and back into the rear propeller where it promptly wrapped around the propeller hub, while still attached to the landing gear — thus dragging the rear engine to a stop. So there he was with his landing gear still only partly extended and his rear engine dead. There is no record of how he explained the lanyard fastened to the landing gear after completing his subsequent gear-up landing. Must have been one hell of a story.

Candid Camera • FACs were also responsible for providing visual reconnaissance (VR) of the areas they were assigned to monitor. Information on cables across the rivers, enemy truck parks, enemy repair facilities, new construction, and anything else that might be of military significance was reported during the FACs' intelligence debriefing. Many times, the FACs were issued 35mm cameras with a modest zoom lens, and they'd take pictures of the enemy activity. Most of the FACs obeyed the

• *Several O-2s in revetments at Pleiku, South Vietnam, in 1972* •
(Fred McNeill)

restrictions and stayed above 1,000-feet AGL, but there were those who not only busted the minimum altitude but returned with clear photographic evidence — oil drums filling the frame the way they might if the photo was taken from a much lower altitude. These pilots were first chastised — and then congratulated for excellent intelligence shots.

Another infrequent arrangement was to mount a KB-18A strike camera in a V-shaped protrusion under the right seat. The KB-18A was a panoramic motion picture camera designed for daylight low-level photography. It was able to record 180 degrees fore-and-aft and 40 degrees side-to-side. There were two controls and one indicator mounted on the upper left of the pilot's instrument panel — a Camera Power Switch, a Camera Run Switch, and a Film Out Light. Sometimes, a still camera was mounted instead of the motion picture camera. Lambert remembered wondering, "You're gonna do what to my airplane? And I'm gonna fly what? I'd never seen one of those before because we never got any checkout [with the camera]."

Later in the war, each FAC was issued an Asahi Pentax 35mm camera with a pistol grip (to make single-handed operation easier) and a long lens (for better close-ups). They only used black-and-white film in these cameras, and the FACs themselves were responsible for developing the film. Having the "official" camera did not keep many FACs from carrying personal cameras and recording a more personal view of the war from an O-2. During the waning days of United States involvement in Vietnam, many young fighter pilots, looking for a combat tour to get their "ticket punched," volunteered to serve as FACs. One young FAC assigned to the 20th TASS in 1972 shortly before the unit was shutdown, decided to record his exploits on his personal 8mm movie camera. The particular mission involved heavy anti-aircraft fire from the NVA forces below, several flights of fighters dropping load after load of ordnance, and the young FAC firing numerous marking rockets — all caught on film. In addition, he caught cockpit views of himself executing loops and sloppy eight-point rolls (the only kind an O-2 can do) as he pulled off his rocket passes. One night in the club at Pleiku, he proceeded to regale his comrades with verbal explanations to accompany his combat screen test. Unfortunately, the squadron commander walked in — and he was not amused.

Splash One Water Buffalo • Sometimes FACs became bored when patrolling an area where clearly nothing much was happening. One of the things they looked for was evidence that perhaps the water buffalo were being used as "military pack animals." When patrolling particularly desolate stretches with no discernible targets,

• *An O-2 on final approach at Dong Ha, South Vietnam, in 1967* •
(Kansas Aviation Museum/Empire News Service)

• *An armament technician loads a "Willie Pete" rocket into the launcher on the right wing of an O-2A.*
This photo was taken at Dong Ha in 1967 •
(Kansas Aviation Museum/Empire News Service)

them amazingly detonated right in the middle of the mountaintop clearing. McNeill overflew the spot and was surprised to find a Russian truck loaded with tires recently abandoned with the doors still swinging open. If the truck crew had been there, the sudden attack of more than a dozen white phosphorous warheads must have spooked them into getting far away fast, even on foot. For the next several days, FACs repeatedly called in airstrikes on that lonely truck, bombs burst all around it but none destroyed it. A Marine A-4 finally hit it and tipped it over — all the tires spilled out and rolled across the clearing. A standing joke among FACs hinged on the disappearance of any derelict truck not attacked for more than a couple of days — it was said the "great green tree frog" got them. A few days after the A-4 hit the Russian truck, the "great green tree frog" struck again.

the temptation would arise to practice a little marksmanship using the roaming herds of "military pack animals" as targets of opportunity. It has been reported that, when hit with a white phosphorous marking rocket, a water buffalo bursts like a huge watermelon exploding.

How Far Will It Go? • Fred McNeill recalled flying a "Steel Tiger" mission over the southern tip of Laos during the dry season. On that perfectly clear day, he approached the end of his four-hour mission with two full rocket pods and "no sign of a war anywhere." There was an unwritten code that dictated one did not return to base with ordnance, so he began to look around for someplace to expend his "Willie Petes" while wondering just how far one of those 2.75-inch rockets could travel. He spotted a road, perhaps 6-miles away, winding around a mountain top that had apparently been attacked frequently, judging from the denuded area around it. He pulled his nose up 45° to get maximum range, and ripple-fired all 14 of his rockets in the general direction of the clearing. He then lowered his nose and began heading for the spot, waiting for the rockets to impact. Several minutes later, after McNeill had decided the rockets must have somehow gone astray, all 14 of

• *Fred McNeill lands at Pleiku in 1972. The Pleiku tower can be seen just to the left of the*
gun sight. The grease pencil marks on the window, just to the right of his helmet, are the
aftermath of his note taking during the mission. The photo was taken with a
USAF-issue camera •
(Fred McNeill)

All Alone • The 20th TASS O-2 FACs were the first to fly missions inside Cambodia, a very difficult area in which to direct airstrikes. The terrain consisted of high plains, which were very flat and featureless with no prominent landmarks. Once over the mountains separating South Vietnam from Cambodia, the FACs had to operate low if they hoped to find the targets — too low to receive TACAN navigational signals and too far away to contact anyone except the C-130 Airborne Command and Control Center (ABCCC) aircraft, which operated under the radio call-sign of Hillsboro. Fred McNeill, who was one of the first to fly the O-2 into Cambodia, said the FACs were

• *Shown here in February of 1972, Major Fred McNeill, Covey 502, is about to mount up at Pleiku for another combat sortie in II Corps* •
(Fred McNeill)

"really all alone out there." Although a FAC might find a target and radio Hillsboro for an immediate airstrike, he actually was provided with fighter support only about 10 percent of the time. Two of the top priority targets, almost guaranteed to get quick attention, were bulldozers working to repair previously bombed-out roads and vehicles pulling radar vans for the surface-to-air missiles.

Shall We Deconflict? • Sometimes, the coordination among the many different aircraft and missions in an area proved less than optimum. Several aircraft, including the O-2B, were used to dispense leaflets over enemy territory, hoping to induce some desertion among the NVA or Viet Cong troops. Darell Lambert was flying along, somewhat bored, one day just south of Ban Laboy in Laos, flying with one hand and holding the binoculars with his other, when he just happened to lower the binoculars and look directly in front of him.

"All I could see in my whole windshield was this sparkly stuff in front of me," he says. "I thought, What the hell? I'm about to die. I had no idea what it was, but I was going to run into it and there wasn't anything I could do. Well, when I ran into it, they were just leaflets."

Without prior coordination, the "litterbug" (a Helio Courier U-10) out of NKP was dropping leaflets in the same area from a slightly higher altitude and crossed in front of him while dispensing the propaganda.

Some of the threats to FACs came from the very fighters with whom they were supposed to work. After all, the fighters were usually flying fast and frequently low, while the FACs were flying slow airplanes that, despite their short turn radius, simply could not get out of the way without some advance warning. And

• *Fred McNeill rolls in to launch a target-marking rocket at a 12.7mm NVA gun site in the Central Highlands northwest of Kantoum* •
(Fred McNeill)

• Smoke from the "Willie Pete" rocket blossoms in the clearing around the 12.7mm gun, allowing fighters to locate it. "Hit my smoke!" •
(Fred McNeill)

FACs, after all, were out there to pay close attention to what was happening on the ground — that was their job, not watching the skies. And throughout the war in South Vietnam, there was never an enemy threat from above. John Wiley recalled a few heart-stopping encounters: one day, he suddenly noted a fast-moving shadow below him, picked up a wing to see where it was coming from, and found an RF-101 Voodoo barreling straight into him (somehow they avoided a collision); he was also almost run down by a flight of South Vietnamese Air Force (VNAF) A-1Es and another flight of VNAF F-5s busting through his area unannounced and unexpected.

Rescues • Another common FAC role throughout the war zone was to assist with coordinating the rescue of downed pilots, although usually the A-1E Skyraiders would take over to provide air cover as well as coordinate with other fighters. When a downed pilot was safely rescued and returned to the base at NKP, there was a ritual welcoming ceremony — they spray-painted the pilot's bare buttocks with green paint and hoisted him up to the ceiling to "make his mark." He would then sign the splotch with his name and the date of his rescue. The ceiling of the base's club was soon almost filled with such green splotches.

Lambert can claim the dubious distinction of flying two "last" missions out of NKP to end his tour of duty. While Lambert was completing his intended last mission, one of his squadron mates was working the rescue of

a downed Navy McDonnell Douglas A-4 Skyhawk pilot and had to transfer control of the rescue to a Rockwell OV-10 Bronco due to running low on fuel. While they were both concentrating on the ground situation, they ran into each other. The OV-10 pilot was forced to eject — now they had two pilots to rescue. The O-2 pilot was able to continue flying despite having suffered severe damage to one of his tail booms from one of the OV-10's propellers, including severing of the elevator and rudder cables on that side. During his final approach into a near-by Air America airstrip, a C-47 pulled out for takeoff. The O-2 pilot made a barely successful go-around with minimal flight controls but lost control turning final for a second attempt. The aircraft was destroyed but neither the pilot nor his Laotian observer were injured beyond friction burns from the shoulder harness straps. When Lambert landed at NKP, relieved to be finished and ready to start packing, he was told the FAC who was to replace him had been diverted to the rescue operation. Lambert was told to go back out and cover his area for another five-hour mission. Lambert said "They just gave me a couple hamburgers and a couple cokes, and I went back out and flew another five hour mission."

FAC Life • A typical week for a FAC was to fly two days, take one day off, then fly three days, and take another day off. There was quite a difference in the "feel" of

• Napalm explodes as a result of a fighter airstrike directed by McNeill •
(Fred McNeill)

war between bases in Thailand and bases in South Vietnam, as well as between individual bases within Thailand. In South Vietnam, there was always the threat of mortar attacks from just beyond the perimeter, and at some of the dispersed Operating Locations (OLs) sapper attacks while just getting to and from the airstrips were possible. In Thailand, once on the ground, the pilots were removed from the front-line threats and could relax more. In Thailand, the FACs lived in barracks with a central communal bathroom and two to four beds in each room. At the 23rd TASS's Ubon OL, living conditions were almost like at a stateside

• *The aftermath of a mortar attack on Long Thanh North. The aircraft sustained damage to the elevator after being moved into revetment. None of the other O-2s were in revetments at the time, and none of them were damaged by the mortar attack* •
(John Wiley)

• *An O-2A taxis out at Binh Thuy, South Vietnam, as other O-2s remain in revetments and a C-47 sits in the background. The photo was taken in October of 1967* •
(Kansas Aviation Museum/Empire News Service)

assignment with a modern downtown just beyond the gates. Back at NKP, however, the town and conditions were different — the difference was like crossing the border from San Diego to Tijuana. On base, though, they had all the necessities, such as a party hooch, volleyball court, picnic tables — and a large bunker. With the war rarely encroaching on the base, the NKP bunker was rarely used, except to tease the maids — if they did not do good work, they were told they might be put down in the bunker with "big snakes."

When Wiley first arrived at Long Than North in mid-1969, he found himself logging 100 flying hours per month, but that gradually tapered off to an average of 60-70 flying hours per month. Flying out of NKP, Lambert generally logged 60-70 hours per month but flew closer to 100 hours per month during a brief deployment to Ubon to fly night missions. No matter how you look at it, FACs flew a lot, they flew solo, and they rarely had other aircraft for support unless they called for an airstrike.

The 20th TASS pilots based at Pleiku, at a field elevation of 5,000 feet in the central highlands of South Vietnam, enjoyed much milder weather than most of the rest of the FAC bases. In fact, Pleiku was about the only base in Southeast Asia where air conditioning was just not needed. The 20th TASS O-2s were ferried down to their main squadron base at Da Nang for anything other than

• *The operations shack for the 20th TASS, Pleiku. The unit flew both O-2s and OV-10s •*
(Fred NcNeill)

routine maintenance. When one of their pilots started bitching too much about life at Pleiku, he was dispatched to Da Nang — by the time he returned to Pleiku he appreciated the much improved weather.

Most O-2 FACs preferred not to work an airstrike, with its requirement for a lot of jinking and maneuvering, until they had been airborne for at least an hour. This reduced their gross weight and made the aircraft more maneuverable. Typical sortie lengths varied depending on how far the FAC had to travel to get to his assigned area. FACs working in the II Corps area of South Vietnam typically operated relatively close to their home bases, at lower altitudes over the flatlands, and averaged about three and a half hours per sortie. In comparision, Thailand FACs travelled well up into Laos and maintained higher altitudes in the mountains and averaged closer to five hours per sortie.

FAC losses were relatively common (after all, they were essentially unarmed, unarmored, and operating down low at slow airspeeds). During his one-year tour with the 23rd TASS at NKP, Lambert noted the loss of six 23rd TASS O-2 pilots. Two were killed in a nighttime final turn accident. One, Captain Robert Rex, was a

---

TO ALL WHO SHALL SEE THESE PRESENTS GREETINGS

"THE ORDER OF THE BRASS BALLS"

BE IT KNOWN THAT

FIRST LIEUTENANT DARRELL R. LAMBERT

Distinguished himself as a Forward Air Controller from 14 November 1968 to 21 October 1969, while stationed at Naked Fanny Royal Thai Air Force Base, Thailand. While engaged in aerial operations against a hostile force, he performed in an unpredictable and never-to-be-duplicated manner; directing the devastation of numerous village picnic grounds, tree parks, and suspected V.C. vegetable gardens in the extreme western DMZ. Though faced with threats of Cricket, Hillsboro, fast moving FAC's, and red smoking balls ascending from the ground, Lieutenant Lambert, in his unarmed aircraft, could always be counted on to confusedly and erratically direct fighter aircraft against the logistic complexes of the hostile foe. Despite severe air sickness and excruciating pain caused by a combination of unsynchronized props, uncoordinated flying and not being able to use a relief tube, he frequently flew when scheduled, generally took off on time, and occasionally flew the entire period. His exploits and achievements, both real and imagined, reflect great credit upon himself and the United States Air Force, demonstrating that he truly possesses <u>balls of brass</u>.

• *Lieutenant Lambert's <u>unofficial</u> certificate on completing his tour of duty in Thailand •*
(Darrell Lambert)

confirmed fatality, shot down over Laos. Two others, Captain Robert Luna and Lieutenant Philip Mascari, were listed as Missing In Action due to missions over Laos — their fate was never learned, or as Lambert noted in his tour scrapbook, "Unknown but to God." Lieutenant Steve Long, Lambert's close friend since pilot training, was also shot down over Laos and interned as a Prisoner of War — he was released in 1973 and eventually returned to USAF flying status.

One of the problems with the twelve-month tours of duty in Vietnam was the amount of truly productive time a FAC was able to serve. The initial in-country checkout, followed by a local combat checkout at the FAC's assigned unit absorbed two months or more. A new FAC then required usually another two to three months to get really familiar with his assigned working area and to understand what was going on and how the system worked. During a FAC's last month in-country, he was given fewer and fewer sorties — since he was then a "double-digit midget" (double digit referring to less than 100 days of his tour remaining). Those sorties were badly needed to get replacement pilots trained and combat-ready. In addition, a week was "lost" to a mid-tour leave for R&R. As a result, for almost six months of a FAC's tour he was less than a 100-percent mission-ready asset to his unit.

Cancel That Request • Flying into Laos, the Nail FACs from NKP could clearly see the leftover influence of the French colonial occupation of the area. There were typically French chateaus in the lush countryside, although most had long since been bombed and had no roofs. And approaching the Plain of Jars on the way to Nape Pass, there was a line of 15 or 20 trucks left

---

FOR THE BEST FAC ASK FOR A NAIL

NKP   NAIL 66   UBON

LT. DARRELL R. LAMBERT
FLYING THE ONLY USAF PUSH-PULL O-2 AIRCRAFT
"HIT MY SMOKE" FOR 100/100

BDA WILL INCLUDE BUT IS NOT LIMITED TO: GUNS

TRUCKS	KBA-WBA	HOOTCHES
BULLDOZERS	COOLIES	COMM-LINES
MOTORCYCLES	BUFFALO	ROAD CUT-FORDS
BICYCLES	BRIDGES	VEGETABLE GARDENS

• Lieutenant Lambert's "business card" as Nail 66 •
(Darrell Lambert)

• Two pilots from Bien Hoa on a checkout sortie over Can Tho in 1967 •
(Kansas Aviation Museum/Empire News Service)

behind by the French, sitting out in the open in single-file as though they had been on the way to someplace. Very few fresh bomb craters were around them. New FACs encountering the display for the first time frequently got excited and called for fighters to attack the trucks. As he flew closer, he would realize they were bombed out hulks and then would have to call to cancel his request for fighters.

So That's What It's All About • John Wiley clearly remembers the first real airstrike he conducted against a supply depot. All of his previous sorties had been with fighters carrying practice bombs that made little sound and only enough smoke to be spotted. On his first live strike in Vietnam he controlled a flight of USAF North American F-100 Super Sabres loaded with M-117 750-pound bombs. Wiley marked the target with a "Willie Pete" rocket, pulled away, and called, "Hit my smoke." The lead F-100 rolled-in, released, and pulled off the target. A huge explosion rocked the little O-2, taking Wiley completely by surprise. Soon, he realized it was just the bombs detonating, but his initial reaction was anything but calm. Nobody had warned him of what to expect.

Fill 'Er Up • Not all of the hazards in Vietnam were due to enemy activity. One day while working with some troops in contact, Wiley received a radio call from his command post informing him the weather had deteriorated at his home base and he should consider diverting to Vung Tao or Ban Me Thuot. He soon found out that both of those bases were below approach minimums already. He had been taking time at the end of his missions to practice GCA approaches to maintain his instrument flying proficiency, so he decided to try to land at the field with which he was most familiar — his home base. At 200 feet AGL (the GCA minimums) he still could not see the runway but told the controller to continue with his instructions. He finally popped out of the clouds at about 50 feet off the runway and landed safely. Due to the unexpected weather delays, he landed with very little fuel remaining — they pumped 116 gallons into the O-2's tanks with their 122-gallon capacity! At maximum endurance power settings, the O-2's two IO-360 engines burned at least 7-gallons of fuel per hour each, not taking into account fuel gauge inaccuracies or whether those tanks were really completely full at takeoff!

Joint Ops • FACs out of Long Tanh North set-up a joint operation with an Army hunter-killer unit working out of Di An. The Army used an OH-6 helicopter working down very low to find possible targets and an AH-1 Cobra helicopter gunship flying cover. The 19th TASS added an O-2 to the team, flying at about 1,500-feet. If the

• *An O-2A at Long Thanh North after the pilot allowed the landing gear handle to snap to the UP position during a pre-takeoff gear door*
retraction sequence. The uplock failed and the nose gear retracted •
(John Wiley)

*• Lieutenant Wiley heads out in his O-2 on a joint mission with an Army OH-6 helicopter,
which is visible just off the O-2's wing •*
(John Wiley)

UH-1 identified a target, the O-2 called in the request for an airstrike through the DASC. If the O-2 spotted a likely target, the OH-6 flew in low and close for confirmation. The aircrews frequently flew in each other's aircraft on the missions.

50 KBA, Sir • Sometimes, the bureaucracy of the tactical air support system overcame good judgement and common sense. On one such occasion, DASC called Wiley with word of a supply depot used by the 274th NVA. Wiley was working with an Army hunter-killer team and had the OH-6 check it out. There was a bunker at the designated location, but it had obviously been abandoned for some time — it was "cold." The DASC Commander listened to his on-sight eyes and ears and ordered them to launch an attack. An RAAF Canberra was sent in, Wiley marked the alleged target, and the Canberra crew dropped a pair of 1000-pounders on it. The OH-6 flew back over the area and there was still no sign of anyone having been there. Wiley, frustrated with the DASC's unwillingness to accept his earlier report, reported a BDA of "2,000 crates of supplies and 50 KBA." When the DASC Commander smugly noted Wiley's earlier "cold" report, Wiley replied, "Sir, you said they were

there and they're not now. So, they must be dead." The DASC Commander failed to appreciate the humor.

I Can Fly Too • One 19th TASS O-2 was lost to nothing more than stupidity. One of the O-2 crew chiefs apparently decided anyone could fly an Oscar Duck. With no flight training whatsoever, he stole one for a joy ride. His joy was short-lived when he discovered that taking off and flying was possible, while landing was much more difficult. He died trying to return to base.

We Know Who You Are • When "business" was slow or when all assigned missions were finished for the day, the O-2 pilots frequently used any excess fuel for a little recreation. Most FACs were frustrated rather-be fighter pilots with a fighter pilot's aggressiveness and sense of adventure. Those very qualities led to quite a bit of unauthorized activity whenever suitable opportunities arose. As the reports of low-level buzzing of indigenous hamlets and of mock aerial combat between the FACs filtered up to the various unit headquarters, the commanders became determined to stop it. The problem, however, was that one O-2 looked like another O-2 — gray with black-and-white markings and white upper wing surfaces. Unless an observer was able to read the tail numbers, there was no way to pin the violation on a specific unit or specific pilots unless they happened to be the only ones airborne in the area at the time. But, even in combat zones, bureaucracies can be creative. So, in an alleged attempt to foster unit morale, the order was issued to paint unit-specific stripes on the vertical stabilizers and rudder tips of all the O-2s. At the very least, headquarters would be able to pinpoint a particular unit when reports of buzzing and rat-racing were received. The units and pilots resisted, but eventually all the aircraft sported distinctive tail markings.

Gear Down? • One O-2A pilot, a Captain assigned to the 20th TASS, was struck by some of a volley of 10-20 rounds of automatic small arms fire. He had been patrolling at 1,200-feet AGL and was struck by shots fired from directly below him. He could not detect any evidence of fuel leaks, fire, or any other aircraft or engine malfunction, so he circled the area to locate the source of the ground fire. According to his report, after 15 to 20 minutes, he still "could not see or hear any more fire." On entering the traffic pattern, however, he finally identified the one aircraft malfunction caused by the enemy fire — his landing gear would not extend. After being looked over by the pilots of two other O-2s and consulting with the 20th TASS Operations and Maintenance staffs, the pilot of the stricken aircraft tried various means to get the landing gear down. The manual extension method (using a hand pump mounted on the floor between the front seats) was only able to get the nose gear down and locked — the main gear were only partially extended. Several other suggested techniques were attempted, including pulling 3.5 Gs a few times, using the manual method with all electrical power turned off, and alternating negative and positive Gs. Nothing worked. Finally, with no more options, the runway was foamed and the pilot setup for a landing, after retracting the nose gear. For the approach and landing, the pilot stated in his report that he "decided to go by the book and feather the front engine,

• *O-2s in revetments at Binh Thuy, South Vietnam, in 1967* •
(Kansas Aviation Museum/Empire News Service)

shutting down the rear engine on final once I had the landing assured in the foam." Other than some minor belly damage and the bullet damage to the landing gear circuitry, the ensuing landing was uneventful.

Oscar Duck Movie Star • One O-2 and its pilot have been immortalized on celluloid. When missile intelligence expert Lieutenant Colonel Iceal Hambleton was shot down on a mission over North Vietnam, the "powers that be" deemed it imperative to rescue him, even more so than other pilots, to preclude the vital information he possessed from falling into North Vietnamese hands. Captain Bartholomew Clark, an O-2 FAC, was able to contact Hambleton, whose call-sign was Bat 21, and flew repeated missions to maintain contact while a rescue effort could be coordinated. Hambleton was eventually rescued by helicopter, despite being injured and pursued by NVA forces. The episode later became a book and a movie — "Bat 21." In the movie, Gene Hackman played Lieutenant Colonel Hambleton and Danny Glover portrayed Captain Clark. The O-2 flown by Clark is now on display in the Dover Air Force Historical Center museum at Dover AFB, Delaware.

Parachutes For FACs

Parachutes, or at least their use, were periodic points of contention between the FACs and their command chain. At first, the FACs carried their issued parachutes in the aircraft — but left them in the back rather than wearing them. Commanders groused and fussed, and finally ordered that the equipment would be in the seats occupied by the crew. Not to be so easily foiled by mere orders, most of the FACs complied — sort of, anyway. They put the chutes behind them in the seats, but did not slip into the harnesses. The parachutes were then little more than lumpy, uncomfortable seat cushions. When headquarters realized the subterfuge being employed to meet the letter, if not the spirit, of the regulation, they responded with explicit instructions that every FAC would wear a parachute on every mission, arms and legs through the harness and buckles buckled! Reluctantly, the FACs complied. In the Southeast Asian heat and humidity, flying an un-air-conditioned aircraft for four or five hours while twisting and turning in the seat to observe the ground and observe the fighters' attack runs, those parachutes, although offering some escape potential, were simply viewed as a nuisance. Without ejection capability and with the jettisonable door being on the right, most did not really believe they had much of a chance to evacuate a stricken aircraft.

However, a pair of O-2 FACs proved a parachute could, indeed, be a lifesaver. — even with two pilots on board trying to scramble through that single door. The two were flying along at about 3,500 feet above the jungle, wearing their parachutes properly, when an unexpected crew-served weapon (probably a 23mm) opened fire on them. The aircraft was hit and dropped quickly into a spin. Unbeknownst to the two pilots, the ground fire had blown off a portion of the empennage and severed whatever control cables were left. The left-seat pilot struggled to regain control, repeatedly applying spin recovery techniques, but to no avail, and finally commanded a bailout. The right seat pilot jettisoned the door, slid his seat full aft, unfastened his lap belt and shoulder harness, disconnected his helmet con-

nections, and dove out. The left seat pilot then slid his seat aft, unhooked from the aircraft, scrambled across the right seat, and dove overboard himself. Despite all the in-cockpit activity in the out-of-control aircraft, both pilots had time to watch their O-2 spin for several seconds while they floated earthward under full parachute canopies. Despite an uncontrollable airplane and a relatively low initial altitude, adrenaline ensured the two pilots completed all their emergency egress procedures with time to spare.

It Takes Some Skill

During the Vietnam War, three different aircraft were used for FAC duties (plus some special "Fast FAC" operators working deep in North Vietnam in two-seat fighters such as F-100s): the O-1 Bird Dog, the OV-10 Bronco, and the O-2. The first two were both purpose-built FAC aircraft with excellent visibility and designed-in features to make the job simpler. The O-2, on the other hand, had been developed from an off-the-shelf businessman's airplane, modified and Rube-Goldberged into an acceptable platform for the demanding FAC mission.

Although the aircraft proved quite effective and continued in service long after the war for which it was intended, it was always a challenge to observe ground activity and mark targets while keeping the fighters in sight during an intense air strike. O-2s could always be seen banking

• *An O-2 on final in the "preferred" configuration* •
(Kansas Aviation Museum/Empire News Service)

• *A helicopter hovers above a couple O-2s in revetments at Dong Ha South Vietnam in 1967* •
(Kansas Aviation Museum/Empire News Service)

first one way and then the other as the pilot worked to keep track of all the activity around him while compensating for the aircraft's visibility shortcomings. Not to disparage the talents and skill of other FACs, but merely to reflect the inherent disadvantages faced by an O-2 FAC, John Wiley observes, "Anybody can work an air strike from an OV-10, and a competent pilot can do it from an O-1, but you've got to be good to do it from an O-2!"

Oscar Deuce Heroes

Although no O-2 pilots were awarded the nation's highest combat medal (the Medal of Honor), at least seven earned the USAF's second highest medal — the Air Force Cross. In fact, the first O-2 pilot to be awarded the Air Force Cross, Captain Donald Stevens, received the medal for his actions on 19 August 1967, only a few months after the first O-2s arrived in-country. Captain Stevens flew cover and provided radio relay for a downed pilot for eight hours until the stricken aviator could be picked-up by helicopter. On Christmas Day of that same year, another O-2 FAC, Captain Jerry Sellers, earned a posthumous Air Force Cross for deliberately provoking enemy ground fire to allow him to locate the enemy and direct fighter aircraft strikes.

Combat action on 30 January 1968 resulted in the awarding of Air Force Crosses to three O-2 pilots. Captain Kenneth Sellers earned his AF Cross by providing close air support for Army ground troops from his lightly armed O-2. Lieutenant Colonel Karl Feurriegal directed air strikes despite heavy ground fire to prevent an enemy overrun of friendly forces and was awarded an AF Cross. And, during missions which began on 30 January and ended on 1 February, Lieutenant Colonel Allan Baer demonstrated "extraordinary heroism" in the face of enemy ground fire, including difficult nighttime FAC missions, for which he was awarded the AF Cross.

Captain Phillip Maywald's AF Cross was awarded for providing support and directing air cover for a downed pilot for over two hours while coordinating a helicopter pickup. On 12 November 1968, Captain Donald Marx intentionally drew enemy fire away from unarmed support aircraft and was awarded his AF Cross.

This may not represent all of the O-2 pilots who earned Air Force Crosses during the Vietnam War. It most certainly is not an exhaustive listing of all who showed courage and heroism while flying Cessna Skymasters in a shooting war. It is, however, a sample of the kind of courage evidenced by the many brave FACs who repeatedly faced enemy fire in an unarmored and barely armed lightplane, and yet launched on the next mission anyway.

Despite these significant combat awards, the ratio of AF Crosses, Air Medals, and Distinguished Flying Crosses (DFC) to total number of FAC pilots seemed low, at least to the FACs. Part of this might be attributed to a perception on the part of some commanders that FACs just did not really deserve such awards. At one point, the Commanding Officer of the 504th Special Operations Squadron told his FAC pilots he had "never heard or read of a FAC mission that deserved a DFC." In fact, on one strike, the pair of F-100 pilots and the O-2 FAC were all submitted for DFCs — the fighter pilots were awarded theirs, but the FAC was not.

One FAC who was awarded a DFC was Major Fred McNeill — for his last mission in the O-2 on 11 March 1972. McNeill did not actually receive the award until after he had retired from the USAF some years later and was a law school student. A large brown envelope arrived with the medal and accompanying citation. In March 1972, all American forces had withdrawn from the northern portion of South Vietnam, with the exception of some Army advisors serving with Army of the Republic of Vietnam (ARVN) troops and the members of the 20th TASS at Pleiku. At the time, official estimates put the number of NVA regular forces in that area at around 300,000. The 20th TASS had to provide all its own perimeter defenses besides flying the FAC sorties and maintaining the aircraft. By March, all of the members of the unit had received their orders for other assignments, and Fred McNeill had his orders to join the unit operating the C-130 ABCCC aircraft.

On the evening of 10 March, McNeill took a call from the Seventh Air Force Operations Center asking him to set-up a mission for first light the following day to conduct an airstrike in support of the 81st ARVN Ranger Battalion that was pinned down in a tight section of the Plei Trap Valley. A two-ship of Navy A-7s was already scheduled for the mission. McNeill told them to have the A-7s loaded with all the napalm they could carry. When he arrived on the scene the next morning, the entire valley was covered in clouds from the peak of a nearby 7,000-foot mountain right down to the ground. The U.S. Army advisor on the scene told him they had already suffered 40 percent casualties and needed tactical air support right away or they would be overrun. He also told McNeill that the visibility was only about 200 meters and it was raining. Since McNeill knew that particular valley intimately, he made a run-in down through the clouds and popped out at about 300 feet over a familiar stream and near a known footbridge. The Army troops listened for his engines and steered him toward them — he passed right over their heads and climbed back out of the valley into the clear just as the A-7s arrived.

McNeill explained the problem and asked the A-7 leader if he would be willing to follow the little O-2 down through the clouds on little more than a compass heading into the obscured valley in an attempt to save the Rangers and their American advisors — "one pass and haul ass," he assured them. The Navy pilots agreed. McNeill pushed

• An O-2 in landing configuration, tucked in tight for the camera. Note how both pilots are peering around the blind spot caused by the original side window •
(Kansas Aviation Museum/Empire News Service)

his O-2 at its maximum speed with the two A-7s wallowing along just behind him at what was, for them, a slow speed. He placed one "Willie Pete" rocket at the start of a ridgeline and the second one at the other end. The A-7s laid down their napalm along that ridge as the NVA opened fire with everything they had — McNeill looked back and saw the sky and clouds behind him turn bright red with burning napalm. The two A-7s zoomed up out of the valley to return to their ship. The ARVN troops and their advisors were ecstatic as the bombing successfully broke up the enemy attack. The ARVN commander credited that attack with over 400 KBA.

VNAF Gets O-2s

In late 1972 and into 1973, as U.S. and North Vietnamese negotiators developed the ceasefire accords that would inevitably lead to the disengagement of U.S. forces from the war, Project Enhance was initiated. This was a U.S. military program to modernize the equipment and upgrade the capabilities of the South Vietnamese armed forces, replacing combat losses and enabling South Vietnam to counter the expected North Vietnamese attacks. Soon after Project Enhance had been completed, Project Enhance Plus was initiated to further buildup the South Vietnamese military capabilities. For its part, the VNAF received a wide array of aircraft including C/RC/EC-47s, C/AC-119s, C-7s, C-130s, A-1s, UH-1s, CH-47s, T-37s, A-37s, F-5s, and 35 O-2As (for a total of over 700 added aircraft, bringing VNAF strength up to more than 2,000 aircraft).

Imperial Iranian O-2s

In the summer of 1969, the Imperial Iranian Air Force expressed an interest in purchasing some O-2s and spare parts. Cessna's invoice number IIAF-2, 11 June 1969, details the costs as follows:

12	O-2A Aircraft	$1,601,964
4	Portable Stretchers	$551
6	Passenger Seats	$1,826
6	Spare Engines	$39,186
	Airframe Spare Parts	$118,328
	Engine Spare Parts	$42,525
	Ferry Delivery, Wichita-New Orleans	$31,536
	Crating, Shipping, Ocean Freight	$66,152
	TOTAL	**$1,902,068**

On 4 May 1970, Derby Frye, Cessna Vice President for Military Relations, presented the twelve aircraft to Colonel

• *An O-2A on its way to a II Corps combat sortie in 1969* •
(Kansas Aviation Museum/Empire News Service)

M. M. Rokni, representing the Embassy of Iran, at a ceremony in Wichita. The Imperial Iranian Air Force intended to use the aircraft for pilot training in addition to liaison and observation missions.

Modifications and Follow-Ons

Although research was unable to uncover substantiating official records, there remains a persistent rumor of at least one O-2A modified into a sort of mini-gunship, much like the arrangement used in the AC-47 or AC-130 gunships. This modification, allegedly tested in the mid-1960s in Southeast Asia under "Project Little Brother," involved mounting a medium-caliber machine gun (perhaps a .50 caliber) to fire sideways out of the right side of the aircraft. Given the military penchant for making the most of

• The view from an O-2 as Major McNeill returns from a combat sortie. This is the kind of cloudy, hazy day that made forward air controlling more difficult than usual •
(Fred McNeill)

available assets, and the documented instances of machine guns being mounted on the much lighter O-1 Bird Dog, it is difficult to totally discount these rumors. However, it is clear that the modification was never pursued beyond the initial tests, probably due to the conversions of C-47s and C-119s into gunships at approximately the same time — aircraft able to carry and deliver significantly more attacking "punch" with larger machine guns.

Before the first O-2As were delivered to the TASS units in South Vietnam, the USAF had asked Cessna to determine the feasibility of major modifications to the

basic O-2 design to create a new FAC aircraft. The new design was to eliminate the shortcomings of the O-2 while capitalizing on the positive features that led to its selection in the first place. A design team (consisting of John Benn, Paul Weiss, Sam Snyder, and Henry Ditmmer) quickly developed Cessna Preliminary Design Memorandum Report No. 26, titled "Model 348 2-Place Tandem Turboprop Military FAC Aircraft," and issued it on 17 March 1967. In the report's introduction, they stated that the "purpose of the this report is to present a military FAC aircraft based on the centerline thrust concept and powered by Allison 250-B14 turboprop engines rated at 370 HP." The salient features of the proposed Model 348 were described as:

- Cabin top and fuselage from rear doorpost aft identical to the O-2A.
- O-2A wing and empennage structurally beefed-up to allow gross weights of up to 4,800-pounds (5,500-pounds with external stores).
- Tandem seating with the rear seat observer located just slightly aft of the wing leading edge.
- New fuselage forward of rear doorpost, narrowed to allow visibility down on both sides for both crew members.

• The "office" in which USAF O-2 FACs spent many hours during combat missions in Vietnam •
(Kansas Aviation Museum/Robert J. Pickett Collection)

- Provisions for enhanced electronics and avionics.
- Provisions for forward looking infrared surveillance equipment and a downward looking camera.
- Provisions for a side firing minigun installation.
- Psy-ops provisions for loudspeakers and leaflet distribution systems (similar to those in the O-2B).
- Provisions for three weapons hardpoints on each wing (the outboard hardpoints were intended primarily for external fuel tanks to increase operating range).
- Entry and exit through the hinged side windows (designed to allow opening in flight, at reduced airspeed, to improve visibility).
- A 12-inch wide center bullet-resistant windshield section.
- Centerline-mounted push-pull Allison turboprop engines driving 86-inch diameter, two-bladed, constant speed, reversing propellers.

Cessna claimed the Model 348, with its turboprop engines and additional avionics, would have an empty weight of 2,590 pounds, compared to the O-2A's empty weight of 3,226 pounds — 636 pounds less propelled through the air by 320 more horsepower! The proposed Model 348 would have been able to carry 2,900 pounds internally (including crew and internal fuel) and up to 3,600 pounds with external stores. The plan was to develop a modification kit to be installed in the field — reusing the fuselage section from behind the front seats to the rear firewall, as well as the tail booms, wings, main landing gear, and flight control surfaces. The modified aircraft's advantages were touted to be increased payload, improved short field performance, reduced external noise levels, improved climb rate and top speed, and minimized development time. Estimated performance for the "Super O-2" illustrates the significant increase in capability over the performance of the basic O-2A (performance at 4,800 pounds):

- Maximum Cruise Speed . . . . .200 KIAS
- Cruise Speed (75% Power) . . . . .185 KIAS
- Rate of Climb (Sea Level) . . . . .2,800 fpm
- Service Ceiling (Both Engines) . . . . .28,800 ft.
- Service Ceiling (Single Engine) . . . . . . .17,700 ft.
- Maximum Range . . . . .773 nm
- Takeoff Over 50-Foot Obstacle . . . . .1,210 ft.
- Landing Over 50-Foot Obstacle . . . . .1,645 ft.

Shortly after the initial design concept was developed, Cessna and the USAF redesignated the project as the O-2TT ("TT" for Tandem Turboprop). On 9 September 1968, Cessna's Cost Estimating Department issued inter-office memo CE9468-1182, titled "Estimated

• An Imperial Iranian Air Force O-2A on its acceptance test flight near Wichita, Kansas, in 1970 •
(Kansas Aviation Museum/Robert J. Pickett Collection)

Kit Cost to Modify O-2A Aircraft to O-2TT Configuration," estimating the basic recurring cost of kits at $38,150 per aircraft (assuming that the Allison engines were provided to the contractor as Government Furnished Equipment — GFE). Non-recurring engineering and technical data costs were estimated at $143,710, plus the cost of jigs to hold the fuselage while the modifications were made. The total cost to deliver and install 100 kits on existing USAF O-2s was quoted as $12,300,000. Cessna determined that the first kit could be delivered to the field 17 months after receipt of an order from the USAF, and that each kit would require 532 manhours to install. The 532-hour process to complete the conversion included the following steps:

- Disassemble the aircraft (removing empennage, tail booms, wings, and struts).
- Modify the fuselage section:
  - Remove main landing gear, cowlings, engines, plumbing, wiring, radios and rack.
  - Install fuselage in new mating jig and cut away front section at the aft doorpost bulkhead.
  - Install new forward fuselage and lower rear cowl sections and rivet it to the rest of the fuselage.
  - Reinstall main landing gear and lower fuselage from jig onto its landing gear.

- Install new plumbing, wiring, engines, cowlings, propellers, and battery.
- Modify the wings (one wing in jig at a time):
  - Remove flaps, ailerons, wing tips, landing lights, fuel tanks, and plumbing.
  - Install wing in new wing jig, cut away center section skins from fuel bay, and remove four ribs.
  - Install new ribs, new extended wing tips, new flap and flap/aileron interconnect system, and new aileron pushrods.
  - Install new fuel tanks, attachments, plumbing, wiring, and fuel bay covers.
  - Install new wing leading edges and original stall warning transducer.
  - Remove wing from jig and reinstall ailerons and flaps.
- Install aileron extensions, modify tail booms and fins, and install new horizontal stabilizer extensions, elevator, and elevator extensions.
- Reattach struts, wings, booms, empennage.
- Connect control cables, plumbing, radios, and wiring.
- Rig flight controls, checkout landing gear and electrical and hydraulic systems, and repaint aircraft.

While the Model 348 concept was being developed, a parallel effort was underway to define the Model 351 CLT

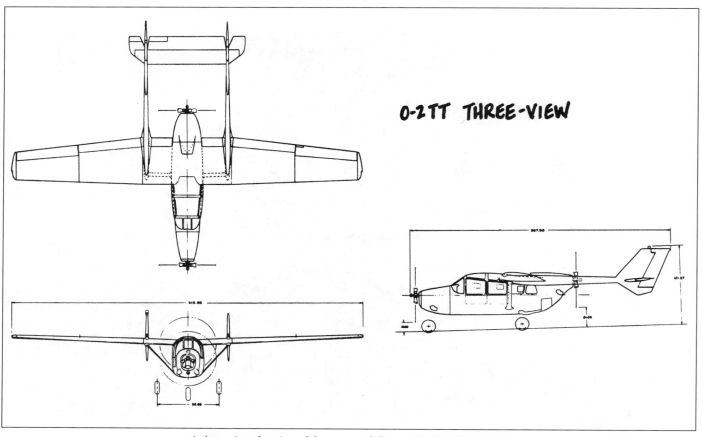

O-2TT THREE-VIEW

• A three-view drawing of the proposed Cessna Model 348 (O-2TT) •
(Kansas Aviation Museum)

• *Cessna's O-2TT mock-up, complete with dummies in the cockpit* •
(Kansas Aviation Museum/Robert J. Pickett Collection)

- Integral, but removable, minigun pods faired into the tail boom fairings under each wing.

The Model 351's empty weight was planned to be 3,826 pounds with a 3,150-pound useful load bringing its maximum gross weight up to 6,900 pounds (including up to 1,400 pounds of external stores). The modification would result in an aircraft capable of cruising at 225 KIAS while stalling at a mere 55 KIAS. Total takeoff distance required to clear a 50-foot obstacle would be a short 520 feet, and only 490 feet to come back and land over that same obstacle! A service ceiling of 24,000 feet and an initial climb rate of 2,530 feet-per-minute were claimed.

as a Cessna Product Improvement Proposal. In a briefing presented to USAF officials in February of 1968, Cessna's opening chart declared:

"Center Line Thrust combined with Turbine Power presents the Optimum FAC Aircraft for Mission Cost Effectiveness."

The Model 351 CLT enhanced O-2 would have employed a pair of 550-horsepower, Pratt & Whitney PT6A-20 engines to provide speeds up to 228 KIAS. The larger engines would allow a FAC, once on-station, to shutdown the front engine and loiter on the rear engine only — cutting fuel consumption in half. With this iteration of the O-2 basic design, the resulting aircraft was beginning to look even more like the Rockwell OV-10 with which the USAF was already planning to replace its O-2, including a high-mounted horizontal stabilizer between the vertical stabilizers and an integral machine gun capability. The tandem-seating Model 351 was proposed with the following features:

- Zero-zero ejection seats (allowing ejection at ground level and zero airspeed).
- Self-sealing, foam-filled fuel tanks.
- High flotation tires, high-lift wings, and reversible propellers.
- Provisions for external microphones (for pinpointing the source of ground fire) and passive self-defense (such as electronic countermeasures equipment).
- Three external stores hardpoints on each wing.

Cessna offered to roll-out the initial prototype Model 351 within 18 months of contractual go-ahead and the first production aircraft 18 months later.

However, USAF interest seemed to center more on the Model 348, so Cessna created a second version of that configuration, the Model 348-2, to find a middle ground between the two designs. A Cessna briefing on 19 April 1968 describes this further modification of the basic Model 348 proposal. It used the same Allison 370-horsepower turboprop engines but with three-bladed propellers, lighter avionics, additional fuel capacity, and a maximum gross weight boosted to 6,300 pounds (with up to 1,663 pounds for external stores). The wings, fuselage, and tail booms would have required further structural enhancements to handle the extra weight and higher speeds. Cessna prepared to deliver the initial prototype within eight months of contract award and the first production modification kits within 30 months.

The final design configuration of the Model 348, described in a 25 November 1968 Cessna press release simply as the O-2TT, used the basic Model 348 fuselage layout, four underwing weapons pylons, and Allison 250-B15 engines rated at 317 horsepower at takeoff power. Derby Frye, Cessna Director of Military Relations, noted that, "We retained the plus features of the O-2, such as the high wing and the fore and aft mounted engines. We then provided for additional performance requirements with the Allison engines and designed a new forward fuselage capsule with a bubble canopy for greater visibility and tandem seating." The new design included constant radius wing leading edges, drooped ailerons interconnected with single-slotted flaps, and 220 square feet of wing area in a 3,220-pound empty weight aircraft — all of which contributed to excellent short takeoff and landing (STOL) performance and the ability to carry up to 1,780 pounds of useful load.

To validate the design for the USAF, Cessna constructed a full-scale mockup of the O-2TT and modified an existing O-2A with everything except the redesigned fuselage, calling the aircraft an O-2T

• *The prototype of the turbine-powered O-2 (the O-2T) taking off at Wichita, Kansas. Note that the rear engine is not operating, as the front turbine engine is providing all the power* •
(Kansas Aviation Museum/Robert J. Pickett Collection)

(turbine). Although performance was impressive, the USAF just could not justify the expense of upgrading its O-2s while at the same time purchasing an entire fleet of the new Rockwell OV-10 Broncos.

In the 1960s, Wren Aircraft Corporation of Fort Worth, Texas, established itself as one of the premier manufacturers of STOL modifications for light aircraft, such as their Wren 460 version of the Cessna Skylane. In 1968, the company modified a USAF O-2A, s/n 67-21299, with those same STOL devices — full-span, double-slotted flaps; synchronized wing-mounted drag devices; a nose-mounted, high-lift flying canard to augment pitch control at slow speeds; and the Wren Beta-Control system to provide reverse propeller pitch for steep approaches and short landing rollouts. The aircraft, which had been one of the original flight test aircraft at Edwards AFB, was transferred to Wren in May 1968.

Although the modified aircraft was developed and flight tested on company funded research and development, no production orders were received. Only one prototype was ever made. Flight tests determined that the five stall fence "teeth" used on the top of each wing on the modified O-2 and the Wren 460 were of little value, so they were replaced with a single "tooth" on

• *One of the original flight test O-2A aircraft (the one temporarily modified by Wren Aircraft) being restored by Darrel Porter of Brighton, Colorado, in 1994.* •
(Ed Reints)

each wingtip. The aircraft was transferred to the USAF Special Air Warfare Center (SAWC) at Eglin AFB, Florida, in May of 1969 where it was flown for 40 hours of flight tests. In January of 1971, Cessna Aircraft's Pawnee Plant returned the aircraft to O-2A configuration. This and other similar expensive projects that failed to reach production helped push Wren Aircraft into financial difficulty. When the Wren engineering vice president was later killed in an aircraft accident, the company was sold.

The Sandcrab

Dropping the O-2TT and Wren O-2 projects did not necessarily mean that all possible modifications for the O-2 aircraft were dropped permanently. In early 1982, Brico Ltd., an Arlington, Virginia, management company, contracted with Robertson Aircraft Corporation of Everett, Washington, for a prototype O-2ST ("ST" apparently referring to the single turboprop configuration). The prototype was first flown six months later. Brico's contract was with the Saudi Arabian government with some contract assistance (and possible official interest) from the USAF.

This modification involved a unique rear-engine-only configuration with a single 700-horsepower Allison 250-C30 turboprop turning an eight-foot, six-inch diameter pusher propeller through a new gearbox designed by Soloy Conversions of Chehalis, Washington. The Allison engine was later replaced by a Pratt & Whitney of Canada 700-horsepower PT6A turboprop engine providing. The O-2ST incorporated a version of Robertson's high-lift system, including increased wing leading edge camber, wing upper surface stall fences, and drooped ailerons. The O-2ST's empennage had a third vertical stabilizer mounted at the midpoint of the horizontal stabilizer to improve control at slow airspeeds. Both the horizontal stabilizer and elevator were extended outboard of the original vertical fins. The fuselage was stretched ahead of the wing to allow six-place seating and, for initial flight test purposes, the tricycle landing gear was fixed. For production, a retractable landing gear was to be installed.

Brico designed an optional composite annular propeller shroud with a narrow chord to increase thrust by about 25 percent without excessive drag penalties at

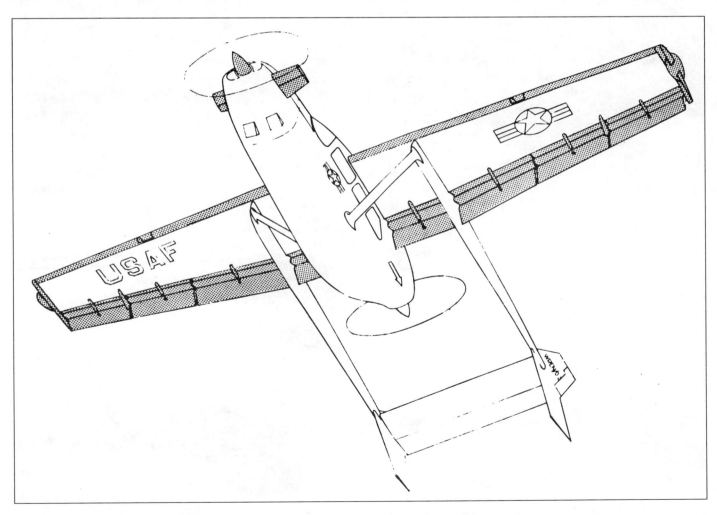

• *A drawing of Wren Aircraft modifications for the O-2. The shading indicates new components, which include the flying canards mounted on each side of the front engine* •
(Todd Peterson)

cruise airspeeds. The project's prime design goals were to produce a multipurpose aircraft able to operate off the loose sands in desert environments, with short takeoff and landing capabilities (with a takeoff roll of 945 feet and a landing roll of 470 feet), a 185-KTAS cruise speed, and a 1,520-mile range. Empty weight was targeted at 3,250 pounds with the potential for up to 2,250 pounds of useful load. Robertson dubbed the aircraft the Sandcrab.

Although the initial contract with the Saudi Arabian government was targeted at remote oil field operations in the desert, provisions were being retained for a light attack version using the O-2's underwing hardpoints for weapons. After the U.S. flight tests were completed, the prototype aircraft was shipped to Saudi Arabia for further tests and demonstrations. The aircraft was later dismantled and shipped back to the United States and turned over to a university.

After the War

When the U.S. military withdrew from South Vietnam, the previously mentioned 35 O-2As were left behind to serve with the armed forces of the beleaguered and soon-to-be-overrun Republic of South Vietnam. When North Vietnam finally overran South Vietnam, there were 31 O-2As in flyable storage. It's not clear what became of those aircraft.

Most of the remaining O-2s were scattered throughout the USAF bases around the world, serving in the Pacific Air Force in Hawaii, the Alaskan Air Command at Eielson AFB near Fairbanks, the United States Air Force Europe (USAFE) bases in West Germany, the U.S. Southern Command's base in the Panama Canal Zone, and at many Tactical Air Command bases throughout the Continental United States. Gradually, many of the aircraft were parcelled out to Air

• *An artist's concept of operational use of the Sandcrab* •
(Sierra Industries)

• A prototype Sandcrab (O-2ST) in flight with another Model 337 flying chase •
(Sierra Industries)

National Guard units until eventually being replaced by either the OV-10 Bronco or the OA-37 Dragonfly.

Five aircraft were assigned to flight test duties, two at the AFFTC at Edwards AFB, California, and three at the Utah Test and Training Range at Hill AFB, Utah. The aircraft at Edwards AFB were used as low-speed chase aircraft and for logistics and flight test support duties, the ones at Hill AFB (actually AFFTC assets as well) were used to support AFFTC test programs operating in the Hill AFB area. At Edwards AFB, the O-2s provided low-speed chase capability for the YC-14 and YC-15 prototype test programs in the mid-1970s during short takeoff and landing tests.

As the focus of USAF preparedness shifted from Southeast Asia to the everpresent threat of a serious attack through central Europe by the now-disassembled Soviet Union, the tactics practiced by the O-2 units changed. Where once the preferred tactics were to remain above small-arms fire range (around 3,500 feet) without worrying about air-to-air threats from above (since air superiority in South Vietnam, Laos, and Cambodia was assured), the new tactics recognized the realities of modern high-threat warfare. Although many O-2 FACs in the 1970s and into the 1980s (the author included) felt that survivability of the slow, not very maneuverable, and unarmed "Oscar Duck" was somewhat of a bad joke, the tactics were, nonetheless, developed and practiced.

Soon, every O-2 FAC had to be qualified to operate and navigate at altitudes between 100 and 500 feet AGL. Terrain masking and contour navigation became common points of discussion among the pilots. A typical scenario might require the O-2 pilot to navigate to a target area at 100 feet AGL, find a target, provide the coordinates and an Initial Point (IP) to the inbound fighters (also flying at very low altitudes), and plan his maneuvers to be in a position to mark the target at the right time. Once the fighters reported approaching the IP, the FAC provided an appropriate run-in heading and time to the flight lead, and then popped-up (to all of maybe 800 feet in the O-2), rolled over and down on the target, fired his "Willie Pete" marking rocket, and jinked out of the immediate area at low altitude once more. After the fighters completed their attacks, the FAC would again pop-up briefly to assess the damage and provide the BDA. The tactics and training were fun, but probably of dubious practicality in an O-2.

When the author was flying O-2s in the Michigan Air National Guard's 172nd TASS in the late 1970s, the

• A Sandcrab with the Brico-designed propeller shroud •
(Sierra Industries)

USAF proposed that we switch to the OV-10. Given the type of threats likely to be encountered in any central European war, we did not feel that the OV-10 was a significant improvement (despite somewhat more speed and agility). The standard squadron joke was that the O-2 was actually more survivable — since it would take us longer to get to the target area in an O-2.

Not all O-2 "war stories" involved combat. In the late 1970s, a certain ex-F-4/F-105 pilot, a senior Captain, was relegated to flying O-2s to maintain his flying proficiency and flight pay while serving in a non-flying staff job. Seems this was the first propeller-driven aircraft said 5,000-hour pilot had ever flown, despite his years of experience. While on a local solo sortie, the Captain declared an emergency and maneuvered for a landing at a local airport. The aircraft crashed on final in the dense woods, and the pilot was severely injured and transported to the hospital. When questioned by the accident investigators, he claimed he had experienced a runaway rear propeller and had to shutdown that engine. He said he restarted it once, but it repeated its earlier runaway performance. Under further questioning, he admitted that, although everything felt and sounded perfectly normal, the rear-engine tachometer was pegged fully clockwise — ergo, a run-

away prop! On short final for his single-engine approach, the front engine quit. Seems the Captain had left the fuel selector on the empty auxiliary tank — and that errant rear engine was actually in perfect running condition except for a malfunctioning tachometer. Experience is one thing — appropriate experience is another.

In 1978, a pair of active duty USAF pilots found themselves unable to get all three gear down-and-locked — the right main dangled downward but would not lock into place. But these were resourceful pilots. The right seater clambered into the rear baggage area, opened the baggage door, and lassoed the gear with a long piece of nylon cord. He had to bodily hang out of the baggage door to about his waist to accomplish this feat of derring-do. By carefully passing the free end of the cord from hand-to-hand from the baggage door to the open side window, he managed to get into a position from which he was able to yank the gear into its forward locked position. The intrepid crew proceeded to land safely and write-up their exploits for dissemination to all O-2 units, with a recommendation from their local Flying Safety Officer that a more appropriate and sturdier piece of rope be developed as a standard part of airborne O-2 equipment. The author recalled vividly when this report was read aloud at an

• *An Alaskan Air Command O-2A, with high-visibility Arctic orange paint on its nose and tail,*
flying over Alaskan Mountains in 1980 •
(U.S. Air Force)

ANG Flying Safety meeting — and the guffaws and disbelief of the O-2 pilots in attendance. We were sure it was all in jest, which it was not. Most O-2s were flown solo, and it would have been almost impossible to lasso that gear safely while maintaining aircraft control. Besides, O-2s had been landed many times gear-up (both intentionally and unintentionally) and had sustained only minor damage. The potential for pilot injury was greater by following the dubious procedure than by simply bellying the aircraft onto the runway. Within a few days, the USAF Flight Safety Center had rescinded any mention of the "gear pulling rope."

• An O-2B assigned to AFFTC at Edwards AFB, California, in 1985 •
(U.S. Air Force)

There is also a story of a certain Tactical Air Support Group Commander who did not maintain weapons qualification in the O-2 and usually only flew the unit's single O-2B. One day, however, he taxied out for a short flight in an A-Model, complete with an empty rocket pod under each wing. Now, the B-Model had no weapons pylons and, therefore, no "Emergency Jettison Button" (labeled "Salvo") mounted on the dash in front of the pilot. The A-Model aircraft did. Both aircraft had a manual slaving button for the heading indicator, also mounted directly in front of the pilot. During the initial takeoff roll, Group Commander noted that he had failed to properly slave his heading indicator so he reached up and casually punched the button — the wrong button, of course. The pair of LAU-32A/A rocket pods promptly departed the aircraft and raced his O-2A down the runway. And, by the way, the "Salvo" button was recessed and surrounded by a collar to preclude such inadvertent activation.

By the end of Fiscal Year 1985, USAF records showed only 68 operational O-2s on the active roster. Their average age was 15.7 years. Another 163 aircraft were sitting in the military "Bone Yard" at Davis-Monthan AFB, Arizona — the Military Aerospace Maintenance and Regeneration Center. In September 1986, according to an official press release in the Air Force Times, "The last operational O-2 used as a forward air control aircraft has been retired from the active fleet by the 21st Tactical Air Support Squadron at Shaw AFB, South Carolina."

For the next year, only a handful of O-2s remained in active service, fulfilling various non-tactical, mission support roles. However, in December 1987, the last three O-2s in the USAF inventory took off from Edwards AFB enroute to Kelly AFB, Texas, where they were retired from active USAF service. Major John Litton, Chief of the Edwards AFB

• An O-2A of the Michigan Air National Guard's 172nd TASS, flying near Cold Lake, Canada, on Operation Cold Flag in June of 1978 •
(Walt Shiel)

• *Jim Grenier's ex-Army O-2A, s/n 68-11150, faithfully restored to the way it served in the Berlin Aviation Detachment* •
(Geoffrey P. Jones)

6510 Test Wing's Operations Center, led the three-ship formation shortly before his own retirement. Major Litton's first operational assignment as a USAF pilot in 1968 was flying the O-2A as a FAC in South Vietnam. Shortly before the mission, he noted, "It's ironic that after 19 years, I end up retiring the aircraft from active service as I prepare for my own retirement."

Army & Navy "Ducks"

On 20 December 1974, the U.S. Army's Berlin Aviation Detachment acquired two O-2A aircraft (serial numbers 68-11149 and 68-11150) from the USAF's 86th Tactical Fighter Wing. These aircraft replaced a pair of Army U-6A Beavers to provide mission support throughout the 20-statute mile radius Berlin Control Zone, under the command of the U.S. Commander of Berlin (this was long before the infamous Berlin Wall was demolished and the divided city of Berlin was reunified). In January 1975, the two O-2s were repainted to standard Army color schemes for mission support aircraft by the Army's 582nd Transportation Company. Since the 1946 Berlin Air Agreement prohibited the operation of combat aircraft within the Berlin Control Zone, the wing hardpoints were removed from both aircraft. While assigned to the Berlin Aviation Detachment, the aircraft were maintained under contract by ten German civilian mechanics.

By 1979, these two aircraft had been replaced by the Swiss-manufactured UV-20 Pilatus Porter and returned to USAF inventory. In September 1994, the entire Berlin Aviation Detachment was deactivated.

The best available information indicates that these erstwhile Army O-2s later served with the Georgia Air National Guard. Serial number 68-11149 was eventually found, in December of 1991, in a state of severe disrepair at Georgia's Stone Mountain Airport. Although it belonged to the Georgia Aviation Museum, possession had seen transferred to the South Georgia Technical Institute in Americus, Georgia. Serial number 68-11150 fared somewhat better. It had served with a local Georgia police force and had been well maintained. Jerry Blue of Lilburn, Georgia, acquired the aircraft and restored it to U.S. Army specifications — it is now owned by Jim Grenier of Westboro, Massachusetts, and has been seen regularly at air shows.

In August of 1982, the U.S. Navy accepted four O-2A aircraft from USAF inventory and another two in 1983. The USAF serial numbers of these aircraft are not recorded but the Navy BuNos were: 721300, 721318, 721349, 721365, 721404, and 721414. The aircraft were used for routine mission support duties and were stricken from the Navy inventory in 1990. At least two examples have been privately acquired, restored to Navy specifications, and can be seen regularly at air shows.

Other Countries, Other Wars

In the late 1970s and early 1980s, Nicaragua's Fuerza Aerea de Nicaragua (FAN) operated both modified civilian Cessna Model 337D aircraft and O-2A aircraft acquired from the USAF. In June 1980, the FAN used its C-337D aircraft, in conjunction with AT-28D aircraft, in attacks against rebel positions in the Matagalpa mountains. Both napalm and defoliants were used.

In 1984, the Contras escalated their attacks against Nicaraguan positions, and in September, an O-2A flown by a contract pilot was shot down during a skirmish near Jalapa.

After rebels destroyed or severely damaged over 20 aircraft in a January 1982 raid on an airfield at Ilopango, El Salvador, the United States provided replacement aircraft, including four O-2As. After further losses in 1984, the United States once again supplied replacement aircraft, this time including two additional O-2s.

Although not technically O-2s, numerous countries

• *An O-2A on display at a Texas airshow in 1994, wearing the emblem "Viet Cong Hunting Club"* •
(Walt Shiel)

have used Cessna's Model 337 in military service. The Rhodesian Air Force's No. 4 Squadron used at least 21 Cessna FTB.337G aircraft, called the Lynx in Rhodesia, for counterinsurgency, reconnaissance, and FAC roles with underwing hard points for rocket pods and a unique overwing mounting for a minigun pod on each wing. Apparently, none of these aircraft were shot down. Some of the Rhodesian Skymasters had been imported in 1977 despite an international arms embargo.

Chad's air force possessed and flew several C-337s in the 1980s. In the late 1980s, reports surfaced that numerous British and Pakistani pilots were flying for the Sri Lankan Air Force (SLAF) and conducting strikes on rebel positions on the Jaffna Peninsula — the No. 2 Squadron possessed at least a few Cessna Model 337s at the time, operating out of Ramalana. The No. 3 Maritime Squadron of the SLAF still operates six Model 337s for reconnais-sance duties out of Trincomalee.

In 1980, Summit Aviation of Delaware sold numerous highly modified Model 337Gs (designated the O2-337) to foreign countries, including Thailand, Bermuda, Haiti, and Jamaica. Summit bought used aircraft, refurbished them to zero-time condition, and upgraded them with tur-bocharged, 225-horsepower Continental TSIO-360 engines, larger fuel tanks, upgraded navigation and communication radios, a head-up display for a gunsight, and four underwing hardpoints for NATO standard MALL-4A weapons pylons. The pylons were certified for carriage of up to 350 pounds apiece and were capable of carrying the usual variety of light weapons (rockets, small bombs, flares, etc.) as well as either 7.62mm or 12.7mm minigun pods. The Royal Thai Navy purchased 10 of the aircraft for its No. 3 Squadron for use in counterinsurgency and antipiracy activities — at least five are still in use.

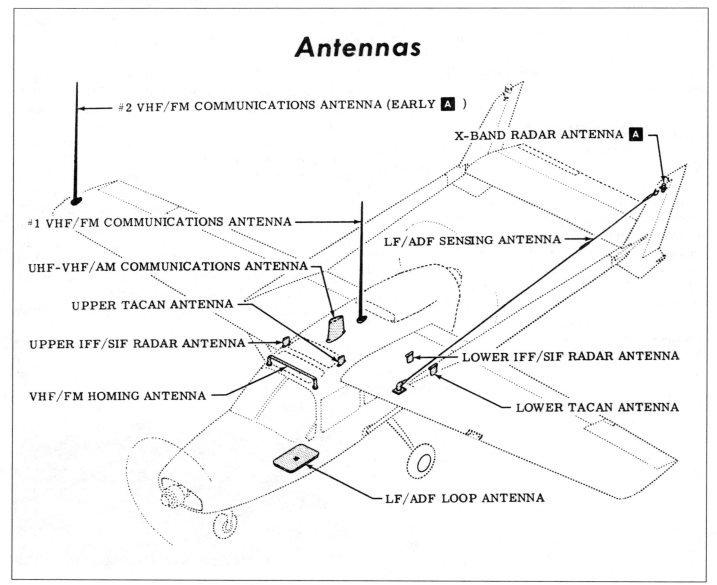

Antennas

#2 VHF/FM COMMUNICATIONS ANTENNA (EARLY **A**)

X-BAND RADAR ANTENNA **A**

#1 VHF/FM COMMUNICATIONS ANTENNA

LF/ADF SENSING ANTENNA

UHF-VHF/AM COMMUNICATIONS ANTENNA

UPPER TACAN ANTENNA

UPPER IFF/SIF RADAR ANTENNA

LOWER IFF/SIF RADAR ANTENNA

VHF/FM HOMING ANTENNA

LOWER TACAN ANTENNA

LF/ADF LOOP ANTENNA

• *Typical antenna arrangement of a "Fighting Skymaster"* •
(Air Force Flight Manual)

Where Are They Now?

Once the USAF retired its O-2s to the boneyard at Davis-Monthan AFB, Arizona, pilots naturally began trying to acquire them for private use — to be seen alongside the many civilian operated Cessna L-19s and O-1s. It was not long before the USAF began releasing them through government auctions. As a result, attend most any weekend airshow that draws Warbirds and you will likely find one or more O-2s on proud display. Besides a large number of USAF O-2s, there are at least two flying in Navy colors and one in Army colors to commemorate those services' involvement, however brief, with the "Oscar Deuce."

There are at least 21 O-2 aircraft on display around the country in various museum collections, including:

- *Pima Air & Space Museum*, Tucson, Arizona
- *Castle Air Museum*, Castle AFB, Atwater, California
- *Travis Air Force Museum*, Vacaville, California
- *March Field Museum*, March AFB, Riverside, California
- *AF Flight Test Center Museum*, Edwards AFB, California
- *Hurlburt Field Air Park*, Fort Walton Beach, Florida
- *USAF Armament Museum*, Valparaiso, Florida
- *Museum of Aviation*, Warner Robins, Georgia
- *Grissom Air Park*, Grissom AFB, Peru, Indiana
- *Selfridge Military Air Museum*, Mt. Clemens, Michigan
- *USAF Museum*, Wright-Patterson AFB, Dayton, Ohio
- *S. Dakota Air & Space Museum*, Rapid City, South Dakota
- *Dyess Air Park*, Dyess AFB, Abilene, Texas
- *History & Traditions Museum*, San Antonio, Texas
- *Kelly Field Heritage Museum*, San Antonio, Texas
- *Hill Aerospace Museum*, Hill AFB, Ogden, Utah
- Dover Air Force Historical Center, AFB, Delaware
- Ellsworth Air Museum, Ellsworth AFB, South Dakota
- Shaw Air Park, Shaw AFB, South Carolina
- 105th Airlift Group, Stewart International Aitport, Newburgh, New York
- 121st Air Refueling Wing, Rickenbacker ANGB, Columbus AFB, Ohio

As the USAF releases more of the aircraft from storage at Davis-Monthan AFB, civilian-operated authentic military O-2s should become even more prevalent. ✝

Specifications

Wingspan. . . . . 38 ft., 0 in.
Length
        O-2A . . . . 29 ft., 2 in.
        O-2B . . . . 29 ft., 9 in.
Height . . . . 9 ft., 5 in.
Engines
        O-2A (Both Engines). . . . . Continental IO-360-D, 210 HP
        O-2B
                Front Engine . . . . Continental IO-360-C, 210 HP
                Rear Engine. . . . . Continental IO-360-D, 210 HP
Weight
        Empty
                O-2A . . . . 3,226 lbs.
                O-2B . . . . 3,268 lbs.
        Maximum Allowable
                O-2A . . . . 4,850 lbs.
                                (all weight over 4,400 lbs. must be on external stations)
                O-2B . . . . 4,600 lbs.
        Maximum for Landing. . . . . 4,400 lbs.
Fuel Capacity
        Main Tanks (2) . . . . 44.2 U.S. gallons ea.
        Auxiliary Tanks (2) . . . . 18 U.S. gallons ea.
        Total Usable . . . . 122 U.S. gallons
Best Glide Speed. . . . . 100 KIAS
Glide Ratio 10.9:1
Maximum Speed
        Maximum, No Flaps . . . . 192 KIAS
        Maximum, Full Flaps . . . . 104 KIAS
        Maximum, Gear Down . . . . 139 KIAS
Maneuvering Speed. . . . . 131 KIAS
G Limits . . . . +3.8/-1.5
Stall Speed (Power Off)
        4,850 lbs., No Flaps. . . . . 72 KIAS
        4,850 lbs., Full Flaps . . . . 66 KIAS
        4,000 lbs., No Flaps . . . . 64 KIAS
        4,000 lbs., Full Flaps . . . . 59 KIAS
Takeoff Ground Roll . . . . 1,850 ft.
Takeoff Distance Over 50-Foot Obstacle . . . . 2,950 ft.
Normal Liftoff Speed . . . . 75 KIAS
Service Ceiling
        No External Stores
                Two Engines . . . . 17,000 ft.
                Single Engine . . . . 2,000 ft.

Specifications continue on next page...

Specifications

...Continued from page 256

Service Ceiling (continued)
    Two Rocket Pods with Rockets
        Two Engines . . . . 14,600 ft.
        Single Engine . . . . Sea Level
Single Engine Rate of Climb at Sea Level
    No External Stores
        Front Engine . . . . 150 fpm
        Rear Engine . . . . 220 fpm
    Two Rocket Pods with Rockets
        Front Engine . . . . 65 fpm
        Rear Engine . . . . 135 fpm
Normal Cruise
    No External Stores
        Airspeed . . . . 140 KTAS
        Fuel Flow . . . . 18.6 gph
        Range (No Reserves) . . . . 860 nm
    Two Rocket Pods with Rockets
        Airspeed . . . . 133 KTAS
        Fuel Flow . . . . 18.6 gph
        Range (No Reserves) . . . . 820 nm
Maximum Range Cruise
    No External Stores
        Airspeed . . . . 124 KTAS
        Fuel Flow . . . . 16.4 gph
        Range (No Reserves) . . . . 900 nm
    Two Rocket Pods with Rockets
        Airspeed . . . . 124 KTAS
        Fuel Flow . . . . 17.4 gph
        Range (No Reserves) . . . . 850 nm
Landing Ground Roll . . . . 540 ft.
Landing Distance Over 50-Foot Obstacle . . . . 1,250 ft.

T-41 Mescalero

-chapter 12-

Although jets began replacing prop aircraft in the USAF inventory in the late 1940s, the service continued using propeller-driven trainers for primary training until April 1961 — aircraft like the T-6, the T-28, and the T-34. So what happened in 1961 to lure the USAF into dropping piston-engine trainers? By that time, the Cessna twin-jet T-37 had proven itself as a primary trainer, prompting the USAF to experiment with an "all-through jet" training syllabus. Officials figured the new jet trainer was so easy and cheap to fly propeller-driven trainers were no longer needed. Besides, with a soon-to-be-all-jet inventory, why train with propeller-driven anachronisms?

Best Laid Plans...

As with so many seemingly well-thought-out plans, reality soon intervened. The USAF discovered that even the T-37, despite its small 1,025-pound-thrust turbojets, cost too much to operate in that entry-level pilot screening role. Students who were unable to overcome physiological deficiencies (such things as active airsickness, claustrophobia, fear of flying, etc.), who were incapable of attaining the required proficiency in the time allotted, or who were merely unsuited for the regimentation of military flying used up a lot of expensive resources before being eliminated from training.

After only three years of the all-jet experiment, the USAF's Air Training Command (ATC) set about reinventing the wheel and went shopping for a piston-engine trainer. When the military reinvents the wheel, it tends to reinvent the whole concept of round. So, the USAF decided that the new trainers should be flown and maintained by civilian flight schools under government contracts,

• Cessna's proposed Civil Air Patrol Model 172 in 1960 •
(Kansas Aviation Museum/Robert J. Pickett Collection)

similar to the civilian contract aviation cadet and primary flight schools operated during World War II and into the late 1950s. In fact, the original T-37s were operated under civilian contracts.

On 31 May 1960, in an attempt to gain a foothold in a semi-military organization, Cessna Aircraft proposed to the USAF that its adjunct civilian search-and-rescue organization, the Civil Air Patrol (CAP), be re-equipped with a combination of Cessna Model 150s and Model 172s. Cessna prepared a new 172 in a special CAP paint scheme to demonstrate its product. The proposal was never accepted.

Off the Shelf

In 1964, the USAF published the requirements for an off-the-shelf civilian trainer, insisting on a fixed-pitch propeller for simplicity. In contrast with the state of general aviation today, in 1964 there were many suitable civilian trainers rolling out of general aviation factories. Piper, Beech, and Cessna all responded to the USAF Request for Proposals with a total of eight variations on their existing training aircraft to compete for the lucrative contract. Cessna offered three aircraft for evaluation — a standard 182, a standard 172, and a 180-horsepower 172,

all with the USAF-mandated fixed-pitch propellers. Piper offered three Cherokee variants. Beech offered two models. Although all three of the Cessna models met the USAF requirements, Cessna elected to provide a firm bid for only the basic Model 172. This basic 172 with the 145-horsepower Continental O-300-D engine, with only the front seats installed, won the contract at a fly-away price of $7,000 apiece.

The USAF designated the new aircraft the T-41A Mescalero (Mescaleros being a branch of the Apaches who inhabited part of what is now Texas and New Mexico). As the T-41A was intended for day VFR primary training only, the instrument panel included only basic flight instruments (altimeter, airspeed indicator, vertical velocity indicator, heading indicator, turn-and-slip indicator, attitude indicator), a single VHF communication radio, and a single VOR navigation receiver. On 31 July 1964, the USAF and Cessna signed a fixed-price, $1.2-million contract for 170 T-41A aircraft (Models 172F and 172G). At the time of the contract award, Cessna had already sold 8,799 civilian Model 172s, making it the most popular private aircraft in the world. The first aircraft were delivered to the USAF under this contract in September of 1964, with final delivery of the 170th air-

• *A USAF T-41A from the first production lot. This photo was taken in 1965* •
(Cessna Aircraft)

craft in July of 1965. A second contract for 34 more T-41A (Model 172H) aircraft was issued in July of 1967. The aircraft were assigned to the eight Undergraduate Pilot Training (UPT) bases active at that time:

• Moody AFB, Valdosta, Georgia.
• Craig AFB, Selma, Alabama.
• Vance AFB, Enid, Oklahoma.
• Reese AFB, Lubbock, Texas.
• Webb AFB, Big Spring, Texas.
• Laughlin AFB, Del Rio, Texas.
• Laredo AFB, Laredo, Texas.
• Williams AFB, Chandler, Arizona.

By 1973, when the demand for pilots for the war in Southeast Asia reached its peak of approximately 3,000 new USAF pilots per year, another UPT base was activated and received T-41s: Columbus AFB, Columbus, Mississippi.

Separate contracts were signed for civilian operation and maintenance of the aircraft at general aviation airports near

• *A typical sparse USAF T-41 instrument panel, intended for day VFR flying only* •
(Walt Shiel)

each of the UPT bases. For the next 30 years, every USAF pilot received his or her first military flight training in the T-41, including the author (I won't say how long ago, but some of the aircraft still smelled new). A few years after earning my Air Force wings, I found myself once again flying the T-41 — this time as an instructor, accumulating some 800 hours in four years at three different locations. Although there was a touch of chagrin at wearing USAF wings while flying the same aircraft thousands of private pilots were flying, I enjoyed the assignment and the opportunity to work closely with civilian flight instructors whose log books reflected a wide range of experience vastly different from that of most of my military cohorts.

Quasi-Military Operations

All USAF aircraft were delivered with both military s/n and civilian registration "N" numbers, since they were destined to be maintained to Federal Aviation Administration (FAA) standards by civilian mechanics. The "N" numbers were chosen to roughly parallel the military serial number, which ran sequentially from 65-5100 through 65-5269 for the first lot of T-41A aircraft and from 67-14959 through 67-14992 for the second lot. An additional seven T-41As (Model 172K) were delivered in 1970 with the 150-horsepower Lycoming O-320-E2D for delivery to foreign air forces under the Military Assistance Program (MAP).

These contract operations were managed by a civilian contract manager. One of his senior instructors was designated as a flight commander or operations officer — the 15-20 civilian instructor pilots worked for him. All of the instructors had to be FAA certified flight instructors, have

a minimum of 300 hours flying time, and pass a checkride administered by the USAF. Maintenance was handled by a civilian chief of maintenance (who had to be an FAA-certified Aircraft Inspector) with a team of maintenance technicians working for him, most of whom possessed FAA Airframe and Powerplant certificates. The contract manager enforced discipline and standardization among his instructors, including requiring some sort of uniform (usually just a pair of dark slacks and an open-neck white shirt with name tag and epaulets). The contract managers, many of the civilian supervisors, and some of the instructors were, in fact, ex-military or retired military pilots.

Each T-41 contract required a local contingent of military personnel to supervise and administer the contract, and to ensure compliance with its terms. A team of three military instructor pilots provided oversight for the flight operations portion of the contract — typically one major or lieutenant colonel and a pair of captains. As one of the assigned captain instructor pilots working with the civilian contract at Howard County Airport, Big Spring, Texas, I was responsible for standardization and evaluation of the civilian instructors. The military detachment included a handful of maintenance personnel, usually supervised by a master sergeant or above, who made sure that the contractor maintenance was completed in accordance with contract and FAA requirements.

When a new instructor pilot was hired, the civilian contractor had to train him or her in three areas: USAF-specific maneuver requirements, ATC standard instructional techniques, and local flying area procedures. When the contractor certified that the new instructor was ready for duty, one of the three military instructors administered an ATC-standard instructional checkride. We also administered twice-a-year checkrides to all civilian instructors and to each other. On most of the contracts, a new-hire did not actually go on the payroll until passing the USAF checkride — and was likewise removed from that payroll upon failing his or her semi-annual checkride. I suppose that was a form of incentive for them to take the checkrides seriously, but it also put the younger and less experienced instructors under considerable pressure. After all, they were usually only barely making minimum wage. Flying for one of the T-41 contracts was, however, a good way for a young civilian pilot to build a lot of flying time quickly, albeit only day VFR flying hours. Most of the civilian instructors were scheduled to fly three or four sorties every day, averaging about 1.3 hours per sortie.

• A Peruvian Air Force T-41A •
(Kansas Aviation Museum/Robert J. Pickett Collection)

The contracts required USAF instructor pilots to fly at least 25 percent of all final student checkrides, but we usually flew more than the minimum. In addition, we flew regularly with a variety of students on normal instructional sorties — to help get a class through training on time or just because it was better than sitting behind a desk. Every few months, we took on a student as the primary instructor just so we did not forget what was involved in teaching a new student and shepherding him through that all-important first solo.

One of my more enduring memories of the Howard County T-41 program occurred when a new lieutenant colonel was assigned. He had not flown a lightplane since primary pilot training in the T-34, sixteen years earlier. Most of his flying time had been in high-performance aircraft like the Republic F-105 Thunderchief and he had most recently been an instructor in the supersonic Northrop T-38 Talon. Five years earlier, he had flown a combat tour in Vietnam in the Douglas A-1E Skyraider — a truly macho propeller-driven beast with a 2,700-horsepower radial engine. I took on the task of bringing him up-to-speed in the little T-41A assuming it would be easy for a pilot of his experience.

Airwork went smoothly, although he did have some trouble adjusting to the idea of a control wheel rather than a stick. Landings, however, were another matter entirely. I had assumed that

• Although technically not a T-41, this Singapore Defense Force Model 172K (s/n 109) was almost indentical. This was photographed at Seletar, Singapore, in December of 1971•
(Kansas Aviation Museum/Robert J. Pickett Collection)

• A Royal Saudi Air Force T-41A •
(Kansas Aviation Museum/Robert J. Pickett Collection)

Anything a damn captain can do, I can do." He then proceeded to fly progressively better landings for the rest of the mission. By the end of the following sortie, his landings were consistently fine. I had just discovered a new technique to add to my instructional techniques repertoire of fear, sarcasm, and ridicule — humiliation!

Fast-Paced Training

The original USAF T-41 flight training syllabus included two distinct tracks: an 18-hour program for those already possessing at least a private license and a 30-hour program for all others. The basic standards paralleled those of the FAA private pilot requirements, but without the cross-country navigation and with only minimal solo flight time. The course included the basics plus chandelles and lazy eights. The syllabus included two solo flights, an initial solo flown strictly in the traffic pattern and another one out to the practice area. There were mid-phase and final checkrides, administered primarily by civilian check pilots but with at least 25 percent administered by the military instructors. Classroom instruction for the T-41 pro-

anyone who could master rudder control in a hairy brute like the A-1E could certainly manage adequate rudder control in the benign T-41. However, every takeoff and landing with my new boss was a new adventure. We landed on all three wheels simultaneously and proceeded to swerve back and forth across the runway in ever-increasing arcs. We landed nosewheel first and "porpoised" down the runway until he gave up in frustration and added power to abort the attempt. Once airborne, everything was fine. On one particularly dazzling display of airmanship, we seemed to be cycling repeatedly between the nosewheel, the left main wheel, and the right main wheel — while pumping the control wheel fore-and-aft. Student flying had ended for the day and all of the civilian instructors had gone home. I was the only witness to the exhibition. As he fought valiantly for control, I burst out laughing — against my better judgement. I just could no longer hold it in. As he jammed the throttle forward and popped the airplane off the runway to escape from the humiliation, he snarled, "What the hell are you laughing at, Shiel?" I swallowed the last of my laughter and asked if he'd like another demonstration. Through clenched teeth, he said, "No.

• A three-ship of USAF T-41A aircraft from the first lot, enroute to their ATC assignment •
(Kansas Aviation Museum/Robert J. Pickett Collection)

gram, including an introduction to aerodynamics, was conducted by military instructors as part of the normal UPT academic curriculum. All training was completed over a two-month period.

Army Jumps on the Bandwagon

By 1966, the USAF had demonstrated the cost-effectiveness of the T-41, and the Army jumped on the bandwagon. They ordered 255 copies of the R-172E, designated the T-41B, for primary training of its fixed-wing pilots (to replace the O-1 Bird Dog and make it available for other duties in Southeast Asia) and for other miscellaneous support duties. This order

• *A military T-41 instructor congratulates his student on a successful first solo* •
United States Air Force

was the result of a competitive procurement conducted by the Army Aviation Materiel Command at St. Louis, Missouri, and resulted in a $4-million contract for Cessna.

Army serial numbers for the new T-41B trainers ran from 67-15000 through 67-15254. The Army order was based on the prototype R-172E developed and tested in Wichita but intended for production at the Reims factory in France as the Cessna-Reims Rocket R-172E. The Army took delivery of the first six Army T-41B aircraft in November of 1966 and the remaining 249 by March of 1967. All were delivered in a three-tone paint scheme of olive drab, white, and Day-Glo orange.

The Army T-41Bs were delivered with the more powerful 210-horsepower Continental IO-360-D engine to meet its requirement for operation from short, unpaved runways at high altitudes and temperatures. Cessna had experience with this engine both on the Reims Rocket and on the Model 337. The T-41B application required some minor only working on the engine cooling modifications. These aircraft were all delivered with a 28-volt electrical system and a constant-speed prop. The Army requirements meant boosting the T-41's gross weight to 2,500 pounds, so Cessna conducted additional stability and control flight tests and verified the performance data. The Army contract required some other modifications as well:

- Strengthened firewall.
- No baggage door.
- 6.00 x 6 nosewheel to replace the usual 5.00 x 5 nosewheel for rough field use.
- Jettisonable doors.
- External power receptacle.
- Larger 52-gallon fuel tanks.
- Opening right-hand window.

• *A T-41A pilot demonstrates the preferred landing method — main landing gear first* •
(United States Air Force)

• *An early U.S. Army T-41B, s/n 67-15072* •
(Kansas Aviaiton Museum/Robert J. Pickett Collection)

Air Force Academy Adds to the Fleet

In 1968, the USAF ordered an additional 52 T-41s for training use at the USAF Academy in Colorado Springs, Colorado. These aircraft were R-172Es with the same IO-360-D ordered by the Army but with a fixed-pitch propeller to simplify power management. The bigger engine was selected to compensate for Colorado Springs' mile-high elevation and hot summertime temperatures. Larger 46-gallon fuel tanks were included to offset the higher fuel consumption of the bigger engine. This new version, designated the T-41C, was delivered with s/n 68-7866 through 68-7910 and 69-7750 through 69-7756.

• Added step on the fuselage just forward of the lift strut and another on the strut itself to simplify refueling without a stepladder (a grab handle was also added just forward of the windshield).

Most of the initial Army deliveries were made to Fort Stewart, Georgia, and Fort Rucker, Alabama, for fixed-wing pilot training. Some were dispersed to Army bases around the world for supply support, personnel transport, and proficiency flying duties. As the Army aircraft were used for much more than pilot training, they were equipped with better avionics than their USAF counterparts, including ADF receivers, up to four communications radios (such as FM radios for communications with Army ground units), and an FM homing capability.

The Army T-41B contract required a full-function intercom, audio control panel for all the radios, push-to-talk switches on both control wheels, and a push-to-talk switch built into the headset cord for the backseat observer (the copilot also had a foot-operated microphone switch).

A number of Army T-41B aircraft were later converted to the Lycoming O-360 engine — although there was no official conversion program. Some 25 B-Models were later refurbished and distributed to foreign air forces under the MAP.

Fuel metering for the fuel-injected engine proved to be a problem with the fixed-pitch propeller, but the Air Force insisted on the configuration. At high altitudes, engine flooding during dives and fuel starvation during power-on stalls were typical. In addition, fuel tended to pool in the muffler during idle-power, high-speed descents, leading to periodic backfiring when the hot fuel ignited. Continental worked on an improved fuel metering schedule while Cessna developed a simple swing-out mechanical stop to prevent USAF Academy cadets from leaning the mixture too much. Whenever operating above 6,000-feet — like taxi and takeoff at Colorado Springs, for instance — the stop had to be in-place. At lower altitudes, the stop was to be swung back to allow full power. Although the cadets proved quite capable of handling this

• *The first U.S. Army T-41B arrives at Fort Stewart, Georgia in November of 1966* •
(U. S. Army Aviation Museum)

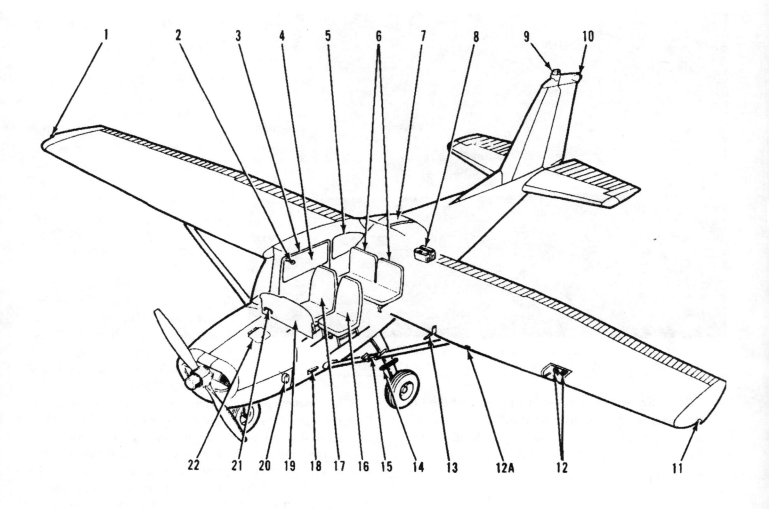

Equipment Not illustrated for Clarity

Operator's manual	Aircraft tow bar
Flight controls lock	Pilot's checklist
First aid kit (1)	Power computer
Fire extinguisher	Hoisting rings

1. Right wing navigation light
2. Free air temperature gage
3. Cabin door (both sides)
4. Cabin door window (both sides)
5. Cabin rear side window (both sides)
6. Rear seats
7. Cabin rear window
8. Battery
9. Rotating beacon
10. Tail navigation light
11. Left wing navigation light
12. Landing and taxi lights
12A. Stall warning port
13. Pilot tube
14. Entry assist step
15. Fueling step
16. Pilot's seat
17. Copilot's seat
18. Fueling step
19. Instrument panel
20. External power receptacle
21. Refueling assist handle
22. Engine compartment access door

• *Typical layout diagram for the Army T-41B, showing the locations for the refueling assist handle (21), the fueling step (18), and the external power receptacle(20)* •
(U.S. Army Flight Manual)

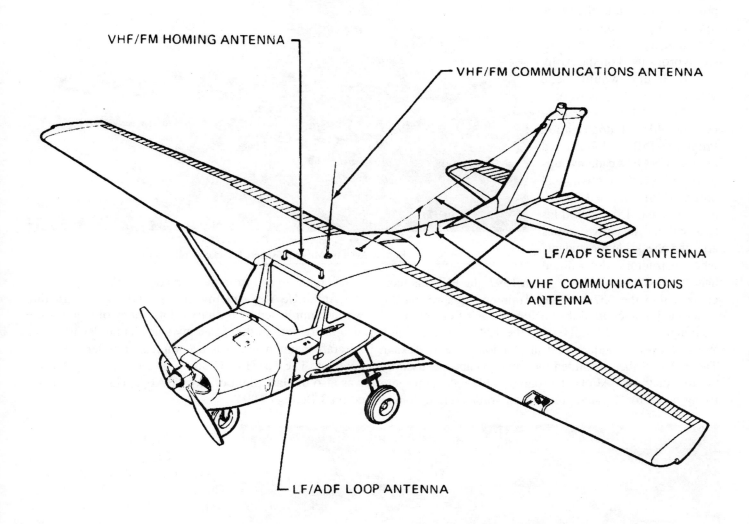

VHF/FM HOMING ANTENNA

VHF/FM COMMUNICATIONS ANTENNA

LF/ADF SENSE ANTENNA

VHF COMMUNICATIONS ANTENNA

LF/ADF LOOP ANTENNA

• *Typical antenna layout for the Army T-41B, illustrating the range of installed radio equipment (as opposed to the USAF T-41A which featured only one VHF/AM communication radio and one VOR navigation receiver)* •
(U.S. Army Flight Manual)

extra fuel management chore, sometimes engines still quit during landing roll-outs.

Eventually, an aneroid mixture control was incorporated on all T-41C aircraft to correct the problem. Since the problem was due to the inter-relationship of power, fuel flow, and rpm, the constant-speed props used on the Army T-41B likely would have solved the problem as well.

These T-41Cs were used in the Pilot Indoctrination Program (PIP), administered by the USAF Academy primarily as a cadet motivational program. PIP included 20 flying hours and 15 sorties (plus two optional incentive sorties after the checkride for students who instructors determined had "earned" them). However, in 1993, the PIP was reorganized into the 557th Flying Training Squadron (FTS) under the jurisdiction of the Air Force's Air Education and Training Command (AETC) and the 12th Flying Training Wing (FTW) (headquartered at Randolph AFB, Texas). The 557 FTS then instituted the same syllabus as used by the rest of the USAF T-41 program, although with more flying hours for the same number of sorties due to longer

• *Columbian Air Force T-41B* •
(Kansas Aviation Museum/Robert J. Pickett Collection)

transit times to and from their practice areas.

At the USAF Academy, ground and flight instruction was accomplished by military pilots, many of whom were also instructors in the Academy's academic departments. Aircraft maintenance was accomplished under a civilian contract. The last T-41C sortie at the Academy (which was also the last flight of any USAF T-41) was completed on 3 October 1994.

• *USAF Academy T-41C, s/n 68-7869, on the ramp at the Academy's Falcon Field in Colorado Springs, Colorado in August of 1994* •
(Walt Shiel)

Final Version

In 1968, another model of the T-41, the T-41D, was produced. These were essentially T-41B aircraft with a few additional "goodies" and were intended primarily for overseas sales under the MAP. Although D-models tended to vary depending on the desires of the receiving country, most were delivered with four seats, bonded cabin and baggage doors, reinforced wing flaps and ailerons, boots on the horizontal stabilizer to protect against abrasion, and corrosion-proofed skins in load-bearing areas — plus wing hardpoints for installing pylons for possible weapons (such as rocket pods). However, these aircraft were delivered in small lots spanning many years and each contract

• *A pair of 557th FTS T-41C instructor pilots prepare for an instructional proficiency sortie* •
(Walt Shiel)

• *USAF Academy T-41C — the component mounted on the engine just forward of the air intake is the aneroid mixture control* •
(Walt Shiel)

lot tended to be unique. Since the D-Model varied little from the earlier B- and C-Models, almost no additional flight testing was required.

Sales of the T-41D totaled 328 aircraft between 1968 and 1974 (Models R-172H through R-172K), including some R-172H models that incorporated the elongated dorsal fin of the C-172I (although not its tubular steel landing gear — all T-41s were delivered with the original flat, tapered spring-type landing gear).

Over the years, some USAF T-41C aircraft were modified with the addition of a constant-speed propeller and redesignated as T-41Ds. Currently, the last two remaining T-41D aircraft in U.S. military service are operated by the USAF Academy as part of its

• A USAF Academy T-41 student respondes to a question on proper application of an emergency procedure during the daily operations briefing •
(U.S. Air Force)

Aeronautical Engineering 456 course. These aircraft are used by students carefully screened and selected to fly flight test profiles. Approximately 16 cadets are selected each semester. After learning the academics in the classroom, they develop the flight test profiles and compute the expected results. They then fly the profiles — which include sawtooth climbs and descents, constant power performance measurements, and handling qualities evaluation — and complete the data reduction and comparison of actual performance against their preflight computations. The conversion to constant-speed props was necessary due to the types of maneuvers and flight profiles flown. These two T-41D aircraft are also used for flight proficiency for colonel-pilots assigned to the Academy.

When the Academy's T-41Cs were phased-out in late 1994, the Academy's Aeronautical Engineering department acquired an additional T-41C and converted it to the D-model configuration.

Consolidation

In 1973, with pilot output decreasing due to the waning United States involvement in Vietnam, the USAF decided to capitalize on potential economies of scale and consolidate the nine T-41 contract programs at a long-since closed USAF navigator training base at Hondo, Texas, approximately 40 miles west of San Antonio. The USAF Academy's PIP was not affected. As part of the change, the dual track 18- and 30-hour syllabi were reduced to a single 14-hour syllabus with only one solo flight and only one checkride. The revamped program was christened the consolidated Flight Screening Program

• A USAF Academy T-41 student starts the engine under the supervision of a 557th FTS instructor pilot •
(U.S. Air Forc)

• USAF Academy T-41Cs line up to await takeoff clearances •
(U.S. Air Force)

USAF Academy T-41Cs had been transferred to Stinson Field on the southeast side of San Antonio, Texas, for use on a separate contract — a primary training program established specifically for South Vietnamese Air Force (VNAF) students as a lead-in to the VNAF T-28 training program at Keesler AFB in Biloxi, Mississippi. Once the Hondo FSP was activated, the VNAF T-41 program was merged into the new program and expanded to include all other foreign military students under the Security Assistance Training Program (SATP). When the consolidation was complete, the T-41Cs were transferred back to the USAF Academy. All training was accomplished in the FSP's T-41A aircraft, although the syllabus used for training foreign students allowed for up to 30 hours of flying time.

(FSP) and placed under the operational command of the Officer Training School at Lackland AFB in San Antonio, Texas. More than 90 aircraft were transferred to Hondo, and the first class of students entered training in May of 1973.

Prior to the birth of the Hondo FSP, some of the eign students allowed for up to 30 hours of flying time.

Having instructed in the T-41C at Stinson, I can attest to the significant performance gain over the standard-engined T-41 and C-172. We routinely climbed out at an indicated 100 miles-per-hour so as to afford a reasonable view over the nose, while still maintaining a climb rate of close to 1,000 feet-per-minute in the hot, humid south Texas summers.

A typical training day at Hondo used the parallel 17-35 runways with the American students flying off the west runway and the foreign students flying off the east runway. In addition, the foreign program used an auxiliary field at Castroville Airport, located 15 miles east of Hondo, for most of their touch-and-go work. Foreign students were primarily from South Vietnam (until 1975 when the United States abandoned that besieged country), Iran (until the fall of the Shah in 1979) and Saudi Arabia,

• A T-41D with a rocket pod under each wing •
(Kansas Aviation Museum/Robert J. Pickett Collection)

although students from Africa, Europe, and Central America were also trained at Hondo.

We experienced a few "cultural" differences in dealing with the large number of foreign students at Hondo. One student, in an attempt to express his appreciation to the military instructor who had just given him a passing grade on his checkride, asked the captain if he liked sports cars. When the captain informed him he could not accept such gifts, the student asked if he liked Rolex watches. Again the captain explained the rules against gratuities from students. How about Chivas Regal?

• A typical fixed gunsight used on armament trainer T-41D aircraft •
(Kansas Aviation Museum/Robert J. Pickett Collection)

After further attempts, the student finally gave up — accepting the fact that the captain just could not legally accept the offers. Our commander, a full colonel, was given a beautiful crystal chandelier by one group of Iranian students — a gift that had to be turned over to USAF authorities who stored it where all such excessive gifts are stored (don't ask me where that is).

We also had an episode that highlighted a significant disparity between American ethics and the ethics of a certain Middle Eastern country. We had caught almost an entire class of students from that country cheating on an exam and were not quite sure what to do with them. We notified their liaison officer, a lieutenant colonel in their air force, who showed up, took the entire group into a classroom, and shut the door — after asking us to just leave him alone for a while. There was a lot of shouting in that room for quite some time, as well as some noise indicating that corporal punishment was being administered. One of our enlisted personnel spoke the language just enough to determine, from the hallway outside, that what the liaison officer was really upset about was that the students were so dumb as to get caught cheating and cause a resultant loss of face for their country.

All of our foreign students had completed a set of Defense Language Institute (DLI) courses run by the U.S. Army — basic English, as well as technical English for all the pilot candidates. During final progress checkrides (the last "make-it-or-break-it" evaluation always conducted by a military instructor),

• A T-41D of the Peruvian Air Force •
(Kansas Aviation Museum/Robert J. Pickett Collection)

• *A close-up of a USAF Academy T-41D's right wing — the brackets under the wing are used to mount flight test instrumentation and atmospheric sampling equipment* •
(Walt Shiel)

Oxford. The Nigerian was well over six feet tall, black as the West Texas night, and still bore the remains of scars from tribal initiation marks across both cheeks. Our SATP manager at the time had spent many years working with and instructing Vietnamese and Iranian students and had developed a unique communication style — a combination of pigeon English and hand signals that had enabled him to converse effectively with those students even in the stressful and noisy environment of an airplane's cockpit. One day, while I was pulling duty as the military supervisor of flying in the T-41 training operations center, the SATP manager was on duty as the civilian supervisor of flying (we always had both) and the Nigerian was doing the honors at the sign-out desk (logging student and instructor names and aircraft tail numbers for each sortie flown). The SATP manager was scheduled to fly with the Nigerian on his first T-41 sortie during the following training period and decided to dis-

we began to hear complaints from the students that they were having trouble understanding their instructors or that they just did not understand the aviation terminology being used. Finally, one of our academic instructors visited the DLI school, monitored some of the classes, and acquired a copy of the aviation-specific textbook. Every term used during their T-41 training could be found in those books. Every student had passed an examination to prove he knew those terms. And every student was allowed to keep his DLI textbooks. From then on, whenever a student complained about his poor English or the technical jargon — we referred him to those books. Once they realized we knew exactly what kind of training they had received, they stopped trying to use ignorance as an excuse.

On at least one occasion language was more of a problem for the instructor than for the student. In 1974, several Nigerian students entered flight training at Hondo. One in particular was the son of a wealthy tribal chieftain and had completed his education in England, including college at

• *USAF Academy T-41D on the ramp at the Academy's Falcon Field* •
(Walt Shiel)

cuss the mission during a lull in the activity.

Manager: "You, me....we go fly." (While pointing first at himself and then the student.)

Student (looking puzzled): "Yes, sir."

Manager (assuming puzzlement meant lack of comprehension): "You, me, airplane...fly." (This time also pointing out the window at a taxiing airplane and then simulating a takeoff with his open hand.)

Student (looking even more puzzled) merely nodded.

Manager: "We climb...turn...glide...and land." (Making suitable gestures and even exaggerated facial expressions.)

Student (nodding), "Yes, sir."

Shortly after this exchange, the manager left to take care of some contract business. Thoroughly perplexed, the student then turned to me and said, with the diction and accent of Richard Burton, "I say, that gentleman certainly does speak strangely." I had to explain to him why the SATP manager was talking that way. He merely shook his head and returned to his work.

Training Improvements for Hondo

A new hangar (with classrooms, offices for the military and civilian contract administrators, and facilities for aircraft maintenance and cleaning) was still under construction at Hondo when the first class started. With construction running late, the first classes were conducted using an existing World War II-vintage classroom — a building sitting on pilings with open rafters overhead and wood plank floors underfoot. There was no insulation or air conditioning, just ancient ceiling fans — in south Texas in the summer!

I recall a visit by General McKee, the ATC commander, in July of 1973. We flew him and a few of his staff members from Randolph AFB to Hondo in our T-41s. The dilapidated old classroom was packed with students and civilian and military instructors. The general stomped up the rickety stairs, the door flew open, somebody shouted, "Room, attenhut!" and the assemblage dutifully obeyed. The raised wood floor thundered as some 60 people leaped to their feet and the military personnel snapped to attention. The whole building shook. Flakes of decaying paint fluttered down to land on General McKee's immaculate uniform. With a frown, the General turned to his aide and asked when the new building was to be completed. When told that it should have been completed two months earlier but that the contractor was running late, General McKee responded, "I want it finished by the first of August!" And it was — for which we were all grateful.

Three significant modifications were made to the T-41 fleet after the Hondo consolidation: a new predominantly white-with-black-trim paint scheme (for improved visibility when flying in the summer haze) replaced the previous bare aluminum; three-point inertia reel shoulder

• USAF Flight Screeing Program T-41A on final at Hondo Municipal Airport •
(U.S. Air Force)

harnesses replaced the lap belts; and a voice-activated intercom with headsets was added. This last was a major improvement and reduced the amount of ad hoc "sign language" required to communicate effectively with some of our foreign students, who sometimes seemed to forget the English they had just learned at DLI as soon as the aircraft lifted off the runway.

Another major construction project at Hondo was approved thanks to the violent thunderstorms that frequent south Texas. One particularly virulent storm bombarded our fleet of almost 100 T-41s with large, wind-driven hail, leaving behind dimpled aluminum skins and a few cracked windshields. Rather than risk a repeat performance, ten wall-less but roofed hail shelters were built. These were not the traditional airport T-hangars since all aircraft faced the same direction to preclude the need for aircraft to taxi in opposite directions in the narrow aisles between the hangars. The appearance of those rows of corrugated-roof hangars placed so close together earned them the nickname "chicken coops."

By the fall of 1973, we were training about 180 American students every three weeks and about 40 foreign students every six weeks at Hondo. Washout rates (the percentage of students eliminated from training for everything from flying deficiency to fear-of-flying) ran as high as 30% in the 1973-1974 period. However, a year later, with Vietnam no longer a factor in USAF planning, the student loads declined and, partly due to more selective recruitment and partly due to a change in ATC philosophy, washout rates also decreased — down to around 10% or less per class by 1976.

Flying Safety

One of the points of pride in the Hondo T-41 program since its inception had been the lack of serious accidents, despite routinely flying through the high winds and weather vagaries of west Texas and the rigors of cramming 30 hours of flight training into a three-week, 14-hour syllabus. At one month's instructor standardization meeting in 1974, the contractor's flying safety officer noted with satisfaction that there had never been a fatal accident in the T-41's 10 year history. A few weeks later, that changed.

Instructors for our SATP program were chosen both for their instructional ability and their sensitivity to the language and cultural problems of our foreign students. In late 1973, a pair of twin brothers were hired by the contractor — brothers who had been in the United States less than a year themselves. They had come from Norway and had completed their flying training in the United States, hoping to eventually return to Norway and get hired by their national airline. Flight training was much cheaper in the United States. They proved to be excellent instructors and were assigned to work with the SATP program — after all, who better to understand the problems of training in a foreign language? Their students performed at least as well

• A T-41C undergoes routine preventive maintenance •
(Walt Shiel)

as anyone else's on their checkrides.

One day, both brothers were trying to solo their students at our auxiliary airfield at Castroville. One brother succeeded and got out of the airplane to watch his student fly the customary first-solo three traffic patterns and landings. The other brother's student was not doing as well, so they continued their traffic pattern work dual. On the solo student's second pattern, he made his turn to base and final at the usual place. His instructor's brother, meanwhile, was flying just ahead of the solo in the pattern and having a difficult time with his student. They extended their final approach and did not hear the warning radio calls from the instructor-controller. The solo student did not respond to the radio calls, either. While the one brother watched from beside the runway, his solo student turned final on top of his brother's airplane. His propeller sliced through the tail of the dual airplane, severing the control cables. The aircraft nosed over and plunged straight down into the ground. The solo managed to control his aircraft and land safe-

• An Ecuadoran Navy T-41D •
(Kansas Aviation Museum/ Robert J. Pickett Collection)

ly. This was the first, and last, fatal accident in the entire 30-year history of the USAF T-41 program.

West Texas Winds

Operating the T-41 in West Texas with the pressure imposed by ATC headquarters to finish each class on time regardless of weather was a challenge at times. Two of the biggest challenges we faced running the Hondo program were (1) the fog that seemingly could form in the space of a single breath thanks to the warm, moisture-laden air that infiltrated from the Gulf of Mexico and (2) the winds. Fog was frequently a challenge, but wind was more often a hazard.

Hondo Municipal Airport, the home of the T-41 program from 1973, was a typical World War II training base — with lots of runways — the two parallel north-south runways, an east-west runway, and a northeast-southwest runway. Most of the time, we used the parallel runways simultaneously to allow generation of the maximum number of sorties. When crosswinds kicked-up, we shifted to single runway operations on one of the other two runways. Sometimes, the gusty and highly variable winds made landing a sporting affair no matter the runway. Every T-

• A T-41D assigned to the VNAF Air Training Center at Nha Trang, South Vietnam •
(Kansas Aviaiton Museum/Robert J. Pickett Collection)

41 instructor quickly became adept at landing with winds well beyond the T-41s "demonstrated maximum crosswind." Even if the strong winds were not producing nasty crosswinds, taxiing in those conditions could be unpleasant. We soon developed a standard procedure to ensure the aircraft's safe return to the chocks.

When the wind conditions necessitated a recall of all airborne aircraft, we rounded up every maintenance technician and every student and instructor who was not flying, packed them into military and contractor vehicles, and hauled them to the runway's first taxiway turnoff to form wingwalker teams. As each returning T-41 reached the turnoff, it stopped. The student got out and seized the left wing strut, one of the other wingwalkers grabbed the right strut, and a third placed himself on the aft fuselage just forward of the horizontal stabilizer. Once all were in place, the instructor taxied slowly back to the chocks, with the aircraft rocking back and forth in the gusts. The wingwalkers were instructed to try to hold the wings and tail level — but to let go and get out of the way if the wind was clearly about to roll it over. We never had an incident of any kind with

• A Honduran Air Force T-41D •
(Kansas Aviation Museum/Robert J. Pickett Collection)

• An Ecuadoran Army Air Service T-41D •
(Kansas Aviaiton Museum/Robert J. Pickett Collection)

this operation, but there were some exciting moments as an aircraft tipped precariously turning downwind off the runway.

Manifestations of Appprehension

The Flight Screening Program's main goals were to give the students their first exposure to military aviation before they were sent on to fly the Cessna T-37 jet trainer — and to inexpensively determine which of them were not suited for further training. There were several reasons a student might be eliminated — inability to learn to fly in the time-constrained and high-pressure military training environment, inability to learn the required academics in the time allotted, inability to adapt to the "military way," and something ATC referred to as "manifestations of apprehension" (MOA).

Now, MOA covered a variety of symptoms that all were deemed likely to stem from an innate fear of flying. Symptoms of MOA ranged from obvious nervousness and an inability to concentrate on the task of learning to fly to hyperventilation and active airsickness. Active airsickness, however, was not necessarily the result of MOA — it might be no more than a matter of learning to adjust to the new and strange sensations of flying. Hyperventilation, for some

• An Argentinian Air Force T-41D •
Kansas Aviation Museum/Robert J. Pickett Collection

reason, was a much worse problem when dealing with our South Vietnamese students than any other nationality. It was never clear why. Many times, T-41 instructors at Hondo returned early from a sortie with a Vietnamese student so deeply in the throes of a hyperventilation episode that his muscles had contracted and he was on the verge of passing out. We would get him out of the airplane and onto a stretcher, elevate his feet slightly, and then try to place a plastic bag over his head to force his breathing rate back to normal. This was never easy, since one of the first faculties lost at these times was English comprehension. We had to learn to deal with the student's panic as we lowered the bag over his head. He was usually certain we were trying to asphyxiate him! After a few, such episodes, we had one of the hyperventilating students own classmates standing by as an interpreter just in case.

• A Columbian Air Force T-41D •
(Kansas Aviation Museum/Robert J. Pickett Collection)

Around the World

Military Assistance Program sales of T-41s, mostly D-models, included Columbia, Argentina, Ecuador, Greece, Honduras, Israel, Peru, Philippines, and South Vietnam. In 1967, eight T-41A aircraft were produced and delivered to the Ecuadoran Air Force (EAF) under the MAP — Cessna trained nine EAF pilots and three EAF mechanics in Wichita for a week before formally turning the aircraft over to them. This EAF contingent then flew the aircraft back to Ecuador. Five others were provided to the Honduran Air Force, and a further lot of 26 T-41A aircraft were delivered later to the Peruvian Air Force under the MAP. More were provided during the Vietnam War to the Khmer Air Force of Cambodia in 1971 through 1974 as part of Project Flycatcher after a North Vietnamese raid destroyed most of their aircraft. In all, at least 34 T-41A and 238 T-41D trainers were provided to foreign countries.

In 1965, then-Captain Fred McNeill was stationed at McConnell AFB in Wichita, Kansas, flying U-6 Beavers equipped with Robertson short takeoff and landing kits and crosswind landing gear on support missions to the dozen or so new ICBM' missile sites scattered throughout the area. He and five other U-6 pilots were assigned to ferry four factory-new T-41D aircraft from the Cessna factory to Santiago, Chile, for delivery to the Chilean Air Force. The entire trip took about 10 days. McNeill says it was not a standard military-style operation since they all would just crank-up and head for the runway, relegating flight lead duties to whomever made it airborne first.

• An Army T-41B demonstrates its ability to meet the "landing over a 50-foot obstacle" performance requirement (note the string of flags just below the aircraft) •
(United States Army Aviation Museum)

They had no maintenance problems with the new airplanes, flying about four hours on each leg between refuelings.

Although technically not T-41s, in 1975 the Angolan military commandeered numerous civilian aircraft including at least one Cessna 172 for reconnaissance and transport missions out of airstrips near Nagage and Ambriz. The Irish Air Corps was still conducting border patrols with Cessna-Reims FR172H aircraft based at Gormanston in the early 1990s.

The total remaining Cessna 172 fleet of military trainers serving with the following air forces includes about

140 T-41s (predominately D-Models) and perhaps 30 stock civilian Model 172s: Angola, Argentina, Bangladesh, Bolivia, Botswana, Burundi, Chile, Colombia, Dominican Republic, Ecuador, El Salvador, Greece, Haiti, Honduras, Ivory Coast, Madagascar, Mexico, Peru, Philippines, Saudi Arabia, Seychelles, South Korea, Sri Lanka, Turkey, Uruguay, and Zaire.

The Fleet Retires

In the 1980s, the U.S. Army began retiring its T-41s from active service, delivering most of them to foreign countries under the Military Assistance Program. By 1988, only 77 aircraft remained in active Army service, almost exclusively used as trainers. By the early 1990s, none still served. Today, one example of the Army B-Model remains on rotating display in the U.S. Army Aviation Museum at Fort Rucker, Alabama.

In 1990, the USAF decided the time had come to retire the aging T-41 and to replace it with an aircraft with better capabilities for screening potential USAF pilots. A formal Request for Proposals, mandating an off-the-shelf aerobatic aircraft with side-by-side seating, was issued and a replacement was chosen in April of 1992 — the Slingsby T67-M260, designated the T-3A Firefly by the USAF. In November of 1993, the last T-41A left Hondo to join the others in military aero clubs around the world. One T-41A was donated to the Air Force Museum, Wright-Patterson AFB, Ohio, where it is on display.

Beginning in September 1994, the USAF Academy began phasing out its 47 T-41s and replacing them with the T-3A Firefly. Four of the T-41Cs were transferred to the Academy's Cadet Competition Flying Team to replace the modified C-150s operated by the 94th Airmanship Training Squadron. The team has competed in National Intercollegiate Flying Association meets since 1972.

By mid-1995, there will be no T-41s in service in the U.S. military. An era will have ended — ironically just as the passage of the General Aviation Revitalization Act of 1994 holds out the possibility of new C-172s rolling out of the Cessna factory in the not-too-distant future. +

• A USAF T-41A retired from the Hondo Flight Screening Program and now on display at the Air Force Museum •
(U.S. Air Force)

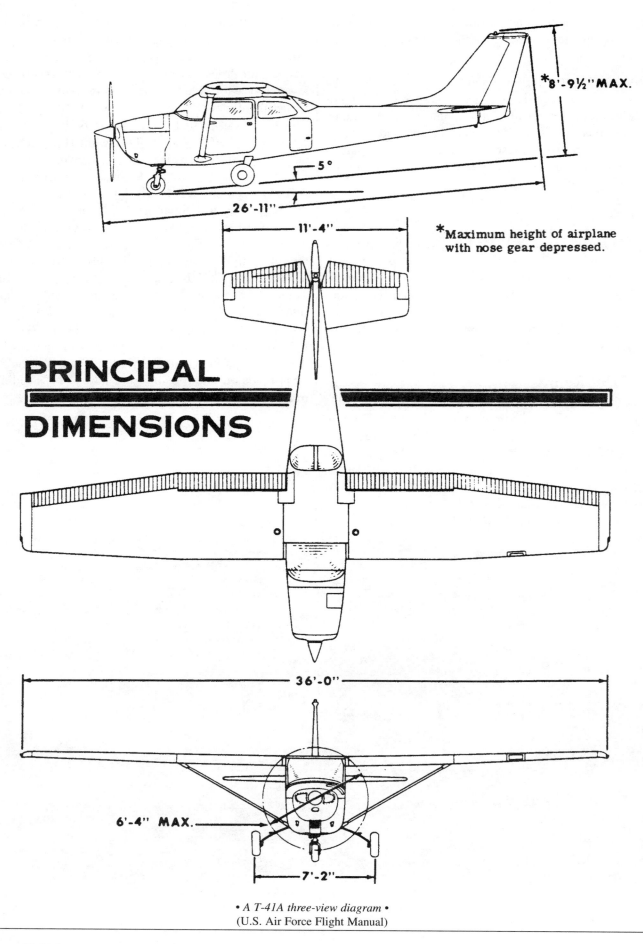

PRINCIPAL

DIMENSIONS

*8'-9½"MAX.

5°

26'-11"

11'-4"

*Maximum height of airplane
with nose gear depressed.

36'-0"

6'-4" MAX.

7'-2"

• *A T-41A three-view diagram* •
(U.S. Air Force Flight Manual)

Specifications

	T-41A	T-41B	T-41C	T-41D
Wingspan	36 ft. 0 in.	36 ft. 2 in.	36 ft. 2 in.	36 ft. 2 in.
Length	26 ft. 11 in.	26 ft. 4.5 in.	25 ft. 11 in.	26 ft. 4.5 in.
Height	8 ft. 9.5 in.	8 ft. 10.5 in.	8 ft. 9.5 in.	8 ft. 10.5 in.
Wheel Track	7 ft. 2 in.	7 ft. 2 in.	7 ft. 2 in.	7 ft. 2 in.
Engine	O-300-D	IO-360-D	IO-360-D	IO-360-D
Horsepower	145 @ 2700 rpm	210 @ 2800 rpm	210 @ 2800 rpm	210 @ 2800 rpm
Propeller	Fixed Pitch	Constant Speed	Fixed Pitch	Constant Speed
Gross Weight	2,000 lbs.	2,500 lbs.	2,500 lbs.	2,500 lbs.
Electrical System	14 volt	28 volt	14 volt	(varies)
Max. IAS	174 mph	182 mph	182 mph	182 mph
Maneuvering IAS	122 mph	127 mph	127 mph	127 mph
Max. Cruising IAS	140 mph	145 mph	145 mph	145 mph
Max. Glide IAS	75 mph	85 mph	85 mph	85 mph
Glide Ratio	8.8:1	8.8:1	8.8:1	8.8:1
Stall IAS				
No Flaps	53 mph	64 mph	64 mph	64 mph
Stall IAS–				
Full Flaps	46 mph	53 mph	53 mph	53 mph
Takeoff				
Roll	630 ft.	655 ft.	860 ft.	655 ft.
50 feet obstacle	1,095 ft.	1,075 ft.	1,360 ft.	1,075 ft.
Climb Rate	840 fpm	915 fpm	880 fpm	915 fpm
Normal Cruise (75% Power, 5,000 feet)				
TAS	128 mph	127 mph	138 mph	127 mph
Fuel Flow	8.4 gph	12.4 gph	11.6 gph	12.4 gph
Range	600 st mi	540 st mi	545 st mi	540 st mi
Landing				
Roll	520 ft.	405 ft.	610 ft.	405 ft.
50 feet obstacle	1,250 ft.	870 ft.	1,320 ft.	870 ft.

YH-41 Seneca

-chapter 13-

In 1951, sensing the likely end of L-19 production, Cessna President Dwane Wallace searched for another niche market for military sales. The U.S. Army had shown an interest in the just-developing helicopter market, and the commercial market for helicopters showed every sign of a vibrant future. Wallace knew he did not have the time to create an in-house technical base if he was to be able to gain an early foothold in the fledgling market and successfully compete. He found his answer right in Wichita — the Seibel Helicopter Company — a company that had accomplished what Wallace recognized as a significant achievement. With a budget of only $125,000 and a total staff of four, Charles M. Seibel had designed, built, and acquired CAA certification for a new helicopter — the S-4B. By doing so, Seibel became only the fifth American company with a CAA-certified helicopter. In fact, the U.S. Army purchased two of the Seibel helicopters for evaluation, designating them YH-24s. They did not, however, show any interest in further orders.

Charles Seibel was a pioneer in helicopter aviation, having earned a Master's degree in Aeronautical Engineering in 1943 from California Institute of Technology after completing his thesis on helicopter design and aerodynamics. In 1947, Seibel designed and built his first helicopter — a single-seat, 800-pound gross weight aircraft powered by a 65-horsepower Franklin engine. This innovative aircraft was capable of cruising at 70 MPH, with a top speed of 90 MPH and a service ceiling of 12,000 feet. This was the first helicopter to incorporate the patented Seibel Control System. At the time, Seibel was unable to market his design and went to work for Bell Helicopter as an engineer on that company's first

• The prototype CH-1 during its flight demonstrations in 1954 •
(Kansas Aviation Museum/Robert J. Pickett Collection)

helicopter designs. In 1950, Seibel formed his own company and designed the S-4B.

Once he saw what Seibel had accomplished, Wallace wasted no time making an offer to purchase Seibel Helicopter — an offer that was quickly accepted by the cash-strapped start-up. In March 1952, Seibel Helicopter Company became the Cessna Helicopter Division. Cessna planned to combine Wallace's leadership and Seibel's technical expertise to take Seibel's design from its rudimentary prototype stage to full-scale production of a sophisticated, and commercially viable, aircraft. Wallace infused the new division with Cessna personnel and selected a general manager from within the Cessna management ranks. He appointed Charles Seibel as the Helicopter Chief Engineer to capitalize on his engineering know-how.

To achieve the commercial success Wallace envisioned for the new product, the Helicopter Division set out to solve what they considered the fundamental shortcomings of the existing helicopters. Cessna wanted to design a helicopter that could hover both in and out of ground effect at much higher altitudes than other helicopters of the early 1950s, without sacrificing cruising speed. To meet these performance demands, they selected a supercharged engine, the Continental FSO-470 — an engine able to generate 260-horsepower at altitudes up to 10,000 feet. Cessna also needed a rotor with excellent lifting ability and decided to incorporate the new Prewitt all-steel rotor. Finally, the designers greatly improved the aerodynamics of the fuselage itself. They had settled on the new design's basic configuration by mid-1952, giving it the official nomenclature as Cessna Helicopter #1, or simply the CH-1.

Insisting on simplicity as a primary design requirement, Seibel used his unique drive system that used only five drive gears — two gears for the tail rotor and three for the transmission. Although this system weighed more than competing systems, it was simple and exceptionally robust. The drive shaft for the tail rotor used no bearing supports between the engine power takeoff and the rotor itself, and all main rotor rotational controls were contained within the rotor shaft.

Five years earlier, Charles Seibel had written an article in the December 1947 issue of "American Helicopter" touting the design simplicity of his tail rotor shaft design:

"Usually for standard auxiliary rotor units seven or eight bearings are used to support the shaft along the complete length of the tail boom. This arrangement is costly and offers alignment and access problems in service. In this new helicopter design only two bearings are used, one at each end of the shaft. . .A friction damper device is located near the center of the shaft to prevent excessive deflections."

Cessna retained the unique Seibel Control System on the CH-1 — a patented means of attaching the main rotor blades to the rotor hub via a "blade attaching angle" that permitted blade pitch changes without the use, and complexity, of the usual antifriction bearings. Charles Seibel had used this method on his helicopter designs since his original 1947 prototype. The only bearings used in the main rotor were a pair of needle bearings within the rotor hub. The hub required two intermeshed castings, with a sheet metal angle attached to each casting. The outer end of each angle, in turn, attached to one of the rotor blades. Control inputs twisted these "blade attaching angles" and changed rotor blade pitch.

Although other helicopters kept the engine behind the cockpit, Cessna located the CH-1's engine forward of the cabin with only the enclosed main rotor shaft penetrating up through the cabin's volume. They mounted the battery and the generator in tail boom compartments to offset the forward engine weight. This combination allowed the maximum amount of useful payload to be carried near the aircraft's center-of-gravity, under the main rotor, and provided ample space for four seats. A nose cowl enclosed the entire engine assembly and easily slid forward to allow waist-high maintenance access. By mounting the engine independently of the transmission and rotor, it was possible to work on these components separately without

• The second YH-41, s/n 56-4237, delivered to the U.S. Army •
(U.S. Army Aviation Museum)

removing extra components or having to work around them. Cessna used two-blade designs for both the main rotor and the tail rotor.

The initial flying test bed, consisting of only the necessary power and mechanical components in an open-frame fuselage, flew in the summer of 1953. At the same time, a ground test unit for the engine and drive system accumulated the required 500 hours of operating time to meet CAA certification requirements. One year later, the initial prototype first flew, with CAA certification following in 1955. To prove that the new helicopter could meet its high-altitude hover goals, the prototype was flown to Colorado for mountain performance tests. Army and Cessna test pilots alternated as flight crew for the demonstrations. According to Charles Seibel in William Thompson's book "Cessna, Wings for the World," among the milestones achieved during these tests were:

- First direct helicopter flight from mile-high Fort Carson at Colorado Springs to 10,000-foot Camp Hale at Leadville, maintaining a cruise altitude of 17,600 feet.
- Four-soldier payload flown into and out of Camp Hale.
- Several 14,000-foot elevation landings.
- First Pike's Peak helicopter landing, after hovering at the peak with three people on board, on 13 September 1955, followed by a flight to deliver Army Major General Van Houten back to his Fort Carson command post.

These demonstrations sufficiently impressed the Army that they issued a contract for ten CH-1A helicopters, designated the YH-41 Seneca (serial numbers 56-4236 through 56-4245), with delivery to begin in September of 1957. However, Continental had been experiencing erratic performance from the supercharger on the FSO-470 engine as well as some early failures of the fan drive belts. Unable to solve these problems, Continental suggested switching to the FSO-526-A engine developed originally for Cessna's ill-fated four-engine Model 620, which never proceeded beyond the prototype stage. The FSO-526-A engine employed gear drive rather than the FSO-470's belt drive and produced an additional ten horsepower. To implement the change, Cessna had to recertify the aircraft with the new engine and drive system. The new configuration was designated by Cessna the CH-1B and became the baseline configuration for the

Army's YH-41s. Despite the engine delays, Cessna delivered the Army aircraft on time.

At the time the YH-41s were being assembled, a jet-engined French Alouette II held the helicopter absolute altitude record — 26,931 feet. Cessna decided to further demonstrate the YH-41's altitude potential by challenging the absolute altitude record with its piston-powered YH-41. Cessna test pilots made several test flights in a stripped down aircraft with a supercharger specifically tuned for the higher altitudes. According to Charles Seibel, "With careful control of airspeed and rpm we could fly the narrow corridor between retreating blade stall and the advancing blade tip compressibility limit."

When the day came for the final official assault on

• *Captain James Bowman and the record-setting YH-41 on 29 December 1957* •
(U.S. Army Aviation Museum)

the helicopter altitude record, the flight test crew removed the landing gear to reduce the weight even more. An Army test pilot, Captain James E. Bowman of the Army Aviation Board at Fort Rucker, Alabama, was chosen for the record flights. On 29 December 1957, Captain Bowman flew the YH-41 twice and established new helicopter records in two weight categories as well as in the unlimited category. The official barograph installed by the National Bureau of Standards recorded 29,777 feet, while Cessna's own calibrated altimeter showed 30,335 feet. Only jet-engined helicopters have ever broken those records. Cessna Aircraft Company presented a plaque to the U.S. Army Aviation Board, commanded by Colonel Robert R. Williams, stating:

"On 29 December 1957, Captain James E. Bowman flew a Cessna YH-41 helicopter to establish three World Altitude Records for helicopters: 29,777 feet for the unlimited class, 29,777 feet for the 1102-2204 lb. class, 28,090 feet for the 2204-3585 lb. class, as certified by the Federation Aeronautique International."

The "YH" portion of the YH-41's Army designation indicated that these aircraft were intended as test aircraft. The aircraft were, according to the Army's official test report, "procured as an off-the-shelf CAA-certificated commercial helicopter." The Army's Technical Compliance Committee Board chose not to have Cessna make the alterations that had been identified during the Contract Technical Compliance Inspection since the aircraft were intended solely for test purposes and already met all CAA requirements for civilian certification. The Army test aircraft were flown and maintained by Fort Rucker personnel "to determine [their] suitability as a light observation helicopter." The Army operated the aircraft at varying gross weights and center-of-gravity loadings up to the CAA certification limits. In addition, "tests to determine the suitability of the YH-41 as an Army instrument trainer were made in conjunction with the Army Aviation School."

Although Jack Zimmerman, Cessna's helicopter test pilot, considered the aircraft's flying qualities acceptable, the Army's evaluation of its first two YH-41s uncovered inherent flaws that caused considerable consternation at Cessna. In the official report issued in March of 1958, the Army Aviation Board discussed the pros and cons of the new helicopter. The major advantage offered by the YH-41 was its high-altitude capability, the primary disadvantage unfortunately involved stability and control concerns — leading ultimately to the Board's recommendation that

• *A U.S. Army YH-41 hovering in ground effect* •
(U.S. Army Aviation Museum)

the Army not procure any more YH-41s until Cessna corrected the deficiencies.

During the flight tests, seven experienced Army helicopter pilots were trained and qualified to fly the aircraft, averaging about four hours of flight time per pilot for qualification — two hours devoted to "getting the feel of the aircraft and the other two in gaining proficiency in performing autorotations."

The need for pilot familiarity with the characteristics of the YH-41 in autorotation maneuvers was due to one of the stability deficiencies noted in the report: "When the power was reduced abruptly, the helicopter dropped off to the left, requiring major displacement of cyclic control to the right in order to level the aircraft. This was especially noticeable in a hovering autorotation because. . .nearly full right cyclic displacement is required." The report also noted that pilot reaction to a power loss was critical, due to a more rapid rotor speed decay than other Army light helicopters and a tendency for the collective pitch reducer to drop rotor rpm below the minimum acceptable rpm if the pilot's reaction was delayed by more than one second. The collective pitch reducer, the report noted, "was only reliable about 50 percent of the time and could not be depended upon to lessen pilot reaction time in an emergency."

Basic stability was worse than the light helicopters then in use by the Army, particularly in even mildly turbulent conditions. This problem was aggravated by a pronounced rolling moment whenever the power setting was changed. When combined with very sensitive controls, these stability problems led to frequent overcontrolling by the pilots. Although the Army was impressed with the

• *The U.S. Army's "Flying Cloud," s/n 56-4241, in flight* •
(U.S. Army Aviation Museum)

high-altitude hovering ability of the YH-41, the sensitive controls and previously noted rolling tendencies meant that pilots simply had to work harder to take advantage of the aircraft's capabilities.

The Army considered both normal and maximum-performance takeoff and landing performance satisfactory. Directional control was adequate and visibility was excellent, but steep approaches required the pilot to fly in the caution area of the height-velocity curves defined by Cessna. Control in flight was adequate, although flight at maximum speed with a full aft center-of-gravity loading required maintaining full forward displacement of the cyclic — leaving no reserve to counter pitch-ups due to turbulence.

The report noted that "the aircraft was unstable about all three axes" and that "whenever a passenger in the rear was changing his seating position or moving about in his seat the condition was worsened." Rapid decelerations also aggravated the aircraft's inherent instability, although adequate control authority was available to counteract the problem — this tended to keep the pilot very busy. Range was also a problem, unless the loads were reduced, since the gross weight limitation would not permit a full cabin load with full fuel. The Army determined that the YH-41's maximum range with a 30-minute reserve was only about 170 nautical miles, at maximum gross weight and 6,000 feet.

The Army felt that leg room for rear seat passengers was inadequate, and the ventilation system, although able to bring plenty of outside air into the cabin, was marginal. All ventilating air was heated, whether heat was wanted or not, as it was routed past the engine into the cabin air inlets. When the outside air temperature was 68°F, the vented air temperature was 84°F. The only way to keep cabin temperature comfortable during warm weather was to fly with the cabin doors removed!

As might be expected, the YH-41's inflight instability meant the aircraft was not well suited to use as a helicopter instrument flight trainer. In even light turbulence, heading control could only be maintained within 15-degrees of assigned heading and airspeed control was erratic at best, with fluctuations of up to 30 KIAS. There was no friction lock on the collective, which tended to creep upward. This combination of instability and collective creep "resulted in a higher rate of pilot fatigue when flying under simulated instrument conditions."

However, the Army's flight test report was not all bad news. The report summary noted:

"**a.** The YH-41 Helicopter was superior to standard light observation helicopters in the performance of the following missions:
(1) All missions requiring operation at high density altitudes.
(2) Air reconnaissance.
(3) Messenger service and liaison.

b. The YH-41 Helicopter is satisfactory in the performance of the following missions:
(1) [Artillery] Fire adjustment.
(2) Emergency resupply.
(3) Troop transport."

The primary deficiencies were the aircraft's instability and its limited gross weight and resulting payload/range limitations. The full report was provided to Cessna with a Board recommendation that the aircraft be reevaluated if the deficiencies were corrected.

• A U.S. Army YH-41 with the engineering modifications installed, including the horizontal stabilizer on the tail boom •
(U.S. Army Aviation Museum)

In William Thompson's book, Charles Seibel admitted that "with our fixation on performance we had neglected handling qualities." Cessna immediately launched a thorough program to correct all the deficiencies noted by the Army Aviation Board. The initial corrections were aimed at solving the instability problem. First, Cessna installed a gyroscope under the cabin floor, mechanically driven through a shaft from the main rotor gear box, to automate lateral cyclic control corrective inputs and provide roll damping. In addition, they added a pivoting horizontal stabilizer on the tail boom linked to the collective stick to improve longitudinal stability — this was allowed to free-float below 40 KIAS and to feather automatically into the main rotor downwash in hover mode. To counter the roll coupling with power changes problem that the Army had noted in its report, Cessna added a pressure cylinder to the supercharger, using the pressure variations from power changes to make counteracting cyclic control inputs. Finally, they increased the collective pitch range to improve the autorotation capability.

The Army was still flight testing their ten YH-41s as Cessna completed the first modified aircraft. Two Army officials travelled to Wichita to evaluate the resulting redesign. Following their evaluation, an appendix was added to the official Army Aviation Board report to note that "Cessna personnel demonstrated fixes for every major problem area that has been found on the H-41 ... This progress is commendable compared to past experience with other contractors in the rotary wing industry."

To demonstrate the stability of the revised aircraft, Cessna test pilot Jerry Polen put the helicopter into a hover — and then climbed into the rear seat and sat there for four minutes! In the summer of 1959, the CAA approved the new Cessna CH-1C for certification. After a few minor additional modifications, the CH-1C became the first helicopter CAA-certified for flight in instrument conditions. In 1961, Cessna began delivering commercial models of the CH-1C, the Skyhook, through its existing airplane dealer and distributor

• An Iranian Army YH-41 Seneca in 1963 •
(Kansas Aviation Museum/Robert J. Pickett Collection)

network. The new aircraft quickly gained popularity for a wide range of commercial operations. During the 1962 Seattle World's Fair, Seattle Helicopter Airways carried some 10,000 passengers on sightseeing flights throughout the Puget Sound area in their CH-1Cs.

Cessna bought back six of the Army's original ten YH-41s and rebuilt them as CH-1Cs for commercial sales. Of the total production run of 29 CH-1C aircraft, 11 were built for foreign military services as YH-41 Senecas under the Military Assistance Program in 1962 and 1963, five were delivered to the U.S. Army and provided to Iran, and six were delivered to the USAF and provided to Ecuador.

Numerous problems were encountered during commercial usage, including a fatal accident in October of 1962 attributed most likely to pilot error. Other problems included a crankshaft failure and several connecting rod failures. The Army also uncovered some engine structural deficiencies during its evaluation. Since Cessna had already cancelled the Model 620, the only other aircraft using the Continental FSO-526-A engine, Continental was in no hurry to remedy these engine deficiencies. The

bottom-mounted exhaust was also prone to starting grass fires during landings in open fields — a major limitation for Sky Hook, Inc. of Durango, Colorado, which provided brush control services throughout the National Forests in Colorado, Arizona, Utah, and New Mexico under contract to the U.S. Forestry Service.

The landing gear arrangement in the helicopter consisted of a single piece of 3.5-inch steel tubing that mounted through holes in the fuselage and was prone to damage in hard touchdowns. According to Duane Moore, Cessna's Military Division Production Manager at the time, the design meant that whenever the gear was damaged beyond repair this entire assembly had to be replaced — an expensive proposition. With the short production run of the helicopters, Moore says Cessna still had 75 complete landing gear assemblies in stock in 1980. They were apparently planning ahead for expected replacements of damaged gear.

In 1962, Cessna developed and received certification for the CH-1D model, which was designed to correct the problems that had been encountered. One of the fixes was to reroute the exhaust through the tail boom to prevent starting grass fires. In addition, the maximum gross weight was boosted to 3,200 pounds — increasing the aircraft's payload by 100 pounds. The aircraft, however, was never produced.

An Air Force test pilot, Major Robert G. Ferry, was awarded the Ivan Kinchloe "Outstanding Test Pilot of the Year" Award by the Experimental Test Pilots Association in 1959 for a rescue with a YH-41 assigned for testing to the Air Force Flight Test Center (AFFTC) at Edwards AFB, California. A civilian, Grant Brady, was thrown from his horse while riding on the slopes of California's Mount Whitney, in the Sequoia National Forest, and suffered multiple injuries. Major Ferry flew the AFFTC YH-41 to the scene, accompanied by his crew chief, Airman First Class R. L. Sparks, and his flight test project engineer, First Lieutenant E. A. Koelle. They found the injured man at 9,300 feet within a clearing in the 100-foot-tall trees on a 30-degree slope. Thanks to the excellent high-altitude hovering capabilities of the Seneca, Major Ferry was able to complete a vertical descent between the trees, pickup Brady, and ascend vertically with all four personnel on board. The injured Brady was then flown across the mountains to the Porterville Airport and met by an ambulance. Major Perry praised the aircraft, noting that any other helicopter available at that time would have been either too big to squeeze into the small clearing, or incapable of the vertical descent and ascent at the high altitude.

At about the same time, Cessna developed a unique concept to meet the Army's requirement for a lightweight, economical vertical takeoff and landing (VTOL) aircraft for the liaison and observation missions — a hybrid helicopter and gyrocopter. This concept, called the Kinedyne 2, incorporated a single, small, rear-mounted jet engine, a pusher propeller between twin tail booms for forward flight, and a modern rotary wing (à la helicopters) mounted above the cabin.

The Kinedyne 2 was touted by Cessna as taking advantage of the "storage of kinetic energy prior to takeoff, to be used during the ascent." This kinetic energy storage was to be accomplished by spinning the overhead rotor up to an rpm much higher than that used in normal cruising flight and setting the rotor blades at a negative collective pitch. This combination allegedly would make "a large amount of energy" available to the mass of the blades and created an upflow of air through the rotor. Once the spinning rotor was running at this high rpm, the drive to the rotor was to be disengaged and engine power routed to the rear-mounted constant speed propeller as the rotor pitch was increased. The "stored energy" in the rotor would be used to generate the extra lifting power for a vertical takeoff. For landing, the rotor rpm would be increased above cruising rpm — then, as the ground was approached, power to the rear propeller was reduced to nearly zero and the rotor's stored kinetic energy used for a landing flare. If a vertical takeoff or landing was not needed, the rear propeller could be used to control the aircraft just as in a conventional aircraft. The Kinedyne 2 never made its way beyond the drawing board stage.

Another proposal developed during this time was a

• *A full-scale mock-up of the proposed jet-engined CH-41* •
(Kansas Aviation Museum/Robert J. Pickett Collection)

jet-engined version of the YH-41, designated the CH-41. This concept was taken further than the Kinedyne 2 — all the way to a full-scale mockup. This model retained the general arrangement, size, and layout of the original YH-41, but with a small jet engine installed in the nose engine compartment. As the Army expressed no interest, the concept never proceeded into development.

Despite the apparent commercial success of the Cessna helicopters, the adverse publicity from the civilian crashes prompted Cessna in late 1962 to discontinue helicopter manufacturing and to repurchase every remaining commercial model Skyhook. These were promptly destroyed to eliminate potential product liability claims and to preclude problems

• The engine installation on the CH-41 mock-up •
(Kansas Aviation Museum/Robert J. Pickett Collection)

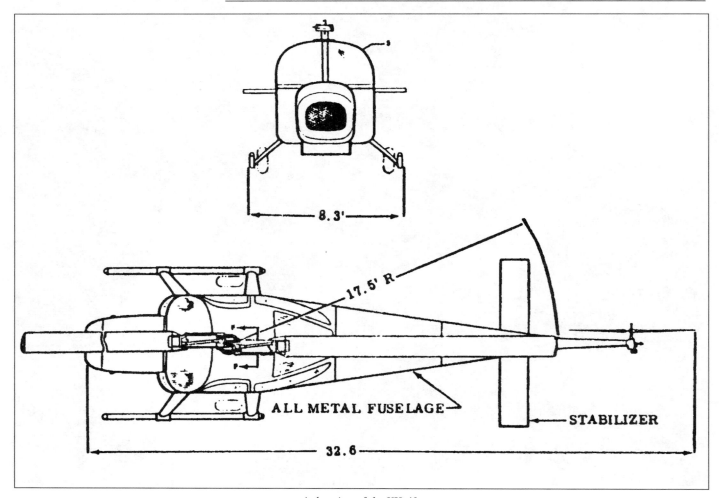

• A drawing of the YH-41 •
(Kansas Aviation Museum)

Production Summary

Skyhook/Seneca

Seibel S-4B Prototype 1

CH-1 Prototype (Note 1) 2

CH-1B Prototype (Note 2) 1

Army YH-41 Seneca (Note 3) 10

CH-1C Prototype 1

CH-1C Production (Note 4) 29

TOTAL **44**

Note 1: One CH-1 prototype was rebuilt as a CH-1A and the other was used as a boundary layer control flight test aircraft.

Note 2: This prototype was used as the YH-41 demonstration aircraft.

Note 3: Six of the original Army YH-41 aircraft were repurchased by Cessna, rebuilt, and sold as civilian CH-1C aircraft.

Note 4: Eleven of these 29 aircraft were provided to foreign military services — six to Ecuador and five to Iran.

with continuing service support. Duane Moore says they salvaged the parts from those helicopters, which netted them over $2 million. In fact, with the exception of a few champions within the company, Cessna's management infrastructure had never really been fully committed to idea of manufacturing and selling helicopters. The word from the top at Cessna, according to Cessna employee Bob Roberts in a March 1971 letter, was "to wipe the word helicopter from the Cessna vocabulary."

The remaining 10 YH-41s were used by the Army and USAF for several more years in a variety of flight test programs and experiments with high-altitude helicopter operations. In 1962, they were all redesignated NH-41A (the "N" prefix indicating the aircraft's new status as permanent Special Test Aircraft).

As for the military Senecas that had been sold overseas, they were operated for several years by both Ecuador and Iran but apparently none survived — thus, the one and only remaining Cessna helicopter, a YH-41 (serial number 56-4244), is the one on display at the U.S. Army Aviation Museum at Fort Rucker, Alabama. ✛

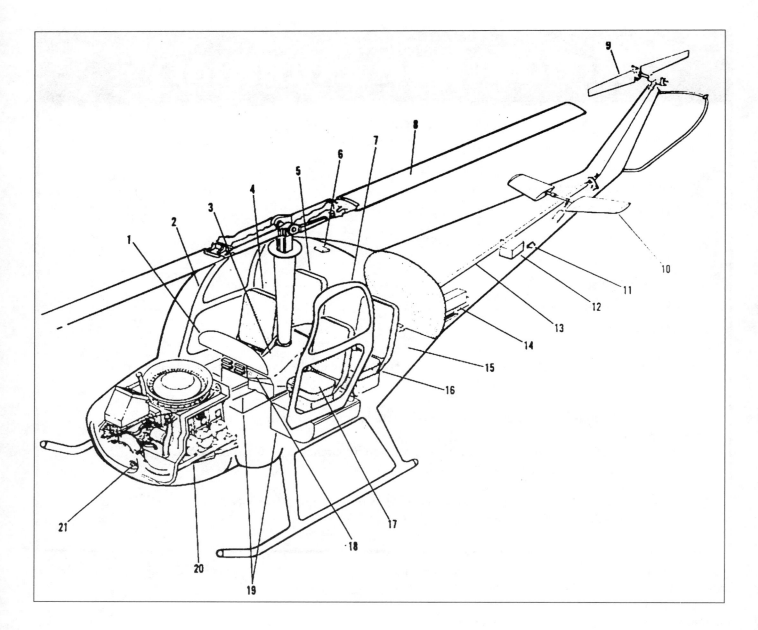

General Arrangement

1. Instrument Panel
2. Right Door
3. Transmission Upholstery Cover
4. Pilot's Seat
5. Right Rear Passenger Seat
6. Dome Light
7. Left Door
8. Main Rotor
9. Tail Rotor
10. Stabilizer
11. External Power Source
12. Batteries
13. Tail Rotor Drive System
14. Radio Equipment
15. Stowage Compartment
16. Left Rear Passenger Seat
17. Copilot's Seat
18. Console (Switch & Circuit Breaker Panel)
19. Fuel Cells
20. Engine
21. Landing Light

• YH-41 Seneca internal arrangement drawing •
(Kansas Aviation Museum)

Specifications

Y-41 Seneca

Length

    Including Rotors . . . . .42 ft. 6 in.

    Fuselage . . . . .29 ft. 5 in.

Width

    Including Landing Gear . . . . .8 ft. 4 in.

    Fuselage . . . . .5 ft. 4 in.

Height

    Including Tail Rotor . . . . .11 ft. 5 in.

    To Top of Main Rotor . . . . .8 ft. 5 in.

    To Top of Cabin . . . . .7 ft. 2 in.

Weight

    Empty . . . . .2,080 lbs.

    Maximum . . . . .3,100 lbs.

    Useful Load . . . . .1,020 lbs.

Fuel Capacity

    Standard Tanks . . . . .60 U.S. gallons

    With Auxiliary Tanks . . . . .90 U.S. gallons

Engine . . . . .Continental FSO-526-A, 270 hp

    Average Fuel Consumption (75 KIAS) . . . . .21 gph

    Maximum Continuous Operation . . . . 3,000 rpm

    Maximum for Takeoff (up to 5 minutes) . . . . .3,200 rpm

Rotors

    Main Rotor Diameter . . . . .35 ft.

    Main Rotor Chord . . . . .13 in.

    Tail Rotor Diameter . . . . .7 ft.

Performance (at 3,100 pounds)

    Maximum Speed . . . . .106 KIAS

    Normal Cruise . . . . .78-104 KIAS

    Maximum Range Cruise . . . . .75 KIAS

    Rate of Climb at 8,000 Feet MSL . . . . .1,030 fpm

    Time to Climb to 10,000 Feet MSL . . . . .10.3 min.

    Hovering Ceiling in Ground Effect . . . . .9,600 ft.

Range and Endurance (Standard Tanks)

    Maximum (No Reserves) . . . . .230 nm

    Maximum (30 Minute Reserve) . . . . .190 nm

    Maximum Endurance . . . . .3 hrs. 20 min.

U-17

Cessna 180s and 185s Go to War

- chapter 14 -

In 1952, Cessna introduced the all-metal, four-place Model 180, the first Cessna with a squared-off vertical stabilizer rather than a rounded one. The aircraft was intended as a higher-performance follow-on to the popular Model 170 and was priced lower than the Model 190/195series. Cessna incorporated its Para-Lift flap system (large, slotted, semi-Fowler flaps like the ones used on the L-19/O-1 Bird Dog), spring steel landing gear, and a steerable tailwheel in the new aircraft. The designers chose the horizontally opposed, 225-horsepower, six-cylinder Continental O-470-A engine and a two-bladed, metal, constant speed Hartzell propeller. The Model 180 enjoyed a long production run, with the last Model 180K rolling out of the Cessna factory in 1981, after a total production of almost 6,200 aircraft.

• *A civilian 1959 Cessna 180* •
(Tracy and Charles Ake)

The Model 180 was designed for aerodynamic efficiency, as can be seen from the use of flush rivets on the leading edges of the wing and on the engine cowling, as well as the incorporation of cowl flaps, wheel fairings, a flush-mounted carburetor air inlet, and an adjustable horizontal stabilizer (to reduce drag at cruise airspeeds). Cessna designed a larger rudder and vertical stabilizer and added a dorsal fin to preclude excessive yaw angles in cruising flight. The heavier engine required a more powerful elevator to offset its weight and ensure satisfactory three-point landings. Cessna used rubberized fuel bladders in the wings, as were being routinely used in larger military and commercial aircraft. However, as the bladders aged, they tended to wrinkle and interfere with fuel flow to the tank outlets. As William Thompson notes

in *Cessna, Wing for the World*, "In hindsight, one would have to say that the continuation of aluminum tanks until wet-wing technology was perfected would have been a better choice."

William Thompson completed the first flight of the Model 180 prototype on 26 May 1952 — but not until the rudder cables were reconnected properly. They had been installed backwards and created a bit of excitement in the initial taxi attempt. The big engine in the little aircraft resulted in very high vibration and noise levels. Numerous changes were made during initial flight testing to reduce these levels — such as shortening the propeller, installing improved crankshaft dampeners, redesigning the muffler, adding insulation under the aluminum skin and beneath the upholstery, thickening the windows, and improving the door seals.

The Military 180

Between 1962 and 1970, the USAF purchased 17 Model 180E and Model 180H aircraft off-the-shelf to be provided to several foreign countries under the Military Assistance Program (MAP). By that time, the engine had been changed to the 230-horsepower Continental O-470-R, boosting maximum speed from 165 mph to 170 mph. The only change from the basic civilian aircraft for these military contracts was the military exterior paint scheme. The USAF purchased eight aircraft in 1962 and three each in 1966, 1967, and 1970. The following Cessna constructor numbers and USAF serial numbers were assigned to these military Model 180s, designated U-17C by the military:

- **1962 Model 180E**
  C/N: 18051134, 18051143, 18051145, 18051147, 18051149, 18051151, 18051153, and 18051155
  S/N: Unknown
- **1966 Model 180H**
  C/N: 18051649, 18051653, and 18051687
  S/N: 65-12771, 62-12770, & 67-14602, respectively
- **1967 Model 180H**
  C/N: 18051795, 18051796, and 18051851
  S/N: 67-14580, 67-14581, and 67-14603
- **1970 Model 180H**
  C/N: 18052145, 18052172, and 18052174
  S/N: 70-1624, 70-2034, and 70-2035

In the mid-1950s, the Mexican Navy purchased some Model 180s for support duties, but the exact number is unknown.

Australian 180s

According to Steve Eather in his book "Target Charlie," the Royal Australian Air Force (RAAF) independently purchased eight Model 180A aircraft in 1959, seven Model 180D aircraft in 1961, and four Model 180E aircraft in 1962. The RAAF later transferred these aircraft to the 16 Army Light Aircraft Squadron based initially at Canberra, later at Amberly, and finally at Oakey. At least three of these aircraft were used by the 161 Independent Reconnaissance Flight (the "Possums") of the First Battalion, Royal Australian Regiment (later the First Australian Task Force) in South Vietnam from 1965 until 1972, under command of the U.S. Army's 173rd Airborne Brigade. With its Model 180s, the 161 Flight flew visual reconnaissance, liaison, and aerial command post support missions. Before long, the 161 Flight added ammunition resupply, casualty evacuation, forward air control, leaflet dropping, and propaganda broadcasting missions, as well. For their FAC role, the Cessna 180s were outfitted with underwing hardpoints to allow use of the usual FAC white phosphorous ("Willie Pete") target marking rockets. The pilots of the 161 Flight, however, generally flew with a mix of Willie Pete and high explosive rockets, to allow for some "organic" attack capability.

• A Cessna U-17C ready for delivery to a foreign air force under the Military Assistance Program •
(Cessna Aircraft Company)

In 1969, the Australian Army began replacing its 180s with Swiss Pilatus Porter aircraft. The last Australian Model 180 retired from Army service in September of 1974. During their Vietnam service, the Australian Cessna 180s maintained a mission ready rate of 92 percent. The Australian Army assigned the following serial numbers to their aircraft:

- **1959 Model 180A**
  S/N: A98-336, A98-338, A98-340, A98-342 through A98-344, A98-350, and A98-351.
- **1961 Model 180D**
  S/N: A98-041 through A98-046, and A98-063.
- **1962 Model 180E**
  S/N: A98-144, A98-146, A98-148, and A98-150.

In 1966, the unit's Cessna 180s and an O-1 Bird Dog "on loan" from the U.S. Army initiated daily morning road reconnaissance ("road recce") flights along the roads of Phuoc Tuy Province to identify new Viet Cong roadblocks and booby traps. The fixed wing pilots of 161 Flight also helped direct the Australian Centurion tanks through the dense Vietnamese jungle in their efforts to provide needed support for the infantry. Then, in 1967, due to the delays caused by the normal weekly mail couri-

er service, 161 Flight's 180s began making almost daily "Possum Post" mail runs from Phuoc Tuy province direct to the Tan Son Nhut Airport for shipment back home to Australia. In mid-1968, 161 Flight relocated to fire support bases in Bien Hoa Province, where the Viet Cong took to setting up machine gun positions just beyond the bases' perimeters. One of the unit's 180s was struck by fire from a Viet Cong 50-caliber machine gun while on final approach for landing; it was grounded for a week while the missing chunks of wing and fuselage were repaired.

On 13 January 1969, a 161 Flight Cessna 180 was damaged by ground fire during a "road recce" mission, but the pilot managed to call for an airstrike before bringing his stricken aircraft home. The same aircraft was fired on again on 23 February, taking hits in the propeller, wing, fuselage, elevator, and flaps. Another 180 was destroyed in a takeoff accident at one of the fire support bases in gusty winds complicated by downdrafts from nearby hovering helicopters — the pilot and his passengers were, however, uninjured. On 17 July 1969, five Viet Cong machine gunners opened fire on a single Cessna 180 flying just above the treetops. After landing, numerous bullet holes were found in the wings, engine compartment, and even in the overhead window above the pilot. A few days later, the

• A U-17A flying over Kansas prior to delivery to the USAF •
(Kansas Aviation Museum/Robert J. Pickett Collection)

same pilot brewed some homemade "napalm" by filling plastic gas cans with gasoline, which began reacting with the plastic as the cans were attached to the pylons of his 180. The pilot flew out to a Viet Cong vegetable garden he had been monitoring, dumped his explosive load, and ignited the spreading mixture by tossing white phosphorous grenades out of the window — the garden was listed as "killed in action" in the after-action report.

Model 180 Variants

The differences among the variants of the Model 180 were mostly minor and cosmetic. The 180A, introduced in 1957, included a revised instrument panel, a single-action parking brake, improved tailwheel steering, and a maximum gross weight increase of 100-pounds to 2,650-pounds total. The 180D of 1961 incorporated further instrument panel revisions and a front mounted air intake filter. The 180E was introduced in 1962 with redesigned fuel tank outlet ports, increased fuel capacity, and new wing tips and position light mounts. In 1964, the Model 180G was introduced with the Model 185's larger fuselage and six-place seating capability. The Model 180H, introduced in 1965, featured an array of improvements by 1967, such as:

- Center-mounted avionics in a redesigned instrument panel
- Improved fuel strainer and door latches
- Pointed propeller spinner
- Increased baggage compartment capacity
- Optional left-side entry door
- New rotating beacon

By 1970, the Model 180H had incorporated stowable rudder pedals on the right side, new wingtips, and provisions for an external 300-pound cargo pack. Gross weight again increased, this time to 2,800-pounds maximum.

• A U-17A undergoing field maintenance •
(Kansas Aviation Museum/Robert J. Pickett Collection)

And Then Came the 185

Although the success of the Model 180 eroded as more buyers opted for the easier-to-land Model 172 and Model 182 with their tricycle landing gear, Cessna introduced a second aircraft, almost identical to the 180 — the Model 185 Skywagon. The 185 was designed to capitalize on the utility aspects of the design. First flight of the new aircraft was in July of 1960, and the first production aircraft rolled out of the factory in March of 1961. The new aircraft was an upgraded Model 180 designed specifically as a heavy load-hauler, with an empty weight of 1,520-pounds and a useful payload of 1,620-pounds! To provide space for all that payload, Cessna lengthened the baggage compartment by 32-inches.

The aircraft incorporated heavy-duty axles, tires, and landing gear plus provisions for the Model 180H's 300-pound cargo pack (this cargo pack cut speeds almost 10 mph and climb rate about 40-feet-per-minute). The only obvious physical difference between the 180 and the 185 was the deeper and less angular dorsal fin. In fact, the larger dorsal fin was actually incorporated in later Model 180s to maintain commonality on the production line. Cessna produced almost 4,000 Model 185s between 1961 and 1985.

A fuel-injected, six-cylinder, 260-horsepower Continental IO-470-F engine powered the six-passenger aircraft via a two-bladed, constant speed Hartzell propeller. To keep the fuel-injection system from trying to suck air from an empty fuel tank, Cessna engineers designed a fuselage-mounted fuel accumulator tank.

• A U-17B on the Cessna ramp in Wichita, preparing for an acceptance test flight •
(Kansas Aviation Museum/Robert J. Picket Collection)

The Model 185 evolved slowly in the ensuing years. The 1962 185A sported new wingtips, increased wing span, vernier throttle and mixture controls, and electric auxiliary fuel pumps. The 185B, introduced in 1963, added diecast magnesium rudder pedals and an overhead light console. The 185C in 1964 incorporated a manual tailwheel lock (to counter a problem with violent shimmy when landing in strong crosswinds), dual brake linings, and an uprated 52-ampere alternator. In 1965, the 185D provided an instrument panel with center-mount avionics and an integrated engine instrument cluster.

The 185E in 1966 came out with a 100-pound increase in gross weight and a sister ship, the A185E, which had a 150-pound weight increase due to its 285-horsepower Continental IO-520-D engine. In 1967, the bigger engine became standard equipment on the Model A185E along with a pointed propeller spinner, larger rear cabin, separate center passenger seats (rather than a single bench seat), and a 60-ampere alternator. In 1968, the A185E's gross weight was upped by 50 more pounds and an automatic air induction system was incorporated, along with a new baggage door. The only improvement made in the 1969 Model 185E was to switch to newer 300/400 series ARC avionics. In 1970, the A185E offered an optional left-side baggage door and incorporated conical camber wingtips. An improved wing, the Cessna "Camber-Lift," was added to the Skywagon with the introduction of the A185F in 1973.

• Ecuadoran army officials accept delivery of a Cessna Model 185 •
(Kansas Aviation Museum/Robert J. Pickett Collection)

Military 185s

In 1963, the USAF purchased 63 Model 185B Skywagons off-the-shelf for the Military Assistance Program, primarily for South Vietnam and Laos, designating them U-17A. An additional 202 aircraft were purchased between 1964 and 1967 for a total U-17A buy of 265 aircraft. U-17s were provided to numerous foreign countries, including Bolivia, Costa Rica, Greece, Indonesia, Laos, Nicaragua, Turkey, and South Vietnam. South Vietnam used U-17s as liaison, training, and FAC aircraft, and even outfitted some with powerful loudspeakers mounted in the passenger compartment for psychological warfare operations (broadcasting propaganda to the enemy). Numbers purchased by year were:

- **1963 Model 185B:** 63 spread throughout Cessna constructor numbers 185-0513 to 185-0653
- **1964 Model 185C:** 34 spread throughout Cessna constructor numbers 185-0654 to 185-0776
- **1965 Model 185D:** 83 spread throughout Cessna constructor numbers 185-0777 to 185-01300
- **1966 Model 185E:** 72 spread throughout Cessna constructor numbers 185-0777 to 185-01300
- **1967 Model 185E:** 13 spread throughout Cessna constructor numbers 185-0777 to 185-01300

Between 1967 and 1973 the USAF purchased 215 Model A185E and A185F aircraft, designated U-17B. All these 185s were spread throughout Cessna constructor numbers 185-1150 to 185-02310, and each featured the 285-horsepower engine. The quantity of planes purchased by year was:

• An Iranian Gendarmerie Model 185 •
(Kansas Aviation Museum/Robert J. Pickett Collection)

- **1967 Model A185E:** 26
- **1968 Model A185E:** 9
- **1969 Model A185E:** 26
- **1970 Model A185E:** 94
- **1971 Model A185E:** 12
- **1972 Model A185E:** 38
- **1973 Model A185F:** 10

A unique and inexpensive crosswind landing gear system was developed by John Geisse and flight tested on the Model 170. During taxi operations, the main wheels are allowed to caster, although in flight, a coil spring centered the wheels. To reduce shimmy with this arrangement, a braking method was devised mounted in the exterior of the wheel housings. The resulting system was quite effective in reducing the frequency of ground loops, but the penalty was increased drag from the bulkier wheel assemblies. Cessna engineers proceeded to develop a similar system mounted almost completely inside the main gear axles, thus eliminating the drag problem. This Geisse crosswind landing gear system was installed on all U-17A and U-17B aircraft. When the first U-17A aircraft were flown into Nha Trang, South Vietnam, in July 1963, the Vietnamese frequently came out to watch the castering

wheels as the aircraft touched down in a crab with its main wheels pointing down the runway.

Many nations have purchased Model 185 aircraft directly from Cessna and many of those have shown up in military service around the world. The South African Air Force (SAAF) operated Model 185s in their Nos. 40, 41, and 42 Squadrons from 1962 to 1974 at various bases, primarily for FAC missions. From the late 1970s through the early 1980s, these SAAF Model 185s were reassigned to Nos. 11 and 43 Squadrons for FAC, liaison, and communications roles. On 21 December 1975 in the war in Angola, the SAAF lost a Cessna 185 to small arms fire northwest of Cela.

The Rhodesian Air Force's No. 3 Squadron operated a number of 185s out of New Sarum in the late 1970s and early 1980s and the Fuerza Aero de Nicaragua operated Model 185s as liaison aircraft in combined helicopter/fixed wing units. The Philippines Air Force operated six U-17A and U-17B aircraft as liaison aircraft in the 240th Composite Wing and another 15 of the aircraft as trainers in their 100th Training Wing.

Raven U-17s

Throughout the covert USAF involvement in Laos

• A Phillipine Air Force U-17A •
(Kansas Aviation Museum/Robert J. Pickett Collection)

during the Vietnam War, numerous U-17s were used for a variety of liaison and FAC missions. These USAF pilots and aircraft were part of the Raven program (see the L-19/O-1 chapter for more information on the Ravens). Christopher Robbins, in "The Ravens," details the complete history of this incredible unit — including the following stories.

In 1967, the first Raven aircraft to be lost in combat was a U-17 when the engine lost power due to contaminated fuel. The aircraft stalled, hit the ground, and rolled into an old French minefield dating from perhaps the 1930s. Rather than risk walking out across the old land mines, the pilot stayed with his aircraft until an Air America helicopter picked him up.

In 1969, a Raven pilot flying a U-17 with a young Meo observer directed nine separate T-28 airstrikes against enemy positions, and then was hit by a 14.5mm anti-aircraft gun. The round shattered the Meo's leg, causing him to start slowly bleeding to death as the Raven nursed their stricken aircraft home. The Raven used his Bowie knife to amputate the man's leg as he held the Meo down with his other hand and flew the aircraft with his feet. The young Meo survived.

One Raven pilot died while flying a U-17 over the Plain of Jars in central Laos. Three 37mm anti-aircraft rounds struck the aircraft, ripping a large hole in one wing. While another Raven watched from a T-28, the U-17 exploded.

Where Are They Now?

Although a perusal of recent issues of "Trade-A-Plane" did not turn up any U-17s for sale, there are numerous Model 180s and 185s offered. There are some civilian-owned U-17s that regularly show up at airshows. A check of North American aviation museums showed only two Cessna 180s on display — one in the National Museum of Naval Aviation in Pensacola, Florida, and another in the Bushplane Heritage Museum in Sault Ste. Marie, Ontario, Canada. ☩

• A civilian-owned U-17C, which once served with the Royal Thai Air Force. This Cessna features a paint scheme typical of USAF utility planes that served in Southeast Asia •
(Walt Shiel)

Specifications

U-17A

Wingspan	.36 ft. 2 in.
Length	.25 ft. 9 in.
Height	.7 ft. 9 in.
Gross Weight	.3,200 lbs. (1963-1965)
	3,300 lbs. (1966-1967)
Engine	Continental IO-470-F
Horsepower	.260
Cruise Speed	.150 mph
Maximum Speed	.172 mph
Service Ceiling	.16,600 feet
Range	.725 sm
Takeoff Roll	.770 ft.
Landing Roll	.480 ft.

Specifications

U-17B

Wingspan	.36 ft. 2 in.
Length	.25 ft. 9 in.
Height	.7 ft. 9 in.
Gross Weight	.3,350 lbs.
Engine	Continental IO-520-D
Horsepower	.285
Cruise Speed	.160 mph
Maximum Speed	.178 mph
Service Ceiling	.17,150 ft.
Range	.725 sm
Takeoff Roll	.770 ft.
Landing Roll	.480 ft.

Specifications

U-17C

Wingspan	36 ft.
Length	25 ft. 6 in.
Height	7 ft. 6.5 in.
Gross Weight	2,650 lbs.
Engine	Continental O-470-R
Horsepower	230
Cruise Speed	145 mph
Maximum Speed	170 mph
Service Ceiling	21,500 ft.
Range	660 sm
Takeoff Roll	625 ft.
Landing Roll	480 ft.

T-47
Navy Citations

-chapter 15-

In the early 1980s, the U.S. Navy decided to replace the fleet of aging North American Rockwell T-39D aircraft it had been using to train navigators and Radar Intercept Officers (RIOs) in its Undergraduate Naval Flight Officer (UNFO) program. RIOs were the officers who rode in the back seats of aircraft like the Northrop Grumman F-14 Tomcat, operating the radar and providing target intercept guidance to the pilot. Following a competitive procurement process, the Navy awarded Cessna Aircraft a contract for 15 modified Citation S/II aircraft in 1984. Cessna called the new version the Model 552, and the Navy designated it the T-47A. The primary differences between the basic Citation S/II and the T-47A were:

- More powerful Pratt & Whitney of Canada JT15D-5 turbofan engines to replace the S/II's JT15D-4B engines.
- Reduced wingspan from the S/II's 52.2-foot span to 46.5 feet on the T-47A.
- Increased fuselage length from 47.2 feet on the S/II to 47.9 feet on the T-47A necessary to accommodate the nose-mounted Emerson APQ-159 radar.
- Addition of three student radar stations in the main cabin to replace the S/II's executive seating.

The combination of more powerful engines and a shorter wingspan provided better acceleration, an improved rate of climb, and a higher top speed. The basic

• *A U.S. Navy leased Citation Model 552/T-47A* •
(Kansas Aviation Museum/Robert J. Pickett Collection)

Citation S/II was capable of a maximum level speed of Mach 0.721 (412 KTAS) at 40,000 feet, while the T-47A could achieve Mach 0.733 (420 KTAS) at the same altitude, enough to meet the Navy's specified performance requirements. The basic Citation S/II incorporated the supercritical wing design of the Citation III on its long, straight wing. First flight of the production version of the civilian Model 550 Citation S/II took place on 14 February 1984, and FAA certification (including a single-pilot authorization) was awarded in July 1984. FAA certification for the T-47A (Model 552) version was received on 21 November 1984 with initial deliveries to the Navy completed the following month.

The supercritical wing used on the Model 550 and T-47A significantly reduced high-speed drag without affecting the Citation's already excellent slow-speed handling characteristics. In addition, the most inboard section of the T-47's wing leading edge on each side was extended forward to increase the wing's total area and, thus, the lift it produced — as well as providing room to enlarge the internal wing fuel tanks. Cessna redesigned the engine pylons to reduce the drag produced by them, faired the wing flap covers, and sealed the gaps between the ailerons and top-mounted speed brakes. These changes reduced drag, improved climb rate, and increased maximum speed.

The Navy issued a $160-million, five-year UNFO/Training System Upgrade contract (with an optional extension for three years) for a complete turnkey training package. This lucrative contract helped to pull Cessna out of 1983's slump (and $18-million loss) and to generate an $0.9M profit in 1984. To provide the necessary complete training program (pilots, maintenance personnel, and simulators), Cessna teamed with Northrop Worldwide Aircraft Services, Inc. (NWASI) for pilots and maintenance personnel, Pratt & Whitney of Canada, Ltd. for the engines, and Singer/Link for the air-to-air and air-to-ground radar training simulators. Fifteen T-47A aircraft were delivered to the Navy's Training Air Wing Six (TAW-6) and its two training squadrons, VT-86 and VT-10, at Naval Air Station Pensacola, Florida. The Navy assigned the aircraft sequential BuNos (162755 through 162769) but retained civilian "N" numbers on the tail with "NAVY" stenciled just below the horizontal stabilizer and the U.S. military star-and-bars insignia on each engine pod.

Deliveries to the Navy were about six months later than originally scheduled due to problems clearing up some initial operational deficiencies. To achieve the required roll rates, Cessna installed an aileron boost system and geared aileron trim tabs. Some minor flight control and aerodynamic changes were made to correct what the Navy considered excessive lateral and longitudinal forces during maneuvering. The aircraft was required to operate at low altitude at speeds up to 350 KIAS. To achieve that goal with adequate crew safety, Cessna

developed and tested an impact resistant polycarbonate windscreen. The new windshield proved able to prevent penetration of a five-pound bird at up to 455 KIAS.

Initial tests showed unexpected range limitations for target acquisition with the APQ-167 radar, but these problems were quickly corrected. Cessna designed and installed hydraulically-actuated, graphite-composite Fowler flaps that extended farther inboard than the standard flaps to improve the lift-to-drag ratio in the landing configuration.

Instructor Pilots

The first pilots for the T-47A program were hired in January of 1985 by NWASI. Although the contract did not specify that all pilots must be ex-military pilots, the Navy, Cessna, and NWASI all preferred such experience. Previous knowledge of military procedures, flying techniques, and terminology were all considered a plus, as was prior fighter aircraft flying time. NWASI management carefully screened all pilot candidates, who had to be approved by the Navy's T-47 Training System Manager at Pensacola, after which Cessna hired them.

The first stop for new T-47A pilots was at Flight Safety International's training facility in Wichita, Kansas, for training in the Citation S/II and an appropriate FAA aircraft type rating. After completing the Flight Safety training program, the new pilots received mission-specific transition training from Cessna instructors and, finally, a checkride administered by one of two assigned Navy T-47A instructor pilots.

Although the contractor's T-47A pilots had no responsibilities for evaluation of student performance, they were still called instructor pilots. Their job was to follow the guidance provided by the student navigators and RIOs in the back of the airplane during departures, arrivals, and a variety of airborne intercept profiles. An NFO instructor closely supervised the students during all missions.

Fighters and Bogies

The standard UNFO training mission required two T-47A aircraft with two or three students and one instructor NFO on each aircraft. An unusual feature was that the instructor NFO (a non-pilot) was actually the mission commander, and his authority included all facets of the mission, including veto rights when a decision might affect the safety of the flight.

The typical pre-mission activities involved up to two hours of student briefings, during which the instructor NFO covered flight safety, mission objectives and requirements, the specific departure and arrival profiles to be flown, and the intercept problems planned for the mission. Afterward, the students coordinated the mission with their assigned T-47A pilots, who were expected to

• *Navy T-47A head-on over the florida panhandle* •
(Kansas Aviation Museum/Robert J. Pickett Collection)

draw on their own experience to discuss the upcoming mission with the students. This was an informal process encouraged by the Navy, validating the wisdom of employing ex-military pilots. In fact, NWASI included this portion of the briefing as part of their routine evaluation of each pilot's performance.

With its single-pilot operation authorization, each T-47 required only one pilot for the mission. One of the NFO students was selected on each mission to fly in the right (co-pilot) seat to monitor aircraft performance and provide direction to the pilot on the specific routing and altitude restrictions of the instrument departure. This student also participated with the pilot in the preflight walk-around inspection of the aircraft.

Once in the training area out over the Gulf of Mexico, a ground controlled intercept (GCI) officer vectored the two T-47s assigned to each mission. Missions were assigned to one of three altitude blocks — low altitude (7,000- to 12,000-feet), medium altitude (13,000- to 17,000-feet), or high altitude (19,000- to 23,000-feet). The two T-47s alternated in the role of interceptor (fighter) and attacker (bogey). The GCI controller assigned the fighter a cruise altitude 1,000-feet above the floor of the altitude block and put the bogey within 500-feet of the fighter's altitude for the initial intercept setup.

The GCI controller established the two aircraft on appropriate intercept headings for the planned scenario and vectored the fighter for the intercept. Once the student on the designated fighter confirmed that he had radar contact on the T-47's APQ-159 radar, he took over the intercept and issued directions to the pilot. The goal was to vector the pilot into position on the bogey's six o'clock position. For some scenarios, the student directed the fighter on an opposite-direction identification pass and then quickly provided appropriate directions to turn-in a mile or two behind the bogey with enough overtake to ensure a "kill."

On each three-hour intercept training mission, the students in each aircraft alternated NFO responsibility. At the conclusion of the intercept mission, one of the student NFOs again assumed right-seat duties and assisted the pilot with instrument approach and airport arrival procedures and associated checklists.

Doing It Down Low

In addition to intercept training missions, the Navy used the T-47s to introduce students to low-level navigation procedures. The T-47s flew these missions over the flat, featureless inland terrain of Florida and southern Alabama at 500 feet AGL at groundspeeds between 270 and 330 KIAS.

The students took turns directing the pilot on these sorties, as well. Their responsibilities included vectoring the pilot to the entry point for the low level route, directing pilot corrections of aircraft speed and course, and calculating wind drift and fuel consumption.

Retirement

The Navy extended the initial Cessna T-47A contract for three years, through 1992, when they were replaced again by contractor-operated North American Sabreliner T-39s. (This change meant the Navy was, once again, operating the same aging aircraft in their UNFO program they had been using prior to the Cessna T-47A contract.) Over their seven years of operation, the 15 aircraft in the T-47A fleet logged over 100,000 flight hours with no major accidents and only a handful of minor incidents. Overall fleet mission completion rates were better than 95 percent.

In 1989, Cessna entered a variation of the Navy T-47A in competition for the potentially lucrative USAF Tanker-Transport Training System (TTTS) aircraft, teaming with General Dynamics (which owned Cessna at that time) for system integration and CAE-Link for the ground-based portion of the training system. The Cessna entry easily met all defined performance requirements and had an excellent record in the Navy's UNFO program, including many hours in the demanding low-level navigation role (considered the most difficult portion of the USAF TTTS requirements for the candidate off-the-shelf, albeit missionized, business aircraft). Ultimately, however, acquisition cost drove the USAF to select the newly developed, and relatively untried, Beech Aircraft BeechJet — now serving in USAF Undergraduate Pilot Training as the T-1A Jayhawk.

The 15 T-47As were put in storage at Forbes Field in Topeka, Kansas. Later, a new roof was being installed on the storage hangar and a fire broke out. Within minutes, the entire hangar had burned to the ground, destroying 13 of the aircraft.

Clandestine T-47s?

As a follow on to the history of Cessna's T-47, on 13 June 1995, Cessna was awarded another contract for a similar aircraft — although apparently for a very different mission. The official USAF contract award announcement read:

"Cessna Aircraft Company, Wichita, Kansas, is being awarded a $40,787,500 Firm Fixed Price contract for the procurement of five OT-47B Tracker aircraft and provides for integration of the APG-66(V) radar and the WF-360TL imaging system onto the aircraft. Contract is expected to be completed March 1997. One firm was solicited and one proposal was received. Solicitation began November 1994 and negotiations were complete April 1995. Aeronautical Systems Center, WrightPatterson Air Force Base, Ohio is the contracting activity."

When Cessna was contacted, they said they were unable to comment in any way on the contract or the aircraft and that all questions were being referred to the USAF. USAF Public Affairs at the Pentagon referred me to an official at the Reconnaissance Systems Program Office at WrightPatterson AFB — the acquisitions agency for this contract. The official would only confirm that the aircraft is, in fact, "similar" to the T-47A aircraft and that it would be used in operations where the Rules of Engagement were uncertain and where the "bad guys" were indeed truly "bad." The lives of service personnel likely would be jeopardized if any information were released on either the aircraft, the using agency, or the intended mission. As of September 1995, no further information had been released. ✛

• *U.S. Navy T-47A* •
(Kansas Aviation Museum/Robert J. Pickett Collection)

Specifications

Wingspan ....46 ft. 6 in.

      Length...47 ft. 10.75 in.

      Height ....14 ft. 9.75 in.

Cabin Dimensions

      Length...20 ft. 10.75 in.

      Width ....+ 4 ft. 10.75 in.

      Height .... 4 ft. 9.5 in.

Empty Weight..9,035 lbs.

Maximum Takeoff Weight ....15,000 lbs.

Maximum Speeds

      Up to 8,000 ft..261 KIAS

      8,000 to 29,315 ft..276 KIAS

      Above 29,315 ft ....Mach 0.733

Cruise Speed at 35,000 ft. ....403 KIAS

Stall Speed, Clean ....94 KCAS

Stall Speed, Gear & Flaps Down ....82 KCAS

Maximum Rate of Climb, Both Engines ....3,040 ft./min.

Maximum Rate of Climb, One Engine ....860 ft./min.

Service Ceiling, Both Engines..43,000 ft.

Service Ceiling, One Engine ....24,000 ft.

Takeoff Runway Length ....3,240 ft

Landing Runway Length ....2,640 ft.

Range, With Reserves ....2,000 miles

Other Cessnas That Served

-chapter 16-

Although, to this point, this book has concentrated on the various Cessna models developed specifically for the military or those purchased off-the-shelf by the military and assigned military nomenclatures, many others have been used by a variety of military forces around the world. In fact, if you were to look hard enough and dig deep enough, you would probably discover that virtually every Cessna model ever built has seen military service of some kind somewhere in the world. I do not pretend to have done that kind of exhaustive search, but I will share the results of my more limited research that turned up various odd military applications. The following should be considered merely examples of how military forces have employed lightplanes, in this case Cessnas, for military purposes.

Cadet Competitors

The USAF Academy in Colorado Springs, Colorado, flew three Cessna Model 150 aircraft in its 94th Airmanship Training Squadron until 1995 when they were replaced by four T-41Cs retired from the training fleet of the 557th Flying Training Squadron. These aircraft belonged to the Cadet Competition Flying Team (CCFT) and were used in National Intercollegiate Flying Association (NIFA) competitions. In 1993 through 1995, Captain Jim Bergstrom was the USAF officer assigned to supervise the program. Each cadet member of the CCFT had to have earned his or her private pilot license to apply for the team. They were given a battery of tests, a flight proficiency evaluation, and put through an extensive interview process. Most of the CCFT cadets had flown close to 100 hours before joining the team. The CCFT C-150s had three major Supplemental Type Certificates incorporated:

- Original engine replaced with 150-horsepower Lycoming O-320 to allow the team to practice at the 6,500-foot Academy field elevation and up to 10,000-foot density altitudes in the summer.
- Installation of 38-gallon long-range fuel tanks.
- Allowable gross weight increased from 1,600-pounds to 1,760-pounds to accommodate the extra fuel.

The Academy aircraft were late 1970s C-150M models. According to Captain Bergstrom, "They're civilian aircraft searched for and located through Trade-A-Plane, purchased with donations from the Association of Graduates of the Academy." The CCFT was set-up in 1972 by a handful of cadets who rented airplanes from the Academy aero club until putting together the funds to purchase their own airplanes. The performance of the CCFT has been steadily improving, moving up from fifth place overall in the NIFA 1990-1991 season to second place out of 24 teams in 1993-1994. A total of 23 cadets participated in the program in 1993-1994, 39 in 1994-1995.

Other Cessnas

In 1961, the Canadian Army ordered four Cessna Model 182D aircraft, built to their specifications. Oddly enough, these aircraft were designated as L-19L aircraft by the Canadians. The Model 182 was a tricycle gear, four-seat aircraft powered by a normally aspirated 230-horsepower Continental engine.

Both the Liberian Army and the Brazilian Air Force currently own and operate Model 208 Caravan I aircraft in a variety of mission support roles. The Pratt & Whitney PT6-powered Caravan I is a 10-14 seat utility aircraft with a 3,000-pound payload capacity, developed in the early 1980s. While not exactly a military use, both the U.S. Central Intelligence Agency and the U.S. State Department operate the Caravan I aircraft as the U-27A. Other U-27s were procured by the U.S. Army for various foreign military services under the Foreign Military Sales program. The French Army operates some more-powerful Caravan IIs as mission support aircraft, for aerial target towing missions and anti-aircraft gunnery training.

The Angolan Army commandeered a significant number of civilian aircraft in 1975. Among them were several Cessna aircraft (C-172, C-180, C-310), which were relegated to personnel and light cargo transport duties.

In 1979, the Royal Rhodesian Air Force operated 19 aircraft as part of No. 3 Squadron's mixed fleet of C-402s and C-185s out of New Sarum Base. The Royal

• *Captain Jim Bergstrom with one of the USAF Academy Cadet Competition Flying Team Cessna 150M aircraft* •
(Walt Shiel)

Malaysian Air Force also flies a dozen C-402s as either multi-engine trainer aircraft or for photographic and liaison duties. The Model 402 Utililiner was developed in the mid-1960s as a 10-seat passenger and freight transport, powered by a pair of turbocharged, fuel-injected 300-horsepower Continental engines.

In the mid-1980s, the Sri Lanka Air Force allegedly initiated air strikes on the Jaffna Peninsula against rebel positions, using a variety of Cessna aircraft (C-150, C-206, C-337, and C-421) that were used for reconnaissance and light attack with unspecified external stores. Some were supposedly flown by British and Pakistani pilots. The Model 206 was first produced in 1964 with a single fuel-injected 300-horsepower Continental engine and seating for up to six. The Model 421 was a pressurized light twin that first flew in 1965 and was powered by a pair of 375-horsepower turbocharged, fuel-injected Continental engines.

In Surinam, rebels tried to overthrow the government repeatedly throughout the 1980s. On one occasion, they captured a Cessna Model 205 (a six-seat derivative of the Model 182 with a 260-horsepower fuel-injected Continental engine), intending to use it on a bombing raid against government forces, although it was apparently never used.

In 1978, the U.S. Navy acquired one Cessna Model 404 Titan as an off-the-shelf purchase for cargo and personnel transport duties. The Navy designation was C-28. The Model 404 was an 8,400-pound gross weight aircraft powered by two turbocharged, fuel-injected 375-horsepower Continental engines. +

JPATS
CitationJet

-chapter 17-

In 1989, the U.S. Congress directed the USAF and the U.S. Navy to procure a single replacement aircraft for the USAF Cessna T-37B and the Navy Beechcraft T-34C trainers. Both services' trainers had been purchased originally in the 1950s and 1960s, and the need for more modern aircraft was apparent. Since the primary pilot training requirements in both services were similar and there was an overall push for more "jointness" to unify operations in the various services and to conserve precious defense procurement dollars, Congress mandated the joint program over initially strong military objectives.

The basic requirements for the joint USAF-Navy trainer and the associated fielding schedule were defined in the Department of Defense's 1989 Trainer Aircraft Master Plan (TAMP). The TAMP also dictated that the new aircraft must be a Non-Developmental Item (NDI)—no from-the-ground-up design and development concepts need apply. From the outset, this seemed to limit the field to foreign contenders, since it seemed that none of the U.S. aircraft manufacturers had a suitable aircraft adaptable to the military needs.

In the early 1980s, under the Next Generation Trainer program, the USAF had attempted to replace its Cessna T-37s with the Fairchild T-46, an aircraft that closely resembled the T-37 in general configuration and performance. Both aircraft were approximately the same size, had side-by-side seating arrangements, had long straight wings, and were powered by twin jet engines. The two prototype T-46As, however, were plagued by one problem after another (including performance shortcomings) during flight testing at Edwards AFB, California. Finally, with resolution of the problems still uncertain, the USAF terminated the contract on 13 March 1987. The entire episode left a residual bad memory in the minds of many senior officials, although the need to replace those old T-37s remained unfulfilled. By 1994, the USAF T-37 fleet of 600 aircraft averaged 32 years of age and was flying an average of 500-hours per year. The original T-37 design had been for a 8,000-hour airframe, which had been

extended to 18,000-hours. By 1998, the average T-37 will have logged those 18,000-hours and will need replacing to avoid serious safety problems.

The U.S. Navy, meanwhile, had pursued an advanced trainer replacement for its capable but worn-out Rockwell T-2 Buckeyes and McDonnell Douglas TA-4J Skyhawks. The winner of that competition was the BAe Hawk trainer, manufactured in the U.S. by McDonnell Douglas as the T4-5A Goshawk. This program, alas, was also not without its problems as the missionization of the proven Hawk produced an overweight and underperforming aircraft. Eventually, those problems were corrected, but once more the U.S. military had failed to impress Congress with its skill in developing something as simple as a training aircraft.

The initial Joint System Operational Requirements Document (JSORD), a rather general treatise on the services' expectations for the new aircraft, was issued in October of 1991. The first of two editions of the final Operational Requirements Document (ORD) for the Joint Primary Aircraft Training System (JPATS) was published in mid-1992, with the final edition issued in January 1994. The aircraft manufacturers, faced with too few potential military contracts for the number of companies in the market, wasted no time forming teams and proposing solutions to meet the ORD specifications.

The ORD specified the following performance requirements for the six-billion-dollar contract, which could result in USAF and Navy purchases of 650 to 760 aircraft (and maybe 800 more overseas sales):

- Climb from sea level to 8,000-feet, with full fuel on a standard day, in no more than eight minutes.
- Takeoff and land with a crosswind component of 25 knots.
- Operate normally from -9 F to +109 F.
- Enter the standard military 360° overhead traffic pattern at airspeeds between 170 KCAS and 250 KCAS at airfield elevations from 800-feet MSL through 7,000-feet MSL.

• First prototype Cessna JPATS CitationJet (Model 526) •
(Cessna Aircraft Company)

- Include Global Positioning System navigational equipment.
- Include on-board collision avoidance system.
- Incorporate flat-panel instrument displays.
- Perform standard student training missions of up to one hour and 45 minutes.
- Perform a 250-nautical-mile low-level navigation mission beginning and ending 45 nautical miles from base, with reserves for a 125-nautical-mile diversion.
- Perform a steady-state +2G turn at 22,000-feet.
- Provide a stable formation training platform at speeds down to 170 KIAS.
- Provide predictable spin entry and recovery capabilities.
- Include cockpit pressurization.
- Provide a canopy able to withstand the impact of a four-pound bird at up to 250 KTAS (270 KTAS preferred).
- Include provisions for a head-up display (although the display itself is not required in the basic proposal).
- Provide single-point ground refueling capability.
- Provide tandem seating with a raised instructor's cockpit.
- Incorporate ejection seats with at least zero altitude and 60 KIAS capability (zero-zero preferred).
- Be stressed for at least +6G and -3G load factors.
- Allow a service life of 20-24 years at an annual utilization rate of 700 flying hours per aircraft.

After considerable internal disagreements and lengthy discussions among the USAF and Navy program office personnel, the ORD did not specify either turboprop or jet power for the new trainer's engines, thus opening the competition to a broader range of candidate aircraft. The initial plans called for awarding a single contract for the aircraft, the ground-based training system (including the flight simulators), and contractor logistics support for the entire training system. However, the JPATS program office changed that last year by deciding to select the best aircraft and then allow the aircraft prime contractor to select the most cost-effective ground-based training system contractor (with guidance from the JPATS program office).

By 1990, 25 JPATS hopefuls were jockeying for position in the race for the trainer roses. However, as the requirements kept changing and the demands on contending companies finances increased, many dropped out. Besides the U.S. military market, the Australian government was about to issue their own requirements for a fighter training aircraft, but had delayed their announcement until after the U.S. made its JPATS selection (the Australians were adamant that they wanted no part of the program if the U.S. military selected a turboprop trainer). By early 1992, only six companies remained in the running — with Cessna still on the sidelines. All of the six competing teams included a U.S. partner to assemble an aircraft designed by an overseas firm:

- Beech/Pilatus (Switzerland) turboprop PC-9 Mk II.
- Northrop Grumman/Embraer (Brazil) turboprop EMB-312H Super Tucano.
- Northrop Grumman/Agusta (Spain) turbofan S.211A.
- Northrop Grumman/FMA (Argentina) turbofan Pampa 2000.
- Rockwell/DASA (Germany) turbofan Ranger 2000.
- Lockheed Martin/Aermacchi (Italy) turbojet MB-339 T-Bird II.

In November of 1992, Cessna announced that it was joining the JPATS competition with an all-American team creating a missionized version of its successful Model 525 CitationJet, with military versions of the small, lightweight Williams International FJ44 1,900-pound-thrust turbofan engines (designated F129 by the military). The Cessna entry became the only twin engine aircraft in the competition.

The original CitationJet completed its maiden flight in May 1991 and received its FAA certification on 16 October 1992. The first prototype Model 526 JPATS CitationJet flew on 20 December 1993, and the second on 2 March 1994. In fact, the second prototype completed three flight test missions on its first day. Cessna predicted that the civilian CitationJet fleet will have logged over one million flying hours before the first JPATS aircraft would be delivered to the military.

In late 1994, following a couple of accidents, the Department of Defense eliminated the Northrop Grumman/FMA Pampa 2000 from further consideration, leaving Northrop Grumman with only two contenders. Pentagon officials cited safety concerns and problems with pilot-induced oscillations during the takeoff phase as well as unsatisfactory spin characteristics. With the field of candidates narrowed to six, the Pentagon announced a restructuring of the production phase of the program from the planned 12 years to 20 years with the last deliveries slipped to the year 2016.

In creating the JPATS version of its business-oriented CitationJet, Cessna planned to capitalize on its existing production line by reusing the following Model 525 components in the new Model 526 (resulting in a 75 percent design commonality):

- Natural laminar flow wings.
- FJ44 turbofan engines (derated to 1,500-pounds of thrust to increase engine life).
- Landing gear.
- Hydraulic (1,500-psi) and electrical (28-volt DC) systems.
- Flight controls (straightforward mechanical system).
- Fuel system (multi-cell single-tank arrangement to eliminate fuel management concerns).

To meet the specific requirements of the JPATS competition, Cessna had to develop a new fuselage, empennage, cockpit section, canopy, avionics, ejection escape system, and on-board oxygen generation system (to eliminate the need for carrying bottles of compressed or liquid oxygen).

To ensure easy maintenance access to aircraft systems and to simplify maintenance procedures, Cessna constructed a complete aircraft mock-up of the Model 526 to validate the overall design's maintainability.

The anticipated date for announcing the winner of the competition was delayed several times. The original plan had been to award the initial contract for 168 aircraft in early 1994, then it was mid-1994, then January of 1995, and the latest slip was to summer 1995. In early 1995, industry experts estimated that the program was costing each competitor approximately one million dollars per month, making further program delays very costly for the teams involved.

On 16 March 1994, Cessna completed a highly successful series of tests of the ejection system for the Model 526. The overall escape system was designed by Cessna using Universal Propulsion Company (UPCO) S-IIIS-3RW ejection seats with full zero altitude, zero airspeed ejection capability. The tests were conducted on UPCO's Hurricane Mesa Test Track using anthropometric dummies to represent both the largest and smallest pilots allowed by USAF and Navy standards, the tests included a through-the-canopy ejection sequence.

The FAA fully certified the Model 526 JPATS CitationJet under Federal Aviation Regulations Part 23 aerobatic criteria on 22 June 1994, just six months after first flight of the first prototype. The flight test program

• *Both prototype JPATS CitationJets (note the thrust deflectors installed on N526JT* •
(Cessna Aircraft Company)

that led to the final certification consisted of over 500 hours and more than 850 spins. According to Cessna's Senior Vice President for Aircraft Development, Bruce Peterman, "The receipt of this type of certificate represents the successful culmination of 18 months of intensive effort by a dedicated Cessna and subcontractor team to design, build, and certify a state-of-the-art training airplane specifically for the JPATS. . .Awarding of the contract to Cessna would result in the addition of more than 2,000 U.S.-based jobs at the peak of the program."

Following the FAA certification announcement, Jon Huffman, Cessna JPATS program manager, noted, "We know the value of designing an aircraft specifically for the primary training mission since we built the T-37 for exactly the same role." Forty years later, the T-37 was still providing an excellent training platform for its third generation of pilots.

However, on 22 June 1995, the Department of Defense announced that the winner of the JPATS competition was the Beech/Pilatus team with its missionized Pilatus PC-9, dubbed the MkII. Despite the optimism of Cessna management, Cessna once more lost a major U.S. military trainer contract to Beech (a version of the Cessna Citation T-47 competed for the USAF tanker-airlift trainer won by the Beech T-1A Jayhawk in 1990). The next major U.S. military trainer contract is not expected for maybe 10 years when the USAF will have to begin replacing its aged supersonic Northrop T-38 Talon trainers. Will this offer Cessna another chance to get back into the military trainer game once its rugged Tweet has been retired? ✛

Associations & Museums

Warbird Associations

Army Aviation Association of America
49 Richmondville Avenue
Suite 205
Westport, CT 06880-2000
(203) 226-8184

Association of Naval Aviation
5205 Leesburg Pike
Suite 200
Falls Church, VA 22041
(703) 998-7733

Classic Jet Aircraft Association
Kermit Weeks Flight Research Center
P. O. Box 3086
Oshkosh, WI 54903-3065
(414) 426-4800

Confederate Air Force
Midland International Airport
P. O. Box 62000
Midland, TX 79711-2000
(915) 563-1000

International Bird Dog Association
3939 C-8 San Pedro, N.E.
Albuquerque, NM 87110
(505) 884-4822

International Liaison Pilot and Aircraft Association
16518 Ledgestone
San Antonio, TX 78232
(512) 490-4572

Marine Corps Aviation Association
P. O. Box 296
Quantico, VA 22134
(800) 336-0291

National World War II Glider Pilots Association
136 West Main Street
Freehold, NJ 07728
(201) 462-1838

Naval Aircraft Restorers Association
3320 Northridge Drive
Grand Junction, CO 81506
(303) 245-7899

Warbirds of America (Experimental Aircraft Association)
EAA Aviation Center
P. O. Box 3086
Oshkosh, WI 54903-3086
(414) 426-4800

Warbird Restoration Society
20 Emerald Court
Airdrie, Alberta, Canada T4B 1B8
(403) 948-7432

Warbirds Worldwide, Limited
5 White Heart Chambers
16 White Heart Street
Mansfield Notts NG18 1DG
England
(0623) 24288

Warbird Museums (With Cessnas)

Alabama
Maxwell Aircraft Museum
502 ABW/PA
50 LeMay Plaza South
Maxwell AFB, AL 36112-5001
(205) 953-2014

US Army Aviation Museum
P. O. Box 620610
Fort Rucker, AL 36362-0610
(205) 255-2893

Arizona
Pima Air And Space Museum
6000 East Valencia Road
Tucson, AZ 85706
(602) 574-9658

California
Air Force Flight Test Center Museum
6500 SW/CCM
Edwards AFB, CA 93523-5000
(805) 277-8050

Castle Air Museum
P. O. Box 488
Atwater, CA 95301
(209) 723-2178

March Field Museum
22 ARW/CYM
16222 I-215, Building 1917
March AFB, CA 92518-2400
(909) 655-3725

Travis Air Force Museum
P. O. Box 1565
Travis AFB, CA 94535
(707) 424-5605

Yanks Air Museum
13470 Dalewood Street
Baldwin Park, CA 91706
(714) 597-1734

Colorado
Wings Over The Rockies
Lowry Heritage Museum Foundation
P. O. Box 30035
Lowry AFB, CO 80230-4757
(303) 676-3028

Delaware
Dover Air Force Historical Center
436 AW/CM
Building 790
Dover AFB, DE 19902-5144
(302) 677-5938

Florida
Florida Military Aviation Museum
P. O. Box 17322
Clearwater, FL 34622
(813) 535-9007

Hurlburt Field Air Park
16 SOW/CVIE
131 Bartley Street, Suite 315
Hurlburt Field, FL 32544-5269
(904) 884-7172

National Museum of Naval Aviation
Building 3465

NAS Pensacola, FL 32508
(904) 452-3604

US Air Force Armament Museum
646 ABW/AM
Eglin AFB, FL 32542-5000
(904) 882-4062

Valiant Air Command
6600 Tico Road
Titusville, FL 32780
(407) 268-1941

Georgia
Museum of Aviation at Warner Robbins
P. O. Box 2469
Warner Robbins, GA 31099
(912) 926-6870

Indiana
Grissom Air Park
Heritage Museum Foundation
6500 Hoosier Boulevard
Grissom AFB, IN 46971
(317) 688-2654

Kansas
Kansas Aviation Museum
3350 George Washington Boulevard
Wichita, KS 67210
(316) 683-9242

Liberal Air Museum
P. O. Box 2585
Liberal, KS 67905
(316) 624-5263

Michigan
Kalamazoo Aviation History Museum
3101 East Wilham Road
Kalamozoo, MI 49002-1700
(616) 382-6555

Selfridge Military Air Museum
Box 745
Selfridge ANG Base, MI 48045-0745
(313) 307-5035

Ohio
US Air Force Museum
1100 Spaatz Street
Wright-Patterson AFB, Dayton, OH 45433-7102
(513) 255-3286

Oklahoma
Fort Sill Museum
437 Quanah Road
Fort Sill, OK 73503-5100
(405) 351-5123

The 45th Infantry Division Museum
2145 N.E. 36th Street
Oklahoma City, OK 73111
(405) 424-5313

Oregon
Oregon Air and Space Museum
90377 Boeing Drive
Eugene, OR 97402
(503) 942-9129

South Dakota
South Dakota Air and Space Museum
Ellsworth Heritage Foundation
P. O. Box 871
Box Elder, SD 57719-0871
(605) 385-5188

Texas
American Airpower Heritage Museum
P. O. Box 62000
Midland, TX 79711-2000
(915) 563-1000

Cavanaugh Flight Museum
Addison Airport
4572 Claire Chenault
Dallas, TX 75248
(214) 380-8800

Dyess Air Park
96th Wing/CVM
Dyess AFB, TX 79607-5000
(915) 696-2196

History and Traditions Museum
Lackland AFB
San Antonio, TX 78236
(512) 671-3444

Kelly Field Heritage Museum
SA-ALC/HQ
Kelly AFB, TX 78241-5000
(512) 925-5551

Lone Star Flight Museum
2002 Terminal Drive

Galveston, TX 77554
(409) 740-7722

Sheppard AFB Air Park
STTC/PA
Sheppard AFB, TX 76311
(817) 676-2733

Utah
Hill Aerospace Museum
649 ABG/XPM
Hill AFB, UT 84056-5842
(801) 777-6868

Virginia
U.S. Army Transportation Museum
Building 300, Besson Hall
ATTN: ATZF-PTM
Fort Eustis, VA 23604-5260
(804) 878-1115

Canada
Aerospace Museum of Calgary
Hangar #10
64 McTavish Place, N.E.
Calgary, Alberta, Canada T2E 7H1
(403) 250-3752

Canada's Aviation Hall of Fame
P. O. Box 6360
Wetaskiwin, Alberta, Canada T9A 2G1
(403) 352-5855

Canadian Warplane Heritage Museum
Unit 300
9300 Airport Road
Mount Hope, Ontario, Canada, L0R 1W0
(905) 679-4183

Commonwealth Air Training Plan Museum
Box 1481
Brandon, Manitoba, Canada, R7A 6N3
(204) 727-2444

Saskatchewan Western Development Museum
Box 185
Moose Jaw, Saskatchewan, Canada, S6H 4N8
(306) 693-6556

Western Canada Aviation Museum
Hangar T2
958 Ferry Road
Winnipeg, Manitoba, Canada, R3H 0Y8
(204) 786-5503

Bibliography

Adcock, Al. *O-1 Bird Dog in Action,* Carrollton, TX: Squadron/Signal Publications, Inc., 1988.

AN 01-125 CA-A1, Handbook, Flight Operating Instructions, USAF Series LC-126A, LC-126B, LC-126C Aircraft, 30 June 1951.

ATC Manual 51-4, Primary Flying, Jet, USAF Air Training Command, 30 November 1971.

Berger, Carl, ed. *The United States Air Force in Southeast Asia, 1961-1973: An Illustrated Account,* Office of Air Force History, Washington, DC, 1984.

Cessna Model 172K (Air Force Model T-41A) Flight Handbook, April 1970.

Cessna Model R-172E (Air Force Model T-41C) Flight Handbook.

Conroy, Kenneth. *War in Laos, 1954-1975,* Carrollton, TX: Squadron/Signal Publications, Inc., 1994.

Doll, Thomas E. *USN/USMC Over Korea, U.S. Navy/Marine Corps Air Operations Over Korea 1950-53,* Carrollton, TX: Squadron/Signal Publications, Inc., 1988.

Eather, Steve. *Target Charlie,* Weston Creek, Australia: Aerospace Publications Pty Ltd.,1993.

Flintham, Victor. *Air Wars And Aircraft, A Detailed Record of Air Combat, 1945 to the Present,* New York: Facts on File, 1990.

Harding, Stephen. *U.S. Army Aircraft Since 1947,* Stillwater, MN: Specialty Press, Inc., 1990.

Love, Terry. *A-37/T-37 Dragonfly in Action*, Carrollton, TX: Squadron/Signal Publications, Inc., 1991.

Mesko, Jim. *VNAF, South Vietnamese Air Force, 1945-1975,* Carrollton, TX: Squadron/Signal Publications, Inc., 1987.

Phillips, Edward H. *Wings of Cessna, Model 120 to the Citation X,* Eagan, MN: Flying Books International, 1994.

Politella, Dario. *Operation Grasshopper,* Tyler, TX: The Robert R. Longo Company, Inc., 1958.

Robbins, Christopher. *The Ravens, The Men Who Flew in America's Secret War in Laos,* New York: Crown Pulishers, Inc., 1987.

Stone, Ronald B., ed. *North American Aircraft & Aerospace Museum Guide, 6th Edition,* Olathe, Kansas: Bruce/Beeson Publishers.

Swanborough, Gordon & Peter M. Bowers. *United States Military Aircraft Since 1909,* Washington, DC: Smithsonian Institution Press, 1989.

Taylor, Michael J. H. ed., *Jane's Encyclopedia of Aviation,* New York: Crescent Books, 1989.

Thompson, William D. *Cessna, Wings For The World, The Single-Engine Development Story,* Bend, OR: Maverick Publications, Inc., 1991.

TM 55-1510-202-10, Operator's and Crew Member's Instructions, Army Model L-19A, L-19E, TL-19A, TL-19D, TL-19E Airplanes (Cessna), April 1961.

TM 55-1510-216-10, Operator's Manual, Army Models U-3A and U-3B Aircraft, 11 December 1978.

TM 55-1510-212-10, Operator's Instructions, Army Model T-41B.

T.O. 1A-37B-1, USAF Series A-37B Aircraft Flight Manual, 1 April 1973.

T.O. 1L-2A-1, USAF Series O-2A and O-2B Aircraft Flight Manual, 10 June 1977.

T.O. 1L-2A-34-1-1, USAF Series O-2A Aircraft Aircrew Weapons Delivery Manual (Non-Nuclear), 10 June 1977.

T.O. 1T-37B-1, USAF Series T-37B Aircraft Flight Manual, 1 August 1972.

T.O. No. 01-125-1, Pilot's Flight Operating Instructions for Army Models AT-17 Series and UC-78 Series, Navy Model JRC-1, and British Models Crane I and Ia Airplanes, 25 July 1943.

Corrections

Thank you for taking the time to help us improve *Cessna Warbirds* for your input is considered quite valuable. We hope you enjoy the book.

Please describe any corrections or suggestions in the space provided.

Page Number   Correction/Addition Necessary

_____   _____

_____   _____

_____   _____

_____   _____

_____   _____

_____   _____

_____   _____

_____   _____

Send to:
Catalog Correction
Jones Publishing, Inc.
P.O. Box 5000
Iola, WI 54945
FAX: (715) 445-4053

We are asking for corrections in this form to ensure proper handling. Thank you.

ORDER FORM FOR

Cessna Warbirds
A Detailed and Personal History of Cessna's Involvement in the Armed Forces

Telephone Orders: Call 1-800-331-0038
Have your Mastercard, Visa, or American Express card ready.
Please mention code "10894."

Fax Orders: Complete this form and fax it to 715/445-4053.

Mail Orders: Mail this form, along with your check (unless paying by credit card), to:
Jones Publishing, Inc.
Book Orders, Dept. 10894
P.O. Box 5000
Iola, WI 54945-5000

Address:
Company Name: _____
Name: _____
Address: _____
City: _____ State: _____ Zip: _____

Quantity	Title	Price Per Book	Total
_____	Cessna Warbirds	$29.95	$_____

Shipping & Handling

	USA	Foreign
$14.00 to $29.99	$4.00	$12.00
$30.00 to $49.99	$5.00	$15,00
$50.00 to 64.99	$5.50	$18.80
$65.00 & over	$6.00	Inquire

Subtotal (from above) $_____
5.5% Sales Tax (Wisconsin residents only) $_____
Shipping & Handling (see chart to the left) $_____
Grand Total $_____

Payment:
❏ Check (U.S. Funds)
❏ Visa   ❏ Mastercard   ❏ American Express

Card Number: _____ Expiration Date: _____
Name on card: _____
Signature: _____